Speed Up Your Site: Web Site Optimization

Contents at a Glance

Speed Up Your Site:
Web Site Optimization

Andrew B. King

www.newriders.com

201 West 103rd Street, Indianapolis, Indiana 46290
An Imprint of Pearson Education
Boston • Indianapolis • London • Munich • New York • San Francisco

Speed Up Your Site: Web Site Optimization

International Standard Book Number: 0-7357-1324-3

Library of Congress Catalog Card Number: 2002110031

Printed in the United States of America

First edition: January 2003

07 06 05 04 03   7 6 5 4 3 2 1

Interpretation of the printing code: The rightmost double-digit number is the year of the book's printing; the rightmost single-digit number is the number of the book's printing. For example, the printing code 03-1 shows that the first printing of the book occurred in 2003.

Trademarks

Warning and Disclaimer

Publisher
David Dwyer

Associate Publisher
Stephanie Wall

Editor in Chief
Chris Nelson

Production Manager
Gina Kanouse

Senior Product Marketing Manager
Tammy Detrich

Publicity Manager
Susan Nixon

Acquisitions Editor
Elise Walter

Development Editors
Laura Loveall
Lisa Thibault

Senior Editor
Sarah Kearns

Project Editor
Kelley Thornton

Copy Editor
Kathy Murray

Indexer
Lisa Stumpf

Proofreader
Linda Seifert

Manufacturing Coordinator
Dan Uhrig

Interior Designer/ Compositor
Kim Scott

Cover Designer
Aren Howell

Table of Contents

About the Author

Andrew B. King (Andy) is the founder of WebReference.com and JavaScript.com, both award-winning web developer sites. Created in 1995 and subsequently acquired by Mecklermedia (now Jupitermedia) in 1997, WebReference has grown into one of the most popular developer sites on the Internet. WebReference.com has won more than 100 awards, including *PC Magazine*'s Top 100 Web Sites (nine-time winner).

As Managing Editor of WebReference.com and JavaScript.com, Andy became the "Usability Czar" at internet.com, optimizing the speed and usability of their sites. He continues to write the three weekly newsletters he started for WebReference.com and JavaScript.com.

Andy has been studying, practicing, and teaching optimization techniques for more than 20 years. For his BSME and MSME from the University of Michigan, he specialized in design optimization. Recruited by NASA, he chose instead to join the fast-paced world of engineering consulting at ETA, Inc., a structural engineering firm. He worked for Ford and GM, optimizing entire automotive structures and suspensions with finite element analysis.

In 1993, he discovered the web. Volunteer work with a local Free-net in 1993 led to a position as one of the first employees of Internet Connect, Inc., a web design firm. He's been working the web ever since.

In addition to his work with WebReference.com, Andy has also written for *MacWeek* and *Web Techniques* (now *New Architect*), and contributed to Jim Heid's *HTML & Web Publishing Secrets*. When he's not optimizing web sites or writing newsletters, you'll find Andy out taking pictures, sailing, or bicycling. Contact Andy through the companion site to this book at `http://www.WebSiteOptimization.com`.

About the Contributing Authors

Konstantin Balashov wrote Chapter 18, "Compressing the Web," and co-wrote Chapter 12, "Optimizing Web Graphics." Jason Wolf wrote Chapter 13, "Minimizing Multimedia," and Chapter 14, "Case Study: Apple.com."

Konstantin Balashov was born in 1971 in Minsk, Belarus. In 1988, he completed high school, and in 1993, he received a degree from Belarussian State University in Informatics and Radio Electronics, where he was part of the Computer Science faculty. After graduation, he worked as a software engineer in the state Science and Research Institute AGAT; then in a pharmaceutical company; and then in a banking software company. From the very beginning, Konstantin was fascinated with data compression algorithms. He published his first work about data compression in 1991, when he was a university student.

In 1996, he founded the first Russian Internet data compression resource—cotty.mebius.net (later moved to cotty.16x16.com). In early 1998, Konstantin met several people on the Internet who changed his life—Peter Cranstone, CEO of Remote Communications, Inc., from Denver, Colorado; and Professor David Akopian from Signal Processing Research Center, Tampere University of Technology, Finland. Shortly thereafter, he became Chief Scientific Officer of RCI. At the same time, Konstantin started postgraduate work in the Institute of Scientific Cybernetics, Belarussian Academy of Science in Minsk. In the summer of 1999, he decided to focus on data compression and quit his prestigious full-time job.

At the very beginning, he had just a corner in a friend's office, but in half a year he moved to a two-room office and hired four engineers. They created data compression software for Remote Communications and did some jobs for some other U.S. companies. Currently this group is known as Miraplacid. In August 1999, Konstantin met Robert Caruso on the Internet. Shortly thereafter they founded OnMercial, Inc., a rich-media email advertising company, later renamed to eyeMotiv. Konstantin was the CIO of the company. Also in 1999, Konstantin spent several months working in a university in Tampere, Finland, as an image compression researcher. In January 2001, Konstantin arrived in the United States at Beaverton, Oregon, and started working for OnMercial on a full-time basis. In addition to the other products, he developed a simple and efficient animated image format (AMF) with a compression ratio about 1.5 times higher than GIF. In June 2002, Konstantin left eyeMotiv and currently is working at Shop All America, Inc. Konstantin has 11 publications regarding data compression to his credit. You can contact him at cotty@miraplacid.com.

Jason Wolf is founder and president of Wolf Studios in San Francisco (http://www.jasonwolf.com). Wolf Studios is one of the true remaining traditional multimedia engineering firms. Jason has created landmark Internet and multimedia pieces, ranging from interactive CDs, DVDs, web sites, Shockwave games, TV commercials, films, documentaries, 3D visual effects, 3D animation, and video production, all of which is blended with traditional artistic values.

Jason is a best-selling author who has published many books and articles on the topics of technology and multimedia, including *Shockwave 3D* (New Riders, 2002). Jason's work over the years has won awards from *Communication Arts* and has been featured in hundreds of publications and books. Wolf Studios has worked with clients such as Apple, Levi's, VISA, Nike, GM, Macromedia, Sony, Pixar, Williams-Sonoma, TBWA Chiat-Day, Eleven Inc., Virtual City Tours, and many others.

Prior to founding Wolf Studios, Jason was the Executive Director of Research & Development at marchFIRST, the Director of Multimedia at USWeb, and the Manager of Technology for CKS Partners. Jason has also worked for other companies such as LucasFilms (ILM) and Koei Corporation (Japan). He can be contacted through his web site at http://www.jasonwolf.com.

About the Technical Reviewers

These reviewers contributed their considerable hands-on expertise to the entire development process for *Speed Up Your Site: Web Site Optimization*. As the book was being written, these dedicated professionals reviewed all the material for technical content, organization, and flow. Their feedback was critical to ensuring that *Speed Up Your Site* fits our readers' need for the highest-quality technical information.

Porter Glendinning has spent the last several years designing and developing interfaces to web-based applications for an Internet consulting company in the Washington, D.C./Baltimore area. He lives in Olney, Maryland, with his wife, Laura, who puts up with his obsession of the Internet, and their very large yellow Lab, Arrow, who eats his socks. Porter can be found online at www.glendinning.org and www.cerebellion.com. He co-administers the Babble mailing list, a forum for discussions on advanced web design topics of all sorts (www.babblelist.com), and is a member of the Web Standards Project Steering Committee (www.webstandards.org).

Bert Van Kets became involved with computers at the age of 15 with a Sinclair Spectrum 48K and, later, a PC XT. Ever since, every aspect of IT has been his passion. As a self-tutor, he has been in DTP, hardware, service providing, digital printing, CD development, networking, Internet hosting, and finally, web development, using ASP first and then XML, XSLT, and Java. Always seeking to find the best way to build the ultimate web sites, search engine optimization and browser compatibility have become a state of mind.

Bert is working as a consultant for The Vision Web Belgium, where he can use his knowledge to the fullest extent by doing Internet development and providing courses in developing search engine-optimized web sites.

You can find out all about his passion—radio-controlled planes and helicopters—on his personal web site at www.dream-models.com.

Acknowledgments

I'd like to thank the following people for their inspiration and help in making this book possible. First I'd like to thank Professor Panos Papalambros at the University of Michigan for inspiring me to pursue engineering and optimization as a career. I'd like to thank my business partner, Bob Peyser, for helping me make WebReference a successful enterprise, and Dan Ragle and Scott Clark for carrying the flame. Thanks to Tammie Bruneau and Bradley Glonka for their last-minute help with the Elivad.com prototype. Thanks also to Lou Rosenfeld and Wendy Peck for their book-authoring advice.

Thanks to WebReference content providers Peter Belesis, Michael Classen, Jonathan Eisenzopf, Daniel Giordan, Nick Heinle, Dmitry Kirsanov, Mark Merkow, Wendy Peck, Stephanos Piperoglou, Robert Polevoi, Yehuda and Tomer Shiran, and Richard Wiggins. Thanks also to all the employees who worked for us over the years. You all helped make WebReference the success that it is today.

Thanks to Mihaly Csikszentmihalyi, Ph.D., Jakob Nielsen, Ph.D., Chris Roast, Ph.D., Benjamin Shneiderman, Ph.D., Marceli Wein, Ph.D., and Ken Winter, Ph.D for their research and input on Part I, "The Psychology of Performance."

Part II, "Optimizing Markup: HTML and XHTML:" Thanks to Travis Anton (`boxtopsoft.com`) for Mizer (now SpaceAgent), Bob Clary (Netscape), Bradley Glonka (`internet.com`), Michael Schröpl for his compression input and wonderful `mod_gzip` site, Johannes Selbach for his input and VSE Web Site Turbo, and Jeffrey Zeldman for his tireless advocacy of web standards, and A List Apart.

Part III, "DHTML Optimization: CSS and JavaScript:" Thanks to Kwon Ekstrom, Mike Hall (`brainjar.com`), Eric Meyer (`meyerweb.com`), Stuart Robinson (`designmeme.com`), and Christopher Schmitt (`cssbook.com`) for their CSS input.

Thanks to Douglass Bagnall (`halo.gen.nz`) for his 5K chess game; Peter Belesis (`dhtml.com`) for his hierarchical menus and invaluable input over the years; Aaron Boodman (`youngpup.net`) for all his help; Lon Boonan (`q42.nl`) for his avatar code, chapter review, and online tools; John Bandhauer (`netscape.com`) for his work on Venkman; Stuart Butterfield (`sylloge.com`) and Eric Costello (`glish.com`) for the 5K contest; Robert Chandler (helpware.net); Mike Hall (brainjar.com); Bob Ippolito (threeoh.com); Jim Ley (jibbering.com) for the JavaScript FAQ; Thomas Loo (saltstorm.net); Chris Nott (dithered.com); Michel Plungjan (irt.org); Scott Porter (JavaScript-Games.org) for his performance insights; Michael Schröpl for his input on JavaScript and compression; and Yehuda and Tomer Shiran (docjs.com).

Part IV, "Graphics and Multimedia Optimization:" Thanks to Jack Berlin (jpg.com), Chuck Duff (spinwave.com), and Greg Roelofs (http://www.libpng.org/pub/png/) for their insights. Thanks to Toyin Akinmusuru for his Flashes of brilliance. Thanks to Jim Bean (jpg.com) for being so helpful.

Part V, "Search Engine Optimization:" Thanks to Fredrick Marckini (iProspect.com), Danny Sullivan (searchenginewatch.com), and Bert Van Kets (www.dream-models.com) for their expertise.

Part VI, "Advanced Optimization Techniques:" Thanks to Ralph Engelschall for creating mod_rewrite (engelschall.com), Bradley Glonka (internet.com), Chuck Hagenbuch (horde.org), Peter Hegedus (internet.com), Richard Litofsky (cyscape.com) for the last-minute JSP code, Darrell King (webctr.com), and Dan Ragle (internet.com).

Thanks to my editor, Laura Loveall, for keeping me on track, and Elise Walter for recognizing my idea. Thanks to my technical editors, Bert Van Kets and Porter Glendinning, for their superb feedback. Thanks to unofficial editors, Peggy Morgan and Wendy Peck. A big thank-you to Jason Wolf and Konstantin Balashov for their chapters. Last but not least, thanks to my parents, John and Jean King, for their support and unconditional love.

Andy King
Ann Arbor, Michigan
November 2002

Tell Us What You Think

As the reader of this book, you are the most important critic and commentator. We value your opinion and want to know what we're doing right, what we could do better, in what areas you'd like to see us publish, and any other words of wisdom you're willing to pass our way.

As the Associate Publisher for New Riders Publishing, I welcome your comments. You can fax, email, or write me directly to let me know what you did or didn't like about this book—as well as what we can do to make our books stronger. When you write, please be sure to include this book's title, ISBN, and author, as well as your name and phone or fax number. I will carefully review your comments and share them with the author and editors who worked on the book.

Please note that I cannot help you with technical problems related to the topic of this book, and that due to the high volume of email I receive, I might not be able to reply to every message.

Fax: 317-581-4663
Email: stephanie.wall@newriders.com
Mail: Stephanie Wall
         Associate Publisher
         New Riders Publishing
         201 West 103rd Street
         Indianapolis, IN 46290 USA

Look for This Related Title from New Riders:

Search Engine Visibility

Shari Thurow

0-7357-1256-5

See a chapter excerpt from *Search Engine Visibility*
in the back of this book.

Foreword

Users rarely agree about user interface design questions. Should the "add to shopping cart" button be red, orange, yellow, or blue? You will probably get about 25 percent in favor of each option if you ask your customers. For this, and many other reasons, you shouldn't design web sites by asking users for their preference. It is much better to learn by watching—see what people *do* and not what they say. Then make the button the color that works best in user testing.

There are two exceptions to the general rule on which users disagree; two questions where the answers are the same for virtually all users, year after year. Since my first Web usability studies in 1994, I have heard the following two comments in almost every test:

- I don't like to read a lot of text on a computer screen.
- I don't want to wait for slow pages to download.

This book doesn't talk much about the first problem, so let me give you a quick usability guideline: Cut your word count in half for online readers.

The second problem is where this book shines and should be mandatory reading for all web designers and Internet executives: Nobody likes slow pages, but we don't have to accept sluggish performance. Make it fast. Employ the optimization techniques you will learn in this book, and any web site will grow its base of loyal users and paying customers.

It is astounding how negatively users react to slow sites. Slow sites are difficult to navigate because users lose their sense of place and progress—human short-term memory is fickle. Even worse, if a site is slow, it communicates contempt for customers and their time. Users will assume that additional pages will be slow as well, and that it will be painful to navigate the site. The back-button beckons.

Some web designers are in denial and think that *their* pages are so good that users will be willing to wait. Sometimes, this is even true: If users have specifically asked for something and know what they will be getting, they are sometimes willing to wait for higher-quality illustrations or other heavy design elements. The most common case is a user who has clicked on a thumbnail image to request a high-resolution scan. Mostly, though, faster is better.

This is the simplest equation in the entire field of Internet strategy. Many other issues can be debated hotly, and there is no easy answer. But to repeat, faster is better. This is a one-dimensional criterion where there is no doubt as to the preferred direction.

I have sometimes posed a challenge to those designers who believe that slow response times are acceptable: Artificially delay each of your page views by ten seconds for a day and see what that does to your online business. (Of course, it would be an even better experiment to speed up every page by ten seconds, but that requires you to actually read the book and redesign the pages. In contrast, it's easy to temporarily reduce performance.) So far, nobody has taken me up on this challenge. If you do, please send me the results.

There are an estimated 600 million Internet users in the world. Every year, these users waste about 6 billion hours waiting for web pages to download. This is the equivalent of about 3 million person—years of full-time work—or about the labor force of Denmark.

We can't totally eliminate download delays, but let's set a goal of reducing the World Wide Wait to half its current magnitude by 2005. That would gain the world economy almost $60 billion in recovered productivity. More important for you, the reader, it will increase customers' satisfaction with your web site.

Jakob Nielsen
Fremont, CA
November 2002

Introduction

Don't make me wait!

That's the message web users give us in survey after survey. Even high-bandwidth users find web sites too slow. And with millions of sites to choose from, they simply won't wait for slow sites.

The problem? Bloated web pages. True, server load and network bottlenecks can hurt, but page size and complexity are the real satisfaction killers.[1]

The solution? Web site optimization (WSO). To win your share of users, you've got to adopt the WSO mantra: "*every byte counts.*" Every extra byte you send puts a barrier between you and your users. In this book, you'll discover techniques that can save anywhere from a few bytes to 30 to 60 percent off your entire bandwidth bill.

Think fast and small. Simplify. Whether you're a gazelle or a web designer, the Darwinian law of the jungle still applies—and the law of this jungle is survival of the fastest. Users migrate from slow to fast web pages. Are you willing to risk your business on slow, outdated web pages? I didn't think so.

Everyone has experienced slow response times on the web. While researching this book, I participated in a conference call and online demo from an optimization firm. To demonstrate their optimization services, they paradoxically used slow-loading pages. This mismatch of expected to actual performance is jarring for most users.

This book is designed to make occurrences like this uncommon. As you will see, even though bandwidth is increasing, consumer sites are actually getting slower. Most users now experience slower response times than they did last year, or even ten years ago.

---

1. Jing Zhi, "Web Page Design and Download Time," *CMG Journal of Computer Resource Management*, no. 102 (2001): 40–55.

Every Site Can Benefit from WSO

WSO is design and technology agnostic. Media-rich artistic sites or news-oriented information sites can all benefit from WSO. Standards compliant or not, low-tech or high, (X)HTML or XML, CSS or XSLT—the same principles apply. Along the way, you will learn techniques that I learned only through ten years of web development and teaching developers how to create better sites at WebReference.com and JavaScript.com.

What About Broadband?

I know what you're thinking: "What about broadband? Won't more bandwidth make WSO irrelevant?" Nope.

Even users with fast connections can get frustrated. Just ask the users of a certain west coast publication who called with a classic complexity conundrum. They said that even their *cable modem* users were complaining about the speed of their pages.

Cable modems are typically capable of providing throughput of 1 to 6Mbps when the whole block isn't online at once. On our T1, the pages for their site took more than a minute to display. Even though high-speed users downloaded their 100K HTML pages in a matter of seconds, page complexity and the sheer number of objects slowed rendering to a crawl.

Bandwidth Trends

Despite the best efforts of broadband providers, last-mile bandwidth is increasing more slowly than some have predicted. According to Nielsen//NetRatings, as of September of 2002, 71.9 percent of home users connect to the Internet at 56K or less (see Figure I.1). Broadband use has steadily increased from 5.4 percent in October of 1999 to 28.1 percent in September of 2002. At this growth rate, broadband use in the United States will exceed 50 percent by late 2004.

Site Speed Trends

Although bandwidth is increasing, most users access the Internet at 56Kbps or less. As you will learn in Part I, "The Psychology of Performance," user satisfaction is directly related to snappy response times and feedback. Although B2B sites have gotten the message,[2] consumer sites are actually becoming slower.

Figure I.1
Web connection speed trends—U.S. home users.

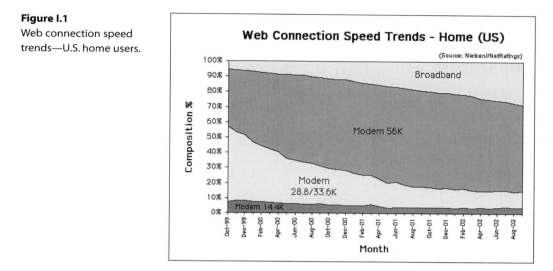

According to Keynote Systems, the average download time for 56K modems of the top 40 consumer sites increased from 19.5 seconds in August of 2001 to 21.4 seconds in September of 2002 (see Figure I.2). Without feedback (and even with feedback), this is well over the attention threshold of most users.

Figure I.2
Download times of Keynote Consumer 40 for 56K modems.

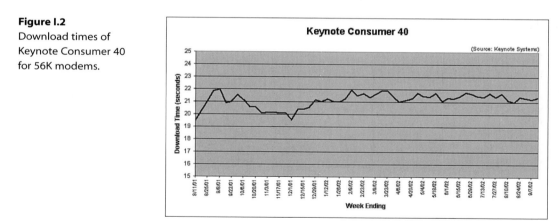

---

2. Patrick Mills and Chris Loosley, "A Performance Analysis of 40 e-Business Web Sites," *CMG Journal of Computer Resource Management*, no. 102 (2001): 28–33. From Oct. 1997 to Jan. 2001, B2B sites cut their average response times from 12 to 2.6 seconds.

Although our computers are getting faster, the speed of our connections can't keep up. With Moore's law leading Metcalf's, CPU processing power is increasing faster than bandwidth.[3]

Who Should Read This Book

This book will appeal to intermediate to advanced designers and developers, and to anyone in management who wants a competitive web site. It assumes that you have some familiarity with the web and its various components, and won't waste your time rehashing the basics of web design. Anyone designing web sites can get something useful from this book, however—especially from Part I, "The Psychology of Performance."

Although the primary emphasis is on optimizing client-side technologies, this book also covers advanced server-side techniques and compression to squeeze the maximum performance out of your site. These are all techniques that most designers and authors can control. Instead of focusing on esoteric server-side tuning limited to system administrators, this book focuses on optimizing the content that you deliver.

For a server-oriented look at performance, see *Web Performance Tuning, 2nd ed.* by Patrick Killelea (O'Reilly, 2002). For an advanced guide to web design, including a chapter on speed, see *The Art & Science of Web Design* by Jeffrey Veen (New Riders, 2001). For baked-in usability, including a section on response times, try *Designing Web Usability* by Jakob Nielsen (New Riders, 2000).

Who This Book Is Not For

This book is not for beginners. This book assumes some previous knowledge of web design and includes a number of before-and-after code samples. If you are a novice, I can enthusiastically recommend *Designing Web Graphics 4* by Lynda Weinman (New Riders, 2003) and *Web Style Guide, 2nd ed.* by Patrick Lynch and Sarah Horton (Yale University Press, 2002).

---

3. Jakob Nielsen, "Nielsen's Law of Internet Bandwidth," in *Alertbox* [online], (April 5, 1998 [cited 11 November 2002]), available from the Internet at http://www.useit.com/alertbox/980405.html.

For a distilled reference, see *Web Design in a Nutshell, 2ⁿᵈ ed.* by Jennifer Niederst (O'Reilly, 2001).

How This Book Is Organized

This book is organized into six major sections covering everything from psychology to advanced optimization techniques. Each section covers a particular area of web site design.

Part I, "The Psychology of Performance," explores the role of response times, feedback, and flow in user satisfaction on the web. How fast is fast enough? What makes users happy? This section distills existing research of user satisfaction and performance into understandable language to give you a solid foundation on how people react to delay, and gives web design guidelines based on this research. Chapter 1, "Response Time: Eight Seconds, Plus or Minus Two" (a somewhat tongue-in-cheek homage to Miller's 1956 classic article on memory span[4]) explores how response time delays affect user satisfaction. You'll learn where all those 8- and 10-second rules come from, and why they are not always correct. This chapter includes an interview with Dr. Ben Shneiderman, one of the leading researchers in the field. Chapter 2, "Flow in Web Design," explores the concept of flow on the web, where you'll discover what web site characteristics induce flow in their users. It features an interview with Dr. Mihaly Csikszentmihalyi, who first studied and wrote about flow.

Part II, "Optimizing Markup: HTML and XHTML," shows techniques that you can use to minimize the size of your (X)HTML pages, which is critical to user satisfaction. Chapter 6, "Case Study: PopularMechanics.com," demonstrates these techniques by optimizing a bloated page to one sixteenth of its original size.

Part III, "DHTML Optimization: CSS and JavaScript," explores ways to transform your code, shrink your style sheets, and make your scripts download and execute faster. Chapter 11, "Case Study: DHTML.com," shows the dramatic effects of crunching and compression on an actual script.

---

4. George A. Miller, "The Magical Number Seven, Plus or Minus Two: Some Limits on Our Capacity for Processing Information," *Psychological Review* 63, no. 2 (1956): 81–97.

In Part IV, "Graphics and Multimedia Optimization," you learn ways to shrink the content that generates the bulk of Internet traffic. Chapter 12, "Optimizing Web Graphics," takes an in-depth look at web graphic formats with everything from capturing and enhancing photographs, designing for compression algorithms, to tools and techniques. In Chapter 13, "Minimizing Multimedia," Jason Wolf shows you the best ways to capture and optimize audio and video, and adds in some Flash and PDF optimization tips. In Chapter 14, "Case Study: Apple.com," Jason puts these techniques to work optimizing an actual video he helped produce for Apple Computer.

Part V, "Search Engine Optimization," shows you how to optimize your keywords to maximize the number of relevant visitors to your site. In Chapter 15, "Keyword Optimization," you look over my shoulder as I optimize the keywords to the companion site to this book, WebSiteOptimization.com. Chapter 16, "Case Studies: PopularMechanics.com and iProspect.com," breaks down the wrong way and the right way to optimize your keywords.

Part VI, "Advanced Optimization Techniques," explores advanced server-based techniques to squeeze the maximum speed out of your web site, including server-side sniffing, URL abbreviation, and compression. In Chapter 18, "Compressing the Web," Konstantin Balashov shows how compressing your content can shrink your bandwidth bills by 30 to 50 percent and dramatically speed up your site. Chapter 19, "Case Studies: Yahoo.com and WebReference.com," demonstrates how automatic URL abbreviation can save 20 to 30 percent off high-traffic pages.

Companion Web Site

You'll find examples, sample chapters, optimization tools, and resources on the companion web site for this book at `http://www.WebSiteOptimization.com`. In addition to numbered code listings and working examples, this site will act as a clearinghouse for optimization-related information.

Conventions

This book follows a few typographical conventions:

- A new term is set in *italic* the first time it is introduced.
- Program text, functions, variables, and other "computer language" are set in a fixed-pitch font—for example:

```
for (var i=iter;i>0;i--) {}
```

I

The Psychology of Performance

1

Response Time: Eight Seconds, Plus or Minus Two

People hate to wait.

You're the fourth person in a six-person line at the supermarket. You spot a clerk moving toward the closed register in the next lane. Is she going to open it? If you bail out too early and she's just looking for bags, it's the back of the line for you. Wait too long and the clerk could call over the next person in line. What do you do?

On the Internet, this kind of choice is simple. If the page you're waiting for takes more than a few seconds to open, you just bail out to another site. No bodies to jostle, no icy stares from the slower crowd. Just exercise your freedom of choice with a twitch of a finger. To hell with the owners of the slower site you just left. Survival of the fittest, right? It's all rosy—unless, of course, you happen to be the owner of that slower site and it's a part of your business. In that case, it's a good thing you have this book.

In survey after survey, the most common complaint of Internet users is lack of speed. After waiting past a certain "attention threshold," users bail out to look for a faster site. Of course, exactly where that threshold is depends on many factors. How compelling is the experience? Is there effective feedback? This chapter explores the psychology of delay in order to discover why we are so impatient, and how fast is fast enough.

Lack of Speed Is the Most Common Complaint

Slow web sites are a universal phenomenon. Researchers have confirmed our need for speed in study after study:

- "GVU's Tenth World Wide Web User Survey," by Colleen Kehoe et al. (1999) `http://www.gvu.gatech.edu/user_surveys/survey-1998-10/tenthreport.html`— Over half of those surveyed cited slow downloads as a problem.

- In "The Top Ten *New* Mistakes of Web Design" (1999) `http://www.useit.com/alertbox/990530.html`—Jakob Nielsen found that 84 percent of 20 prominent sites had slow download times.

- *Designing Web Usability: The Practice of Simplicity* by Jakob Nielsen (New Riders Publishing, 2000)—"...fast response times are the most important design criterion for web pages."

- In "System Response Time and User Satisfaction: An Experimental Study of Browser-based Applications," in *Proceedings of the Association of Information Systems Americas Conference* (2000), John Hoxmeier and Chris DiCesare found that user satisfaction is inversely related to response time. They said that response time "could be the single most important variable when it comes to user satisfaction."

The study of this psychology is called *Human-Computer Interaction* (HCI). This chapter focuses on the speed aspects of HCI. How does delay affect user satisfaction? Why do we become so frustrated when we have to wait? This chapter distills this research into understandable language and web page design guidelines.

Flow: The Compelling Experience

It's one thing to optimize a web site for speed and get satisfactory results. It's quite another to help your users achieve flow. *Flow* is an optimal state that is characterized by intense yet effortless concentration, a sense of being at one with a larger good, clarity of goals with challenges met, and actualization. Is it possible that optimal web design can lead to users experiencing this optimal state? You'll find out in Chapter 2, "Flow in Web Design."

With the rapid expansion of the web and increasing bandwidth, you would think that the problem of slow system response would have gone away. As you learned in the Introduction, the opposite is true: Consumer sites are actually becoming slower.[1] In fact, Zona estimates that over $25 billion in potential sales is lost online due to web performance issues. HCI research is just as relevant today as it was a decade ago.

Speed: A Key Component of Usability

Speed is a key component of usability, which helps determine system acceptability.[2] How acceptable a system is determines its adoption rate. With over half of the IT projects deployed in the U.S. abandoned or underutilized,[3] it is important to make systems and sites (many of which are big IT projects themselves) that people actually use.

---

1. Zona Research, "The Need for Speed II" [online], (Redwood City, CA: Zona Research, 2001 [cited 9 November 2002]), available from the Internet at http://www.keynote.com/downloads/Zona_Need_For_Speed.pdf. Found that although B2B sites have doubled their speed, consumer sites have become 20 percent slower.
2. Brian Shackel, "Usability—context, framework, definition, design, and evaluation," in *Human Factors for Informatics Usability*, ed. Brian Shackel and Simon Richardson (Cambridge, UK: Cambridge University Press, 1991), 21–37.
3. Thomas K. Landauer, *The Trouble with Computers: Usefulness, Usability, and Productivity* (Cambridge, MA: MIT Press, 1995). "…sadly, most reengineering efforts fail." A sobering book on computers and productivity.

Shackel's Acceptability Paradigm

Part of our psyche, it seems, is devoted to understanding whether a particular system will have a big enough payoff to warrant the necessary expenditure of our time and energy. Brian Shackel characterized this paradigm as "system acceptability," which is a tradeoff between three dimensions:

- **Utility**—Or perceived usefulness. Is it functionally efficient?
- **Usability**—Or perceived ease of use. Can users work the system successfully?
- **Likability**—The user's subjective attitude about using the system. Do users feel it is suitable?

All of these factors are weighed against each other and the cost of using the system (see Figure 1.1). Seen through Shackel's lens, when users make decisions about using a web site, they weigh how useful it will be, its perceived ease of use, its suitability to the task, and how much it will cost them both financially and socially. That's why sometimes we are willing to put up with difficult sites if the reward for doing so is large enough.

Figure 1.1
Shackel's Acceptability
Paradigm.

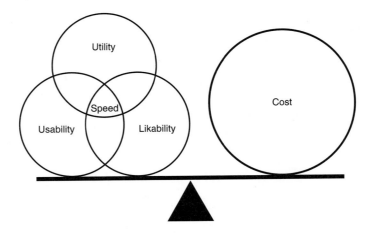

Traditionally, HCI research has focused on the quantification of Shackel's second dimension, usability. There is compelling evidence, however, that the utility of a technology should first be measured before any usability analysis occurs.[4,5] If you can't accomplish a task, it doesn't matter how easy the system is to use. Likability, Shackel's third dimension of acceptability, is most closely associated with "flow,"[6] or emotional appeal.

User Experience and Usability

The relative importance of usability changes over time. At first, usability has a strong effect on system use. As users gain more experience, they become more confident and believe they can accomplish more tasks with a desired level of performance (also known as *self-efficacy*[7]). As a result, ease of use fades in importance and utility, and likability increase in relative importance. Usability then indirectly influences usage through utility (usability -> utility -> usage).

Designers tend to favor ease of use over utility. Davis found that utility has far more influence on usage than usability, however. "No amount of ease of can compensate for a system that does not perform a useful function."[8]

Speed plays a key role in all of these dimensions, especially usability and likability, so it is an important determinant of system acceptability and usage. In other words, how responsive your site is will in large part determine its adoption rate, which in turn affects your bottom line.

---

4. Fred D. Davis, "Perceived Usefulness, Perceived Ease of Use, and User Acceptance of Information Technology," *MIS Quarterly* 13 (1989): 319–340. Found that perceived usefulness "had a significantly greater correlation with usage behavior" than perceived ease of use.

5. Brian R. Gaines, Lee Li-Jen Chen, and Mildred L. G. Shaw, "Modeling the Human Factors of Scholarly Communities Supported Through the Internet and World Wide Web," *Journal of the American Society for Information Science* 48, no. 11 (1997): 987–1003.

6. Mihaly Csikszentmihalyi, *Beyond Boredom and Anxiety: Experiencing Flow in Work and Play* (San Francisco: Jossey-Bass, 1975). This landmark book introduced the concept of flow to the public.

7. Albert Bandura, *Self-Efficacy: The Exercise of Control* (New York: W. H. Freeman, 1997).

8. Davis, "Perceived Usefulness," 333.

A Brief History of Web Performance

Soon after the birth of the web, HCI researchers started studying online environments. Networked environments like the Internet add another dimension to the mix—namely, network latency. Unlike the closed computing environments that HCI researchers studied in the past, on the Internet the delay between requesting a resource and receiving it is unpredictable. The more resources a page has (graphics, multimedia), the less predictable the response rate.

Initially researchers studied the effects of fixed response times on user satisfaction. Later studies simulated variable response rates for more real-world results. Their metrics changed from user satisfaction and performance to measures such as attunability, quality of service, quality of experience, and credibility.

In the late 1990s and early 2000s, researchers started looking at Shackel's likability dimension by studying the effects of download delays on user perceptions of web sites, flow states,[9] and emotional appeal.

Users form negative impressions from web site delays. Users perceive fast-loading pages to be of high quality, while they perceive slow-loading pages to be of low quality and untrustworthy. A user's tolerance for delay also decreases with experience. These topics are covered in more depth later in this chapter.

In fact, slow-loading web pages can cause users to believe that an error has occurred, because the computer has not responded in an appropriate amount of time.[10]

Affective Computing

Some researchers theorize that if a computer could respond "supportively" to delay-induced frustration, any negative emotional effects could be mitigated. According to

---

9. Donna L. Hoffman and Thomas P. Novak, "Marketing in Hypermedia Computer-Mediated Environments: Conceptual Foundations," *Journal of Marketing* 60 (July 1996): 50–68.

10. Jonathan Lazar and Yan Huang, "Designing Improved Error Messages for Web Browsers," in *Human Factors and Web Development*, 2d edition, ed. Julie Ratner (Mahwah, NJ: Lawrence Erlbaum Associates, 2002).

Pre-Attentive Recognition

In their classic book on the psychology of human performance, Wickens and Hollands describe parallel processing in visual searching, or *pre-attentive recognition*.[11] We can recognize features much more quickly on the screen using color or grouping than we can locate a word in a body of text. That's why links default to blue; this helps us locate them immediately.

11. Christopher D. Wickens and Justin G. Hollands, *Engineering Psychology and Human Performance*, 3d ed. (Upper Saddle River, NJ: Prentice Hall, 1999), 84–89.

researchers who have studied "affective computing," computers can respond to human emotions in order to lower frustration levels.[12]

Using galvanic skin response and blood volume pressure, Scheirer found that random delays can be a cause of frustration with computers.[13] Rather than ignoring their frustration (the most common condition) or letting them vent, a supportive approach gave users the most relief from frustration.[14] Perhaps we'll soon hear something like: "I'm sorry I'm so slow, Dave. Would you like me to speed up this web site?"

User-Rated Quality Models

More recently, researchers have been attempting to create a grand unified theory of web site quality from a user's perspective. How do users rate web sites? Why do they return to particular web sites and buy products? WebQual™, an overall measure of web site quality, is composed of twelve distinct measures derived from existing research.

12. Rosalind W. Picard, *Affective Computing* (Cambridge, MA: MIT Press, 1997).
13. Jocelyn Scheirer, Raul Fernandez, Jonathan Klein, and Rosalind W. Picard, "Frustrating the User on Purpose: A Step Toward Building an Affective Computer," *Interacting with Computers* 14, no. 2 (2002): 93–118.
14. Jonathan Klein, Youngme Moon, and Rosalind W. Picard, "This Computer Responds to User Frustration: Theory, Design, and Results," *Interacting with Computers* 14, no. 2 (2002): 119–140.

WebQual™ can accurately assess the overall perceived quality of web sites. Response time and emotional appeal both play a major role in perceived web site quality.[15]

Automated Quality Testing

WebTango researchers have developed an automated web site quality rating tool.[16] Their system, which is empirically based, automatically measures web site structure and composition in order to predict how experts will rate sites. Based on web designs judged by experts (Webby Awards), their 157-factor model, which includes page performance, had an average accuracy of 94 percent when quantifying good, average, and poor pages. However, some of the measures of good design are counterintuitive (i.e., more Bobby accessibility errors, see http://bobby.watchfire.com/).

Essentially a mining tool, WebTango analyzes existing web pages to create profiles of good and bad designs, and then applies this data to the design of new sites. This interactive "quality checker" is analogous to a grammar checker for web sites (see Figure 1.2).

Figure 1.2
Web site structure: From information to experience design.

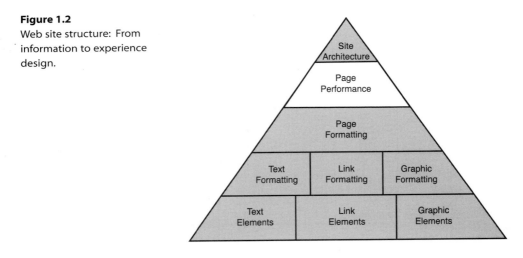

15. Eleanor T. Loiacono, Richard T. Watson, and Dale L. Goodhue, "WebQual™: A Web Site Quality Instrument," *American Marketing Association: Winter Marketing Educators' Conference* 13 (Austin, Texas: American Marketing Association, 2002): 432–438. A 12-factor web quality super-model from a user's perspective. See also http://www.webqual.net/.

16. Melody Y. Ivory and Marti A. Hearst, "Improving Web Site Design," *IEEE Internet Computing, Special Issue on Usability and the World Wide Web* 6, no. 2 (2002): 56–63. Available from the Internet at http://webtango.ischool. washington.edu/.

Set Performance Goals

Usability professionals routinely set usability metrics and goals for particular systems. Web performance is no different. Choose a performance goal for your site, and strive to achieve that goal for all of your pages. Because usability guidelines can be subjective, Shackel suggests quantifying usability in measurable terms.[17] Here is an example of a performance goal checklist:

- **Effectiveness**—Display high-traffic pages faster than eight seconds on 56Kbps modems; display useful content within the first two seconds. Other pages should display useful content in no more than 12 seconds on 56Kbps modems.

- **Learnability**—Achieve a 90 percent success rate on finding particular products within 30 seconds.

- **Flexibility**—Give users the ability to find products by browsing or searching.

- **Attitude**—With an attitude questionnaire on a 5-point scale from "very good" to "very bad," score 80 percent in good or above and only 2 percent below neutral.

- **Overall usability**—Meet 75 percent or more of Nielsen's 207-point usability checklist.[18]

17. Shackel, "Usability—context, framework, definition, design, and evaluation," 27.
18. Jakob Nielsen, Rolf Molich, Carolyn Snyder, and Susan Farrell, *E-Commerce User Experience* (Fremont, CA: Nielsen Norman Group, 2001). This invaluable book revealed the mythical 207 usability design guidelines.

Response Time and User Satisfaction

Shneiderman posed the question best: "How long will users wait for the computer to respond before they become annoyed?"[19] Researchers say "it depends." The delay users will tolerate depends on the perceived complexity of the task, user expertise, and feedback. Variability also plays an important role in delay tolerance. Users can tolerate moderate levels of delay variability, up to plus or minus 50 percent of the mean.

19. Ben Shneiderman, "Response Time and Display Rate in Human Performance with Computers," *Computing Surveys* 16, no. 3 (1984): 265–285. Keep it under 1 to 2 seconds, please.

A number of studies have attempted to quantify computer response times versus user satisfaction. Robert Miller found three threshold levels of human attention:[20]

- **0.1s**—One tenth of a second was viewed as instantaneous.
- **1.0s**—A one-second response time was needed for users to feel they were moving freely through an information space.
- **10s**—A response time below 10 seconds was required for users to keep their attention focused on the task.

Miller proposed that the ideal response time is around two seconds.

Shneiderman agreed with Miller that a two-second limit is appropriate for simple tasks, as long as the cost is not excessive. Shneiderman found that users "pick up the pace" of computer systems, that they were more productive at shorter response rates, and that they "consistently prefer the faster pace," below 1 to 2 seconds.

Although users prefer shorter response rates, the optimum system response time (SRT) depends on task complexity. Fast SRTs cause input errors while longer response times tax short-term memory and frustrate users. Users want consistency in response times.

Because surfing the web is mainly a low-complexity activity, users prefer faster response rates. Usage studies empirically confirm this need for speed; most pages are viewed for less than a second and few for more than 10 seconds.[21]

---

20. Robert B. Miller, "Response Time in Man-Computer Conversational Transactions," in *Proceedings of the AFIPS Fall Joint Computer Conference* 33 (Montvale, NJ: AFIPS Press, 1968), 267–277.

21. Bruce McKenzie and Andy Cockburn, "An Empirical Analysis of Web Page Revisitation," in *Proceedings of the 34th Hawaii International Conference on System Sciences* (Los Alamitos, CA: IEEE Computer Society Press, 2001). Found that web page revisitation is over 80 percent, visits are short, and bookmark lists are long.

An Interview with Ben Shneiderman, Ph.D.

I talked to Dr. Ben Shneiderman, one of the leading experts on HCI, to find out more about the relationship between speed and user satisfaction on the web.

Andy King: How does speed relate to usability and success on the web?

Ben Shneiderman: Usability plays a key role in web success stories…design, graphics, navigation, organization, consistency, etc. all play important roles. Speed is also vital—it's hard to get users to like a slow interface, and satisfaction grows with speed. Google is a good example of an excellent service that is even more valuable and appreciated because it is fast. Speed is the strongest correlate of user satisfaction.

King: Why do we prefer shorter response times?

Shneiderman: Lively interaction keeps the engagement high. For most people, wasted time, especially while just waiting for something to happen, is annoying.

King: What happens when we exceed our attention threshold (8 to 12 seconds)?

Shneiderman: Users not only grow frustrated, but they forget their next step, and have to reconstruct their intentions…often making mistakes that only exacerbate their frustration.

King: What do you think of the flow construct for user satisfaction on the web?

Shneiderman: Rapid movement through complex sequences of actions that move users toward a desired goal contributes to the flow experience. Users should be working just at the right level of challenge, accomplishing something they desire. There is a great thrill of finding what you want, and getting it rapidly so you can move on to the next step.[22]

---

22. Ben Shneiderman, email to author, 24 August 2002.

System Response Time Guidelines

Shneiderman suggests the following guidelines for system response times:[23]

- Users prefer shorter response times.
- Longer response times (> 15 seconds) are disruptive.
- Users change usage profiles with response time.
- Faster is not always better. Users tend to increase the rate of interaction, which may cause corresponding increased error rates.
- Users should be advised of long delays.
- Modest variability in response times is acceptable (plus or minus 50 percent of the mean).
- Unexpected delays may be disruptive.
- Response time should be appropriate to the task:
    - Typing, cursor motion, mouse selection: 50 to 150 milliseconds
    - Simple frequent tasks: 1 second
    - Common tasks: 2 to 4 seconds
    - Complex tasks: 8 to 12 seconds

23. Ben Shneiderman, *Designing the User Interface: Strategies for Effective Human-Computer Interaction*, 3d ed. (Reading, MA: Addison-Wesley, 1998). An excellent HCI book for designers.

Negative Impressions and Perceived Quality

The speed at which your pages display can affect user perceptions of the quality, reliability, and credibility of your web site. Ramsay, Barabesi, and Preece studied the effects of slow-loading pages on user perceptions of web sites.[24] Using delays of two seconds to two minutes (with an interval of 19.5 seconds), they asked users to rate pages on eight

24. Judith Ramsay, Alessandro Barabesi, and Jenny Preece, "A psychological investigation of long retrieval times on the World Wide Web," *Interacting with Computers* 10 (1998): 77–86.

criteria including "interesting content" and scannability. They found that pages with delays of 41 seconds or longer were perceived to be significantly less interesting and harder to scan. Note that the pages in this study loaded incrementally.

Perceived Usability

Jacko, Sears, and Borella studied the effects of network delay and type of document on perceived usability. They found that perceived usability of web sites was dependent on the length of delay and on the media used in web documents. When delays are short, users prefer documents that include graphics. When delays lengthen, however, users prefer text-only documents because graphics are viewed as contributing to the delay. As users become more experienced, their sensitivity to delay increases, increasing the need for "delay reduction mechanisms."[25]

Perceived Quality of Experience

Morris and Turner found that perceived quality of experience (Shackel's utility dimension) affects the adoption rate of IT.[26] How users perceive the quality of a system can affect how much they will actually use it.

They found that interface "enhancements" (graphics, animation, sound, etc.) had little effect on quality of experience "although these features may be aesthetically pleasing…they do little to remove actual barriers to the users' goal attainment."

Perceived Quality of Service

The speed at which your pages display affects their perceived quality and reliability. Bouch, Kuchinsky, and Bhatti investigated the effects of delay on perceived QoS in order to find an acceptable QoS level for e-commerce transactions. They tested delays

---

25. Julie A. Jacko, Andrew Sears, and Michael S. Borella, "The effect of network delay and media on user perceptions of web resources," *Behavior & Information Technology* 19, no. 6 (2000): 427–439.

26. Michael G. Morris and Jason M. Turner, "Assessing Users' Subjective Quality of Experience with the World Wide Web: An Exploratory Examination of Temporal Changes in Technology Acceptance," *International Journal of Human-Computer Studies* 54 (2001): 877–901.

from 2 to 73 seconds for both non-incremental and incrementally loaded pages.[27] Users rated latency quality versus delay on a scale of high, average, to low (see Table 1.1).

Table 1.1   Web Page Quality Rating versus Delay

Quality Rating	Range of Latency: Non-Incremental Display	Range of Latency: Incremental Display
High	0–5 seconds	0–39 seconds
Average	> 5 seconds	> 39 seconds
Low	> 11 seconds	> 56 seconds

The results show a mapping between objective QoS and the users' subjective perception of QoS. Pages that displayed quickly (0–5 seconds) were perceived to be of high quality with high-quality products. Pages that displayed slowly (> 11 seconds) were perceived to be of low quality and untrustworthy. In fact, slower pages caused some users to feel that the security of their purchases may have been compromised, and they abandoned their transactions.

Figure 1.3 shows the actual data behind Table 1.1 for the non-incremental display. This figure plots the number of low, average, and high ratings versus latency. The range where high ratings turn to low is between 8 to 10 seconds for non-incremental downloads, closely matching what Nielsen and others have found.

Figure 1.3
Latency quality ratings show a drop-off at around 8 to 10 seconds.

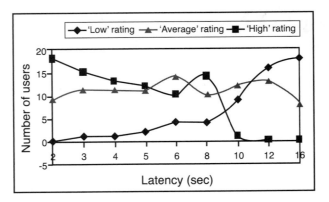

27. Anna Bouch, Allan Kuchinsky, and Nina Bhatti, "Quality is in the Eye of the Beholder: Meeting Users' Requirements for Internet Quality of Service," in *Proceedings of CHI2000 Conference on Human Factors in Computing Systems* (New York: ACM Press, 2000), 297–304.

Users tolerated nearly six times the delay for pages that displayed incrementally, although this tolerance decreased with usage. Test subjects rated pages as "average" with delays up to 39 seconds, and "low" with delays over 56 seconds.

The researchers also tested user requirements for speed by allowing them to click "increase quality" if they found the web page delay to be unacceptable. The average tolerance was 8.6 seconds with a standard deviation of 5.9 seconds. They attribute this large deviation in acceptable download times to contextual factors like web experience and user expectations. *The longer users interact with a site, the less they tolerate delays.*

Users will tolerate longer delays with tasks they perceive to be computationally complex. Users expect database access or complex calculations to take longer than displays of cached or static pages. Users form a conceptual model of system performance, which influences their tolerance for delay.

Credibility

Fogg et al. found that slow-loading pages reduce ease of use, which reduces credibility (or trustworthiness and expertise). Only difficult navigation was found to hurt credibility more.[28]

Bailout Rates and Attention Thresholds

The *bailout rate* is the percentage of users who leave a page before it loads and start looking for a faster, more engaging site. In their first "Need for Speed" study of 1999, Zona Research found that pages larger than 40K had bailout rates of 30 percent.[29] Once the designer reduced the same page to 34K, the bailout rate fell to between 6 and 8 percent, a dramatic decrease for just a few kilobytes. When fat pages were reduced to the recommended maximum of 34K, readership went up 25 percent.[30] These are averages,

28. B. J. Fogg et al., "What Makes Web Sites Credible? A Report on a Large Quantitative Study," in *Proceedings of the SIGCHI Conference on Human Factors in Computing Systems* (New York: ACM Press, 2001), 61–68.

29. Zona Research, "The Economic Impacts of Unacceptable Web-Site Download Speeds," *Zona Market Bulletin* [online], (Redwood City, CA: Zona Research, 1999 [cited 9 November 2002]), available from the Internet at http://www.keynote.com/solutions/assets/applets/wp_downloadspeed.pdf. The oft-quoted "Need for Speed I."

30. Jacob Nielsen, *Designing Web Usability*, 49.

and users with faster connections and processors will experience faster downloads, but they can also become frustrated.

Zona's second study, "Need for Speed II," took into account dynamic transactions in order to modify the so-called "8-second rule."[31] They recommend that designers of dynamic sites cut an additional 0.5 to 1.5 seconds off connection latency in order to stay at the same level of abandonment compared with static web pages. As the web moves from a "plumbing" (pipes delivering pages) to a "transaction" (a series of dynamically generated pages) model, they argue that "cumulative frustration" plays an important role in user satisfaction.

Cumulative Frustration and Time Budgets

Users can change the way they browse a site as they request and view additional pages. As they become more proficient, their learning "spills over," and users reduce their expected number of page views on returning visits. Clickstream-based analysis suggests that visitors trade off the number of pages requested and the time spent at each page.[32] Users may set "time budgets" for particular tasks, even though the tasks may take multiple pages to complete.

Provide Feedback for Longer Tasks

Without effective feedback, users will wait only so long for your pages to load. For longer delays, you can extend the time that users are willing to wait with realistic feedback. Displaying your pages incrementally, a crude form of feedback, can extend user tolerance for delays.

Myers found that users prefer percent-done progress indicators for longer delays.[33] These linear progress bars lower stress by allowing experienced users to estimate completion

---

31. Zona Research, "The Need for Speed II" [online], 2001.
32. Randolph E. Bucklin and Catarina Sismeiro, "A Model of Web Site Browsing Behavior Estimated on Clickstream Data" [online], (Los Angeles, CA: UCLA, 2001 [cited 9 November 2002]), available from the Internet at `http://ecommerce.mit.edu/papers/ERF/ERF129.pdf`.
33. Brad A. Myers, "The Importance of Percent-Done Progress Indicators for Computer-Human Interfaces," in *Proceedings of the ACM Conference on Human Factors in Computing Systems* (New York: ACM Press, 1985), 11–17.

times and plan more effectively. Such progress bars are commonly used in download managers.

Bickford found that with no feedback, half of his test subjects bailed out of applications after 8.5 seconds. Switching to a watch cursor delayed their departure to an average of 20 seconds. "An animated watch cursor was good for over a minute, and a progress bar would keep them waiting until the Second Coming."[34]

Dellaert and Kahn found that wait time negatively affects consumer evaluation of web sites, but that this effect could be mitigated by providing information about the delay.[35] Delay information reduces uncertainty between expected and actual delays. For longer delays, they found that countdown feedback, a form of percent-done indicator, was better than duration feedback.

They also found that delays before viewing pages are less frustrating than delays while viewing pages. In other words, any delay *after* a page has loaded—for example, a sluggish response while users are interacting with the page—is worse than delays *before* a page has loaded.

Response times below two seconds are ideal, but current bandwidths make this speed impractical, so we settle for 8 to 10 seconds. What does this mean for web page design?

Page Design Guidelines

Page size and complexity have a direct effect on page display speed. As you learned in the Introduction, the majority of current users are at 56Kbps or less. That trend will continue until at least 2004, with international users lagging behind until 2007. Table 1.2 shows the maximum allowable page size needed to meet three attention thresholds at different connection speeds (derived from Nielsen, *Designing Web Usability*, 2000).

---

34. Peter Bickford, "Worth the Wait," *Netscape's Developer Edge* [online], (Mountain View, CA: Netscape Communications, 1997 [cited 10 November 2002]), available from the Internet at http://developer.netscape.com/viewsource/bickford_wait.htm.

35. Benedict G. C. Dellaert and Barbara E. Kahn, "How Tolerable Is Delay? Consumers' Evaluations of Internet Web Sites after Waiting," *Journal of Interactive Marketing* 13, no. 1 (1999): 41–54. Found that countdown feedback nearly negates the negative effects of waiting for the web for retrospective evaluations.

Table 1.2   Maximum Page Size for Various Connection Speeds and Attention Thresholds

Bandwidth	Attention Threshold		
	1 Second	2 Seconds	10 Seconds
56.6Kbps	2KB	4KB	34KB
ISDN	8KB	16KB	150KB
T1	100KB	200KB	2MB

These figures assume 0.5-second latency.

You can see that 34KB is about the limit of total page size to achieve the 10-second attention threshold at 56Kbps. Under 30KB would be an appropriate limit for 8.6 seconds at 56Kbps. This is total page size, which includes ads and graphics. Assuming a 10KB banner ad and some small graphics, your HTML should be at most around 20K.

Designers who violate the 30KB limit will pay for their largesse with lost sales, increased bailout rates, and increased bandwidth costs.

The Limits of Short-Term and Working Memory

Chunking is important to the working of short-term memory. For example, we do not easily retain the number 7545551212 but have much less difficulty with 754–555–1212. There are three *chunks* and we know where to expect boundaries. Our short-term memory is limited in the number of "chunks" of information it can hold. As we gain expertise with an activity, we tend to think more abstractly and acquire shortcuts, increasing our overall chunk size and thus increasing how much we can perceive and accomplish.

Shneiderman and others suggest that delays increase user frustration due to the limits of short-term and working memory. Depending on complexity, "people can rapidly recognize approximately" three to "seven 'chunks' of information at a time, and hold them in short-term memory for 15 to 30 seconds."[36]

---

36. Shneiderman, "Response Time and Display Rate in Human Performance with Computers," 267–68.

George Miller's original (and entertaining) "The Magical Number Seven, Plus or Minus Two"[37] study was subsequently shown to be a maximum limit to short-term memory span for simple units of information along one dimension. Broadbent argued that the basic unit of memory is closer to three, where each chunk can perhaps hold three further chunks.[38] LeCompte showed that as word length or unfamiliarity increases, memory span decreases, and Miller's maximum memory span should really be three to cover 90 percent of the population.[39] Mandler said that the magic number is closer to five.[40] Some 44 years after Miller's original paper, Kareev found that the effect of capacity limitations of working memory forces people to rely on samples consisting of seven plus or minus two items, for simple binary variables.[41]

People make plans on what to do next, and form solutions to problems while waiting between tasks. Longer delays (11 to 15 seconds) tax the limits of short-term memory and frustrate users who cannot implement their plans, and errors increase. Extremely short response times also increase errors, but lower their cost, improving productivity and encouraging exploration. More complex tasks require the use of working memory, which slows the optimum response rate. Given their druthers, users prefer short response times to long ones.

---

36. Shneiderman, "Response Time and Display Rate in Human Performance with Computers," 267–68.

37. George A. Miller, "The Magical Number Seven, Plus or Minus Two: Some Limits on Our Capacity for Processing Information," *Psychological Review* 63 (1956): 81–97. "My problem is that I have been persecuted by an integer…"

38. Donald E. Broadbent, "The Magic Number Seven After Fifteen Years," in *Studies in Long-Term Memory*, ed. A. Kennedy and A. Wilkes (New York: Wiley, 1971), 3–18.

39. Denny C. LeCompte, "Seven, Plus or Minus Two, Is Too Much to Bear: Three (or Fewer) Is the Real Magic Number," in *Proceedings of the Human Factors and Ergonomics Society* 43rd Annual Meeting (Santa Monica, CA: HFES, 1999), 289–292.

40. George Mandler, "Organization in Memory," in *The Psychology of Learning and Motivation*, ed. K. W. Spence and J. T. Spence 1 (San Diego: Academic Press, 1967), 327–372.

41. Yaakov Kareev, "Seven (Indeed, Plus or Minus Two) and the Detection of Correlations," *Psychological Review* 107, no. 2 (2000): 397–402.

So what have we learned from all this? Speed of response is certainly one factor in user satisfaction on the web. Consistency of response times is another. But some researchers say that modeling human behavior in real-time environments with fixed performance metrics (like response times below 10 seconds) is too simplified. What we need is a more holistic approach.

Attunability

Some HCI researchers say that it is not so simple: users "attune" to a particular system's response rate regardless of its duration.[42] Ritchie and Roast say that user satisfaction with web performance is more complex than simple numeric response times. Users form a mental model of systems they are dealing with based on system response characteristics. To form this model, users perform a "selection and adjustment [of] *subjective time bases*, and adapting the rate at which the environment is monitored to meet its particular pace."[43] *Attuning* is the process of forming this mental model and adapting our expectations to a particular system's response rate.

Consistent response times and adequate feedback help users attune to a system's pace. Inconsistent response times and poor feedback reduce the "attunability" of a particular system, and "temporal interaction errors" ensue. Thus "the less variable the duration of a particular task, the more likely that users can attune to the environment"[44] and the more accurately users can distinguish tasks of differing duration.

Humans can attune to a remarkably varied range of response rates, anything from years to seconds. Everyone knows that postal mail takes a matter of days, that Domino's delivers pizza within minutes, and that traffic lights change in a matter of seconds. The web is different, however.

---

42. Innes Ritchie and Chris Roast, "Performance, Usability, and the Web," in *Proceedings of the 34th Hawaii International Conference on System Sciences* 5 (Los Alamitos, CA: IEEE Computer Society Press, 2001).
43. Chris Roast, "Designing for Delay in Interactive Information Retrieval," *Interacting with Computers* 10 (1998): 87–104. Introduced the notion of attunability.
44. Ibid., 91.

The Chaotic Web

On large decentralized networks like the web, the effects of latency can exceed the effects of improvements in performance. Conventional performance engineering and evaluation are not possible in this environment.

Chaotic large-scale systems like the web can introduce non-deterministic delays. An external object in a web page can take anywhere from tens of milliseconds to what seems like an eternity (30 to 40 seconds or longer) to download. Rigid performance metrics such as response times under 10 seconds can be less important than consistent response rates.

To meet the needs of users, you need to provide an environment with characteristics to which they can attune. Consistency of response times and feedback allows users to better "attune" to system delays.

Consistent Response Rates

The key to attunability is to minimize the variability of delays. Variability is the difference between the slowest and fastest possible response rates. "The larger this variation, the less well system delays can be associated with a task," and the lower the system's attunability.[45] By minimizing this range, you allow users to model your system more easily and adjust their performance expectations.

Design for Attuning

Designing for attuning implies the adoption of transparency as an architectural principle.[46] By offering feedback mechanisms as pages and objects download, you can ensure that users will minimize "temporal interaction errors" associated with inconsistent response times.

---

45. Ibid., 94.

46. Chris Roast and Innes Ritchie, "Transparency in Time," in *Proceedings of the Workshop on Software Architectures for Cooperative Systems* (Philadelphia: IFIP Working Group 2.7/13.4, 2000).

The idea is to offer feedback that matches user expectations. Linear progress bars, which match user expectations, can be used to give users real-time feedback. Server load, cache state, and file sizes can be displayed with server-side includes. All of these performance cues are designed to let the user know how the system is performing and form a mental model. Here is an example file size cue using SSI:

```
<a href="thisfile.zip">download this file</a>
(<!--#config sizefmt="abbrev" -->
<!--#fsize file="thisfile.zip" -->)
```

This code automatically displays the file size of the referenced file so the user can gauge how long it will take.

The antithesis of this concept is the Windows file copy animation. The system portrays the activity as an animation of pages flying across at a constant rate, independent of the actual progress being made. This is like a spinning watch cursor, which has no relation to the progress bar. The non-linear progress bar stalls near the end of the scale, while pages keep flying (see Figure 1.4). A better solution would be to create a linear progress bar, and change the animation to filling up a page or removing it entirely.

Figure 1.4
The non-linear Windows
file copy animation.

Users "attune" to the speed of the web's response. If your pages are slower than average or are inconsistent in size, users tend to tune out and go elsewhere. Optimizing the size of your pages and making them respond consistently can help users establish a rhythm as they surf through your site. Throw in a compelling experience, and some sites can attain the most elusive of web site goals, flow. You'll learn more about flow in Chapter 2, "Flow in Web Design."

Summary

This research suggests that without feedback, the length of time that users will wait for web pages to load is from 8 to 12 seconds. Nielsen recommends the average of 10 seconds. Bickford, Bouch, and Shneiderman found that most users will bail out of your page at around 8 to 8.6 seconds. Without feedback, that is the limit of people's ability to keep their attention focused while waiting.

If you provide continuous feedback through percent-done indicators, users will tolerate longer delays, up to 20 to 39 seconds, although their tolerance decreases with experience. Users will be more forgiving if you manage their delay experience with performance information. They will also tolerate increased delays if they perceive the task to be computationally complex, like a database access. Try to minimize response time variability by keeping page response times uniform to maximize attunability.

This research suggests the following web page design guidelines:

- Load in under 8.6 seconds (non-incremental display).
- Decrease these load times by 0.5 to 1.5 seconds for dynamic transactions.
- Minimize the number of steps needed to accomplish tasks—to avoid cumulative frustration from exceeding user time budgets.
- Load in under 20 to 30 seconds (incremental display) with useful content within 2 seconds.
- Provide performance information and linear feedback.
- Equalize page download times to minimize delay variability.

Web designers exceed these limits at their peril. Users associate slow-loading pages with inferior quality products and services, compromised security, and low credibility. Lower user satisfaction can lead to abandoned web sites and shopping carts.

Online Resources

- http://www.hcibib.org/—HCI Bibliography offers human-computer interaction resources, by Gary Perlman.

- http://www.keynote.com—Keynote Systems offers web site performance measurement and research.

- http://www.mercuryinteractive.com—Mercury Interactive offers web site performance measurement products and services.

- http://www.useit.com—Jakob Nielsen's usability portal includes his biweekly newsletter, Alertbox.

- http://www.webcriteria.com—Web Criteria offers automated usability tools (Site Analyst) that can find e-commerce bottlenecks to increase conversion rates.

2

Flow in Web Design

Imagine that you're doing your favorite activity—let's say, sailing. You're skimming along the waves, when suddenly the breeze freshens. You hike out to compensate, leaning back into the wind to keep the boat upright. A wave splashes your face. You shake your head and trim the main sheet for more speed. You are entirely focused on the movements of your body, the water rushing past, and keeping the boat right side up.

You're really flying now, just on the edge of control. You're so fully immersed in this activity, there's no room left in your awareness for distractions. Otherwise, you might catch a wave and capsize. You're having so much fun that you want this moment to last forever. Mihaly Csikszentmihalyi calls these exceptional moments *flow experiences.*[1] Flow can occur in practically any activity, including browsing the web.

---

1. Mihaly Csikszentmihalyi, *Finding Flow: The Psychology of Engagement with Everyday Life* (New York: Basic Books, 1997), 29.

This "optimal experience"[2] is "intrinsically enjoyable."[3] Time seems to stand still, and we lose our sense of self. We feel playful and are willing to try (and presumably buy) new things. Although flow can occur anywhere, certain activities like rock climbing, performing surgery, chess, and sailing lend themselves to this optimal state of focused attention. Responsive, well-designed web sites can also induce flow in their users.

On Flow and Mihaly Csikszentmihalyi

Mihaly Csikszentmihalyi, a professor and former chair of the Department of Psychology at the University of Chicago, pioneered the study of flow. He wrote that flow is the "holistic sensation that people feel when they act with total involvement."[4]

Csikszentmihalyi wanted to understand the experience of enjoyment. He asked, what motivates people to perform better? Extrinsic rewards like money and prestige are limited resources that ultimately are about comparisons between people. Status is a zero-sum game; so something else must motivate us humans. Intrinsic rewards, doing activities for the sheer joy of it, are the key to understanding flow.[5]

In order to understand intrinsic motivation, Csikszentmihalyi studied self-rewarding, or *autotelic*, activities. Csikszentmihalyi knew that if he could understand what made us tick, he could revolutionize how we work and play. He observed painters, rock climbers, dancers, musicians, and surgeons, taking surveys and later paging them at random intervals. His goal was to answer one of life's greatest questions: What makes life worth living?

The answer is that life is worth living when we can experience the joy of doing what we want to do, have autotelic experiences, or flow. Without flow "there would be little purpose in living."[6]

---

2. Mihaly Csikszentmihalyi, *Optimal Experience* (New York: Cambridge University Press, 1988).

3. Gayle Privette and Charles M. Bundrick, "Measurement of Experience: Construct and Content Validity of the Experience Questionnaire," *Perceptual and Motor Skills* 65 (1987): 315–332.

4. Mihaly Csikszentmihalyi, *Beyond Boredom and Anxiety: Experiencing Flow in Work and Play* (1975; reprint, with a Preface by Mihaly Csikszentmihalyi, San Francisco: Jossey-Bass, 2000), 36.

5. Ibid., 4.

6. Mihaly Csikszentmihalyi, "Towards a Psychology of Optimal Experience," in *Annual Review of Personality and Social Psychology*, ed. L. Wheeler (Beverly Hills, CA: Sage, 1982), 3:13–36.

Flow is a positive, highly enjoyable state of consciousness that occurs when our perceived skills match the perceived challenges we are undertaking. When our goals are clear, our skills are up to the challenge, and feedback is immediate, we become involved in the activity.

We can become so involved that we lose our sense of self and time distorts. The experience becomes autotelic or intrinsically rewarding; we do it for its own sake. People who have experienced flow consistently report the same nine dimensions:[7]

- Clear goals
- Unambiguous and immediate feedback
- Skills that just match challenges
- Merging of action and awareness
- Centering of attention on a limited stimulus field
- A sense of potential control
- A loss of self-consciousness
- An altered sense of time
- An autotelic experience

Flow depends on how we *perceive* our skills and the challenges at hand. We may feel "anxious one moment, bored the next, and in a state of flow immediately afterward."[8]

As you can imagine, as our skill level improves, we must undertake more difficult challenges to achieve a flow state. Flow encourages us to improve ourselves and our web sites. People tend to repeat activities they enjoy, so flow is like a Darwinian force of nature, subtly changing society.[9] That's why people tend to return to web sites they enjoy.[10] Csikszentmihalyi wrote this about flow and cultural evolution:

---

7. Csikszentmihalyi, *Beyond Boredom and Anxiety*.

8. Ibid., 50.

9. Paolo Inghilleri, *From Subjective Experience to Cultural Change* (New York: Cambridge University Press, 1999).

10. Donna L. Hoffman and Thomas. P. Novak, "Marketing in Hypermedia Computer-Mediated Environments: Conceptual Foundations," *Journal of Marketing* 60 (July 1996): 50–68.

"Flow is a sense that humans have developed in order to recognize patterns of action that are worth preserving and transmitting over time." [11]

The best memes are passed down through generations.

Attention! Supply Is Limited

Our supply of attention (otherwise known as "*bandwidth*") is limited. Csikszentmihalyi estimated that we can process about 126 bits per second, which I'll update in light of recent findings. This is based on our ability to recognize seven chunks of information per unit of time, plus or minus two, and Orme's estimate of our "attentional unit" of $1/18^{th}$ of a second.[12] This gives humans 18×7 or 126 bits per second of processing power.

As you learned in Chapter 1, "Response Time: Eight Seconds, Plus or Minus Two," our span of immediate memory is more on the order of five,[13] or as low as three,[14] which means that our bandwidth is on the order of 90 to 126 bits per second. That gives humans a processing power of around 5,400 to 7,560 bits of information per minute.[15]

What can we accomplish with this limited attention capacity? Csikszentmihalyi estimated that listening to a conversation takes about 40 bits per second, or about one third to one half of our bandwidth. That's why it is so difficult to listen to multiple conversations, or to play engrossing games or sports while listening to a conversation. It's also one reason why designers are told to minimize distractions on the web.

---

11. Csikszentmihalyi, *Optimal Experience*, 34.

12. John E. Orme, *Time, Experience, and Behavior* (London: Iliffe Books, 1969).

13. George Mandler, "Organization in Memory," in *The Psychology of Learning and Motivation*, ed. K. W. Spence and J. T. Spence (New York: Academic Press, 1967), 1:327–372.

14. Denny C. LeCompte, "Seven, Plus or Minus Two, Is Too Much to Bear: Three (or Fewer) Is the Real Magic Number," *Proceedings of the Human Factors and Ergonomics Society 43rd Annual Meeting* (1999): 289–292.

15. Csikszentmihalyi, *Optimal Experience*, 17–18.

What Causes Flow Online?

Speed and control play a big part in establishing flow in online interactions. In 1996, Hoffman and Novak extended Csikszentmihalyi's work to consumer navigation on the web. They proposed that users return to web sites that facilitate flow and suggest that online marketers offer these "flow opportunities."[16] It turns out that marketers are listening. Nearly 45 percent of the users that they surveyed experienced flow online. A subsequent study found that 47 percent of users had experienced flow on a specific web site.[17] Hoffman and Novak defined flow online as:

> *"the state occurring during network navigation which is: (1) characterized by a seamless sequence of responses facilitated by machine interactivity, (2) intrinsically enjoyable, (3) accompanied by a loss of self-consciousness, and (4) self-reinforcing."*[18]

The prerequisites for flow online are similar to those offline. On the web, flow "is determined by (1) high levels of skill and control; (2) high levels of challenge and arousal; and (3) focused attention; and (4) is enhanced by interactivity and telepresence."[19] Telepresence is a new dimension unique to online environments where users feel they are part of the action.[20]

Novak, Hoffman, and Yung tested and refined their conceptual model of flow to create a structural model that describes the factors that make for a compelling online experience. They found that flow is a multidimensional construct with nine variables, including interactive speed.

---

16. Hoffman and Novak, "Marketing in Hypermedia Computer-Mediated Environments," 66.

17. Thomas P. Novak, Donna L. Hoffman, and Yiu-Fai Yung, "Measuring the Customer Experience in Online Environments: A Structural Modeling Approach," *Marketing Science* 19, no. 1 (2000): 22–42.

18. Hoffman and Novak, "Marketing in Hypermedia Computer-Mediated Environments," 57.

19. Novak, Hoffman, and Yung, "Measuring the Customer Experience," 24.

20. Jonathan Steuer, "Defining Virtual Reality: Dimensions Determining Telepresence," *Journal of Communication* 42, no. 4 (1992): 73–93.

Speed and Flow

Hoffman, Novak, and Yung found that the speed of interaction had a "direct positive influence on flow" on feelings of challenge and arousal (which directly influence flow), and on importance. Skill, control, and time distortion also had a direct influence on flow.[21]

The researchers then applied their model to consumer behavior on the web. They tested web applications (chat, newsgroups, and so on) and web shopping, asking subjects to specify which features were most important when shopping on the web.

They found that speed had the greatest effect on the amount of time spent online and on frequency of visits for web applications. For repeat visits, the most important factors were skill/control, length of time on the web, importance, and speed.

So to make your site compelling enough to return to, make sure that it offers a perceived level of control by matching challenges to user skills, important content, and fast response times.

Experiential versus Goal-Directed Flow

Confirming their previous work, the authors found two types of flow: experiential (associated with recreational surfing) and goal-directed (associated with research, shopping, etc.). The authors suggest that these two types of activities require different web site designs to facilitate flow.

Less-experienced users tend to see the web in a hedonic, playful way, while more experienced users tend to view the web in a utilitarian way, or a means to accomplish tasks. The authors found that telepresence/time distortion, exploratory behavior, focused attention, and challenge/arousal correlated with recreational web use, while skill/control, importance, and experience correlated with task-oriented activities, such as research, work, and shopping.

---

21. Novak, Hoffman, and Yung, "Measuring the Customer Experience," 34.

There is some debate over which type of flow is more common on the web. A subsequent study found that flow is more likely to occur during task-oriented activities than during recreational activities.[22] Nantel, Sénécal, and Gharbi found that flow contributes to more hedonic online shopping experiences but not to utilitarian shopping.[23] They suggest that e-tailers offer both types of activities for a compelling shopping experience. Offer "flow opportunities" plus utilitarian features like one-click buying, intuitive searches, and customized pages.

In either case, to facilitate flow, as designers we must offer plenty of speed and "enough challenge to arouse the consumer, but not so much that she becomes frustrated navigating through the site and logs off."[24]

An Interview with Mihaly Csikszentmihalyi

To find out more about flow, speed, and web design, I talked to Dr. Mihaly Csikszentmihalyi, who popularized the notion of flow.

Andy King: You talk about immediate feedback being a prerequisite for the flow state. How does speed of interaction influence flow?

Mihaly Csikszentmihalyi: If you mean the speed at which the program loads, the screens change, the commands are carried out—then indeed speed should correlate with flow. If you are playing a fantasy game, for instance, and it takes time to move from one level to the next, then the interruption allows you to get distracted, to lose the concentration on the alternate reality. You have time to think: "Why am I wasting time on this? Shouldn't I be taking the dog for a walk, or studying?"— and the game is over, psychologically speaking.

King: Responsive feedback of an activity and feelings of control go hand in hand. Can you elaborate on that?

---

22. Donna L. Hoffman, Thomas P. Novak, and Adam Duhachek, "The Influence of Goal-Directed and Experiential Activities on Online Flow Experiences," *Journal of Consumer Psychology* 13 (2002).

23. Jacques Nantel, Sylvain Sénécal, and Jamel Gharbi, "The Influence of the Flow on Hedonic and Utilitarian Shopping Values," *Advances in Consumer Research* 29 (2002).

24. Novak, Hoffman, and Yung, "Measuring the Customer Experience," 39.

Csikszentmihalyi: Actually it's not so much the "feeling" of control, as the fact that you can act without thinking, without interruption, and making your own choices (for example, BEING in control). If a computer program has a mind of its own, is not responsive to your commands, or is so slow as to appear to be a moron, then you are again brought back to "reality" and lose flow.

King: Has your definition of flow changed over the years?

Csikszentmihalyi: The only change has been that we found it takes above average challenges AND skills to get into flow. Also, there seem to be individual differences so that some people prefer to be in control (that is, high skill, moderate challenge) to being in flow.

King: You said that web sites should be like a gourmet meal to enable flow.[25] Can you elaborate?

Csikszentmihalyi: What I meant is that like in a good meal, you should have varieties of tastes and textures, metaphorically speaking.

King: What do you think the key attributes would be of web sites that enable flow?

Csikszentmihalyi: The key attribute is that it should be very user-friendly and transparent at first, but one should immediately be able to find complexity in it, so as to find quickly the right level of opportunities for "action" that match one's skills. These "challenges" include the visual aspects as well as the content.[26]

Shopping Site Design

Hoffman, Novak, and Yung performed an additional survey on web shopping using a list of features that shoppers found important on the Internet. They found customer support to be very important for a "smooth" shopping experience. Speed plays a role in a compelling shopping experience, contributing significantly to ease of contact and variety.[27]

---

25. John Geirland, "Go With The Flow," *Wired* 4, no. 9 (1996): 160–161. Available from the Internet at `http://www.wired.com/wired/archive/4.09/czik.html`.
26. Mihaly Csikszentmihalyi, email to author, 30 August 2002.
27. Novak, Hoffman, and Yung, "Measuring the Customer Experience," 38.

Variety and quality of information are important to consumers. Shoppers don't want cutting-edge technology, however. It just gets in the way of consumer goals.

Flow Can Be Measured

The researchers found that "the degree to which the online experience is compelling can be defined, measured, and related well to important marketing variables."[28] Marketers can use their flow model to discover the secrets of online success.

The Benefits of Flow Online

People who experience flow tend to be more playful,[29] exploratory,[30] and willing to try new things. They tend to stay longer, and return to web sites that facilitate flow. Hoffman and Novak found the following benefits of flow online:[31]

- Increased learning
- Exploratory and positive behavior
- Positive subjective experience
- Perceived sense of control over their interaction

The bottom line is that people in flow are having fun, and truly enjoying themselves. Of course, you can have too much of a good thing. The authors warn that playful people in flow can take longer to complete tasks, although staying longer on your web site isn't necessarily a bad thing. People in flow can also become overinvolved in an activity.

Marketers know that engaged users tend to buy more products, so making your site flow can make a big difference to the bottom line. It is relatively easy to get users to come to your site, but getting them to stay is another matter.

---

28. Ibid., 22.
29. Jane Webster, Linda Trevino, and Lisa Ryan, "The Dimensionality and Correlates of Flow in Human Computer Interactions," *Computers in Human Behavior* 9, no. 4 (1993): 411–426. Flow means fun and playfulness, which increases use.
30. Jawaid A. Ghani and Satish P. Deshpande, "Task Characteristics and the Experience of Optimal Flow in Human-Computer Interaction," *The Journal of Psychology* 128, no. 4 (1994): 381–391.
31. Hoffman and Novak, "Marketing in Hypermedia Computer-Mediated Environments."

Enabling Flow with Web Design

As you have seen, flow occurs under a limited set of circumstances. Users can experience flow only if their trips through cyberspace feel seamless, with fast response, immediate feedback, and few distractions. Users who experience flow feel their skills match available challenges. To enable flow, make sure your site has the following traits:

- **Speed**—Interactive speed is a significant factor in all models of user satisfaction. Make your pages load quickly and minimize the variability of delay. Be especially careful to avoid sluggish response after your pages have loaded.

- **Feedback**—Provide fast, unambiguous feedback for user input and the following elements:

    - Links (include hover, visited, and active styles)

    - Navigation widgets (menus, etc.)

    - Display performance variables (server load, cache state, page/file sizes, download progress bars)

- **Clear navigation**—Include signposts—such as site maps, breadcrumb trails, and "you are here" landmarks—to help visitors find their way so they can easily form a mental model of your site.

- **Match challenges to skills**—Offer an adaptable/adjustable interface that gives users control over their environment's complexity that is appropriate to their skill level. Stage their experience. Make it easy at first, but offer more complex challenges as users gain experience.

- **Simplicity**—Uncluttered layout and minimal features reduce the attention load.

- **Importance**—Make your offerings appear important and credible with professional design, impressive clients, and outside recognition.

- **Design for fun and utility**—Offer a rich yet responsive experience, plus tools to help users accomplish their goals quickly and easily.

- **Avoid cutting-edge technology**—Cutting-edge technology gets in the way of user goals. Research shows that users don't want it; they just want to get their information.

- **Minimize animation**—It distracts users, who often have limited attention.

Summary

No matter how you slice the performance pie, it is clear that to ensure that you have satisfied, repeat customers online, you have to design for speed, feedback, and flow. Offering a consistently fast-loading web site with unambiguous feedback can contribute to a compelling online experience.

Give your users a sense of perceived control by offering them challenges matched to their skills. Use a simple layout with minimal distractions, offer interesting well-chunked and delineated content, and make navigation and performance transparent. Happy users are loyal users who will keep coming back to purchase your products and use your services.

Online Resources

- `http://elab.vanderbilt.edu/`—Vanderbilt's eLab research center is devoted to studying the Internet, including flow.
- `http://www.hcibib.org/`—HCI Bibliography features a searchable database of human-computer interaction resources.
- `http://www.humanfactors.com/`—Human Factors International has an excellent free monthly newsletter on user interface design issues.

II

Optimizing Markup:
HTML and XHTML

3

HTML Optimization

HTML is still the *lingua franca* for publishing hypertext documents on the web. With simple markup tags like <h1> and </h1> used to denote structure, HTML has become the universal language of the web. As designers and browser manufacturers morphed HTML into the web equivalent of PageMaker, however, HTML code became too verbose with presentational tags, scripts, and objects intermixed with structural markup. This chapter and the ones that follow show you how to optimize and simplify your code for maximum speed, while still maintaining the functionality and visual appeal of your site.

Ask any group of users today what makes the web so slow, and you'll hear about large video, Flash, and image files. You might hear about overused and unoptimized Java and JavaScript. What is seldom mentioned is bloated HTML. Yet HTML size is the one web page component that users cannot control. They can turn off JavaScript, images, plug-ins, and Java, but they can't turn off HTML bloat—only designers can.

Because it has looser rules, HTML offers more opportunities for optimization than its newer cousin, XHTML. In HTML, you can omit some end tags and abbreviate attributes and still have a valid document. In XHTML, every tag must be closed, every attribute fully qualified and quoted. Because HTML offers more opportunities for savings and it isn't going away anytime soon, it is the focus of this chapter. Chapter 5, "Extreme XHTML," focuses on optimizing XHTML, which can use a subset of the techniques discussed here.

What Is HTML Optimization?

Often overlooked, HTML optimization is key for fast page display. *HTML optimization* is the process of minimizing HTML file size and complexity to maximize page display speed.[1] The typical web page contains extra information that browsers don't need to render your page. Look inside most pages on the web and you'll find whitespace, comments, and redundant attributes that can all be safely removed with no change in appearance. Unwinding or eliminating complex tables can also help speed up page display.

But HTML optimization doesn't stop there. Through techniques like CSS optimization, URL abbreviation, conditional code, minimization of HTTP requests, and other "shunting" techniques, you can dramatically reduce total HTML file size and complexity.

Why Optimize HTML?

Users hate to wait. As you learned in Chapter 1, "Response Time: Eight Seconds, Plus or Minus Two," users want fast-loading pages. After waiting 8 to 10 seconds (about 34K on 56Kbps modems), users become frustrated and bailout rates jump dramatically. Users also want reasonably uniform response times and linear feedback so that they can attune to the response rate of your site.

Reducing your total page footprint and HTTP-request load can also have a direct impact on your bandwidth costs, especially for busier sites.

---

1. Andrew King, "Extreme HTML Optimization" [online], (Darien, CT: Jupitermedia Corp., 2001 [cited 13 November 2002]), available from the Internet at http://www.webreference.com/authoring/languages/html/optimize/.

Increasing Complexity=Higher Bandwidth Designs

As the web and HTML have rapidly evolved, sites have grown fatter and more complex. With each new version, HTML added new tags and attributes to accommodate new features.[2] As new features are used, file size and complexity invariably increase. Flash, DHTML, Java, audio, and video have become *de rigueur* for higher-profile sites. Complex 2D and 3D animations vie for our attention. Simple text navigation bars have been replaced by complex multi-image JavaScript-powered extravaganzas.

Web Page Size Inflation

The average size and complexity of web pages has increased dramatically since the early days of the web.[3,4] In a brief survey using the Wayback Machine (`http://www.archive.org`), I found that the average "base page," or HTML page size, for five of the busiest sites had increased from 8,297 to 28,290 bytes between 1996 and late 2002. During that time, the bandwidth of most home users increased from around 28.8Kbps to 56.6Kbps.

For example, since 1996, Yahoo.com's home page HTML has increased from 5,998 to 30,887 bytes, over a five-fold increase in HTML page size.

3. Andrew King, "A Brief Homepage Survey" [online], (Ann Arbor, MI: Web Site Optimization, LLC, 2002), available from the Internet at `http://www.WebSiteOptimization.com`. A survey of five of the busiest sites on the web (AOL.com, Disney.com, Lycos.com, Microsoft.com, and Yahoo.com) found that total page size has increased from 40,223 bytes to 86,995 bytes from Oct. 1996 to Sep. 2002.

4. Patrick Mills and Chris Loosley, "A Performance Analysis of 40 e-Business Web Sites," *CMG Journal of Computer Resource Management*, no. 102 (Spring 2001): 28-33, available from the Internet at `http://www.keynote.com/solutions/assets/applets/Performance_Analysis_of_40_e-Business_Web_Sites.pdf`. In January 2002, this study showed that the average "base page" size (HTML) of the top 40 e-business web sites was 28,537 bytes, with a content size of 44,191 and a total size averaging 72,802 bytes composed of 21 objects.

2. W3C, "HyperText Markup Language Home Page" [online], (Cambridge, MA: World Wide Web Consortium (W3C), 1995), available from the Internet at `http://www.w3.org/MarkUp/`.

The Ideal Web Page

The ideal web page is a finely tuned symphony of one or more optimized components working in harmony. In a perfect world (wide web), the content would be clearly marked up with structural tags, while the presentation would be handled by style sheets. Efficient dynamic scripts would be embedded in the page or linked to external files (in the case of XHTML, this is practically a requirement) and "objects" (such as images and Java applets) would be clearly delineated by size and weight. Scripts with three-letter acronyms (CGI/PHP/JSP/ASP) would sip at backend databases on highly tuned HTTP servers in a delicate dance that—when done right—would be a site to behold.

In practice, the picture is not so rosy. What we find is that presentation (in the form of font tags, tables used for layout, etc.) is mixed into content, muddying the waters for automated agents, screen readers, and browsers. Overused images jerkily reflow pages (no dimensions specified), and Java applications and Flash gizmos scream for our attention, scrolling this way and that with the latest recycled news flashes and "skip intro" splash screens. (Sounds a bit like Dr. Seuss here, but I digress.) All this extra noise detracts from what we really want to see, which is content we can use—fast.

HTML (or XHTML, and someday XML) is the glue that binds all these disparate pieces together. What you will learn in this chapter is how to minimize the footprint of your pages so that they fly onto your users' screens. Subsequent chapters address the other components that make up a web page, including CSS, JavaScript, images, multimedia, CGI scripts, some server-based techniques, and HTTP compression.

A Trim Skeleton

You can think of the HTML portion of your page as a skeleton, on which all the various components fall into place. This skeleton in large part determines the initial display speed of your pages.[5] HTML pages cannot be multithreaded and usually are not served from a content delivery network. One glance at your progress bar tells you that 235K

---

5. Mills and Loosley, "Performance Analysis of 40 e-Business Web Sites."

HTML catalog will take some time, while that 15K home page should display fast. If you minimize the initial HTML footprint of your pages, your site can quickly display useful content to your users.

The idea is to use the minimum amount of markup to render a page that still works and validates. This is especially important on high-traffic pages like home pages.

Illegible HTML?

The knock against HTML optimization is that the optimized markup is hard to read and modify. The problem is that most users don't have to read your markup; they just want your information fast. The extra effort required by designers to optimize the size of their high-traffic pages is well worth it, both in terms of happier users with lower bailout rates and happier bosses with lower bandwidth charges and higher conversion rates.

You can put systems into place that will make updating optimized pages easier. At WebReference.com, we used scripts and server-side includes to streamline the updating and optimization process.[6] You can label major areas within your pages without those messy byte-hungry comments. You can employ mapping techniques that make the optimization process reversible for easier maintenance. After a while, you become so familiar with the markup that updating optimized pages by hand becomes second nature.

Bandwidth versus Beauty

Web design is all about balance. Before CSS, web design was largely a tradeoff between bandwidth and beauty; functional utility and aesthetics. CSS changes this equation. Now you can create appealing designs that load quickly, but it takes real skill to find the right balance between appearance and functionality and craft pages that load quickly yet have visual appeal.

---

6. Andrew King, "Evolution of a Home Page" [online], (Darien, CT: Jupitermedia Corporation, 2001), available from the Internet at http://www.webreference.com/dev/evolution/.

The Minimalist Standards School of Design

Recently, there's been a movement toward minimalist standards-based design, reminiscent of the early days of the web. Pioneers like Jeffrey Zeldman[7] (his Web Standards Project in particular), Eric Costello,[8] and Eric Meyer[9] have shown that compelling sites can be made with minimal markup. These standards samurai use low-impact techniques like CSS rollovers to replace bandwidth-hungry image rollovers and external style sheets to replace table-based designs. This "forward compatibility" mindset is beginning to replace a backward-compatible mode. As more users switch over to standards-based browsers, you'll see more sites adopting this approach. We cover these issues in Chapter 5, "Extreme XHTML," and Chapter 8, "Advanced CSS Optimization."

7. Jeffrey Zeldman et al., "The Web Standards Project" [online], (New York: The Web Standards Project, 1998), available from the Internet at `http://www.webstandards.org/`.

8. Owen Briggs, Steve Champeon, Eric Costello, and Matthew Patterson, *Cascading Style Sheets: Separating Content from Presentation* (Birmingham, England: glasshaus, 2002). See also `http://www.glish.com`.

9. Eric A. Meyer, *CSS: The Definitive Guide* (Cambridge, MA: O'Reilly and Associates, 2000). See also `http://www.meyerweb.com`.

How Modern Browsers Work with HTML

Browsers interact with servers on the Internet using TCP/IP and HyperText Transfer Protocol (HTTP).[10] A browser issues a GET request with a page's URI, and an HTTP server responds with a "message" that contains HTML. This message is "a byte stream of ASCII characters." Browsers download this stream of text as fast as possible. They don't download HTML files line by line; these are for human consumption and editing convenience.

10. Roy T. Fielding et al., "Hypertext Transfer Protocol—HTTP/1.1," RFC 2616 [online], (Reston, VA: The Internet Society, 1999), available from the Internet at `http://www.ietf.org/rfc/rfc2616.txt`.

Lines are "delimited by an optional carriage return followed by a mandatory line feed character. The client should not assume that the carriage return will be present. *Lines may be of any length.*"[11]

The browser parses the document according to the specified or implied Document Type Definition (DTD). The parser makes a single pass through the document, starting at the head and working down to the end until all objects and HTML have been rendered. The parser inserts tags where they are implied and ignores or collapses to a single space any excess whitespace characters that appear before, after, and between tags. It does not display comments. Content between tags is displayed according to the associated DTD. Faulty HTML may require extra overhead, slowing display speed especially on slower systems like PDAs.

As the document downloads, browsers send out additional HTTP requests, one per object. An *object* can be any external file like CSS, JavaScript, images, and multimedia. Each HTTP request adds additional time, which can vary considerably, to the total page-display speed due to latency. Modern browsers send out multiple simultaneous HTTP requests (from 2 to 8) to speed downloads, especially on faster connections. That's why CNET's search.com had only four graphics on their home page in 1998, three of which were ads.[12]

Line Length

HTML and XHTML have no official maximum line length; however, some HTML email programs (for example, Microsoft Outlook in Windows NT) give an overflow warning for viruses if your lines are longer than 255 characters. Most text editors have a practical limit due to buffer sizes. If you use vi to edit your files in Unix, you will find that it has an 80-character limit. If you are not emailing your HTML and you want to fully optimize a high-traffic page, feel free to remove most returns.

---

11. Tim Berners-Lee, "The Original HTTP as defined in 1991" [online], (Cambridge, MA: World Wide Web Consortium, 1991), available from the Internet at `http://www.w3.org/Protocols/HTTP/AsImplemented.html`.

12. Matt Rosoff, "More Great Tips from CNET Designers" [online], (San Francisco, CA: CNET Networks, 1998), available from the Internet at `http://www.builder.com/Graphics/CTips2/`.

Older versions of the Oracle Information Server will break all lines longer than 2,048 characters on the fly. If you plan on emailing your HTML pages or want to play it safe, it's best to stick with no more than 255-character lines of HTML markup. If you don't stay within that guideline, make sure that your lines are less than 2,000 characters long.

Because HTML documents typically have shorter lines, removing unnecessary line breaks can save you up to 12 percent off file sizes. Here's an example:

```
<table>
<tr>
<td>speed</td>
</tr>
<tr>
<td>me</td>
</tr>
<tr>
<td>up</td>
</tr>
</table>
```

Becomes:

```
<table><tr><td>speed</td></tr><tr><td>me</td></tr><tr><td>up</td></tr></table>
```

This is a savings of 10 bytes, or 11 percent (10/90).

How to Optimize Your HTML

Optimizing HTML is a matter of using the fewest number of bytes to deliver a valid page that renders properly. There are a number of techniques you can use to shrink your HTML. These include removing whitespace, omitting optional closing tags and quotes, removing redundant tags and attributes, cutting comments, and minimizing HTTP requests. This last point is important to keep in mind. We'll delve more deeply into graphics in Chapter 12, "Optimizing Web Graphics." First, let's start with the DOCTYPE declaration.

Step 1: Choose the Right *DOCTYPE*

As far as speed goes, there are two things to consider when choosing a DOCTYPE and coding style: DOCTYPE switching and parsing speed. By now you've seen the three DTDs you can use at the top of HTML documents (see Chapter 5, "Extreme XHTML" for details). Depending on the DTD that you choose and some internal parameters the browser developers have chosen, browsers switch to one of two or three "modes" to render your HTML document: standards, almost standards, and quirks modes. For more information on "almost standards" mode, see `http://www.mozilla.org/docs/web-developer/quirks/doctypes.html`.

Standards Mode versus Quirks Mode

The "standards" mode can be fastest because the parsing code is smaller and less complex. The browser is most likely to invoke this mode when you use the strict DTD. Keep in mind that there's not a one-to-one relationship between the DOCTYPE you choose and the mode browsers switch into, although they do have an influence.[13] For more details, see Matthias Gutfeldt's article on DOCTYPE switching, available at `http://gutfeldt.ch/matthias/articles/doctypeswitch.html`.

There are some tradeoffs, however. Strict means just that—*strict*. No deprecated tags allowed. Some designers may have to rethink how they lay out pages. A common method some authors use is to first markup and validate the structure of their documents and then add presentation in the form of style sheets.

As you can imagine, quirks mode by its very nature is slower to parse HTML than standards mode. The parsers for quirks mode are necessarily more complex to allow for all the permutations of looser legacy markup.

Coding Style

For HTML, your coding style can affect download and display speed. When you use the strict DTD and close all tags, the browser can use a faster parsing algorithm and does less work inserting and matching tags. Your pages will render faster but will be slightly larger because of the closing tags. On the other hand, omitting optional closing tags can yield smaller pages that will download faster but render slightly slower—yet they will still be valid. Either method is a valid approach, but the former makes for a smoother

---

13. Eric Meyer, "DOCTYPE Grid" [online], (Cleveland, OH: Meyerweb.com, 2002), available from the Internet at `http://www.meyerweb.com/eric/dom/dtype/dtype-grid.html`.

transition to XHTML. One approach is to fully optimize home pages (omit optional closing tags and quotes) and create well-formed interior pages (use XHTML-like HTML with closing tags and fully qualified attributes).

Step 2: Minimize HTTP Requests

Because each HTTP request takes an indeterminate amount of time, it's important to minimize the number of HTTP requests per page. As discussed earlier, the browser issues HTTP GET requests, and the HTTP server responds with the requested object. Each object—including HTML pages, images and multimedia, external style sheets, and JavaScript—takes one HTTP request. To get a better idea of how to improve the conversation between client and server, let's take a look at a real-world example. Let's optimize the prototype of Elivad.com's home page (see Figure 3.1). Elivad claims to boost click-through rates for online ads.

Figure 3.1
Elivad.com prototype with
graphic rollovers.

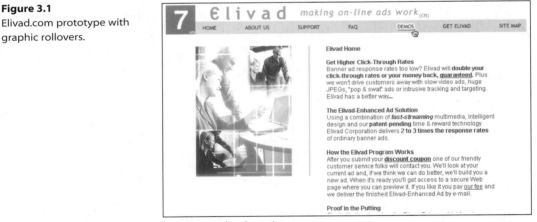

http://www.elivad.com/

Here's an abbreviated log file of Elivad.com, which uses graphic rollovers after loading this page:

```
192.168.1.1 - - [07/Sep/2002:11:07:24 -0400] "GET / HTTP/1.1" 200 6289
192.168.1.1 - - [07/Sep/2002:11:07:26 -0400] "GET /css/company.css HTTP/1.1" 304 503
192.168.1.1 - - [07/Sep/2002:11:07:27 -0400] "GET /pics/logo.gif HTTP/1.1" 304 10582
192.168.1.1 - - [07/Sep/2002:11:07:28 -0400] "GET /pics/toptext450.gif HTTP/1.1" 304 6855
192.168.1.1 - - [07/Sep/2002:11:07:28 -0400] "GET /pics/spacer.gif HTTP/1.1" 304 43
```

```
192.168.1.1 - - [07/Sep/2002:11:07:28 -0400] "GET /pics/home_off.gif HTTP/1.1" 200 305
192.168.1.1 - - [07/Sep/2002:11:07:29 -0400] "GET /pics/map_on.gif HTTP/1.1" 200 421
192.168.1.1 - - [07/Sep/2002:11:07:29 -0400] "GET /pics/get_on.gif HTTP/1.1" 200 468
192.168.1.1 - - [07/Sep/2002:11:07:29 -0400] "GET /pics/demo_on.gif HTTP/1.1" 200 400
192.168.1.1 - - [07/Sep/2002:11:07:29 -0400] "GET /pics/faq_on.gif HTTP/1.1" 200 314
192.168.1.1 - - [07/Sep/2002:11:07:29 -0400] "GET /pics/support_on.gif HTTP/1.1" 200 424
192.168.1.1 - - [07/Sep/2002:11:07:29 -0400] "GET /pics/about_on.gif HTTP/1.1" 200 460
192.168.1.1 - - [07/Sep/2002:11:07:30 -0400] "GET /pics/home_on.gif HTTP/1.1" 200 360
192.168.1.1 - - [07/Sep/2002:11:07:30 -0400] "GET /pics/home_image2.gif HTTP/1.1" 200
21004
192.168.1.1 - - [07/Sep/2002:11:07:30 -0400] "GET /pics/map_off.gif HTTP/1.1" 200 360
192.168.1.1 - - [07/Sep/2002:11:07:30 -0400] "GET /pics/get_off.gif HTTP/1.1" 200 401
192.168.1.1 - - [07/Sep/2002:11:07:30 -0400] "GET /pics/demo_off.gif HTTP/1.1" 200 352
192.168.1.1 - - [07/Sep/2002:11:07:32 -0400] "GET /pics/faq_off.gif HTTP/1.1" 200 281
192.168.1.1 - - [07/Sep/2002:11:07:32 -0400] "GET /pics/support_off.gif HTTP/1.1" 200 366
192.168.1.1 - - [07/Sep/2002:11:07:32 -0400] "GET /pics/about_off.gif HTTP/1.1" 200 392
```

Notice the number of HTTP requests. Each corresponds to an image, an external CSS or JavaScript file, or the HTML file itself. The total number of bytes transferred is 50,580 bytes, with 20 HTTP requests. The seven graphic rollovers account for 14 of these HTTP requests, two for each item.

This home page takes about 15 seconds to download at 56Kbps. This is due to the total size of the page (50,580 bytes at 4,500 bytes per second) and the latency introduced from HTTP requests. Each HTTP request takes an indeterminate about of time, depending on network conditions. Jakob Nielsen found that on average it takes about 1/2 to 2 seconds per HTTP request.[14]

An Optimized Example

Now let's take that same page and optimize it. By converting images and rollovers into text, consolidating and optimizing images, and optimizing JavaScripts and style sheets, you can minimize the number of requests and speed up your pages. By replacing the graphic rollovers and JavaScript with CSS rollovers and any buttons with links and colored backgrounds, you can eliminate the majority of images. So instead of this:

```
<td align="center"><a href="index.html" onMouseOut="imageout(IMG01, 'pics/home_off.gif')"
onMouseOver="imagein(IMG01, 'pics/home_on.gif'); return true"
target="_top"><IMG NAME="IMG01" SRC="pics/home_off.gif" WIDTH="64" HEIGHT="22" BORDER="0"
```

---

14. Jakob Nielsen, *Designing Web Usability: The Practice of Simplicity* (Indianapolis, IN: New Riders Publishing, 2000).

```
ALT="HOME"></A></td>
<td align="center">
<a href="about/" onMouseOut="imageout(IMG02, 'pics/about_off.gif')"
onMouseOver="imagein(IMG02, 'pics/about_on.gif'); return true"
target="_top"><IMG NAME="IMG02" SRC="pics/about_off.gif" WIDTH="105" HEIGHT="22"
BORDER="0" ALT="ABOUT US"></A></td>
```

Do this:

```
.buttons a:hover {background:#fff; color: blue;}
...
<td align="center" class="buttons">HOME</td>
<td align="center" class="buttons"><A HREF="about/">ABOUT US</A></td>
```

Here's the same page after replacing the graphic rollovers with CSS (see Figure 3.2).

Figure 3.2
Elivad.com after optimization.

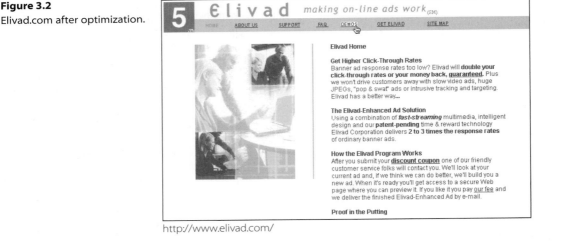

http://www.elivad.com/

Here's the log file after loading this optimized page:

```
192.168.1.1 - - [07/Sep/2002:11:06:22 -0400] "GET /index_new.html HTTP/1.1" 200 4083
192.168.1.1 - - [07/Sep/2002:11:06:24 -0400] "GET /css/company2.css HTTP/1.1" 304 544
192.168.1.1 - - [07/Sep/2002:11:06:25 -0400] "GET /pics/logo.gif HTTP/1.1" 200 3468
192.168.1.1 - - [07/Sep/2002:11:06:25 -0400] "GET /pics/spacer.gif HTTP/1.1" 200 43
192.168.1.1 - - [07/Sep/2002:11:06:25 -0400] "GET /pics/toptext450.gif HTTP/1.1" 200 1505
192.168.1.1 - - [07/Sep/2002:11:06:25 -0400] "GET /pics/home_image.gif HTTP/1.1" 200 12384
```

Notice that the number of HTTP requests decreased from 20 to 6. By replacing the graphic rollovers with CSS, you eliminate 14 HTTP requests. The page now weighs in at 22,027 bytes and takes about six seconds to load on a 56K modem. The HTML is

41 percent smaller, having eliminated the JavaScript rollover code. The CSS is slightly larger, because of the CSS rollover added to the navigation bar links, but that's a small price to pay for the reduced HTTP request load. The images were also optimized to save space. Overall the page feels much faster and has the same functionality as before. Most importantly, we've brought the load time down below eight seconds.

Modern browsers and servers (HTTP 1.1) send out multiple simultaneous requests to save time. Even with HTTP keep-alive, each round trip adds more time because the message has to traverse the Internet from client to server and back again. Each hop in this path adds latency due to packet loss and network load.

By minimizing the number of HTTP requests required by your pages, you can speed up their display, and lower delay variability. This is especially important for any external files in the head of your document, which must be processed before the visible body content. Multiple external CSS and JavaScript files are now common, but they can dramatically slow down your pages. You'll learn how to defer, consolidate, and eliminate these external files in Chapter 7, "CSS Optimization," and Chapter 9, "Optimizing JavaScript for Download Speed."

Step 3: Remove Whitespace

The average web page has between 20 and 35 percent extra whitespace, according to Insider Software (http://www.insidersoftware.com/) and WebTrimmer (http://www.glostart.com/webtrimmer/). Browsers don't care how pretty your markup is; they're just looking between tags—real or implied. Those extra spaces, tabs, and returns make your markup easier to read but slower to display. Spaces between and inside tags can also be removed. Indents are typically used by programmers and WYSIWYG editors to make the markup more legible and the document's structure more obvious.

So instead of this:

```
<table  id="whitespace-repository"  width="800">
     <tr>
          <td>speed</td>
          <td>me</td>
          <td> up </td>
     </tr>
</table>
```

Do this:

```
<table id="better" width="800">
<tr>
<td>speed</td>
<td>me</td>
<td>up</td>
</tr>
</table>
```

Or even better:

```
<table id="best"><tr><td>speed</td><td>me</td><td>up</td></tr></table>
```

Removing whitespace and tightening up things saves over 50 percent for this code snippet.

This whitespace is entirely unnecessary (with some exceptions for JavaScript) for browsers rendering HTML. They see the HTML file as a stream of bytes with tags interspersed around data. Indents and spaces before or at the end of lines are simply wasted bandwidth and are ignored by browsers. If necessary, you can re-beautify your markup for editing by using sophisticated text editors like BBEdit and Homesite or by using regular expressions or short shell scripts.

Step 4: Tighten Up Comma-Delimited Attributes

Some tags allow a comma-delimited list for attribute values. The most common are the `<keywords>` meta tag, the `<map>` coordinate attribute, and the `<style>` tag. Browsers and search engines ignore leading spaces before comma-delimited attributes. You can save some space by omitting spaces when using commas or omitting commas altogether for the `<keywords>` meta tag. See Chapter 15, "Keyword Optimization," for more details.

The `style` tag allows comma-delimited lists. The same principle applies.

So instead of this:

```
<style type="text/css">
<!--
body {
      font-family: arial, helvetica, sans-serif;
        font-size:   1.1 em;
```

```
}
-->
</style>
```

Do this:

```
<style type="text/css">
<!--
body{
font-family:arial,helvetica,sans-serif;
font-size:1.1em;
}
-->
</style>
```

Or even better:

```
<style type="text/css"><!-- body{font-family:arial,helvetica,sans-serif;font-size:1.1em;} --></style>
```

Sharp-eyed readers will see that there is one additional optimization that can be made to this style sheet. For more details, see Chapter 7, "CSS Optimization."

Step 5: Omit Redundant Tags and Attributes

In many cases, attributes or tags are redundant and can be safely eliminated. Elements (formatting or otherwise) need to be placed only around blocks of HTML text. Here's an example:

```
<ol>
<li><font size="+1">Speed</font></li>
<li><font size="+1">Me</font></li>
<li><font size="+1">Up</font></li>
</ol>
```

This code becomes the following (which is invalid markup):

```
<font size="+1">
<ol>
<li>Speed</li>
<li>Me</li>
<li>Up</li>
</ol>
</font>
```

Even better, get rid of the deprecated `<font>` tag and remove optional closing tags,
like this:

```
<style type="text/css">
<!--
.plus{font-size:1.1em;}
--></style>
...
<ol class="plus"><li>Speed<li>Me<li>Up</ol>
```

You could use an `id` instead of a `class` attribute to identify the list element here; however, `id` names must be unique within the document and cannot be used on multiple
elements like `class` can.

Redundant Attributes

Redundant attributes generally specify the default attribute value for that particular
element. These include `align="left"` for p, h1, h2 and other heading tags, `table`, `tr`, and
`td` elements and `border="0"` for non-linked images.

Tables are a common place to find redundant attributes. The `td` tag can be aligned individually, but you also can control the alignment of an entire row by using the `tr` tag,
which saves space. For strict XHTML compliance, use style sheets to align the contents
of tables.

So instead of this:

```
<table>
      <tr>
            <td align="right">tastes great</td>
            <td align="right">less filling</td>
            <td align="right">burma shave</td>
      </tr>
</table>
```

Do this:

```
<table>
<tr align="right">
<td>tastes great</td>
<td>less filling</td>
<td>burma shave</td>
</tr>
</table>
```

Or even better:

```
<style type="text/css">
<!--
table.tr.right{text-align:right;}
-->
</style>
...
<table><tr class="right"><td>tastes great</td><td>less filling</td><td>burma
shave</td></tr></table>
```

Step 6: Omit Optional Quotes, If You Dare

The HTML 4.01 specification allows certain attribute values to be unquoted. Attribute strings that contain only alphanumeric characters (A-Z, a-z, 0-9), hyphens, periods, underscores, and colons can be unquoted. Any attribute values that include other characters must be quoted.

This means that you can do this:

```
<img src="t.gif" width=1 height=1>
```

But not this:

```
<table width=100%>
```

Values with spaces, symbols, or links require quotes in HTML. For example:

```
<a href="/index.html">
```

Browsers are quite liberal in what they accept for HTML markup. Some sites take advantage of this and omit quotes entirely, violating the HTML Recommendation. Yahoo!, the busiest site on the web, omits quotes from their link tags. For example:

```
<font size=3 face=arial><a href=r/ci><b>Computers & Internet</b></a></font><br><a
href=r/in>Internet</a>,
<a href=r/ww>WWW</a>,
<a href=r/sf>Software</a>,
...
```

Note the lack of quotes here. Also notice those funny-looking URLs that start with r/. To abbreviate their URLs, Yahoo! uses redirects to save bandwidth. We'll discuss how to use automatic URL abbreviation in Chapter 4, "Advanced HTML Optimization," and go into more detail in Chapter 17, "Server-Side Techniques."

Omitting quotes for URLs works on all current browsers and saves Yahoo! three percent off their home page,[15] but it is invalid HTML. However, there's no guarantee that future browsers won't require quotes around links. I recommend that you quote all attribute values that require them, and to get ready for XHTML, you may want to consider quoting all attribute values regardless of whether the quotes are needed in HTML.

> **NOTE**
>
> If you are adventurous, you can learn more about Extreme HTML Optimization at `http://www.webreference.com/authoring/languages/html/optimize/`.

Step 7: Omit Optional Closing Tags

A number of elements in HTML don't technically require closing tags because the elements that follow them imply closure. These include p, li, option, and even body and html. Even table row and data closing tags (</td> and </tr>) are not technically required by the HTML specification, but Netscape 3 does not render tables properly without them.

So instead of this:

```
<select ...>
<option>Numero Uno</option>
<option>Numero Dos</option>
etc.
</select>
```

Do this:

```
<select ...>
<option>Numero Uno
```

---

15. Andrew King, author calculation (Feb. 8, 2002). Yahoo.com's home page with link quotes added = 16,360 bytes; without quotes (as is) = 15,869 bytes, a three percent savings.

```
<option>Numero Dos
etc.
</select>
```

Even better:

```
<select ...><option>Numero Uno<option>Numero Dos</select>
```

Keep in mind that this practice violates XHTML where all tags must be closed and attributes fully qualified. Early versions of Netscape 6 also can fail to properly apply CSS and execute dynamically written external JavaScripts when elements are improperly nested. So, make sure that your elements are nested properly and your HTML is validated.[16]

Again, this is a tradeoff between page size and rendering speed. Using HTML with all tags closed makes your pages render slightly faster, whereas using HTML without optional closing tags makes your pages download faster but still validate. At current bandwidth-to-CPU-speed ratios, bandwidth is the limiting factor.

Step 8: Minimize Colors and Character Entities

You can save some space by optimizing your color references and character entities. In HTML 4.01, each offers numeric references and named references to colors and character entities. In some cases, the named reference is shorter; in others, the numeric reference is shorter. Choose the shortest reference to save a few bytes. As color attributes are deprecated in HTML 4.01 and XHTML, you can use style sheets to specify colors to save even more space, because in some cases, they can be optimized to use shorthand hexadecimal colors.

Character References

For characters outside of the default (or specified) character encoding scheme, you can use SGML character references to specify special characters.

---

16. Andrew King, "JavaScripting Netscape 6: No More Sloppy Code" [online], (Darien, CT: Jupitermedia Corporation, 2001 [cited 13 November 2002]), available from the Internet at http://www.webreference.com/programming/javascript/netscape6/.

In HTML, you can specify character entities in two ways:

- Numerically (either decimal [i.e., ©] or hexadecimal)
- Using a named character entity (i.e., ©)

In some cases, using the numeric reference is shorter than the named reference and vice versa (that is, reg and deg). To see the full list of character entities, go to http://www.w3.org/TR/html401/sgml/entities.html.

Colors

Color attributes can be represented numerically or with one of 16 named colors. In HTML, you specify colors using RBG hexadecimal triplets, like #RRGGBB:

- The first pair of digits specifies the red intensity.
- The second pair specifies the green intensity.
- The third pair specifies the blue intensity.

You also can specify colors using named colors. Because Internet Explorer 2 defined only 16 colors, there are 16 colors in the HTML 4.01 specification. Color names are case-insensitive. For example:

```
Blue = "#0000FF"
```

The W3C has deprecated the use of colors in HTML attributes in favor of style sheets, however, so this information applies primarily to style sheets. Named colors outside the 16 listed in the specification are not recommended because different browsers support different numbers and types of named colors. (Remember the infamous 216 browser-safe colors?) The hexadecimal values are unambiguous and can use fewer characters than their named equivalents, although some named colors use less than their hex equivalents ("red," for example). The sixteen named colors are listed here:

- Black = "#000000"   - Green   = "#008000"
- Silver = "#C0C0C0"   - Lime   = "#00FF00"
- Gray   = "#808080"   - Olive   = "#808000"
- White = "#FFFFFF"   - Yellow = "#FFFF00"

- Maroon   = "#800000"   - Navy   = "#000080"

- Red   = "#FF0000"   - Blue   = "#0000FF"

- Purple   = "#800080"   - Teal   = "#008080"

- Fuchsia = "#FF00FF"   - Aqua   = "#00FFFF"

In modern browsers, version 3 and up, except for buggy behavior in Mac IE3,[17] RGB triplets can be abbreviated if each of the R, G, and B hex pairs are the same, thus:

```
Blue = "#00F" is equivalent to "#0000FF"
```

The browser automatically expands three-character colors into six by duplicating the R, G, and B values. You'll learn more about color abbreviation in Chapter 7, "CSS Optimization." For more information, see the HTML 4.01 specification.[18]

Step 9: Cut the Comments

HTML comments are often used to mark major sections of documents. These comments can help teams of designers locate insertion points for new or changed content. Unfortunately, users have to download your entire HTML file including your comments, and browsers don't display them. Therefore, comments should be abbreviated.

So instead of this:

```
<!-- #### Start left column here #### -->
```

Do this:

```
<!-- left col --> or <!-- lcol --> or even <!-- l --> (could use an abbreviation map
here)
```

Abbreviating your comments can dramatically reduce file sizes, especially for heavily commented pages. This technique saves 31 bytes, or 75.6 percent (31/41).

---

17. Eric A. Meyer, "WebReview.com's Style Sheet Reference Guide" [online], (Manhasset, NY: CMP Media, 2002), available from the Internet at `http://style.webreview.com`.

18. Dave Raggett, Arnaud Le Hors, and Ian Jacobs, "HTML 4.01 Specification" [online], (Cambridge, MA: World Wide Web Consortium, 1999), available from the Internet at `http://www.w3.org/TR/html401/`.

Embed Labels in Elements

A more efficient technique is to eliminate comments entirely. Instead of peppering your code with placeholding comments for other designers to key off of, eliminate the comments by shunting them into surrounding elements. For example, you could shunt the preceding comment label into an element's id, like this:

```
<table id="left-column"> or <table id="lcol"> or even <table id="l">

<div id="left-column"> or <div id="lcol"> or even <div id="l">
```

This technique of shunting labels into elements saves 41 bytes or 85 percent over the original (41/48).

By using a template system, you can include any comments you need within the template. A script could then periodically strip out all comments from the page, and output the final optimized page. We use this technique on WebReference.com's home page.[19]

You can eliminate comments and id labels entirely. Using SSI or a content management system, you can merge separate files into one optimized template and have the best of both worlds. Editors can update only the parts of the page that need to change, and the server or content management system can assemble the optimized page.

Pages Are Not Digital Dumping Grounds

HTML files, especially crucial high-traffic pages, are not digital blackboards where designers can freely scrawl comment graffiti. They are not repositories for old or seldom-used commented-out blocks of markup. HTML documents should be designed to make it easy for users to get your information, not for the convenience of designers.

Step 10: Minimize *alt* Values

alt values are important for a number of reasons, not the least of which is the fact that there are over 49 million disabled people in the U.S. alone.[20] Vision-impaired users rely

---

19. King, "Evolution of a Home Page" [online].
20. Total number of disabled in the U.S. is 49,746,248 out of 257,167,527 total people. Or nearly 1 out of every 5 people in the U.S. has a disability. (U.S. Census, 2000. Available from the Internet at http://www.census.gov/.)

Real-World Example

Here's a real-world example of comments run wild from PopularMechanics.com:

```
<!-- END LEFT COLUMN NAVIGATION BAR MARKETING AREA, "button_one" -->
         <!-- BEGIN LEFT COLUMN NAVIGATION BAR MARKETING AREA, "button_two" -->
          <a href="http://popularmechanics.com/cooper" target="new"><img
src="/images/button_two.gif" border="0"></a><table name="left_col_spacer_table4"
width="124" height="15" border="0" cellspacing="0" cellpadding="0"><tr><td width="124"
height="15" align="left" valign="top"><img src="/images/clear.gif" width="124"
height="15" border="0"></td></tr></table>
                    <!-- END LEFT COLUMN NAVIGATION BAR MARKETING AREA, "button_two" -->
         <!-- END ADDITIONAL/NEW 2 LEFT COLUMN NAVIGATION BAR MARKETING AREAS -->
        <!-- xxxxxxxxxx xxxxxxxxxx xxxxxxxxxx xxxxxxxxxx xxxxxxxxxx xxxxxxxxxx -->
        <!-- END LEFT COLUMN NAVIGATION BAR MARKETING AREA -->
```

on alt values to navigate graphics-rich sites. Frequently we're seeing graphics-only designs with *no alt values.* This makes for a beautiful slow-loading site that is not usable with graphics turned off. Available for the applet, area, and img elements, alt attribute values can be optimized and eliminated altogether for non-functional graphics.

So instead of this:

```
<img src="/images/global/transparent-gif1x1.gif" alt="transparent gif" border="0">
```

Do this:

```
<img src="t.gif" alt=""width="1" height="1">
```

For functional graphics, alt values should be descriptive, not generic. Imagine that you are a visually impaired person surfing your site—what would you want to know about that image?

So instead of this:

```
<img src="/art/webreference_logo.gif" alt="our logo">
```

Do this:

```
<img src="/l.gif" alt="webref.com" width="125" height="60">
```

Make your `alt` values short and sweet, and don't try stuffing them with too many keywords. For client-side image maps, `alt` values allow non-graphical browsers to present the map as a list of links identified by the `alt` labels.

Accessibility and Optimization

The Americans with Disabilities Act includes Section 508, which provides accessibility rules for electronic and information technology that is created or procured by a U.S. Federal agency (`http://www.section508.gov/`). These rules/laws have been passed to ensure equal access for all to publicly available information. By providing alternative content, you can remove barriers for people with disabilities and maximize your potential audience. Optimization does not preclude accessibility; it actually enhances it if done properly (see the W3C's "Web Accessibility Guidelines" at `http://www.w3.org/WAI/`). Pages that use text to convey information display faster and are more easily read by people with or without disabilities.

Step 11: Minimize the *head*

Browsers interact with servers in discrete-sized messages and parse HTML pages sequentially. The `head` must be parsed before the rest of your page is rendered. By minimizing the size of the `head` of your pages, you can speed your content's initial display. This is especially important for busy home pages. Excess CSS or JavaScript, especially multiple external files, can both delay content display and lower your page's search engine relevance.

Minimize *meta* Tags

`meta` tags are HTML tags that you place in the `head` section of your page. They let you specify metadata information about your document in a variety of ways. `meta` tags are designed to help automated agents process metadata about your document and to help show where your document fits into the web. Many sites overuse `meta` tags, however, by stuffing in data that could best be omitted or handled more efficiently by the server.

The meta element identifies the properties of a document (such as author, expiration date, a list of keywords, and so on) and assigns values to those properties. For example, one way to specify the author of a document is to use the meta element, as follows:

```
<meta name="Author" content="Dr. Seuss">
```

The meta element specifies a property ("Author") and assigns a value to it ("Dr. Seuss").

meta tags can be used to specify default scripting, style sheet languages, or character sets. They also can be used to specify keywords to help search engines classify your pages. Additionally, meta tags can be used to augment HTTP headers sent from the server (although most of these are redundant) and have even been extended to include taxonomy classification systems like the Dublin Core.[21]

Here's a list of some popular meta tags:

```
<head>
        <meta http-equiv="Content-Type" CONTENT="text/html; charset=us-ascii">
        <meta http-equiv="Content-Script-Type" CONTENT="text/javascript">
        <meta name="resource-type" CONTENT="document">
        <meta name="distribution" CONTENT="Global">
        <META NAME = "keywords" CONTENT = "broadband user-friendly customer service...">
        <META NAME = "Description" CONTENT = "Megatelco is the definitive site...">
        <META NAME = "ROBOTS" CONTENT="ALL">
        <META NAME = "Copyright" CONTENT = "2002, 2003, 2004 Company.com">
        <META NAME = "Author" CONTENT = "author name">
        <META NAME = "Date" CONTENT = "2003-1-1">
        <META http-equiv="Expires" content="Mon, 1 Jan 2004 12:00:00 GMT">
        <META HTTP-EQUIV="PICS-Label" CONTENT = '(PICS-1.1
"http://www.rsac.org/ratingsv01.html" l gen true comment "RSACi North America Server"
by "webmaster@company.com" for "http://company.com/" on "2002.12.31T08:13-0800" r (n 0 s 0
v 0 l 0))'>
        <META NAME="generator" CONTENT"Microsoft FrontPage 7.0">
</head>
```

The only meta tags you really need to use are the description and keywords tags, and possibly the default scripting language. All the others are superfluous or can be handled more efficiently by server settings.

---

21. DCMI, "Dublin Core Meta Data Initiative" [online], (Dublin, OH: DCMI, 1995), available from the Internet at http://www.dublincore.org/.

Summary

The size of your HTML page "framework" determines the initial load time of your pages. To maximize display speed, minimize the number of bytes and objects the browser has to deal with. Here's a summarized list of what you learned in this chapter:

- Use a strict DTD to enable standards mode for maximum rendering speed.
- Minimize HTTP requests: Convert graphic text to text and consolidate.
- Remove whitespace (spaces, tabs, and returns).
- Omit redundant tags and attributes.
- Omit optional quotes and closing tags (this can violate HTML/XHTML).
- Minimize colors and character entities.
- Cut the comments.
- Minimize `alt` values, but make them descriptive, not generic.
- Minimize the `head` to maximize `body` display speed.
- Minimize `meta` tags:
    - Use only the `description` and `keywords` tags.
    - Conditionally include `meta` tags for critical pages.

4

Advanced HTML Optimization

You can only go so far minimizing the code you use in HTML pages. To fully optimize your HTML, you've got to dig a little deeper and transform your code. This chapter shows you how to tune your tables, optimize your forms, auto-abbreviate your links, and compress your HTML for maximum speed. The last two techniques require server access, which I explain in this chapter as well as in Chapter 17, "Server-Side Techniques," and Chapter 18, "Compressing the Web."

Table Tips

It's too bad that tables came out before CSS. Designers who are used to pixel-level placement can be frustrated by HTML's lack of control. Some pioneers, including David Siegel,[1] with his single-pixel GIF trick, realized they could use tables as a crude layout device. The use of tables subsequently exploded.

Intended for tabular data, the overuse of tables has polluted the web with unnecessary presentation in billions of pages. With the advent of modern standards-compliant

---

1. David Siegel, *Creating Killer Web Sites, 2d ed.* (Indianapolis, IN: Hayden Books, 1997).

browsers, there is a better way: CSS2. But, because this is the table section, I suppose that I should talk about some techniques you can use to speed up their display.

Complex Tables=Slow Rendering Speed

Using tables to lay out complex pages is usually a recipe for disaster. Cramming three or four columns' worth of content into a device originally designed to hold scientific data is not the W3C's idea of an optimal solution. What designers and WYSIWYG HTML editors typically do is lay out the page using one large table, placing content within this framework. Often, that content uses other tables, which can contain even more tables. The problem is that table size calculations are dynamic and interrelated.

All this complexity must be parsed and unwound by your browser. That's why many sites are so slow to load, even on high-bandwidth connections. The more complex your table structure, the slower your page displays. This is especially true when numerous images size and fill tables, each taking one HTTP request, further slowing down your page.

The way to speed up your tables is to give browsers as much information as possible about their structure and content, and reduce their complexity. Try to simplify, unwind, and layer your tables for speed. Use CSS to style tables, substitute background colors for background images, and use the fixed table layout option where possible to speed display. Or, ideally, you can transform your code to get rid of tables altogether and use divs and CSS2. But that's a story for another chapter (see Chapter 8, "Advanced CSS Optimization"). Let's start optimizing tables by helping the browser.

Enable Incremental Display

Given enough information, HTML tables are designed to render incrementally as table rows arrive, instead of waiting for all the data before beginning to render. If you want a browser to format a table in one pass, you need to tell the browser the number of columns in the table and their widths. You give browsers this information using the colgroup and col elements. If there are any columns with relative widths, you also must specify the table's width, which defaults to 100 percent. Without this explicit column information, browsers use a two-pass auto-sizing algorithm, finding the number of columns on the first pass. By giving the browser structural information ahead of time, you can speed up the rendering of your tables.[2]

You can group rows and columns in tables to format them as a group. For standards-compliant browsers—like Internet Explorer 5 on the Mac, Internet Explorer 6, Netscape 6, and Opera 6—this can mean big savings from attribute consolidation. The frame, rules, and border attributes can then control how a table's external frame and internal rules appear.

Row Groups

You can group table rows into table head, foot, and body sections by using the thead, tfoot, and tbody elements, respectively. You can format these groups separately and use them for printing longer, multi-page tables when you want header and/or footer information to print on each page.

For example:

```
<table frame="border" rules="groups">
<thead>
      <tr> ...header information...
<tfoot>
      <tr> ...footer information...
<tbody>
      <tr> ...first row of block one data...
      <tr> ...second row of block one data...
<tbody>
      <tr> ...first row of block two data...
      <tr> ...second row of block two data...
      <tr> ...third row of block two data...
</table>
```

The tfoot element must appear before the tbody tag so that the browser can render the foot before receiving all the rows of data. "This is an optimization shared with CALS[3] for dealing with very long tables. It allows the foot to be rendered without having to

---

2. Dave Raggett, Arnaud Le Hors, and Ian Jacobs, "Chapter 11, Tables," in HTML 4.01 Specification [online], (Cambridge, MA: World Wide Web Consortium, 1999), available from the Internet at http://www.w3.org/TR/html401/struct/tables.html.

3. U.S. Navy, "Continuous Acquisition and Life-Cycle Support (CALS)" [online], (Washington, DC: U.S. Navy), available from the Internet at http://navysgml.dt.navy.mil/cals.html.

wait for the entire table to be processed."[4] More important for our purposes is the ability to group and specify the attributes of columns.

Column Groups

Column groups allow you to break up tables structurally and style columns with style sheets or the `rules` attribute of the `table` element.

A table contains either a single implicit column group (no `colgroup` specified) or one or more explicit column groups, each delimited by a `colgroup` element.

The `col` element allows you to assign attributes to one or more columns, using the `span` attribute for multiple columns.[5]

You can specify the `width` attribute of columns either by using the `span` attribute of the `colgroup` element or by including it in each `col` element. Specifying multiple identically sized columns using a `span` is more efficient:

```
<colgroup span="10" width="60">
</colgroup>
```

In contrast, here's the alternative:

```
<colgroup>
        <col width="60">
        <col width="60">
        ...a total of 10 col elements...
</colgroup>
```

Calculating the Number of Columns

In HTML 4.01, you can determine the number of columns in a table in two ways:

- By using the `col` or `colgroup` elements (in that order)
- If no column elements exist, by determining the number of columns required by the rows

---

4. Dave Raggett, Arnaud Le Hors, and Ian Jacobs, "Appendix B: Performance, Implementation, and Design Notes," in HTML 4.01 Specification [online], (Cambridge, MA: World Wide Web Consortium, 1999), available from the Internet at `http://www.w3.org/TR/html401/appendix/notes.html#notes-tables`.

5. Raggett, Le Hors, and Jacobs, "Chapter 11, Tables" [online].

The number of columns in a table is equal to the row with the most cells, including spans. By specifying the column data beforehand, browsers can save themselves a pass inside your table to find how many columns are required.

Calculating the Width of Columns

Once the browser finds the number of columns, it calculates the width of each column. You can specify column widths in three ways:

- **Pixel**—A fixed width (that is, width="125" pixels) enables incremental rendering.
- **Percentage**—Percentage widths (for example, width="33%") are based on the percentage of the horizontal space available to the table. Percentage widths enable incremental rendering.
- **Relative**—Relative widths (such as, width="2*") are based on the horizontal space *required* by a table. If you give the table a fixed width, browsers may still render the table incrementally. If the table does not have a fixed width, however, browsers must receive all the data before they can size the table.[6]

By specifying the number and width of the columns in your tables, you can enable incremental rendering and speed their display. Otherwise, browsers have to wait until the table data arrives in order to allot space. Listing 4.1 shows an example.

Listing 4.1   Table Column Widths Specified

```
<table width="100%">
<colgroup>
        <col width="33%">
        <col width="67%">
</colgroup>
        <tr>
                <td colspan="2">
                        <p>top navigation bar (branding and advertising)</p>
                </td>
        </tr>
        <tr>
                <td>
```

continues

6. Ibid.

Listing 4.1   Table Column Widths Specified   *continued*

```
                <p>left navigation bar</p>
        </td>
        <td>
                <p>main content area</p>
        </td>
    </tr>
<table>
```

Fixed or percentage widths enable incremental rendering. In the same way that authors have no control over users adjusting table and font size, relying on fixed widths can be risky, unless the content is of a known size.

Consolidate Table Attributes

You can save space by using defaults wherever possible and consolidating attributes from the specific to the global. Use one <tr align="center"> instead of many occurrences of <td align="center"> to align rows of cells. Even better, use a row group like thead or tbody to style entire blocks of rows. Listing 4.2 shows an example.

Listing 4.2   Consolidate Attributes

```
<table width="100%" frame="border">
<colgroup>
        <col width="33%">
        <col width="67%">
</colgroup>
    <tr>
            <td colspan="2">
                    <p>top navigation bar (branding and advertising)</p>
            </td>
    </tr>
    <tbody align="center">
    <tr>
            <td>
                    <p>left navigation bar</p>
            </td>
            <td>
                    <p>main content area</p>
            </td>
    </tr>
    </tbody>
</table>
```

The closing tags for row group elements and `col` are optional in HTML (`</thead>`, `</tbody>`, `</tfoot>`, and `</col>`), but required in XHTML. Note that some versions of Netscape 4 mistake the closing `</colgroup>` element for a `div` and can cause unexpected rendering behavior. Similarly, you can use `colgroup` to align one or more columns instead of aligning each individual cell.

For example, use this to align one column:

```
<colgroup align="center">
```

Or use this to align a group of three columns:

```
<colgroup align="center" span="3">
```

This technique works for standards-compliant browsers and degrades gracefully (left aligned) for older browsers. Of course, you can use CSS instead to style your `cols` and `colgroups` (see Listing 4.3).

Listing 4.3   CSS-Styled Table

```
<style type="text/css">
<!--
      table#skel {width:100%;}
      col#left {width:33%;}
      col#right {width:67%;}
      tbody#main {text-align:center;}
-->
</style>
</head>
<body>
<table id="skel" frame="border">
<colgroup>
      <col id="left">
      <col id="right">
</colgroup>
      <tr>
            <td colspan="2">
                  <p>top navigation bar (branding and advertising)</p>
            </td>
      </tr>
      <tbody id="main">
      <tr>
            <td>
```

continues

Listing 4.3   CSS-Styled Table   *continued*

```
                 <p>left navigation bar</p>
           </td>
           <td>
                 <p>main content area</p>
           </td>
      </tr>
      </tbody>
</table>
```

Let's put it all together and throw in one more table turbocharger.

Fast Table Rendering

With browsers that support CSS2,[7] such as IE6 and NS6, tables can get a big speed boost with the new `table-layout` property. The `table-layout` property lets authors control the algorithm browsers use to lay out the table cells, rows, and columns.

Fixed Table Layout

With the faster fixed `table-layout` algorithm, the browser sizes the table horizontally not based on cell contents, but on the width of the table and columns and any borders and spacing. This layout algorithm is faster because the horizontal layout of the table does not depend on every cell's contents; instead, it depends only on specified or default column and table widths. Thus, the browser renders your table in one pass and doesn't have to wait for the rest of the table to load. This can be especially helpful for longer tables.

Here's how fixed table layouts work. For each column, the first cell whose width is not set to auto sets the width for that column. Subsequent cells in each column are set to that width, regardless of their content. Make sure that the first cell is each column is the widest when using the fixed algorithm.

7. Bert Bos et al., "Cascading Style Sheets, level 2 CSS2 Specification" [online], (Cambridge, MA: World Wide Web Consortium, 1998), available from the Internet at http://www.w3.org/TR/REC-CSS2/.

There are three possible values to the `table-layout` property:

- `auto` (the default)
- `fixed`
- `inherit`

For example:

```
table { table-layout: fixed }
col.sum { width: 10em }
```

The default of `auto` can be inefficient, requiring up to two passes to size the table properly because it needs to access all the content within the table.

When you set the `table-layout` property to `fixed`, you are fixing the column widths (and optionally the column heights) for the entire table. Column widths are based on non-auto `col` element widths or, if these are not present, on the first cell in each column. Without `col` elements, the browser can begin to lay out the table after it receives the first row. With `col` elements, even that step is unnecessary. Cells in subsequent rows do not affect column widths.

For CSS2-compliant browsers, this setting greatly increases the parsing and display performance of tables. Microsoft claims a 100-fold speed improvement using the fixed layout option for Internet Explorer 6+. The fixed algorithm allows the table to be rendered progressively to the screen, one row at a time. Listing 4.4 shows an example.

Listing 4.4 Fixed Table Layout Example

```
<style type="text/css">
<!--
    table#skel {table-layout:fixed;width:100%;}
    col#left {width:33%;}
    col#right {width:67%;}
    tbody#main {text-align:center;}
-->
</style>
</head>
<body>
<table id="skel" frame="border">
```

continues

Listing 4.4   Fixed Table Layout Example   *continued*

```
<colgroup>
        <col id="left">
        <col id="right">
</colgroup>
        <tr>
                <td colspan="2">
                        <p>top navigation bar (branding and advertising)</p>
                </td>
        </tr>
        <tbody id="main">
        <tr>
                <td>
                        <p>left navigation bar</p>
                </td>
                <td>
                        <p>main content area</p>
                </td>
        </tr>
        </tbody>
</table>
```

Overflow Control

To be safe, make sure that the first row's cells are the widest in each column. If the contents of a cell exceed the fixed width of a column, the content is wrapped or, if this isn't possible, it is clipped. The CSS2 overflow property allows authors to control the behavior of content that exceeds the width of any block element, including td. Here's an example:

```
<style type="text/css">
<!--
        table#fixed {table-layout:fixed;width:100%;overflow:hidden;}
-->
</style>
</head>
<body>
<table id="fixed">
```

There are four possible values for the overflow property:

- **visible**—Displays the content that exceeds the containing block (the default value).
- **scroll**—Inserts a scrollbar to the block regardless of overflow.
- **hidden**—Clips the overflowed content with the containing block.
- **auto**—Clips overflowed content and adds a scrollbar only when necessary.

Real-World Fixed Table Layout Example

I tried the fixed `table-layout` algorithm on WebReference.com's home page with mixed results. Listing 4.5 shows an excerpt from the source.

Listing 4.5   Real-World Fixed Table Layout

```
<style type="text/css">
...
TABLE#f{table-layout:fixed;width:100%}
COL#a{width:9px;}
COL#b{width:134px;}
COL#c{width:9px;}
COL#d{width:65%;}
COL#e{width:8px;}
COL#f{width:1px;}
COL#g{width:125px;}
</style>
...
<TABLE id=f WIDTH="100%" BORDER=0 CELLSPACING=0 CELLPADDING=0>
<colgroup><col id=a><col id=b><col id=c><col id=d><col id=e><col id=f><col
id=g></colgroup>
<TR VALIGN=TOP><TD WIDTH=9 BGCOLOR="#FFCC00"><IMG SRC="/t.gif" WIDTH=9 HEIGHT=1
ALT=""></TD>
... 134 px TD follows ...
```

After sizing the initial cells properly, the tables flew onto the screen. However, I noticed two problems. Embedded tables sometimes moved down with unsized ads, and increasing to larger fonts caused overflow in NS6.x. Adding a `valign="top"` to the containing `<tr>` solved the first problem. The second was more of a challenge.

Increasing fonts to a larger size in Netscape 6.x sometimes overflowed the text in fixed columns, although reloading corrected most of these problems. IE5 Mac and IE6 for the PC seem to handle larger font sizes better. You can tweak the `overflow` attribute to control this behavior, although it had no effect in NS6.x. When you use a strict `DOCTYPE`, the `overflow` attribute applies to the entire HTML object.

Figure 4.1 shows what happens in Netscape 6.2 when you use the fixed `table-layout` algorithm and then increase the font size.

Figure 4.1
Fixed table layout in
Netscape 6.2.

http://www.webreference.com/

Increasing the initial cell size would solve some of these problems. However, Netscape 7 fixed the reflow problem with larger fonts and the fixed `table-layout` algorithm (see Figure 4.2).

Figure 4.2
Fixed table layout in Mozilla
1.0 (Netscape 7).

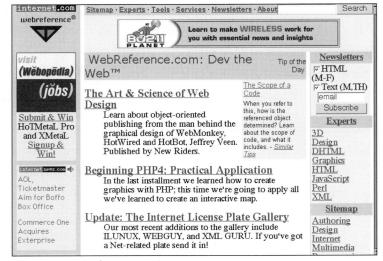

http://www.webreference.com/

With fixed-width contents like graphics, use the `fixed` algorithm. When your content can vary in width, make sure that you test your table at larger font sizes.

I had better luck specifying widths as `col` attributes. Here's an example from WebReference.com's home page:

```
<table id=f width="100%" border=0 cellspacing=0 cellpadding=0>
<colgroup><col width=9><col width=134><col width=9><col width="65%"><col width=8><col
width=1><col width=126>
```

Rather than using style sheets:

```
table#f{table-layout:fixed;width:100%}
table#f{overflow:auto;}
col#a{width:9px;}
col#b{width:134px;}
col#c{width:*;}
col#d{width:8px;}
col#e{width:1px;}
col#f{width:126px;}
```

A happy medium would be to conditionally include the fixed and overflow styles for CSS2-compliant browsers like IE6+ and Netscape 7+, which is based on Mozilla 1.0. Use the `colgroup` and `col` elements for longer tables and use `table-layout` and `overflow` styles where possible.

Setting the row height can further improve rendering speed, because the browser's parser can begin to render the row without examining the content of each cell in the row to determine row height.

Simplify

In those self-improvement seminars, the speakers always seem to be touting simplicity. Simplify your life; remove everything that's non-essential. Reduce your stress level. Take Echinacea. Breathe! The same advice holds for tables (except maybe the breathing and Echinacea parts).

Browsers usually parse tables in stages. First, they look in cells to size what's inside. Then they back out of your table(s), dynamically sizing table cells along the way until the entire thing is rendered. By making your content simpler and easier to "digest," you can speed up your tables. Try removing everything that's non-essential. Take out all those cross-promo buttons you agreed to last year. Yank out those affiliate and advertising links you're not making any money on. Rip out that slow-loading Java news ticker. There, isn't that better?

Leave in only what's new and maybe some decks. I'll even let you leave in a logo for branding. Now your tables will really fly. You can put back in only what your users want, or better yet, let them decide. Removing excess is one of the most effective ways to speed up tables—or pages, for that matter.

Unwind

The deeper you nest tables, the slower they'll display. Even after they've downloaded, browsers must perform numerous calculations to size tables properly. Complex nested tables can tax the CPUs of your users' computers, especially slower machines. Because browsers must render the deepest tables first and then back out, calculating cell sizes as they go, the trick is to unwind your tables by coding more intelligently to reduce their number and depth.

Layer

Many sites use one table to lay out their entire page. In many cases, this means the browser displays the table only after everything is downloaded and sized properly, delaying page display. The trick is to break up your tables into separate tables, like a layer cake.

Perceived Speed

Use a simple fast-loading table at the top and an above-the-fold table underneath. Include useful content—such as a search box or navigation bar—in your first table so that users can navigate quickly. Browsers render tables sequentially, so first give your users something to look at, while the rest of your page loads. This makes your pages feel faster, even though they may load slower overall. Figure 4.3 shows an example from CNET.com's home page.

Figure 4.3
CNET.com's top
navigation bar.

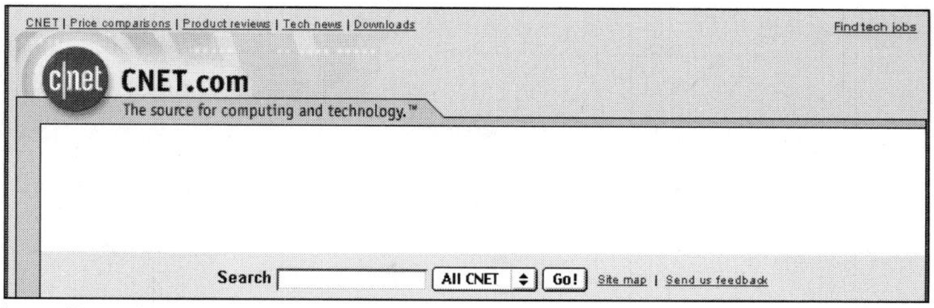

http://www.cnet.com/

Your first table literally pops onto the screen, giving users something to work with instantly. In Chapter 1, you learned that feedback is important. When some useful content instantly appears, users are rewarded for clicking your link. Figure 4.4 shows an example from WebReference.com's home page.

Figure 4.4
WebReference.com top
navigation bar.

http://www.webreference.com/

On the other hand, popping up useless content can annoy users. Showing them your logo or an ad quickly doesn't give them useful content and let them navigate your site. Figure 4.5 shows an example.

Figure 4.5
Onlinenewspapers.com.

onlinenewspapers.com

http://www.onlinenewspapers.com/

Three-Panel Layout

A similar strategy involves rearranging tables to raise relevance along with perceived rendering speed. A typical three-panel layout has the branding and advertising in the top row, navigation in the left column, and content on the right. For an example, see Listing 4.6.

Listing 4.6   Three-Panel Layout

```
<table>
    <tr>
        <td colspan="2">
            <p>top navigation bar (branding and advertising)</p>
```

continues

Listing 4.6   Three-Panel Layout   *continued*

```
            </td>
      </tr>
      <tr>
            <td>
                  <p>left navigation bar</p>
            </td>
            <td>
                  <p>main content area</p>
            </td>
      </tr>
</table>
```

Fortunately, a simple addition to the `table` element provides an alternative. Ever since Netscape 2, authors have had the ability to align tables, similar to images and modern `div`s. This feature allows you to align tables next to each other. Let's break up this table into three parts (see Listing 4.7).

Listing 4.7   Three-Table Layout

```
<table>
      <tr>
            <td colspan="2">
                  <p>top navigation bar (branding and advertising)</p>
            </td>
      </tr>
</table>

<table align="left">
      <tr>
            <td>
                  <p>left navigation bar</p>
            </td>
      </tr>
</table>

<table align="right">
      <tr>
            <td>
                  <p>main content area</p>
            </td>
      </tr>
</table>
```

The tables will now load individually as the HTML byte stream downloads. Now instead of waiting for one large table, the user sees the first table pop onto the screen, while the other tables load sequentially. Even though the markup may be larger, the page *feels* faster. Sharp-eyed readers will notice that this technique is a simulation of divs. You can achieve the same effect more efficiently with divs, but I will save that discussion for Chapter 8, "Advanced CSS Optimization."

I discovered two problems with this technique. The left table (at least in IE5 Mac) has a gap above it. You can eliminate this gap by setting cellspacing to 0. Also, because they're not part of the same table, the left and right tables can have different heights. By using the same background color as your body element for the right main content table cell, you can lessen the impact of this problem.

The Table Trick to Increase Relevance

The problem with these layout approaches is that your main content is buried below navigation and branding. Search engines typically look at the first 2K or 3K of your page, and give higher relevance to content toward the top of your page. There are two ways to raise your content higher in your markup: the rowspan trick and CSS2.

You can move your main content cell above your navigation by using the following markup (see Listing 4.8).

Listing 4.8   The Table Trick

```
<html>
<head>
      <title>The Table Rowspan Trick</title>
</head>
<body>
<table>
      <tr>
            <td colspan="2">
                  <p>top navigation bar (branding and advertising)</p>
            </td>
      </tr>
      <tr>
            <td><!-- leave me empty --></td>
```

continues

Listing 4.8   The Table Trick   *continued*

```
            <td rowspan="2">
                    <p>main content area</p>
            </td>
      </tr>
      <tr>
            <td>
                    <p>left navigation bar</p>
            </td>
      </tr>
</table>
</body>
</html>
```

The trick is the empty td in the second row and the rowspan="2" in the cell next to it. The table displays the left navigation bar with the main content on the right as before, but the main content cell appears before the navigation in the markup, raising its relevance to search engines (see Figure 4.6).

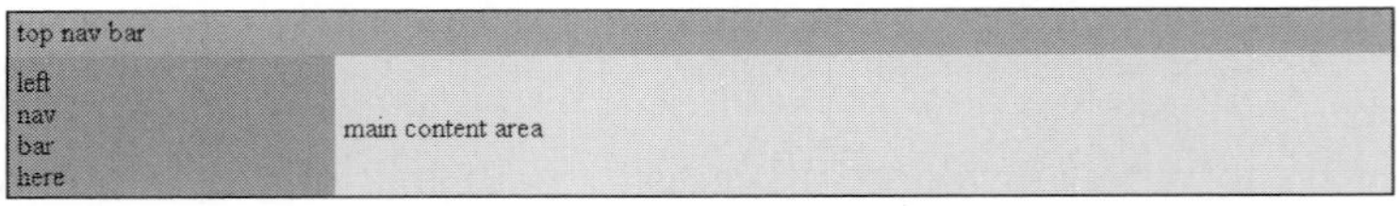

Figure 4.6
The table trick.

Optional Closing Tags

In theory, you can omit the closing table data (</td>) and table row (</tr>) tags from your tables, because HTML 4.01 does not require them. Netscape 3 can choke on this technique, however. You could dynamically include closing </td> and </tr> tags for Netscape 3 only, and all others could receive the more streamlined and valid table. XHTML requires these closing tags, however. For example:

```
<table>
      <tr><td>The<td>emperor
      <tr><td>has no<td>close
</table>
```

Tables and Returns

Netscape 3 (and possibly earlier versions) can add extra space to your table cells if you put a return after a <td>. You can ensure that won't happen, while saving additional bytes, by removing returns after <td> tags, and removing other whitespace from your page. So instead of this:

```
<table>
     <tr>
          <td bgcolor="#ffcc00" align=center>
               <a href="/r/ex"><b>Experts</b></a>
          </td>
     </tr>
     <tr>
          <td>
               <a href="/3d/">3D</a><br>
               <a href="/dlab/">Design</a><br>
...
```

Do this:

```
<table><tr><td bgcolor="#ffcc00" align=center><a href="/r/ex"><b>Experts</b></a></td></tr>
<tr><td><a href="/3d/">3D</a><br><a href="/dlab/">Design</a><br>
...
```

Colored Cells

By replacing background images with background colors, you can save space and a trip to the server. For example:

```
<table>
<tr><td bgcolor="#ffcc00">...
```

This can, of course, also be done with style sheets for version 4+ browsers:

```
<style type="text/css">
<!--
     .dark {background-color:#ffcc00;}
-->
</style></head>
<body>
<table>
     <tr><td class="dark">
```

Even better, optimize the style sheet like this:

```
<style type="text/css">
<!--
.d{background:#fc0;}
-->
```

```
</style></head>
<body>
<table>
<tr><td class="d">
```

For simpler two- or even three-column layouts, you can use CSS2. You learn how this technique can save you space in Chapter 8.

Form Optimization

Forms allow users to interact with web sites. HTML forms consist of controls (buttons, checkboxes, input fields, menus, and so on) that users modify before submitting for processing. Forms act as containers for controls, which in turn can act as containers for other options like select menus. Form optimization is often overlooked, but it can accelerate web pages by saving clicks, HTTP calls, and file space by using client-side processing and eliminating or shunting code to the server.

JavaScript and Forms

JavaScript and forms are a powerful combination. You can save both extra clicks and a trip to the server by using a gracefully degrading JavaScript to process your forms (see Listing 4.9).

Listing 4.9 JavaScript- and CGI-Enabled Form

```
<script language="text/javascript">
<!--
function jmp(form) {
var thesrc = form.url.selectedIndex; // grab the selected index
      if (thesrc >= 0) { // check if valid
           location = form.url.options[thesrc].value;
                        // jump to that option's value
      }
}
-->
</script>
</head>
<body>
<FORM METHOD="POST" ACTION="/cgi-bin/redirect.cgi" onSubmit="return false"><SMALL>Pick a
topic:</SMALL><BR>
<SELECT NAME="url" onChange="jmp(this.form)">
```

```
<OPTION VALUE="/3d/">3D Animation
<OPTION VALUE="/dlab/">Design
...
</SELECT><INPUT TYPE="SUBMIT" VALUE="Go" onClick ="jmp(this.form)">
</FORM>
```

The key is to not rely entirely on JavaScript. Always gracefully degrade for the 11 percent of users who don't have JavaScript.[8]

GET versus POST

The GET method is more efficient than POST because it takes one less trip to the server. When security is not paramount, using GET (or non-parsed headers) can mean faster form processing for your users. You learn more about CGI-related issues in Chapter 17, "Server-Side Techniques."

Form Controls

Users interact with forms through controls. Two controls in particular offer opportunities for optimization: input and select.

Hidden Inputs

Input controls often are used to interact with server-based scripts like search engines or email newsletter subscriptions. HTML authors typically place default values for scripts within hidden input fields like this:

```
<form method="get" action="/cgi-bin/search.cgi">
    <input type="hidden" name="what" value="local">
    <input type="hidden" name="engine" value="au">
    <input type="hidden" name="summary" value="1">
    <input type="hidden" name="startnumber" value="0">
```

---

8. TheCounter.com, "Global Statistics 2002" [online], (Darien, CT: Jupitermedia Corporation, October 2002), available from the Internet at http://www.thecounter.com/stats/. The percentage of users with no JavaScript is 11% as of October 2002.

```
      <input type="hidden" name="batchsize" value="25">
      <input type="hidden" name="relevancethreshold" value="50">
      <input type="text" name="query" size="12">
</form>
```

A better way to set defaults is to shunt these hidden fields to the server inside the CGI script. Then you end up with something like this:

```
<form method="get" action="/cgi-bin/search.cgi">
      <input type="text" name="query" size="12">
</form>
```

Done properly, authors can still override these CGI-based defaults if hidden fields exist. Chapter 17 shows you how.

Replace DHTML Menus with Cascading Select Menus

Select menus are frequently used to offer users options for navigation and other alternatives. The select element creates a multiple-choice menu or scrolling list. This element can contain one or more option elements. It also can contain one or more optgroup elements that group related choices logically, and can create cascading menus. These can replace complex DHTML, Java, or Flash cascading menus with smaller, standards-based code.

The optgroup Element

The optgroup element defines a logical group of options to create submenus. Until recently this element was poorly supported. With the advent of HTML 4 standards-compliant browsers like NS6, IE6, and OP6, optgroup can be used to group related options under one label.

This feature can be especially helpful when users must choose from a long list of options. You can group related choices, making it easier for users to understand and remember selections. In HTML 4, optgroup elements cannot be nested; however, in the specification, they leave the possibility open for the future nesting of optgroup elements.

The sole attribute of optgroup is label, which can be used for hierarchical menus, as you see here:

Label = text—Defines a label to be used when displaying the submenu.

Here's an example (see Listing 4.10):

Listing 4.10   `optgroup` Menu Example

```
<form method="get" action="/cgi-bin/go.cgi">
<select name="nav">
      <optgroup label="DHTML">
            <option value="/dhtml/">DHTML
            <option value="/dhtml/hiermenus">Hiermenus Central
            <option value="/dhtml/dynomat/">Tools
      </optgroup>
      <optgroup label="JavaScript">
            <option value="/js/">JavaScript
            <option value="/js/tips/">JavaScript Tips
            <option value="/js/tools/">Tools
      </optgroup>
      <optgroup label="XML">
             <option value="/xml/">XML
             <option value="/xml/tools">Tools
      </optgroup>
</select>
<input type="submit" value="submit">
</form>
```

For standards-compliant browsers like IE5 Mac, IE5.5 Win, NS6, and OP6, each `optgroup` creates a category header. Older browsers ignore the unrecognized `optgroup` element and display the `options` as before. IE5 Mac displays a cascading menu like the one shown in Figure 4.7.

Figure 4.7
optgroup menu in IE5 Mac.

IE6 and NS6/7 display a visually nested menu, as shown in Figure 4.8.

`optgroup` elements offer a standards-compliant alternative for two-level DHTML hierarchical menus that gracefully degrade. They are an excellent alternative to DHTML hierarchical menus, which can become quite code-intensive.

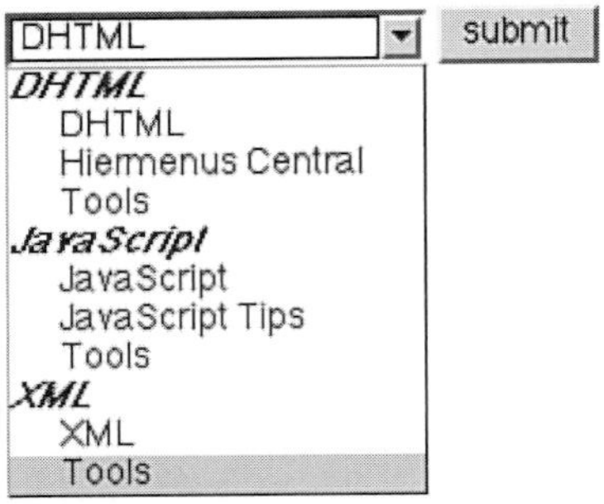

Figure 4.8
optgroup menu in Mozilla 1.0
(Netscape 7.x).

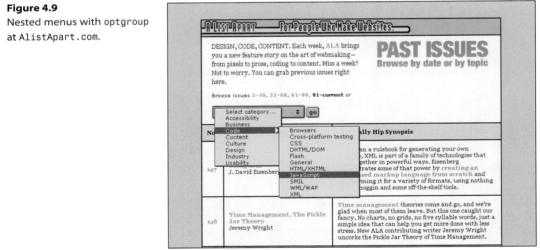

Real-World Example of Nested Menu with optgroup

Real-world examples of nested menus are hard to come by. Figure 4.9 shows one from
A List Apart, an online magazine for developers.

Figure 4.9
Nested menus with optgroup
at AlistApart.com.

http://www.alistapart.com/stories/

Listing 4.11 shows the HTML.

Listing 4.11   optgroup Hierarchical Menu from AlistApart.com

```
/*  Based on Charity Khan's article, Menu Maker Update, on Builder.com
        http://www.builder.com/Programming/Scripter/123097/
*/

function buildArray() {
  var a = buildArray.arguments;
```

```
  for (i=0; i<a.length; i++) {
    this[i] = a[i];
  }
  this.length = a.length;
}

var urls1 = new buildArray("",
"http://www.alistapart.com/stories/indexAccessibility.html",
"http://www.alistapart.com/stories/indexBusiness.html",
"http://www.alistapart.com/stories/indexBrowsers.html",
"http://www.alistapart.com/stories/indexCrossPlatform.html",
"http://www.alistapart.com/stories/indexCSS.html",
"http://www.alistapart.com/stories/indexDHTMLDOM.html",
"http://www.alistapart.com/stories/indexFlash.html",
"http://www.alistapart.com/stories/indexGeneral.html",
"http://www.alistapart.com/stories/indexHTMLXHTML.html",
"http://www.alistapart.com/stories/indexJavaScript.html",
"http://www.alistapart.com/stories/indexSMIL.html",
"http://www.alistapart.com/stories/indexWMLWAP.html",
"http://www.alistapart.com/stories/indexXML.html",
"http://www.alistapart.com/stories/indexContent.html",
"http://www.alistapart.com/stories/indexCulture.html",
"http://www.alistapart.com/stories/indexDesign.html",
"http://www.alistapart.com/stories/indexIndustry.html",
"http://www.alistapart.com/stories/indexUsability.html");

function go(which, num, win) {
  n = which.selectedIndex;
  if (n != 0) {
    var url = eval("urls" + num + "[n]")
    if (win) {
      openWindow(url);
    } else {
      location.href = url;
    }
  }
}

function stdStatus()
{
    window.status = "A List Apart, for people who make websites.";
    return true;
}


<form action="null" method="post">
```

continues

Listing 4.11   optgroup Hierarchical Menu from AlistApart.com   *continued*

```
<fieldset><legend> </legend>
<select class="butt" name="selectCategory">
        <option selected>Select category...</option>
        <option>Accessibility</option>
        <option>Business</option>
        <optgroup label="Code">
                <option>Browsers</option>
                <option>Cross-platform testing</option>
                <option>CSS</option>
                <option>DHTML/DOM</option>
                <option>Flash</option>
                <option>General</option>
                <option>HTML/XHTML</option>
                <option>JavaScript</option>
                <option>SMIL</option>
                <option>WML/WAP</option>
                <option>XML</option>
        </optgroup>
        <option>Content</option>
        <option>Culture</option>
        <option>Design</option>
        <option>Industry</option>
        <option>Usability</option>
</select>
<input class="butt" type="button" name="goButton" value="go"
onClick="go(this.form.selectCategory, 1, false)">
</fieldset>
</form>
```

Notice that the designers use the selected index number to access the array of URLs, instead of embedding the URLs within the form itself. This saves space by shunting the URLs into the external cached JavaScript file and bypasses some bugs in older browsers. This form could be modified to gracefully degrade by adding a fall-back CGI redirect script for browsers without JavaScript. The CGI script could map option values to URLs, similar to the preceding JavaScript.

NOTE

You can use CSS to style forms to customize their look for standards-compliant browsers. You also can fix their width with the fake horizontal rule trick.

URL Abbreviation

URL abbreviation is a little-used yet effective HTML optimization technique. Yahoo!'s home page, the busiest page on the planet, spans the entire web but weighs in at only 22.4K for the HTML. Yet Yahoo.com has over 279 links. How do they do this? Listing 4.12 shows you a snippet of Yahoo!'s abbreviated URLs.

Listing 4.12   Yahoo.com HTML Snippet

```
<html><head><title>Yahoo!</title><base href=http://www.yahoo.com/
target=_top>...<style>a.h{background-color:#ffee99}</style></head><body>
...
<table><tr><td nowrap align=center><small><b>Shop</b> 
<a href=r/a2>Auctions</a> &#183;
<a href=r/cr><b>Autos</b></a> &#183;
<a href=r/cf>Classifieds</a> &#183;
...
```

Yahoo! uses the `mod_rewrite` module to automatically expand their abbreviated URLs to save space. Although each abbreviated URL requires that the server make an HTTP redirect to the longer URL (through a `mod_rewrite` redirect), the faster download speed on high-traffic pages can be worth it.

The idea is to shunt longer URLs to the server to save space. After hand-optimizing WebReference.com's home page to 24K, I thought that was as far as I could go, but as you'll discover, there's always room for improvement. By automatically abbreviating our links using a Perl script and expanding them with the `mod_rewrite` module, we trimmed 5K off our home page, a savings of over 20 percent.[9] You'll find out how in Chapter 17.

Shorter URLs Are Better

On high-traffic pages, shorter URLs can make a big difference in file size, up to a 30 percent savings. Without `mod_rewrite`, you can still name frequently used files with short names. So instead of this:

```
<img src="/images/global/transparent1x1.gif" WIDTH=1 HEIGHT=1 ALT="1-pixel GIF">
```

---

9. Andrew King, "Evolution of a Home Page" [online], (Darien, CT: Jupitermedia Corporation, 2001), available from the Internet at `http://www.webreference.com/dev/evolution/`.

Do this:

```
<img src="t.gif" width=1 height=1 alt="">
```

By placing images and objects high up in your directory structure, you can shorten their URLs. Of course, there's always a tradeoff. Search engines give higher importance to keywords in URLs, which means that keyword-rich web pages can make for longer links. By auto-abbreviating URLs, you can have the best of both worlds: short abbreviated URLs on your home page that resolve to longer keyword-rich URLs.

Also, don't forget to optimize and abbreviate any URLs in your JavaScript.

Trailing Slash

URLs that point to directories technically are supposed to end with a slash to indicate that the URL indeed points to a directory. Authors commonly omit the trailing slash, however, forcing the server to perform a redirect to figure out whether the user is requesting a file or a directory. By including the trailing slash for URLs, you can speed up the response time of directory URLs.

So instead of this:

```
http://www.domain.com/dir
```

Do this:

```
http://www.domain.com/dir/
```

By using directories rather than files, you also can shorten your URLs while making them more universal. So instead of this:

```
http://www.domain.com/dir/about.asp
```

Do this:

```
http://www.domain.com/dir/about/
```

Or even better:

```
http://www.domain.com/about/
```

This way you don't lock yourself into one particular technology. Of course, leaving off the trailing slash saves a byte. A compromise for maximum file size optimization would be to use redirect URLs without trailing slashes, and include them in your redirect file. For example:

```
<a href="r/ab">About</a>
```

In this line, `"r/ab"` maps to `"/about/"`.

HTML and Compression

Compression shrinks the amount of data you have to send from your web server. Browsers decompress this data on the fly, which increases page display speed, despite the additional work necessary for the browser. As external objects make up over 50 percent of the average web page, developers have naturally focused their efforts on compressing images and multimedia to reduce file size.

HTML compression is often overlooked, however. Since 1998–1999, most browsers have been equipped to support the HTTP 1.1 standard known as IETF "content-encoding." *Content encoding* is a publicly defined way to compress (that is, deflate) HTTP content transferred from web servers to browsers using public domain compression algorithms, like gzip. That content of course includes HTML.

HTML is pure ASCII text, which is highly compressible. HTML markup is also highly redundant, with a small set of tags that are used repeatedly. This redundancy makes HTML even more compressible, especially for string replacement algorithms like gzip.

HTML Compression Example

To give you an idea of the savings you can expect from HTML compression, let's take a real-world example. You can create gzipped versions of static files beforehand, and let tools like mod_gzip or PipeBoost do the negotiation for you. Or for more dynamic data, you can let these tools compress your data on the fly and do the content negotiation. (Letting the Apache or IIS servers do the negotiation on their own is possible but problematic.) For example, the home page of PopularMechanics.com can be compressed from 138,548 to 21K using gzip compression (see Table 4.1).

Table 4.1   The Effects of HTML Compression on PopularMechanics.com

	PopularMechanics.com (HTML)	GZIP -9	Percentage Savings
Original	138,548	21,743	84.3%

GZIP compression typically saves from 80 to 85 percent off HTML files. We continue optimizing PM's home page in Chapter 6, "Case Study: PopularMechanics.com."

Although static files can be compressed with `gzip`'s maximum setting of 9, `mod_gzip` actually uses the more moderate compression setting of 6, which gives a good compromise between file size and decompression speed.

The net effect is dramatically smaller files, faster page response, and lower bandwidth bills. In fact, webmasters who have employed content-encoding on their servers have seen bandwidth savings of 30 to 50 percent. The compression ratio depends on the degree of redundancy in your site's content, and the ratio of text to multimedia. Because HTML text files can be highly redundant (especially tables), compression rates for HTML files can be dramatic, with savings up to 90 percent. Because compression of HTML files is almost universally supported, there's really no reason not to support content encoding for HTML files on your site. For more details on content encoding, see Chapter 18, "Compressing the Web."

Summary

In order to fully optimize your HTML, you've got to do more than remove whitespace. Transform your code by tuning your tables or replacing them with positioned `divs`. Optimize your forms and use JavaScript to save clicks and HTTP requests, and replace complex DHTML and Java menus with standards-based cascading select menus. Most importantly, auto-abbreviate your URLs with `mod_rewrite` and use content encoding to compress your content for maximum speed. Here's a summary of what you learned in this chapter:

- Table tips:
    - Use row groups to segment tables for style, accessibility, and printing.
    - Use `colgroups` and `col` to style entire columns.
    - Consolidate attributes (`tr` versus many `tds`, and so on).
    - Enable incremental rendering with sized `col` elements.
    - Use the fixed `table-layout` algorithm where possible (NS7+, IE5+).
    - Simplify, unwind, and layer your tables for maximum speed. Provide useful content in the first table.
    - Use the table trick to raise relevance.
    - Use CSS to style cell backgrounds (version 4+ browsers).

- Forms:
    - Use JavaScript to save clicks and HTTP trips.
    - Gracefully degrade with CGI scripts for non-JavaScript browsers.
    - Use `GET` where possible.
    - Shunt `form` defaults into CGI scripts.
    - Substitute `optgroup` select menus for DHTML hierarchical menus.

- Use trailing slashes on directories.
- Abbreviate your URLs.
- Use compression where possible.

Recommended Reading

Here are some good sources for more information on optimizing HTML:

- `http://www.webreference.com/authoring/languages/html/optimize/`
  "Extreme HTML Optimization," by Andrew King.

- `http://www.gzip.org/`
  The gzip compression format.

- `http://www.w3.org/TR/html401/`
  "The HTML 4.01 Specification" (see also the Performance, Implementation, and Design Notes).

- `http://www.webreference.com/internet/software/servers/http/compression/`
  "HTTP Compression Speeds Up the Web," by Peter Cranstone.

- `http://www.schroepl.net/projekte/mod_gzip/`
  Michael Schroepl's excellent mod_gzip site.

- `http://www.glostart.com/webtrimmer/fluff.html`
  A discussion of waste data in HTML documents, by Cub Lea and Stephen Winter.

5

Extreme XHTML

The "X" in XHTML signifies HTML's addition to a large family of extensible, inter-operable, and self-describing markup languages. This is the Extensible Markup Language (XML) family, which defines a general way to create application-specific markup languages for different purposes.[1] The XML clan frequently welcomes new members, including XHTML, Scalable Vector Graphics (SVG), and Rich Site Summary (RSS) for news syndication. In this chapter, you'll learn how to push XHTML to extremes, but abide by the family rules.

Extensible HTML (XHTML) 1.0 is HTML 4.01 reformulated as XML with many of XML's benefits.[2] A blend of the old and the new, XHTML acts as a bridge between the ad hoc HTML world and the more structured world of XML, the web's meta markup language.

1. Tim Bray et al., "Extensible Markup Language (XML) 1.0," 2d ed. [online], (Cambridge, MA: World Wide Web Consortium, 2000), available from the Internet at `http://www.w3.org/TR/REC-xml`.
2. Steven Pemberton et al., "XHTML 1.0: The Extensible HyperText Markup Language," 2d ed. [online], (Cambridge, MA: World Wide Web Consortium, 2002), available from the Internet at `http://www.w3.org/TR/xhtml1/`. A reformulation of HTML 4 in XML 1.0.

If you want your site to work with the largest possible audience and "future proof" it for the coming XML-based web, converting to XHTML is the way to go. XHTML is the first step toward XML and what Tim Berners-Lee calls "The Semantic Web." [3]

XHTML documents are in fact XML documents with all of XML's syntactical requirements. XHTML documents must be "well-formed;" that is, all elements must be closed and properly nested. All attributes must be fully qualified and surrounded by double quotes. All XHTML elements and attributes must be lowercase, because XML is case sensitive and its DOCTYPEs prohibit mixed- or uppercase markup.

XHTML practically requires external JavaScripts and separate style sheets. Strict XHTML, on which XHTML 1.1 and 2 are based, prohibits presentational tags, forcing separation of presentation from structure. Strict XHTML documents closely resemble the pure structure of XML documents.

These stricter rules give XHTML a consistency unmatched by HTML and make it easier for automated agents and alternative browsers to access your content. Conversely, due to these stricter rules, XHTML offers fewer opportunities for optimization. Fortunately, many of the techniques discussed in Chapter 3, "HTML Optimization," and Chapter 4, "Advanced HTML Optimization," also can be applied to XHTML.

To get you started on the road to standards satori, this chapter first outlines the benefits of XHTML. Then you learn how XHTML works and how its rules differ from HTML. Finally, you discover ways you can optimize XHTML within these stricter confines.

Benefits of XHTML

The benefits of switching to XHTML are many. Valid, well-formed XHTML works well with both new and old browsers. By structuring your content logically and separating presentation into style sheets, you'll save on bandwidth and maintenance costs while increasing accessibility, reach, and interoperability on alternate platforms. (Try viewing that complex table-based layout on a Palm Pilot.)

---

3. Tim Berners-Lee, James Hendler, and Ora Lassila, "The Semantic Web," *Scientific American* 284, no. 5 (May 2001): 34-43. See also http://www.SemanticWeb.org.

Properly designed XHTML documents typically are smaller and less complex than their HTML counterparts and are more easily viewed on older browsers. Valid XHTML documents are XML-conforming, so that they can be viewed, edited, and validated with standard XML tools. Best of all, you can extend XHTML documents with namespaces (collections of element-naming conventions) to combine multiple markup languages and add new tags.[4]

So, instead of this:

```
<html>
<head><title>Presentation-intermingled HTML Document</title>
<script type="text/javascript">
<!--
var = embedded_and_invalid_variables_and_code_goes_here;
-->
</script>
<body topmargin=0 leftmargin=0 ...>
<center><font size=5><b>Fake H1 Here</b></font></center>
<p><font style="arial, helvetica, sans-serif" size="3">Inline styled prose goes here. How
do you change the font site-wide?
</body>
</html>
```

Do this:

```
<?xml version="1.0" encoding="UTF-8"?>
<!DOCTYPE html
     PUBLIC "-//W3C//DTD XHTML 1.0 Strict//EN"
     "http://www.w3.org/TR/xhtml1/DTD/xhtml1-strict.dtd ">
<html xmlns="http://www.w3.org/1999/xhtml" xml:lang="en" lang="en">
<head>
     <title>Strict XHTML Replacement</title>
<script src="/scripts/global.js" type="text/javascript"></script>
<link rel="/css/global.css" type="text/css" />
</head>
<body>
     <h1>Structural Header Here</h1>
     <p>Presentation-free prose goes here. Much cleaner.</p>
</body>
</html>
```

---

4. Tim Bray, Dave Hollander, and Andrew Layman, "Namespaces in XML" [online], (Cambridge, MA: World Wide Web Consortium, 1999), available from the Internet at http://www.w3.org/TR/REC-xml-names/.

Here are some benefits of moving to XHTML:

- **Compatibility**—XHTML is both forward compatible with the structured world of XML and backward compatible with older HTML-based browsers.

- **Interoperability**—XHTML's logical structure allows easier repurposing of content for different platforms.

> **NOTE**
>
> According to Forrester Research, over 75 percent of desktop users will view web pages on alternative platforms, such as mobile phones, kiosks, and Palm Pilots. By 2008, over one third of the world's population will own a wireless device (`http://cyberatlas.internet.com/markets/wireless/article/0,1323,10094_950001,00.html`).

- **Extensibility**—XHTML documents can be extended to add new tags with namespaces. Or, because XHTML is XML, authors can add new tags without namespaces. These tags will be ignored by the browser, but they can be used by XML tools for exchanging data.

- **Productivity**—XHTML helps you improve productivity by separating presentation and behavior from structure. One team (the artists) can concentrate on style sheets while another (the programmers) can concentrate on behavior, and yet another (the XHTML coders) can concentrate on structure. Although this is possible with well-crafted HTML, strict XHTML (and XHTML 1.1 and 2) forces this clean separation.

- **XML Conforming**—XHTML documents have a reliable structure and conform to the rules of XML. XML processors can reliably manipulate and validate these conforming cargos of content for easier document and data exchange. Aggregators like O'Reilly's Meerkat (`meerkat.oreillynet.com`) and Userland's Radio (`radio.userland.com`) use RSS feeds to create meta-news sites and products.

XHTML versus HTML

To get an idea of the differences between XHTML and HTML, let's take a look at the differences between the technologies on which they are based: XML and SGML.

XML versus SGML

By transforming HTML 4.01 into XML-based XHTML, the W3C hopes to avoid the chaotic evolution that HTML experienced. Both HTML and XHTML use Document Type Definitions (DTDs) to constrain the element and attribute "grammar" of their documents. Adding elements to HTML through new SGML DTDs requires a trip through committees, which is not an easy task. Adding new elements to XHTML is much easier: just add the tags and a namespace.

Anatomy of an XHTML Document

The W3C has made learning XHTML easy for HTML authors. XHTML looks like HTML, but it's neater and has a few more mandatory tags thrown in due to its XML heritage. Let's first look at a minimal XHTML document, and then we'll break down the most important parts:

```
<?xml version="1.0" encoding="UTF-8"?>
<!DOCTYPE html
    PUBLIC "-//W3C//DTD XHTML 1.0 Strict//EN"
    "http://www.w3.org/TR/xhtml1/DTD/xhtml1-strict.dtd ">
<html xmlns="http://www.w3.org/1999/xhtml" xml:lang="en" lang="en">
<head>
    <title>A Minimal XHTML Document</title>
</head>
<body>
    <p>Hello <a href="http://world.org/">World.org</a>.</p>
    <hr />
</body>
</html>
```

The first three statements are different from a minimal HTML document, but the rest look just like garden-variety HTML in lowercase with all tags closed. The first three statements declare that this is an XML 1.0-based XHTML document encoded in 8-bit

Unicode (ASCII) using the XHTML 1.0 Strict DTD (wrapped over three lines) and the English XHTML namespace.

The second (DOCTYPE) and third (html namespace) statements are mandatory in XHTML documents, while the first (prologue) is optional. The prologue would presumably be included using conditional SSI for modern XML-savvy browsers (see Chapter 17, "Server-Side Techniques"), or left out to save 39 bytes. The next section explains all these new tags.

Pull the Prologue

All XML documents begin with declarations that tell the browser how to interpret them. The XML declaration, or prologue, precedes the DOCTYPE and namespace declarations and defines a document's type or markup language. For example:

```
<?xml version="1.0" encoding="UTF-8"?>
```

This funny-looking element tells the browser three things:

- The type of document (XML)
- Which version of XML the document uses (1.0)
- The document's character encoding (8-bit Unicode)

Unfortunately, some older browsers choke on the <?xml prologue and display a blank page. Internet Explorer 4 and 5 for the Mac and Netscape Navigator 4 behave badly when they come across a page with an XML prologue because they don't recognize the <?xml syntax. The prologue can also occasionally cause trouble with server-side parsing engines, like PHP.

Wisely, the W3C has made the prologue optional. You can either omit the prologue from your XHTML pages or conditionally include it for newer browsers. But what if you want to use a character set other than the default UTF-8 or UTF-16, and you don't want to use a prologue? You can use a meta http-equiv tag instead:

```
<meta http-equiv="Content-type" content="text.html; charset=EUC-JP" />
```

Even better, you can save some bandwidth by configuring your server to send this as part of the content-type header.

Now that we've got everybody talking the same language, let's look at how the DOCTYPE and namespace declarations work to define the grammar and vocabulary of the language of XML documents.

DOCTYPE Declaration

Both HTML and XHTML use Document Type Declarations (DOCTYPE) to define *markup declarations* that provide a grammar for a class of documents. This grammar is the Document Type Definition (DTD). The DTD can point to an external and/or internal definition of markup declarations. For example:

```
<!DOCTYPE html PUBLIC "-//W3C//DTD XHTML 1.0 Strict//EN" "DTD/xhtml1-strict.dtd">
```

This statement declares that the root element of your document is html, as defined by the DTD whose public identifier is "-//W3C//DTD XHTML 1.0 Strict//EN". The browser either already knows this public DTD, or it can follow the URI to locate the DTD.

Although it is optional in HTML, the DOCTYPE declaration must be included before the "root" HTML element in XHTML documents. Note that some validators give errors for relative DTD URIs. Use absolute URIs instead to ensure forward compatibility and portability. For example:

```
<!DOCTYPE html PUBLIC "-//W3C//DTD XHTML 1.0 Strict//EN"
"http://www.w3.org/TR/xhtml1/DTD/xhtml1-strict.dtd">
```

Keep in mind that relative DTD URIs stored locally would save at least 31 bytes, but would not be as portable as absolute URIs.

DOCTYPE Switching

As you learned in Chapter 4, "Advanced HTML Optimization," modern browsers switch their rendering behavior based on the DOCTYPE you specify. IE6 Win and NS6/Mozilla use DOCTYPE switching among standards and quirks modes. The latest versions of Mozilla/Netscape add a third "almost standards" option to their switching arsenal. IE5 Mac switches into standards mode if you specify a DTD URI for *any* DOCTYPE: strict, transitional, or frameset. For strictly authored XHTML documents, use the full form of the DOCTYPE. For all others, use the abbreviated form or conditionally include the DTD URI for all but IE5 Mac. For more on almost standards mode, see `http://www.mozilla.org/docs/web-developer/quirks/doctypes.html`.

DTDs

Both HTML and XHTML use DTDs to define their constituent parts. The DTD defines rules that constrain the logical structure of a class of XML documents. The DTD lists all legal markup and specifies where and how that markup can be included in a document. This element syntax or grammar defines the semantics of the elements and their attributes. For example:

```
<!DOCTYPE html PUBLIC "-//W3C//DTD XHTML 1.0 Transitional//EN"
    "http://www.w3.org/TR/xhtml1/DTD/xhtml1-transitional.dtd">
```

This DOCTYPE specifies that this document is authored to the XHTML 1.0 Transitional DTD, which allows deprecated elements.

Documents that match the constraints of the DTD are said to be *valid,* or error free. The three DTDs for XHTML correspond to the ones defined by HTML 4.01:

```
<!DOCTYPE html
    PUBLIC "-//W3C//DTD XHTML 1.0 Strict//EN"
    "http://www.w3.org/TR/xhtml1/DTD/xhtml1-strict.dtd ">

<!DOCTYPE html
    PUBLIC "-//W3C//DTD XHTML 1.0 Transitional//EN"
    " http://www.w3.org/TR/xhtml1/DTD/xhtml1-transitional.dtd">

<!DOCTYPE html
    PUBLIC "-//W3C//DTD XHTML 1.0 Frameset//EN"
    "http://www.w3.org/TR/xhtml1/DTD/xhtml1-frameset.dtd">
```

The only differences between the XHTML and HTML DTDs are the ones found in SGML and XML, which impose stricter syntactical constraints. Like HTML, the first DTD is for strict adherence to the XHTML standard, without any deprecated presentational elements like font. The second DTD is transitional and includes deprecated elements and attributes for legacy HTML code. The third DTD is for XHTML documents that use frames.

As I noted previously, using the strict DTD can be faster. Browsers choose among two or three rendering modes, based on their DOCTYPE switching criteria. The transitional parsers are necessarily more complex because they have to handle all of the deprecated tags and attributes in transitional XHTML. By using the strict DTD, you'll separate structure from presentation and behavior, and gain even more benefits from cached CSS files. You'll also be ready for future versions of XHTML that are based on strict XHTML 1.0.

Namespaces

An XML namespace is a collection of element types and attribute names, identified by a URI reference. Every conforming XHTML document must designate the XHTML namespace that it uses in the HTML root element with the xmlns attribute. Here's an example:

```
<html xmlns="http://www.w3.org/1999/xhtml" xml:lang="en" lang="en">
```

In essence, this namespace defines the markup vocabulary for XHTML. The DTD defines the grammar of that vocabulary. Together they define the markup language used in your document so that browsers can more easily grok your code.

Multiple Namespaces

What if you want to include elements and attributes from different document types? You can't combine multiple DTDs for a single document, but you can use multiple namespaces. Namespaces allow authors to use multiple "markup vocabularies" within the same document. Adding new sets of elements is as easy as pointing to another namespace. For example, if you want to include MathML inside an XHTML document, you can include an element with a namespace attribute, like this:

```
<div xmlns="http://www.w3.org/1998/Math/MathML">
    <!-- math elements here -->
</div>
```

An XML-compliant browser would use the `http://www.w3.org/1998/Math/MathML` namespace to find out that what follows is MathML, not XTHML. But what if you want to include multiple instances of MathML for multiple equations? Instead of including a namespace declaration for each equation, you can declare the MathML namespace at the beginning of your document and refer to its shorthand prefix later. So instead of this:

```
<html xmlns="http://www.w3.org/1999/xhtml" xml:lang="en" lang="en">
```

Do this:

```
<html xmlns="http://www.w3.org/1999/xhtml" xml:lang="en" lang="en"
xmlns:math="http://www.w3.org/1998/Math/MathML">
```

Then you can tag each equation `div` with the `math` namespace prefix, like this:

```
<math:div>
    ...
</div>
```

By assigning URIs to each element, namespaces disambiguate elements with the same name to help avoid element name collisions that would confuse XML applications. Namespaces codify your extensions to allow industry-wide data exchange.

The Syntactical Rules of XML

XML imposes stricter rules on XHTML documents than HTML does. The main differences between XHTML and HTML documents are as follows:

- XML documents must be well-formed.
- Attributes must be fully qualified and quoted.
- Lowercase markup.
- Scripts and style elements must conform to the stricter #PCDATA format.
- Fragment identifiers must be of type `id`, not `name`.

Rule #1: Well-Formed Documents

XML documents are by definition well-formed. No, that's not a shapely set of tags; it means essentially that all elements must be closed and properly nested.

There are other requirements of well-formed XML documents, but these are the two that cause the most problems for authors and browsers. So instead of this:

```
<p><a href="../"><em>Extreme</a></em> HTML Optimization
```

Do this:

```
<p><a href="../"><em>Extreme</em></a> HTML Optimization</p>
```

Close All Tags

Unlike HTML, all elements in XHTML documents must be closed. Non-empty tags like `<p></p>` and `<div></div>` must have matching closing tags. So instead of this:

```
<p>This paragraph has no end.
<p>I'm invalid XHTML.
```

Do this:

```
<p>This paragraph has some closure.</p>
<p>This is valid XHTML.</p>
```

This need for closure extends to empty tags, which can lead a lonely existence. Empty tags like `<br>` and `<img>` should be closed by a forward slash like this `<br/>` or `<img src="t.gif"/>` to create a self-closing tag. The W3C recommends that you include a space before the slash to allow older browsers to ignore the slash, as shown here:

```
<br />
```

or

```
<img src="t.gif" width="1" height="1" alt="" />
```

To avoid compatibility problems, the W3C recommends that for empty elements you use the space/trailing slash method rather than a closing tag.

An empty paragraph could be written as `<p />` and an empty data cell could be written as `<td />`. This abbreviated form can confuse HTML-based browsers, however. Either use `<p> </p>` or omit these spacing hacks entirely and use CSS. Here's a list of all the empty HTML tags expressed in XHTML transitional form (the starred elements [*] are not allowed in strict XHTML):

- `<area />`
- `<base />`
- `<basefont />`*
- `<br />`
- `<col />`
- `<frame />`*
- `<hr />`
- `<img />`
- `<input />`
- `<isindex />`*
- `<link />`
- `<meta />`
- `<param />`

Netscape 6: No Sloppy Code Allowed

Improperly nested or orphaned elements can cause rendering problems for some browsers, particularly Netscape 6.x. Standards-compliant browsers like Netscape rely on properly nested and closed elements to apply CSS rules and JavaScript. When we updated our JavaScript news flipper for WebReference.com's front page, we found that Netscape 6 did not properly execute dynamically written external JavaScript with improperly nested code.[5]

---

5. Andrew King, "JavaScripting Netscape 6: No More Sloppy Code" [online], (Darien, CT: Jupitermedia Corporation, 2001), available from the Internet at http://www.webreference.com/programming/javascript/netscape6/.

Rule #2: Quote All Attributes

In HTML, you can omit quotation marks from certain attributes. In XHTML, all attribute values must be quoted. So instead of this:

```
<img src="t.gif" width=1 height=1>
```

Do this:

```
<img src="t.gif" width="1" height="1" alt="" />
```

Rule #3: Don't Minimize Those Attributes

In HTML, you can minimize certain Boolean-like attributes like this:

```
<option selected>The Chosen One</option>
```

XML does not support attribute minimization. The value of all attribute-value pairs, like `checked` and `compact`, must be fully qualified. For example:

```
<option selected="selected">The Properly Chosen One</option>
```

No dangling attributes are allowed. See how well-organized XHTML is? This well-formedness and lack of ambiguity is what gives XML-based documents their power. If XHTML had a bedroom, it would be immaculate.

Note that some older browsers can choke on fully qualified attributes, although HTML 4-compliant browsers don't have this problem. One optimization technique is to use defaults whenever possible (that is, the first option in a select menu is selected by default), or omit attributes entirely. Here is a list of these self-referential attributes (the starred elements [*] are not allowed in strict XHTML):

- `checked="checked"`
- `compact="compact"`*
- `declare="declare"`
- `defer="defer"`
- `disabled="disabled"`
- `ismap="ismap"`

- `nowrap="nowrap"`*
- `multiple="multiple"`
- `nohref="nohref"`
- `noresize="noresize"`*
- `noshade="noshade"`*
- `readonly="readonly"`
- `selected="selected"`

Rule #4: Higher Court Says Lowercase

XHTML tags and attributes must be lowercase because XML is case-sensitive. XHTML documents will not validate without lowercase markup. The character set of XML is ISO 10646, which makes a distinction between upper- and lowercase characters. Accordingly, all three XHTML DTDs define elements and attributes using lowercase letters. So instead of this:

```
<TITLE>The New York Times on the Web</TITLE>
```

Do this:

```
<title>The New York Times on the Web</title>
```

To be compliant, even your style sheet fragment identifiers should be lowercase. Also make your `id` values lowercase for consistency.

Rule #5: Handle Script and Style Differences with Care

Style sheets and especially scripts must be handled with care when you are switching from HTML to XHTML. XHTML changes the content type of script and style elements from unparsed characters for HTML to parsed character data (#CDATA to #PCDATA). This seemingly minor change, caused by the stricter way XML handles files, can mean major changes to style sheets and especially scripts.

#PCDATA, or parsed character data, interprets the less-than sign (<) and ampersand (&) as the start of markup, instead of processing them unparsed as HTML does. The symbols (]]>) and (-) are also prohibited inside #PCDATA blocks. To make matters worse, XML parsers can also silently remove the contents of comments.

Thus, the traditional practice of surrounding embedded style sheets or scripts with comments to make them backward compatible with very old browsers won't work with XHTML files. But fear not, gentle reader; there is a solution.

Embedded Style Sheets and XHTML

With style sheets, this restriction is usually not a problem. You can create most style sheets without using these characters, and embed them in your page like this:

```
<style type="text/css">
code {
    color: red;
    font-family: monospace;
    font-weight: bold;
}
</style>
```

Note that comments are not included here. For very old browsers, the text within style tags may display. You can do one of three things:

- Conditionally include embedded style sheets
- Ignore older browsers
- Use external style sheets

The link element is the traditional way of associating an external style sheet with a document:

```
<link rel="stylesheet" type="text/css" href="/global.css" title="global styles" />
```

Because Netscape 4 can choke on some newer CSS commands, the link element can sometimes be a problem. As a workaround, some authors import style sheets into their documents because Netscape 4 ignores this unrecognized CSS2 command. For example:

```
<style type="text/css">@import url("/global.css");</style>
```

These "at rules" act like CSS2 filters, in the way dynamically written JavaScript 1.2 SRC statements do for some DHTML-compatibility techniques. Another option is to layer your styles with basic Netscape 4-friendly styles in a linked style sheet and more advanced styles in an imported style sheet.

External Style Sheets

External style sheets have some definite advantages. With one small sub-1K CSS style sheet, you can style and lay out your entire site, instead of embedding layout markup in the form of tables or embedded CSS within each file. The CSS file is cached after the first time it loads. Embedding your style sheet can, however, save one HTTP request for high-traffic pages. At WebReference.com, we use a hybrid approach by embedding a stripped-down style sheet within the home page and linking to an external style sheet everywhere else. For more details on linking to external style sheets see Chapter 7, "CSS Optimization."

Embedded Scripts in XHTML?

Embedding JavaScript inside XHTML files is another matter. In theory, you could rewrite your code to avoid the < and & symbols prohibited by XHTML's stricter #PCDATA requirement (for example, x <= y becomes y > x, and (x && y) becomes !(!x || !y)), but this can be a hassle for larger scripts. To embed scripts with these special characters, the XHTML specification recommends that you either escape them (which HTML browsers then misinterpret) or wrap your script within a CDATA section, essentially forcing XHTML to behave like HTML:

```
<script type="text/javascript">
<![CDATA[
    ... unescaped script content ...
]]>
</script>
```

These CDATA sections are recognized by XML processors, which act like HTML-based browsers and process the sections as unparsed data. HTML-based browsers such as Internet Explorer 5 for the Macintosh do not, however, recognize the CDATA command and will produce a script error. There are three solutions to XHTML's fussier handling of embedded scripts:

- Conditionally include recoded JavaScript.
- Ignore older browsers (not recommended now).
- Use external JavaScripts.

You can recode your JavaScripts to exclude problem characters (<, &,],], >, and -), and embed them without comments inside a script tag.

Or just do what most people do—link to an external JavaScript and avoid the problem entirely:

```
<script src="/gomenu.js" type="text/javascript"></script>
```

JavaScript optimization techniques are covered in more detail in Chapter 9, "Optimizing JavaScript for Download Speed," and Chapter 10, "Optimizing JavaScript for Execution Speed."

Rule #6: Fragment Identifiers: *name* and *id*, Please

In XHTML, fragment identifiers are handled differently from HTML. In XHTML, the `id` attribute replaces the `name` attribute. URI references that end in fragment identifiers (such as #review) do not refer to elements with a named attribute. They refer instead to elements with an `id` attribute. In CSS, the `id` attribute is also used to refer to HTML elements. Some existing HTML browsers don't support the `id` attribute; therefore, you should supply both the `id` and `name` attributes to ensure forward and backward compatibility (for example, `<a id="review" name="review">...</a>`). Alternatively, you can ignore older browsers and use only `id` attributes for forward compatibility.

The data type of `name` and `id` attributes also has been changed from `CDATA` to `NMTOKEN`. To make your fragment identifiers backward compatible, use `id` and/or `name` attributes that match the pattern `[A-Za-z][A-Za-z0-9:_.-]*` (for example, use a string starting with "a" through "Z" and zero or more alphanumeric characters).

Converting from HTML to XHTML

Converting a few documents by hand is one thing, but what if you want to convert a hundred—or a *thousand*—web documents to XHTML? You can partially automate this process by using automated tools like HTML Tidy and Dreamweaver extensions.

HTML Tidy

HTML Tidy, a free, standalone, W3C-approved tool, can automatically convert your web pages from uppercase to lowercase markup, your `font` tags to equivalent style sheet rules, and more. Originally developed by HTML 4's primary author Dave Raggett, Tidy is now maintained as open source at SourceForge (`tidy.sourceforge.net`). As its name implies, Tidy can clean up your code, point out problem areas, and pretty-print your (X)HTML. Tidy is quite powerful, so be sure to read the manual and make a backup before you tidy up your code.

One little-known option in Tidy is the `-o` option for optimization. This undocumented flag performs rudimentary whitespace removal to shrink your code.

Tidy has been ported to Java and Perl, a number of platforms (including DOS, Windows, and Mac), and embedded in a number of third-party programs, including BBEdit (`http://www.bbedit.com/`), EVRSoft's 1stPage (`http://www.evrsoft.com/`), HTML Kit Web Editor (`http://www.chami.com/html-kit/`), Notetab (`http://www.notetab.com/`), and Mozquito Technologies' Factory (`http://www.mozquito.com/`).

Dreamweaver Extensions

Jason Dalgarno has created a Dreamweaver extension (`http://home.clara.net/locust-star/`) that converts HTML pages into XHTML. The tool will do the following:

- Add closing tags.
- Close empty tags.
- Add (or replace) DOCTYPE and `xmlns` attributes.
- Quote unquoted attribute values.
- Unminimize Boolean attributes.

In addition, the tool will optionally clean up `<script>` tags, copy name attributes to `id` attributes, add blank `alt` attributes for alt-free images, and run commands site-wide.

Make a backup before making these changes, and be especially careful with site-wide commands. For the latest Dreamweaver extensions, visit Macromedia's Dreamweaver exchange at `http://www.macromedia.com/software/dreamweaver/`.

Optimizing XHTML

What does this all mean for web site optimization? XHTML's persnickety nature means that some of the optimization techniques shown in Chapter 3, "HTML Optimization, and Chapter 4, "Advanced HTML Optimization," cannot be used. Closing tags are not optional and all attributes must be quoted and fully qualified. All these other HTML optimization techniques can be used, however:

- Remove whitespace.
- Minimize HTTP requests (replace images with CSS).
- Cut the comments.
- Minimize `alt` attribute values.
- Use conditional `meta` tags.
- Optimize forms.
- Tune tables with `table-layout:fixed` and `colgroup/col` elements.
- Auto-abbreviate URLs.

Just make sure that you close your tags and quote and fully qualify your attributes. Adopting the quoteless link approach Yahoo! uses is *verboten* in XHTML.

Transform Your Code

You'll gain the most benefit, however, by transforming your code to a more standards-compliant mode. XML's emphasis on structure, not presentation, enables authors to transform their code into a more interoperable format. By separating presentation in the form of style sheets from structure, authors can enable their pages to work well in different contexts.

Think Outlines

When marking up your web documents, think purely in terms of logical structure. Organizing your documents like a traditional outline ensures interoperability:

```
<h1>Primary Topic</h1>
    <p>Introduction...</p>
```

```
<h2>Seconday Topic</h2>
    <p>Secondary text...</p>
    <h3>Tertiary Topic</h3>
```

Avoid using presentational tags like `<b>`, `<font>`, and `<i>`. Use structural markup instead, like `<strong>`, `<hx>`, and `<em>`. Better yet, use style sheets to control the appearance of your document and streamline your code. So instead of this:

```
<h1 align="center">Main Topic</h1>
<p align="right"><font size="+1" face="arial,helvetica,sans-serif" color="#333333">Overly
specified paragraph text goes here.</p>
```

Do this:

```
<h1>Main Topic</h1>
<p>Normal paragraph text goes here.</p>
```

Then use a simple style sheet, which could be reused site-wide.

The W3C reminds us that "HTML documents are supposed to be structured around … paragraphs, headings, and lists."[6] If you muddy the waters with embedded presentational tags and common HTML spacing hacks, you will experience higher maintenance costs and larger files. This will ultimately reduce your audience.

Replace Tables with CSS

Chapter 4 showed you how to get the most out of your tables. Although originally designed to present tabular data, tables have become the traditional way to lay out entire web pages. Table-based layout has some inherent drawbacks, however, mainly because it embeds presentation amidst your content. But there's a new kid on the block-level: CSS2.

CSS2 allows you to separate presentation from structure. This seemingly innocuous statement has rather powerful implications. Pure structural XHTML can be easily repurposed for different formats and platforms. Alternate style sheets can reformat your content for printing, display on handheld devices, and even screen readers for the visually impaired. Best of all, this separation of church and state means faster pages, because CSS-based sites are generally smaller, and the CSS file(s) are cached throughout the site.

---

6. W3C, "Font tag considered harmful," HTML Home Page [online], (Cambridge, MA: World Wide Web Consortium, 2002), available from the Internet at http://www.w3.org/MarkUp/.

Rather than using table rows and columns, you can use positioned `divs` to lay out your pages. Most of CSS2 is supported by over 85 percent of the web's current browsers and it is growing fast, which makes CSS2-based layout a practical alternative to tables. By breaking out of the fixed grid tyranny of tables, you can free up your code to adjust to your user's whims.

Let's rework our three-panel table design in XHTML and CSS2. Here's the original table-based layout:

```
<?xml version="1.0" encoding="UTF-8"?>
<!DOCTYPE html
    PUBLIC "-//W3C//DTD XHTML 1.0 Strict//EN"
    "http://www.w3.org/TR/xhtml1/DTD/xhtml1-strict.dtd ">
<html xmlns="http://www.w3.org/1999/xhtml" xml:lang="en" lang="en">
<head>
    <title>Three-panel table layout</title>
</head><body>
<table>
    <tr>
        <td colspan="2">
            <p>top navigation bar (branding and advertising)</p>
        </td>
    </tr>
    <tr>
        <td>
            <p>left navigation bar</p>
        </td>
        <td>
            <p>main content area</p>
        </td>
    </tr>
</table>
</body>
</html>
```

Here's the XHTML/CSS equivalent:

```
<?xml version="1.0" encoding="UTF-8"?>
<!DOCTYPE html
    PUBLIC "-//W3C//DTD XHTML 1.0 Strict//EN"
    "http://www.w3.org/TR/xhtml1/DTD/xhtml1-strict.dtd ">
<html xmlns="http://www.w3.org/1999/xhtml" xml:lang="en" lang="en">
<head>
    <title>Three-panel XHTML/CSS layout</title>
<link rel="stylesheet" href="/css/layout.css" />
```

```
</head>
<body>
<div id="top">
    <p>top navigation bar (branding and advertising)</p>
</div>
<div id="nav">
    <p>left navigation bar</p>
</div>
<div id="content">
    <p>main content area</p>
</div>
</body>
</html>
```

Note that we use descriptive labels here, not positional ones like "left" or "right." Don't think in terms of positioning when labeling elements; think function instead. You can see that the body of the document is greatly simplified, with its presentational aspects within the style sheet, not intermixed within the HTML.

By combining the use of strict XHTML, CSS1 to replace font tags, and CSS2 to replace tables, you can dramatically reduce the size of your pages and gain layout flexibility in the process. Chapter 8, "Advanced CSS Optimization," delves more deeply into how CSS can streamline your pages and how you can optimize your CSS.

Summary

Because of its stricter rules, optimizing XHTML is more limited than optimizing HTML. For XHTML, however, you can use many of the same techniques we used in Chapter 3 and Chapter 4. You'll reap the greatest performance gains by transforming your code from old-style presentation-intermingled HTML to pure structural XHTML with CSS handling the presentation and JavaScript handling the behavior. Typical results when converting from HTML to XHTML and CSS range from 25 percent to 50 percent smaller files, with essentially the same presentation. Adopting strict XHTML means that your code will be smaller, easier to maintain and repurpose, and faster to display in modern browsers. In addition to the techniques listed previously, here are some optimization and compatibility techniques that you can apply to XHTML:

- Transform your code into a more standards-compliant mode for smaller files and lower maintenance costs.

- Adopt strict XHTML for faster downloads and parsing.

- Create well-formed documents, close all tags, and fully qualify and quote all attributes.

- Use lowercase markup and text.

- Embed style sheets on high-traffic pages and link to external files everywhere else.

- Link to external scripts, and group, compress, and defer where possible.

- Minimize fragment identifiers.

- Validate your XHTML; use HTML Tidy to clean up your code.

Recommended Reading

For more information about XHTML, check out these books and web sites:

- *HTML & XHTML: The Definitive Guide, 5th ed.,* by Chuck Musciano and Bill Kennedy (Cambridge, MA: O'Reilly and Associates, 2002). A great introduction and reference for markup.

- *Inside XML* by Steve Holzner (Indianapolis, IN: New Riders Publishing, 2000). For more details on XML's inner workings.

- http://www.alistapart.com/

- http://validator.w3.org/

- http://www.w3.org/TR/

- http://www.webstandards.org/

- http://www.xhtml.org/

6

Case Study: PopularMechanics.com

For this example of optimizing an actual web page, we turn to Popular-Mechanics.com, the poster child for web site optimization (see Figure 6.1). On Popular Mechanic's page, you'll apply most of the HTML optimization techniques you learned in Chapters 3 and 4 and use some information from other chapters as well—CSS (Chapter 8), JavaScript (Chapter 9), and compression (Chapter 18). First, you remove whitespace and redundant tags and attributes. Then, you optimize the CSS and JavaScript. Next, you tune the tables and cut the comments. Finally, you compress the optimized page to see what kind of savings you can expect.

Figure 6.1
The PopularMechanics.com home page.

http://www.popularmechanics.com/

The HTML source for PopularMechanics.com weighs in at 138,548 bytes. In total, the front page is nearly half a megabyte in size (498,976 bytes), taking about 1.5 minutes to load on a 56K modem. It takes over a minute before any useful content appears, due in part to large amount of JavaScript in the head. As you learned in Chapter 1, "Response Time: Eight Seconds, Plus or Minus Two," few users are willing to wait that long for content.

You can learn a lot by looking at the source for unoptimized pages, and Popular-Mechanics.com is most instructive. Looking at the source code, PopularMechanics.com does almost everything wrong. This site has it all:

- Overspecified and unoptimized CSS (9,986 bytes)
- Overused and unoptimized JavaScript (56,453 bytes)
- Numerous images (196 total objects)
- Long directory and filenames
- Absolute versus relative URLs
- Verbose comments and commented markup
- Whitespace galore
- Overspecified tables, and more

The JavaScript alone in this example is larger than most home pages, and even the CSS is larger than some. It's a wonderful example of what *not* to do on a home page. Listing 6.1 is an abbreviated excerpt.

Listing 6.1   PopularMechanics.com Original HTML Excerpt

```
<html>
<head>
<title>Popular Mechanics</title>
<meta http-equiv="Content-Type" content="text/html; charset=iso-8859-1">
<meta name="site" content="PM_Zone">
<meta name="Description" content="">
<meta name="Keywords" content="">
<meta name="department" content="">
<meta name="date" content="">
<meta name="display" content="">
<SCRIPT LANGUAGE="JavaScript">
```

```
function formHandler(form){
var URL = document.form.site.options[document.form.site.selectedIndex].value;
window.location.href = URL;
}
</SCRIPT>
</HEAD>

<style type="text/css">
<!--
BODY { background-color: #000000; margin-left: 0px; margin-top: 0px; margin-width: 0px;
margin-height: 0px;}

A:link { color: #993333; font-family: Arial, Helvetica, sans-serif; font-size: 12pt;}
...
-->
</style>
<!-- iSyndicate Content Delivery (HTML)Guidelines are the following COMMENT tags around
their actual content:-->
<!-- feed name = "Top News"  -->
<!-- article  -->
<!-- headline  -->
<!-- summary  -->
<!-- url  (supplied in CMS)  -->
<!-- byline  -->
<!-- date  (supplied in CMS) -->
<!-- copyright  (to be supplied in CMS by user/WRITER/EDITOR)  -->
<!-- body  -->
<!-- end article  -->
<!-- end feed  -->
<!-- iSyndicate Content Delivery (HTML)Guidelines  -->
<!-- Begin - pm.js, which holds all javascript functions; and - popup.js, cookie  -->
<script language="Javascript">
function check4popup() {
        top.main.document.contentForm.target = "new_window";
        top.main.document.contentForm.submit();

}


function gotoPreview() {

// "NEXT" after filling in metatag & location information
// this submits the form in the top frame and redirects the bottom frame to the document
with
// Preview & Cancel buttons

       if (top.main.document.contentForm.elements['form[dept]'] &&
```

continues

Listing 6.1   PopularMechanics.com Original HTML Excerpt   *continued*

```
!(top.main.document.contentForm.elements['change-folder'])
... (56.4K later [18 script elements total])
</script>
<!-- End rollovers (yellow_navigational_buttons)  -->
<!-- PowerAd -->
<!-- PowerAd -->
</head>
<!-- feed name ="Top New" -->
<!-- article -->

<BODY OnUnLoad="checkCount()"  leftmargin="0" topmargin="0" marginwidth="0"
marginheight="0"
onLoad="MM_preloadImages('/images/b_auton.gif','/images/b_himpon.gif','/images/b_scion.gif'
,'/images/b_outon.gif','/images/b_techon.gif','/images/b_srcon.gif','/b_whton.gif','/images
/b_shpon.gif','/images/b_crron.gif','/images/b_emlon.gif','/images/b_advon.gif','/images/b_
msgon.gif')">
...
<!-- BEGIN table-1 (top_spacer) -->
<table name="top_spacer" width="805" height="7" border="0" cellspacing="0"
cellpadding="0">
  <tr align="left" valign="top">
    <td width="805" height="7"><img src="/images/clear.gif" width="805" height="7"
border="0"></td>
  </tr>
</table>
<!-- END table-1 (top spacer) -->
<!-- BEGIN table-2 (UPPER LEFT MAGAZINE COVER; ADSERVING L90; homepage LOGO; UPPER RIGHT
SPONSORSHIP; DATE) -->
<table name="table-2" width="805" border="0" cellspacing="0" cellpadding="0" height="153">
```

Most of the techniques you learn in this book can be applied to this page. This page needs a complete overhaul, so I won't make all the changes here, but I'll give you an idea of the savings you can achieve with some automated tools and manual techniques. In Chapter 16, "Case Studies: PopularMechanics.com and iProspect.com," you learn to optimize Popular Mechanic's keywords.

Automatic Optimization

First, use SpaceAgent to remove the comments, whitespace, and optional closing tags (see Figure 6.2).

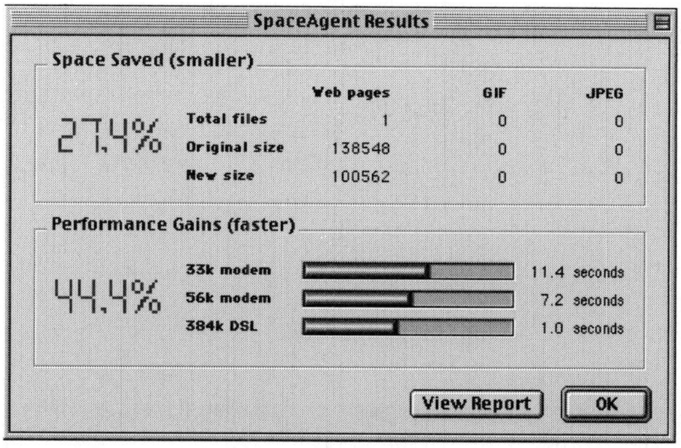

Figure 6.2
SpaceAgent.

SpaceAgent, from Insider Software, automates the removal of excess whitespace (tabs, returns, and spaces) and can remove optional meta and closing tags, and even quotes. For this example, I turned off the optional quote removal for HTML and XHTML compliance. The result is 100,562 bytes, a savings of more than 27 percent. Although still quite large for a busy home page, this savings is significant. So this:

```
<html>
<head>
<title>Popular Mechanics</title>
<meta http-equiv="Content-Type" content="text/html; charset=iso-8859-1">
<meta name="site" content="PM_Zone">
<meta name="Description" content="">
<meta name="Keywords" content="">
<meta name="department" content="">
<meta name="date" content="">
<meta name="display" content="">
<SCRIPT LANGUAGE="JavaScript">
function formHandler(form){
var URL = document.form.site.options[document.form.site.selectedIndex].value;
window.location.href = URL;
}
</SCRIPT>
</HEAD>

<style type="text/css">
<!--
BODY { background-color: #000000; margin-left: 0px; margin-top: 0px; margin-width: 0px;
margin-height: 0px;}

A:link { color: #993333; font-family: Arial, Helvetica, sans-serif; font-size: 12pt;}
```

Becomes this:

```
<html><head><title>Popular Mechanics</title><meta name=Description content=""><meta
name=Keywords content=""><SCRIPT LANGUAGE=JavaScript>function formHandler(form){var
URL=document.form.site.options[document.form.site.selectedIndex].value;window.location.href
=URL;}</SCRIPT><style type="text/css">
<!--
BODY { background-color: #000000; margin-left: 0px; margin-top: 0px; margin-width: 0px;
margin-height: 0px;}
A:link { color: #993333; font-family: Arial, Helvetica, sans-serif; font-size: 12pt;}
```

> **NOTE**
>
> See also VSE Web Site Turbo for a Mac-only optimizer at `http://www.vse-online.com`.

Other than whitespace and redundant tag removal, most HTML optimizers do not
optimize CSS or JavaScript effectively. You could save even more by optimizing the CSS
and using shorthand hex color values and font shorthand properties. For example,
#RRGGBB becomes #RGB, and font-size, font-family, etc., becomes font.

Manual Optimization

Automated optimizers can only go so far. To fully optimize web pages, you've got to do
the job manually. Popular Mechanics overuses unoptimized CSS rules, absolute URLs,
long filenames and directory names, and a good amount of unoptimized JavaScript (18
script elements in all). This section shows you how to take out some of this dead wood.

CSS Optimization

Let's start with the CSS. Popular Mechanics uses nearly 10K of CSS, with redundant
rules aplenty. These can be optimized using shorthand properties like font and shorthand hex notation for colors. In addition, by specifying global fonts for the body (and td
and th) elements, you can avoid the redundant font-family properties strewn throughout the code. So this:

```
<style type="text/css">
<!--
```

```
BODY { background-color: #000000; margin-left: 0px; margin-top: 0px; margin-width: 0px;
margin-height: 0px;}

A:link { color: #993333; font-family: Arial, Helvetica, sans-serif; font-size: 12pt;}

A:active { color: #993333; font-family: Arial, Helvetica, sans-serif; font-size: 12pt;}

A:visited { color: #999999; font-family: Arial, Helvetica, sans-serif; font-size: 12pt;}

td.table4main { background-color: #FFFFFF;}
...
```

Becomes this:

```
<!--
BODY{background:#000;margin:0px;}
BODY TD TH{font:12px arial,helvetica,sans-serif;}
A:link{color:#933;}
A:active{color:#933;}
A:visited{color:#999;}
td.table4main{background:#FFF;}
```

Even better, you can reduce the number of rules and shunt everything into an external
file to raise relevance by using the link tag:

```
<link rel="/css/global.css" type="text/css">
```

Note that they use points to specify font size, which is better suited to print style sheets
than onscreen font sizing. I changed points to pixels for screen display.

JavaScript Optimization

Popular Mechanics uses a whopping 55K of JavaScript in the head of the home page
alone. This amount of code delays the display of visible content and lowers search
engine relevance. Using JavaScript, Popular Mechanics adds hierarchical navigation
menus, a number of pop-up window controls, and an editable home page. There are a
total of 18 script elements in the page, including some ad code snippets. JavaScript also
is included within the body itself for various rollovers, pop-up windows, and navigation
gizmos. This is a great example of JavaScript gone wild, without regard to the user's
experience.

I'd recommend that Popular Mechanics shunt any create-your-own-page code to a CGI script with cookies to save state and streamline or eliminate the menu code. The designers also use pop-up menus and frames extensively, even though there are no frames on the initial home page. All of these features make the code unnecessarily complex. Here's an example JavaScript snippet to confirm canceling a change:

```
function confirmCancelDept() {
        var agree = confirm("Are you sure you want to cancel?  This will undo any changes " +
                            "you've made to this page only and will return you to the dept
tool TOC");

        if (agree) {
                top.main.document.contentForm.target = "main";
                top.main.document.contentForm.action =
"/INTERNAL/genForm/forms/dept_one.phtml?dept=" +
                        top.main.document.contentForm.elements['form[dept]'].value +
"&username=" +
                        top.main.document.contentForm.elements['form[username]'].value +
"&version=" +
                        top.main.document.contentForm.elements['form[version]'].value;
                //top.main.document.contentForm.action =
"/INTERNAL/genForm/forms/dept_one.phtml";
                top.main.document.contentForm.cancel.value = "TRUE";

                top.bottom.document.location.href = "/INTERNAL/edit_dept/bottom.html";

                top.main.document.contentForm.submit();
        }

}
```

The long pathnames could be cached in variables once and referred to later, or eliminated entirely by eliminating frames or pop-up windows:

```
top.main.document.contentForm.etc.
top.main.document.contentForm.target="main";
```

This code becomes:

```
var cf = top.main.document.contentForm;
cf.target="main";
```

Even better, you can remove all but the most essential JavaScript and shunt the remaining optimized code into an external file by using this command:

```
<script src="/js/global.js" type="text/javascript"></script>
```

For maximum speed, Popular Mechanic's site designers could SSI or merge this file into their page. You'll learn more about optimizing JavaScript in Chapter 9, "Optimizing JavaScript for Download Speed," and Chapter 10, "Optimizing JavaScript for Execution Speed."

Trim the Tables

Popular Mechanics overuses overspecified tables throughout the page. The site even uses one to create a vertical gap at the top:

```
<BODY...>
<!-- BEGIN table-1 (top_spacer) -->
<table name="top_spacer" width="805" height="7" border="0" cellspacing="0"
cellpadding="0">
  <tr align="left" valign="top">
    <td width="805" height="7"><img src="/images/clear.gif" width="805" height="7"
border="0"></td>
  </tr>
</table>
<!-- END table-1 (top spacer) -->
```

You can accomplish this with CSS, deprecated body tags, or even a row in the subsequent table. There's no need to use a table to create a seven-pixel top margin. Popular Mechanics already specifies margins in the body tag, as follows:

```
<BODY topmargin="0" marginheight="0" ...>
```

Even better, you could do this with a CSS rule.

Cut the Comments

On high-traffic pages like home pages, excess comments should be abbreviated or eliminated for maximum speed. Instructions to other designers should be included in a separate file or deleted automatically, not carried along in the home page like some poor man's content revision system. The Popular Mechanics site includes the following comments:

- **Long instructions for future designers:**

```
<!-- iSyndicate Content Delivery (HTML)Guidelines are the following COMMENT tags
around their actual content:-->
<!-- feed name = "Top News"  -->
<!-- article  -->
<!-- headline  -->
<!-- summary  -->
<!-- url  (supplied in CMS)  -->
<!-- byline  -->
<!-- date  (supplied in CMS) -->
<!-- copyright  (to be supplied in CMS by user/WRITER/EDITOR)  -->
<!-- body  -->
<!-- end article  -->
<!-- end feed  -->
<!-- iSyndicate Content Delivery (HTML)Guidelines  -->
<!-- Begin - pm.js, which holds all javascript functions; and - popup.js, cookie -
->
```

- **Commented non-functional code:**

```
//top.main.document.contentForm.which_button.value = "Preview";
```

- **Verbose comments throughout the head and body:**

```
<!-- FOR ADDITIONAL/NEW 2 LEFT COLUMN NAVIGATION BAR MARKETING AREAS -->
        <!-- BEGIN LEFT COLUMN NAVIGATION BAR MARKETING AREA, "button_one" -->
        <a
href="http://service.bfast.com/bfast/click?bfmid=36011593&siteid=38248310&bfpage=appl
ication" target="new"><img src="/images/button_one.gif" border="0"></a><table
name="left_col_spacer_table3" width="124" height="15" border="0" cellspacing="0"
cellpadding="0"><tr><td width="124" height="15" align="left" valign="top"><img
src="/images/clear.gif" width="124" height="15" border="0"></td></tr></table>
        <!-- END LEFT COLUMN NAVIGATION BAR MARKETING AREA, "button_one" -->
        <!-- BEGIN LEFT COLUMN NAVIGATION BAR MARKETING AREA, "button_two" -->
        <a
href="http://w1.buysub.com/servlet/OrdersGateway?cds_mag_code=PME&cds_page_id=1015"
target="new"><img src="/images/button_two.gif" border="0"></a><table
name="left_col_spacer_table4" width="124" height="15" border="0" cellspacing="0"
cellpadding="0"><tr><td width="124" height="15" align="left" valign="top"><img
src="/images/clear.gif" width="124" height="15" border="0"></td></tr></table>
            <!-- END LEFT COLUMN NAVIGATION BAR MARKETING AREA, "button_two" -->
        <!-- END ADDITIONAL/NEW 2 LEFT COLUMN NAVIGATION BAR MARKETING AREAS -->
        <!-- xxxxxxxxxx xxxxxxxxxx xxxxxxxxxx xxxxxxxxxx xxxxxxxxxx xxxxxxxxxx -->
        <!-- END LEFT COLUMN NAVIGATION BAR MARKETING AREA -->
```

Perhaps the site's designers wanted to make it easier for all of us who dare view their source to understand the convoluted markup. These comments could all be abbreviated, or better yet, eliminated entirely and shunted into home page documentation (say, index.info). Sharp-eyed readers will see the redundant `align="left"` attribute to the `td` tags, which is the default. Also, many of the table elements, rows, and cells are over-specified with height values (not necessary) and long names.

Use Short Relative URLs

Popular Mechanics uses absolute URLs for some of their links and forms, including a select menu with more than 100 items:

```
<SELECT NAME="SelectURL" size="1">
<option value="">Cover Gallery
<option
value="http://popularmechanics.com/albums/index.phtml?mode=album&album=1902&dispsize=
640">1902
<option
value="http://popularmechanics.com/albums/index.phtml?mode=album&album=1903&dispsize=
640">1903
...
```

You can trim this considerably by using relative links and the `<base href>` tag, as shown here:

```
<base href="http://www.popularmechanics.com">
</head>
<body>
...
<SELECT NAME="SelectURL" size="1">
<option value="">Cover Gallery
<option value="/albums/index.phtml?mode=album&album=1902&dispsize=640">1902
<option value="/albums/index.phtml?mode=album&album=1903&dispsize=640">1903
```

Even better, redesign the CGI/JavaScript form handler to map the numbers to the corresponding URLs, like this:

```
<base href="http://www.popularmechanics.com">
</head>
<body>
...
<SELECT NAME="SelectURL" size="1">
```

```
<option value="">Cover Gallery
<option value="1902">1902
<option value="1903 ">1903
```

Spacer GIF Redux

Popular Mechanics makes a common mistake in using long descriptive filenames for spacer GIFs. Descriptively naming an image whose sole purpose is to take up space in a layout is a waste, and should be avoided. So this:

```
/images/clear.gif
```

Becomes this:

```
/t.gif
```

All told, these changes bring down our SpaceAgent-optimized version to a little under 48K (see Table 6.1).

Table 6.1   PopularMechanics.com HTML Optimization

	HTML Size (bytes)	GZIP -9	Percent Savings over Original
Original	138,548	21,743	84.3%
SpaceAgent	100,562 (27.4%)	16,017	88.4%
+ Manual Optimization	49,118 (64.5%)	8,561	93.8%

Summary

Table 6.1 shows the effects of various optimization and compression levels on the sample home page. By removing unnecessary whitespace, and meta and closing tags, SpaceAgent reduced the page by 27 percent, to 100,562 bytes. Manually optimizing the page to optimize the CSS and JavaScript, and doing some table trimming would reduce this figure well below 100K.

Manual optimization using the preceding techniques brings down the page to a little under 48K. With a 56K modem humming along at 4.5K/second on a clean line, the HTML portion of the HTML page would now load in a little over 10 seconds.

Utilizing compression would bring down the optimized page to 8.4K, which would load in just over two seconds. Sub-eight second display times are desirable, and a two-second load is nearly ideal. *The compressed version of the optimized page is over 16 times smaller than the original.*

Keep in mind that this is a partial optimization. Fully optimizing the page by reworking the tables, using abbreviated links, using optimized CSS and positioning, and simplifying or eliminating the JavaScript would mean even more savings. Compression would achieve similar ratios of 80 to 85 percent over the optimized HTML. HTML optimization and compression can make a big difference in the perceived and actual display speed of your pages and will keep your site visitors coming back for more.

III

DHMTL Optimization: CSS and JavaScript

7

CSS Optimization

CSS optimization is the process of minimizing your markup and CSS files for maximum speed. You can employ some of the same techniques to optimize CSS that you learned in Chapter 3, "HTML Optimization." Whitespace removal, cutting comments, crunching color values, and embedding code with SSI are some of the techniques common to both CSS and HTML optimization. CSS gives you more flexibility than HTML or XHTML, however, because you can make up your own names and group rules together to save space.

You'll reap the greatest rewards by using CSS to transform your code into a more rule-based *modus operandi*. Converting old-style table/font layouts into XHTML/CSS-style code typically saves 25 to 50 percent off file sizes and gives you the benefits of adaptable structure and separate presentation. You can use layering and inheritance to save space and increase compatibility, and use shorthand properties to shrink your CSS code by up to 50 percent. This chapter gives you the tools you need to optimize your CSS.

NOTE

See Jeffrey Veen's *The Art & Science of Web Design* (New Riders, 2001) for more rule-based design ideas.

In Chapter 8, "Advanced CSS Optimization," you'll put these techniques to work with real-world examples showing substitution and optimization in action.

This chapter assumes you have some familiarity with CSS. To learn CSS, I recommend *Cascading Style Sheets: The Definitive Guide* by Eric A. Meyer (O'Reilly, 2000), *Eric Meyer on CSS* (New Riders, 2002), and *Designing CSS Web Pages* by Christopher Schmitt (New Riders, 2002).

Apply Styles Wisely

Before you can optimize CSS, you need to understand the four ways to apply styles to (X)HTML documents :

- External style sheets referenced by a `link` element
- External style sheets referenced by an `@import` rule
- Rules embedded in a `style` element
- Inline declarations in `style` attributes

These methods are listed from the most abstract to the most specific. Let's use a minimal XHTML document to demonstrate them all (see Listing 7.1).

Listing 7.1   Four Ways to Apply Styles

```
<!DOCTYPE html
      PUBLIC "-//W3C//DTD XHTML 1.0 Strict//EN"
      "http://www.w3.org/TR/xhtml1/DTD/xhtml1-strict.dtd ">
<html xmlns="http://www.w3.org/1999/xhtml" xml:lang="en" lang="en">
<head>
<title>Piet Mondrian's Home Page</title>
<link rel="stylesheet" type="text/css" href="/css/global.css" title="default" />
      <style type="text/css" media="screen">
      @import ("/css/local.css");
      h1 {color:green;}
      </style>
</head>
<body>
      <h1>Piet Mondrian: Abstract Impressionist</h1>
<p style="color:red">Mondrian was one of the great abstract masters....</p>
</body>
</html>
```

In honor of Mondrian and efficiency, I recommend being as abstract as possible when applying styles. Try to use external style sheets wherever possible, and avoid embedding style elements and attributes within your (X)HTML. External style sheets are reliably cached, and reduce overall bandwidth usage. For maximum speed on high-traffic pages, however, you can embed rules in a style element or SSI them into the page to avoid an extra HTTP request. For more details on using style sheets and XHTML, see Chapter 5, "Extreme XHTML."

Remove Whitespace

Like (X)HTML and JavaScript, CSS can be optimized by removing whitespace. Spaces and tabs are commonly used to beautify CSS and make it more legible, but browsers ignore this excess formatting. You can save some bytes by eliminating spaces within declarations and around selectors separated by commas, and by eliminating returns. Make sure that you punctuate your declarations with semicolons, and quote any values with embedded spaces first to avoid any problems. So instead of this:

```
body {
    font-family: arial, helvetica, sans-serif;
    font-size:1em;
}
```

Do this:

```
body{font-family:arial,helvetica,sans-serif;font-size:1em}
```

Even better, use the `font` shorthand property:

```
body{font:1em arial,helvetica,sans-serif}
```

We'll look at this CSS form of shorthand in the "Use Shorthand Properties" section later in this chapter.

Cut the Comments

Comments within style sheets start with /* and end with */. They can be useful for documenting more complex style sheets but should be minimized or eliminated on high-traffic pages. Here's a verbose example:

```
h1 {color:purple} /* first-level headers are the color purple */
```

In HTML, CSS also allows SGML comments (<!-- ... -->) to hide style sheets from pre-HTML 3.2 user agents. However, XHTML can strip SGML comments within style or script elements because the data type changed to the more restrictive #PCDATA. You can either use conditional SSI to include embedded styles within XHTML documents, or you can ignore these ancient browsers.

Minimize HTTP Requests

Because style sheets must be in the head of (X)HTML documents, multiple CSS files can slow down the display of your visible content, especially on high-traffic pages. For popular pages, minimize the number of HTTP requests by embedding CSS directly within your page or using SSI. For all pages, try to consolidate multiple external CSS files into fewer files if possible. One CSS file is ideal.

Use Simple Selectors and Substitution

The selector part of a style rule is the link between your styles and your HTML elements. Selectors use pattern matching to determine which style rules apply to which elements in the document tree. Properly used, selectors can save you plenty of space and time tweaking pages. For the smallest CSS rules, use the simplest, highest DOM-hierarchy selectors you can, take advantage of inheritance, and group both selectors and declarations.

Use Type Selectors

Type selectors and the "universal" selector (*) are the simplest and most powerful selectors. "A type selector matches every instance of the element type in the document tree."[1] For example,

```
p { font-family: sans-serif }
```

matches all p elements in the document tree.

A better way to do this would be to use the body element, because all descendants of this element inherit its properties (with some buggy exceptions for Netscape 4), like this:

```
body { font-family: sans-serif }
```

Type selectors are the most general way to style your structure, and therefore they are the most efficient to use.

Use Descendant Selectors to Get Specific

As you'd expect, a descendant selector allows authors to style elements that are the descendants of another element. Suppose that you want to style all code elements inside divs. You do the following:

```
div code {color:red}
```

Now any code fragments inside divs will be styled red.

```
<div>This is a <code>code red</code> alert.</div>
```

This "in context" selector avoids the need to use a class or id selector, saving space and separating style information (class or id attributes) from structure.

CSS2 and CSS3 add some additional contextual selectors like child and sibling selectors, but these can be too specific for effective optimization. CSS2 introduced the notion of

---

1. Bert Bos et al., "Chapter 5, Selectors," in Cascading Style Sheets, level 2 CSS2 Specification [online], (Cambridge, MA: World Wide Web Consortium, 1998), available from the Internet at http://www.w3.org/TR/REC-CSS2/selector.html.

attribute selectors, where you can match elements with certain attribute characteristics. These offer possibilities for optimization, but are not yet widely supported. Once they are, you will be able to do things like this:

```
a[title¦=ext] {color:red} /* color all external links red */
...
<a href="http://www.w3.org/" title="ext-w3c">The World Wide Web Consortium</a>
```

Use Short *class* and *id* Selector Names

The nice thing about CSS compared to (X)HTML is that you are not locked into a fixed set of tags. For high-traffic pages, you can abbreviate `class` and `id` names to one or two characters to save space. You can create a map file that shows the expanded abbreviations for easier updates (for example, `index.cssmap`). In HTML, you can leave off the quotes; in XHTML you must quote all attributes, including `class`. So instead of this:

```
.very-important-section {font-weight: bold;}
```

Do this:

```
.v{font-weight:bold;}
```

Of course, now you lose the advantage of embedding keywords inside your selectors for search engines, but there's always a tradeoff. You could use a dual-pronged approach and fully optimize home pages but use more descriptive selectors on interior pages.

Pseudo Selectors

What if you want to target the "state" of an element or something that's not part of the document tree? That's where pseudo selectors come in. Pseudo-class selectors allow you to target the state of an element (for example, `hover`, `focus`, `active`, etc.) to make them more interactive. In most cases, this means links and forms, or things you interact with inside a web page. CSS1 introduced three pseudo-classes that can be applied to the anchor tag: `link`, `visited`, and `active`. For example:

```
a:link    { color: blue }
a:visited { color: purple }
a:active  { color: red }
```

The colon (:) signifies a pseudo selector. These selectors replace the HTML link, vlink, and alink attributes to the body tag with CSS equivalents.

CSS2 introduced two new dynamic pseudo-classes: hover and focus. "The hover pseudo-class applies while the user 'designates' an element … but does not activate it."[2] This usually means that a cursor is hovering over a link or element. "The focus pseudo-class applies while an element has focus" or will accept input.[2] This can be used to identify a form element that has focus. Here's an example:

```
a:link     { color: blue }       /* unvisited links  */
a:visited  { color: purple }     /* visited links    */
a:hover    { color: yellow }     /* user hovers      */
a:active   { color: red }        /* active links     */
:focus     { background: yellow } /* user gives focus */
```

Note that when you are using pseudo-classes, they must be in this order. A:hover must be after a:link and a:visited, because cascading style sheets will hide the color property of the a:hover rule if it appears before them. Also, to target links specifically, the hover pseudo-class should come after the link and visited pseudo-classes, like this:

```
a:link:hover { color: yellow }   /* more specific hover */
a:visited:hover { color: yellow }  /* more specific hover */
```

For more information, see Chapter 8, "Advanced CSS Optimization," and the CSS2 specification at http://www.w3.org/TR/REC-CSS2/selector.html#dynamic-pseudo-classes.

NOTE

Regarding CSS2 browser support, Netscape 6+, IE5+, and Opera 3.5+ support the hover and focus pseudo-classes.

Substitute CSS2-Based Rollovers

You can use the hover pseudo-class to create dynamic effects without JavaScript or images. JavaScript-free rollovers are possible and much faster with hover. Some authors change the font size or weight on rollover, although browsers are not required to reflow

---

2. Bos et al., Cascading Style Sheets [online].

pages due to pseudo-class selections. In Chapter 8, I show you how to save space by replacing conventional JavaScript-based image rollovers with CSS2 rollovers.

Use Grouping

You can group selectors to apply the same style to multiple elements, and you can group declarations to apply multiple styles to one or more elements. Grouping is a great way to save space in style sheets.

Group Selectors

Suppose that you have multiple instances of headings (or any other element) that you want to style. Without CSS, you'd have to repeat style information within each header, like this:

```
<h1><font color="green">Piet Mondrian</font></h1>
<h2><font color="green">Early Work</font></h2>
```

Using CSS, you could style these headers with multiple rules:

```
h1 {color: green}
h2 {color: green}
...
<h1>Piet Mondrian</h1>
<h2>Early Work</h2>
```

When several selectors share the same declaration, you can save space by grouping them into a single rule by using a comma-separated list:

```
h1, h2 {color:green;}
...
<h1>Piet Mondrian</h1>
<h2>Early Work</h2>
```

Toward the latter part of his career, Mondrian grew to hate the color green. Changing his headings to red takes just one step:

```
h1, h2 {color:red}
```

Note that although the semicolon separates declarations, it is optional for the final declaration of a rule.

Group Declarations

You can group multiple declarations for the same selector into one rule set, separated by semicolons. So instead of this:

```
div { font-size: 1.1em }
div { font-family: arial, helvetica, sans-serif }
div { color: blue }
div { background: yellow }
```

Do this:

```
div {
     font-size: 1.1em;
     font-family: arial, helvetica, sans-serif;
     color: blue;
     background: yellow;
}
```

Even better, you can optimize this rule set further by using shorthand properties (such as `font`) and removing whitespace. You'll learn about these techniques in the "Use Shorthand Properties" section.

Group Selectors and Declarations

You can combine these techniques in powerful ways to apply multiple declarations to multiple selectors. So instead of this:

```
body {font-size: 1.1em; }
body {font-family: arial, helvetica, sans-serif;}
th   {font-size: 1.1em; font-family: arial, helvetica, sans-serif;}
td   {font-size: 1.1em; font-family: arial, helvetica, sans-serif;}
```

Do this:

```
body, th, td {font-size: 1.1em; font-family: arial, helvetica, sans-serif;}
```

Or even better:

```
body,th,td{font:1.1em arial,helvetica,sans-serif;}
```

Use Multiple Classes to Group Common Styles

Modern CSS2-compliant browsers can reference multiple classes within individual elements. For elements that use the same styles (text-align:center, dimensions, etc.), you can create new classes for these common style declarations to save space. Here is an example:

```
<style type="text/css">
    …
    .center {text-align:center;}
</style></head>
<body>
<div id="main" class="main center">…</div>
<div id="nav" class="nav center">…</div>
```

Without the third "center" class, the "text-align:center" declaration must be repeated in both the main and nav classes. By using an additional class, you can group style declarations that are shared by multiple HTML elements into one class to save space.

You can take this technique to its logical conclusion by using DOM-compliant JavaScript to swap classes for individual elements. Here is an example:

```
document.getElementById(id).className = "main common";
```

You can create sophisticated yet lightweight rollover effects by swapping classes to maintain state and change styles. For more details, see Eddie Traversa's articles on using multiple classes at:

http://www.webreference.com/authoring/style/sheets/multiclass/

http://www.dhtmlnirvana.com/multimenus/

Inheritance

Inheritance is a key concept in CSS. Most style properties are passed down from parent to child elements, although margins do not inherit. Descendants of an element in the document tree inherit their parent's style properties. Suppose that you style all h1 elements to be red, as follows:

```
h1 {color: red;}

<h1>Hiermenus <em>Central</em></h1>
```

The word Central also would be red because it is a child of h1.

Take Advantage of Your Inheritance

You can use inheritance to your advantage to save space. Instead of styling all elements individually, use the highest-level parent you can in the document tree. To style the entire document, use the `body` tag. For example:

```
body {font-size: 1em; font-family: sans-serif;}
```

All descendants of the `body` element will inherit this style, unless of course, you're using Netscape 4.

A Strange Inheritance

Unfortunately, Netscape 4 once again is quirky when it comes to interpreting some CSS rules. Netscape 4 does not consistently inherit styles into tables. Some authors work around this quirk by explicitly listing table elements in their top-level body declaration, like this:

```
body, th, td {font-size: 1em; font-family: sans-serif;}
```

Netscape 4 will (usually) use this style throughout the page, including tables. For a list of CSS rules Netscape 4 supports, see `http://www.bobsawyer.com/nn4css.html` and `http://style.webreview.com`.

Specific Is Slow

In CSS, specificity is the enemy of clean, fast code. Contrary to what your English teacher told you, being specific in CSS is much less efficient than being as vague and abstract as possible. The more general you can be in your rules and selectors, the fewer you'll need, and the smaller your files will be. Try to use a few global, simple element selectors to style your pages for maximum speed.

For more details on specificity weighting, see the CSS home page at `http://www.w3.org/Style/CSS/`.

Layer Styles for Speed

With cascading and inheritance built-in, style sheets can be layered from separate global and local styles and gracefully merge together. Multiple style sheets can be overlaid for multiple purposes, each cascading happily over the other according to the cascading rules of CSS.

Use Media Types

You can separate styles for different output media into separate style sheets. For example:

```
<link rel="stylesheet" type="text/css" href="/screen.css" media="screen">
<link rel="stylesheet" type="text/css" href="/print.css" media="print">
```

Presumably you'd use relative units for the screen style sheet and absolute units for the print style sheet. This separation means faster, more efficient pages. It's faster than one all-purpose style sheet because only the style sheet that matches the output media will load, which saves bandwidth.

Use Shorthand Properties

Shorthand properties allow you to specify the values of several properties with a single property. They combine multiple property definitions into a shorter, more abbreviated form. In most cases, any omitted values are assigned an initial value automatically. Combined with grouping, shorthand properties let you shrink your styles to the bare minimum. There are six types of shorthand properties defined in CSS: `font`, `background`, `margin`, `border`, `padding`, and `list`.

The *font* Shorthand Property

The `font` property allows you to set all font-related properties with one abbreviated property. The syntax is based on traditional typographic shorthand notation. The syntax is `font` followed by values separated by spaces, in the following order:

```
{ font: weight style variant size/line-height font-name(s) inherit }
```

A valid `font` value must contain the `size` and `font-name` values in that order or the value will be ignored. The other values can appear in any order before these required values.

To define all the font properties for an element, you use something like this:

```
h1 {
     font-style: italic;
     font-variant: small-caps;
     font-weight: bold; font-size: 1.5em;
     line-height: 1.2;   /* this form is shorter than 1.2em = 120% */
     font-family: arial, helvetica, sans-serif;
}
```

A much more efficient way to specify font properties for the same selector is to use the shorthand `font` property. Here are the same properties expressed in shorthand:

```
h1 {font: italic small-caps bold 1.5em/1.2 arial,helvetica,sans-serif}
```

Leaving out the unnecessary styles, it becomes even shorter:

```
h1 {font:bold 1.5em arial,helvetica,sans-serif}
```

Even better:

```
h1{font:bold 1.5em sans-serif}
```

The *background* Shorthand Property

Like the `font` property, the `background` shorthand property groups all the background-related values into one shorthand property: `background`. The background is the area behind the content plus any padding. "Border colors and styles are set with the `border` property. Margins are always transparent so that the background of the parent box always shines through."[3] Background properties set either the background color or the properties of a background image. Here's the shorthand syntax:

```
{ background: color image repeat attachment position inherit }
```

Background properties do not inherit, but the parent's background shines through by default because `background-color` defaults to "transparent."

---

3. Bert Bos et al., "Colors and Backgrounds," in Cascading Style Sheets, level 2 CSS2 Specification [online], (Cambridge, MA: World Wide Web Consortium, 1998), available from Internet at `http://www.w3.org/TR/REC-CSS2/colors.html`.

The values may be in any order, except the position values must appear together: horizontal, and then vertical. Position values can be percentages, pixels, or keywords (top, left, right, and bottom). Percentages are shorter than keywords, but remember that the default is 0% 0% or the top-left corner of the screen. Here's a longhand example:

```
body {
    background-color: white;
    background-image:url(http://domain.com/logo.gif);
    background-repeat:no-repeat;
    background-attachment:fixed;
    background-position:0% 0%;
    color:black;
}
```

The longhand example becomes this in shorthand:

```
body {
    background: white
    url(http://domain.com/logo.gif) no-repeat fixed 0% 0%;
    color:black;
}
```

Even better, avoid the image entirely, and save an HTTP request, like this:

```
body{background:#fff;color:#000}
```

Here are a couple of caveats for the background property. Netscape 4 understands only the background shorthand property, not background-color. Netscape 4 also doesn't properly apply the background property to the entire content box and padding, but only behind the text itself. To get around this, you can set the border of the element. For example:

```
body {background: white}
p {background: gray; padding: .5em; border: 0.1px solid gray}
```

By setting a border with a style, Netscape 4 colors the entire background, not just the area behind the text. Of course, Netscape 4 then botches the padding, which adds a gap, but that's a story for the "The padding Shorthand Property" section.

It's a good idea to set the foreground color when you set the background color; otherwise, user style sheets could render your text illegible. For example,

```
body {color: white; background: black;} /* user styles */
body {color: black} /* author styles */
```

would result in the following:

```
body {color:black; background: black} /* combined styles */
```

Hey, it's your funeral.

Now that we've got the background down, let's think inside the box. The CSS element box, that is. Figure 7.1 gives you a look at the CSS box model.

Figure 7.1
The CSS box model.

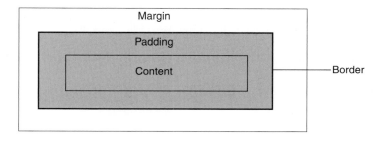

CSS treats every element as though it were surrounded by a series of boxes, consisting of a rectangular content area that is surrounded by padding and enclosed within margins. The border is a line that surrounds the element's contents and any padding.

The *margin* Shorthand Property

The margin shorthand property groups the margin-top, right, bottom, and left margin properties into one shorthand property. The margin properties set the width of blank space around an element's content. You can set any padding, border, and margin values as length units, a percentage, or auto. The syntax is as follows:

```
{ margin: top right bottom left | inherit }
```

Value Replication

Like the border and padding shorthand properties, margin values replicate themselves to fill in any missing values. These shorthand properties have shorthand values! You can specify from one to four values, and any missing values will be provided. For example:

- Set one value, and it applies to all sides:
  ```
  body {margin:2em} = { margin: top/right/bottom/left }
  ```

- Set two values, and the first sets the top and bottom margins, while the second sets the right and left margins:

```
body {margin: 2em 4em} = { margin: top/bottom right/left }
```

- Set three values, and the first sets the top, the second sets the right and left, and the third sets the bottom:

```
body {2em 4em 3em} = { margin: top right/left bottom }
```

- Set all four, and it sets the top, right, bottom, and left margins:

```
body {margin: 2em 4em 3em 5em} = { margin: top right bottom left }
```

Here are some examples:

```
body { margin: 2em }         /* all margins set to 2em */
body { margin: 2em 4em }      /* top & bottom=2em, right & left=4em */
body { margin: 2em 4em 3em } /* top=2em, right&left=4em, bottom=3em */
```

You can use this value duplication to your advantage. In most cases, you can set one margin for all sides. If you need to set only one side for all but margin-bottom, you will find that setting the longhand property is more efficient. So instead of this:

```
div {margin:0 0 0 2em}
```

Do this:

```
div {margin-left:2em}          /* set left margin to 2em */
```

If you are setting margins on two or more sides, it is always more efficient to use the shorthand property.

The *border* Shorthand Properties

The border properties have eight—count 'em, eight—shorthand properties. This is because each border has a width, style, and color, and there are four sides to a border. Finally, there's a shorthand for the shorthands: the border property. Generally anywhere there's a dash, there's a shorthand equivalent.

The border properties set the width, style, and color of a line that surrounds the content and padding of an element. The background extends up to the outer edge of the border. In order for a border to exist, it must have a style, because it defaults to none.

Border colors default to the element's foreground color. Unless explicitly set, borders get the foreground color, which may be explicitly set or inherited. The `border-style`, `border-width`, and `border-color` all have the same syntax:

```
border-style/width/color { top right bottom left | inherit }
```

Let's take the `border-width` shorthand as an example for all three.

The *border-width* Shorthand Property

Once you've assigned a style, you can set an optional width for your border. The `border-width` shorthand property sets the width of each of the four sides of an element's border. The values replicate like the `margin` and `padding` properties. So instead of this:

```
p {
        border-style:solid;
        border-top-width: 1em;
        border-right-width: 10px;
        border-bottom-width: 2em;
        border-left-width: 20px;
}
```

Do this:

```
p { border-style:solid;border-width: 1em 10px 2em 20px }
```

Even better, use the same width all around:

```
p {border-style:solid;border-width:1em}
```

The shorthand `border` property is better suited here, because it sets all four sides at once.

The *border-top*, *border-right*, *border-bottom*, and *border-left* Shorthand Properties

Although there may be some cases in which you'll want to style four borders by `style`, `width`, and `color`, there is a better way: `border` shorthand properties. These properties group `width`, `style`, and `color` into one property for each of the four sides, and the entire border. They all have the same syntax:

```
border-top|right|bottom|left { width style color | inherit }
```

So instead of this:

```
div a {
      display:block;
      border-top-width: thin;
      border-top-style: solid;
      border-top-color: black;
}
```

Do this:

```
div a {display:block;border-top: thin solid black}
```

This rule sets only the top border to a thin black line, leaving the others to their defaults of none. The other border side properties work exactly the same.

You can leave out values that have defaults (`width` and `color`) to create shorter rules. So instead of this:

```
div {border-left: 2px dashed black}
```

Do this:

```
div {border-left: dashed}
```

The border will inherit the foreground color of the `div` (say, black text), and use the default of `medium` for width (usually around three or four pixels). Once again, you give up some control to gain some flexibility and efficiency.

As it turns out, there is even a better way—the ultimate shorthand property: the `border` property.

The *border* Shorthand Property

The `border` shorthand property sets the same values for `width`, `style`, and `color` for all four borders. It is a great way to shrink the size of your border styles to the bare minimum. The syntax is as follows:

```
border { width style color | inherit }
```

So instead of this:

```
p {
      border-top: thin solid black;
      border-right: thin solid black;
      border-bottom: thin solid black;
      border-left: thin solid black;
}
```

Do this:

```
p {border:thin solid black}
```

Even better, inherit the foreground color, like this:

```
p{border:1px solid}
```

Or leave off the `width` entirely and default to `medium`:

```
p{border:solid}
```

Like the other `border` properties, you can use the cascade to your advantage. Suppose that you want a solid border around a paragraph with the top border dashed. You could do the following:

```
p {
      border:solid;
      border-top:dashed;
}
```

Border Gotchas

Netscape 4 once again screws up the way it interprets borders and backgrounds. In order to force Netscape to display a background behind the entire content and padding (not just the text), you can set an invisible border:

```
border {.1px solid none}
```

This will force Netscape to display the background around the entire box. Of course, it then adds extra space between the border and the padding, but there seems to be no way to get rid of this odd behavior.

The *padding* Shorthand Property

The padding shorthand property lets you set the padding on all four sides of an element. The padding properties set the width of the padding area around an element's content. The border is applied to the outer edge of any element's padding. Padding values replicate in the same way margin values do. Here's the syntax:

```
{ padding: top right bottom left | inherit }
```

The default padding value is 0. You can use any length unit or a percentage value for padding. Watch out for percentages, however, because they are based on the width of the parent element. Percentage-sized padding changes with the screen size, not the font size. You're better off with em or pixel units for padding.

Here's the longhand way to set padding around four sides of a div. Instead of this:

```
div {
        padding-top: 1em;
        padding-right: 2em;
        padding-bottom: 3em;
        padding-left: 4em;
}
```

Do this:

```
div {padding: 1em 2em 3em 4em}
```

Even better, spread the same padding all around with this command:

```
div{padding:1em}
```

Similar to the margin property, when you are setting padding on only one side, it is more efficient to use the longhand property, except for padding-bottom. When you are working with two sides or more, it is always more efficient to use the shorthand property.

Padding Gotchas

Because Netscape 4 doesn't extend padding out to the border, you'll get a gap between any background and the border. Use the thin styled border trick you learned in the "The `background` Shorthand Properties" section to force Netscape 4 to color the entire box, not just the area behind the text (see Figure 7.2).

Figure 7.2
The Netscape 4
box model.

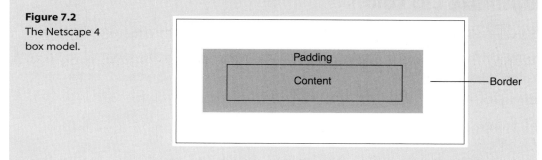

Padding and widths in the same element don't mix well in Internet Explorer 4+. You are better off separating these two properties into nested `div`s to avoid the problem entirely.

The *list-style* Shorthand Property

The `list-style` property sets the three list properties (`list-style-type`, `list-style-image`, and `list-style-position`) in one shorthand notation. These properties are used to affect the bullet type, image, and placement for a list. The syntax is as follows:

```
{ list-style: type position image ¦ inherit }
```

The `list-style` values can appear in any order. Any missing values will be filled in with their defaults of `disc`, `outside`, and `none`. Here's an example:

```
ul li { list-style: url(http://domain.gif/b.gif) square outside }
```

When you are using a bullet image, it's a good idea also to specify the `list-style-type` value because the image may not load. Because `outside` is the default, this could be written as:

```
ul { list-style: url(http://domain.gif/b.gif) square }
```

Be careful with nested lists because list styles are inherited.

CSS2 adds a number of new values to the list-style-type property, and "inherit" to all three properties. CSS2 also adds the marker-offset property, which allows more sophisticated lists but doesn't give us anything as far as optimization goes.

Optimize CSS Colors

You can specify colors five ways in CSS; four use numeric RGB values and one uses named colors. The two most efficient ways to specify colors are hexadecimal and named colors. Hexadecimal colors take two forms: RGB triplets and shorthand. Here's an example:

```
h1 { color: #ff0000 }        /* hexadecimal   #rrggbb */
h1 { color: #f00 }           /* shorthand hex #rgb */
```

Hexadecimal Colors

Hexadecimal values are base-16, which means that they usually are shorter than base-10 numbers. To specify 0 to 255 in hex, you'd use 00 to ff, saving a byte for higher color channels.

Shorthand Hexadecimal Colors

In modern browsers (version 3 and above), RGB triplets can be abbreviated if each of the R, G, and B hex pairs are the same. So instead of this:

```
.dark-yellow {color:#ffcc00}
```

Do this:

```
.dark-yellow {color:#fc0}
```

The browser automatically expands three-character colors into six by replicating the R, G, and B values. You can use this shorthand hex notation to shrink your CSS.

Shorthand Hex Notation

All browsers that support style sheets support this three-character form of hexadecimal colors (#rgb), with the exception of buggy behavior in IE3 Mac.

For more information, see http://style.webreview.com.

Named Colors

Hexadecimal values are unambiguous and can use fewer characters than their named equivalents, although some named colors use less than their hex equivalents. The 16 named colors are shown in Table 7.1.

Table 7.1 Named Color Equivalents

Color	Hex Pair	Short Hex	Color	Hex Pair	Short Hex
Aqua	#00ffff	#0ff	Navy	#000080	
Black	#000000	#000	Olive	#808000	
Blue	#0000ff	#00f	Purple	#800080	
Fuchsia	#ff00ff	#f0f	Red	#ff0000	#f00
Gray	#808080		Silver	#c0c0c0	
Green	#008000		Teal	#008080	
Lime	#00ff00	#0f0	White	#ffffff	#fff
Maroon	#800000		Yellow	#ffff00	#ff0

Use shorthand hex colors wherever possible, unless the named equivalent is shorter (red, for example). Some named equivalents are shorter than their seven-character hex equivalents (silver, gray, maroon, purple, olive, navy, and teal).

Web-Safe Colors

The so-called web-safe color cube is made up of 216 colors that supposedly display identically on different platforms, without any color shifting or dithering. Most of the time they do. Web-safe colors happen to be expressed in multiples of 20% and 51 for

RGB values, and 33 in hex. So to create a web-safe color, use any combination of 00, 33, 66, 99, cc, and ff. These values can be abbreviated to shorthand hex values of 0, 3, 6, 9, c, and f. This means that #fc3, #c6c, #960, and #f00 are all web-safe colors.

For site redesigns, try to use web-safe colors or at least colors that can be abbreviated wherever possible. Finding the closest web-safe color to the one you want is a great way to save space in your pages. In addition to the benefit of not dithering, they offer you the added advantage of shorthand equivalents. For more details, see the CSS specification (http://www.w3.org/TR/REC-CSS2/).

Length Units: Everything Is Relative

Many CSS properties are specified with length measurements, either horizontal or vertical. Length values can be either positive or negative, although some properties other than length are restricted to be positive. The format of a length value is an optional sign (+ or -), followed by a number, followed by a two-letter unit abbreviation—like px (pixels), pt (points), or in (inches). For length values of 0, however, units are optional. Length units can be either relative or absolute.

Relative Length Units

Relative units measure distance relative to another length property. The relative units are em, ex, px, and % (percentage). Here they are in all their glory:

```
body { margin: 0.5em }
h1   { margin: 1ex }
p    { font-size: 12px }
dt   { font-size: 120% }
```

In CSS, em is short for "em-height," and ex is short for "x-height." Both terms will be familiar to those from the typesetting world. One em is traditionally equal to the width of the capital M in the current font. In reality, it is equal to the computed font-size of a given element. The exception is when em is used on the font-size property itself, referring to the font size of the parent element. For example:

```
dt { font-size: 1.2em }
```

Here descriptive terms would be 1.2 times the font size of the parent element, or about 20 percent larger.

The ex unit is supposed to be defined by the font's x-height. However, most browsers simply halve the font size to compute the x-height. Pixels (px) correspond to the pixels on the user's screen, which depends on its resolution. Macs typically have 72 dpi displays, although this isn't guaranteed because font sizing percentage values are relative to another value and work like the em unit.

In practice, most authors use px, em, or % to specify relative length units. Because pixels are resolution dependent, using em and % are the most flexible ways to specify font sizes. For example:

```
p { font-size: 1.1em }
```

Embrace Your Relatives

Relative units automatically scale to the environment in which they are displayed, so they're more suitable for the screen. Designers on the web have no way of knowing beforehand in which resolution, display size, or user settings their pages will be viewed. Relative units automatically adjust to user font size preferences, and they are more accessible than absolute sizes.

You'll read stories about bugs that occur when people use em or percentages to specify font sizes, but these are relatively minor for the majority of browsers in use today. Using pixels to specify font sizes may work everywhere, but it is not a true relative length unit and it defeats one of primary goals of CSS: flexibility.

Absolute Length Units

Absolute units are fixed units of measurement, and they are useful only when you know the dimensions of the output medium; for example, a sheet of 8.5" × 11" paper. They do not scale to the user's display. Although they make a poor choice for the screen, absolute units are perfect for defining style sheets for printed documents. In CSS, the absolute units are as follows: in (inches), cm (centimeters), mm (millimeters), pt (points), and pc (picas). The same optimization techniques you learn in this chapter can be applied both to print and aural style sheets.

Length Units Summary

For maximum flexibility, use em or % to define font sizes. When defining widths for divs, etc., beware of using ems, because Netscape 6 does not automatically scale when the user adjusts the font size (although Netscape 7+ does). Percentage widths do scale properly in Netscape, Explorer, and Opera. Use as few fonts and sizes as possible. Take advantage of inheritance, and set your font properties as high up the document tree as possible. For example:

```
body { margin: 0.5em; font: 1em serif }
```

Summary

CSS allows authors to strip their markup down to structure and style. To optimize your CSS, remove as much whitespace and as many comments as you can, and use short class and id names. Use simple, high DOM-level type selectors and avoid the specific; be as vague and abstract as possible to apply your style in wide swaths across types of structural elements (all body text, paragraphs, or dts, for example). Group selectors and declarations and use shorthand properties to minimize your CSS rule sets. Finally, minimize HTTP requests by grouping external style sheets and embedding where necessary. Here is a list of the topics covered in this chapter:

- Embed or SSI abbreviated styles for maximum speed.
- Minimize HTTP requests by grouping external CSS files.
- Link to external style sheets site-wide to cache in.
- Layer style sheets for speed. Use cascading to combine linked, alternate, and imported style sheets to layer your presentation for older browsers and alternate media (print), and to save bandwidth.

- Group selectors with the same declarations and declarations with the same selectors.
- Use simple selectors high in the document tree to set global and element-wide styles (that is, type styles like `body`, `h1`, `p`, and `dt`).
- Use descendant selectors to get specific without `class` or `id` selectors.
- Take advantage of your inheritance—don't overspecify CSS; let it flow down the document tree.
- Use multiple classes to group common style declarations to save space.
- Use value replication on the `border`, `padding`, and `margin` properties.
- Use shorthand hex colors (such as `#00f`).
- Use shorthand properties to optimize your CSS (including `font`, `background`, `margin`, and `border`).
- Use short `class` and `id` names.
- Use shorthand hexadecimal colors or names, whichever is shorter.
- Use relative lengths for maximum flexibility.
- Remove whitespace.
- Cut the comments.

8

Advanced CSS Optimization

Beyond the oft-cited benefits of cached CSS files and overall bandwidth savings, CSS allows you to substitute lightweight standards-based replacements for older, bandwidth-hungry techniques (like graphic rollover menus). This chapter shows you four general ways you can use CSS to speed up your site:

- Smaller style sheets
- Substitution
- Faster tables
- CSS layout and positioning control

Optimizing CSS Rules

Here you get to put the techniques you learned in Chapter 7, "CSS Optimization," to work and see whether you can optimize WebReference's old style sheet (see Listing 8.1).

Listing 8.1   WebReference.com's Original Style Sheet

```
<style type="text/css">
<!--
form.tb{display:inline;}
.h{text-decoration:none;font-size:9pt;font-family:geneva,arial,sans-serif;}
.c{font-size:80%;font-family:arial,geneva,sans-serif;}
.d{font-size:70%;font-family:arial,geneva,sans-serif;}
dt{font-weight:bold;font-size:120%;margin-top:.8em;}
.w{font-size:125%;font-family:verdana,sans-serif;color:#660099;}
.NSlyr{width:119;position:absolute;visibility:hidden;}
a:hover{background-color:#ffdd33;}
-->
</style>
```

This style sheet already uses a number of techniques discussed earlier. It uses short, one-character class names (like .h and .c), simple type selectors (dt), the :hover pseudo-class, and it is embedded rather than linked. But there's always room for improvement. Let's use the font and background shorthand properties and shorthand hex notation to shrink it even further:

```
<style type="text/css">
<!--
form.tb{display:inline}
.h{text-decoration:none;font:9pt geneva,arial,sans-serif}
.c{font:80% arial,geneva,sans-serif}
.d{font:70% arial,geneva,sans-serif}
dt{font:bold 120% serif;margin-top:.8em}
.w{font:125% verdana,sans-serif;color:#609}
.NSlyr{width:119;position:absolute;visibility:hidden}
a:hover{background:#fd3}
-->
</style>
```

Using these shorthand properties, you save 99 bytes—from 449 to 350 characters. Note that because the font shorthand property requires a font-family value, you may have a problem with your definition lists if the user sets the font-family to "sans-serif." The dts will be serif, and the dds will be without serifs. To get around the problem, you could set the body to "serif," like this:

```
<style type="text/css">
<!--
body{font:1em serif}
form.tb{display:inline}
.h{text-decoration:none;font:9pt geneva,arial,sans-serif}
```

```
.c{font:80% arial,geneva,sans-serif}
.d{font:70% arial,geneva,sans-serif}
dt{font:bold 120% serif;margin-top:.8em}
.w{font:125% verdana,sans-serif;color:#609}
.NSlyr{width:119;position:absolute;visibility:hidden}
a:hover{background:#fd3}
-->
</style>
```

But as it turns out, using longhand for the dt properties and leaving out the font family is shorter (360 versus 364 characters):

```
<style type="text/css">
<!--
form.tb{display:inline}
.h{text-decoration:none;font:9pt geneva,arial,sans-serif}
.c{font:80% arial,geneva,sans-serif}
.d{font:70% arial,geneva,sans-serif}
dt{font-weight:bold;font-size:120%;margin-top:.8em}
.w{font:125% verdana,sans-serif;color:#609}
.NSlyr{width:119;position:absolute;visibility:hidden}
a:hover{background:#fd3}
-->
</style>
```

This is a savings of nearly 20 percent over the original (449 to 360 characters). You could further optimize this style sheet by grouping the font family of three styles and setting their sizes separately:

```
<style type="text/css">
<!--
form.tb{display:inline}
.h,.c,.d{font-family:arial,geneva,sans-serif}
.h{text-decoration:none;font-size:9pt}
.c{font-size:80%}
.d{font-size:70%}
dt{font-weight:bold;font-size:120%;margin-top:.8em}
.w{font:125% verdana,sans-serif;color:#609}
.NSlyr{width:119;position:absolute;visibility:hidden}
a:hover{background:#fd3}
-->
</style>
```

This takes you down to 348 characters. You could save even more by using generic font families, one smaller font size, and the font shorthand property (see Listing 8.2).

Listing 8.2   WebReference.com's Optimized Style Sheet

```
<style type="text/css">
<!--
form.tb{display:inline}
.h,.c,.d{font:80% sans-serif}
.h{text-decoration:none}
dt{font-weight:bold;font-size:120%;margin-top:.8em}
.w{font:125% sans-serif;color:#609}
.NSlyr{width:119;position:absolute;visibility:hidden}
a:hover{background:#fd3}
-->
</style>
```

Now you're down to 276 bytes, over 38-percent smaller than the original. We like the look of the previous one, however. Did you notice that this example combined grouping and a shorthand font property? Note that in the actual style sheet, you would remove the returns (creating up to 255-character lines) and any unnecessary spaces. By using cascading, inheritance, grouping, and shorthand properties, you can shrink unoptimized CSS by over 50 percent.

Substitution

With the widespread support of the CSS2 hover pseudo-class, you can create low-impact rollover effects without JavaScript. There are two general approaches:

- **CSS2 image rollovers**—These use transparent GIFs and colored backgrounds to cut in half the number of images required.
- **Pure CSS2 rollovers**—These use a text-only approach that entirely eliminates the need for images.

Either way, by using CSS to create a rollover effect, you save costly HTTP requests and code.

CSS2 Image Rollovers

CSS2 image rollovers use transparent GIFs and the hover pseudo-class to change the background behind the image on rollover. You get the same effect as conventional rollovers, without the extra images and JavaScript. Stuart Robinson of Designmeme.com demonstrates using this technique to improve Zeldman.com's toolbar (see Figure 8.1).

Figure 8.1
Designmeme.com's CSS2 image rollovers.

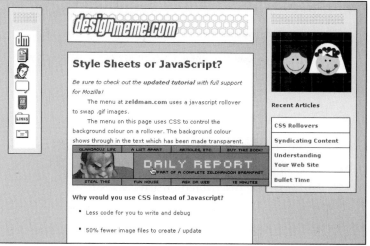

http://www.designmeme.com/zeldman/

All you need are some images with aliased transparent cutouts and a couple lines of CSS:

```
.zeldman a { display:block; width:100px; background-color: #000000;}
.zeldman a:hover { background-color: #CCFF00}
```

The simplified HTML code looks like this:

```
<div class="zeldman">
<table border="0" cellpadding="0" cellspacing="0">
     <tr>
          <td bgcolor="#000000"><a href=http://www.zeldman.com/glamorous/>
               <img name="glam" src="glam.gif" width="100"
               height="16" border="0"
               alt="MY GLAMOROUS LIFE: Tragicomic fodder from the life of Zeldman."
/></a></td>
...
```

This ingenious method changes the background color of the link behind the image on rollover. Because the text within the images is transparent, the background color shines through. You could optimize this further by using the shorthand background property and shorthand hex colors, but you get the idea. This low-impact technique gracefully degrades for older browsers and requires no JavaScript.

For More Information

For more information on CSS2 graphic rollovers, see the following sites:

- `http://www.alistapart.com/stories/rollovers/`
- `http://www.designmeme.com/zeldman/`

Pure CSS2 Rollovers

You can go one step further and use CSS2 to eliminate entirely the need for images. Pure CSS2 rollovers use styled links for both the foreground and background menu items. Authors have discovered creative ways to turn links into rollovers. Some authors create 3D buttons that change on rollover. Some morph their links into block-level elements. Some go the other way and turn lists into inline elements. Whichever way you choose, they all use the `hover` pseudo-class to create pure text rollovers that gracefully degrade.

Simple Text Rollovers

The simplest way to add a rollover effect to your links is to use the `hover` pseudo-class as it was originally intended. Create your links as normal, but add a hover background color:

```
a:hover{background:#fd3}
```

Technically, this technique would affect all anchors—not just the links—to display the hover effect. A more specific way to style hovers on links is the following:

```
a:link:hover{background:#fd3}
a:visited:hover{background:#fd3}
```

These rules change the background color behind links to yellow when users hover over them. To make sure that your background doesn't make your text disappear, you also can set the foreground color when specifying the background color:

```
a:link:hover{background:#fd3;color:#00f}
a:visited:hover{background:#fd3;color:#00f}
```

Putting all the link pseudo-classes together gives you the following:

```
a:link          { color: #00f }   /* unvisited links - blue */
a:visited       { color: #609 }   /* visited links   - purple */
a:link:hover    { color: #fd3 }   /* user hovers      - yellow */
a:visited:hover { color: #fd3 }   /* user hovers      - yellow */
a:link:active   { color: red }    /* active links */
a:visited:active { color: red }   /* active links */
```

You can achieve a reverse effect by flipping the background and foreground colors on rollover:

```
a:link          { color: #00f; background:#fc0 }
a:visited       { color: #609 }
a:link:hover    { color: #fc0; background:#00f }
a:visited:hover { color: #fc0; background:#00f }
a:link:active   { color: red }    /* active links */
a:visited:active { color: red }
```

Chained by Pseudo-Classes

Internet Explorer for Windows can have some trouble with chained pseudo-classes. It seems that IE4, 5, and even 6 can ignore all but the last pseudo-class when you string them together, at least as long as an element identifier is involved. Fortunately in this case, when you set the a:link:hover and a:visited:hover to the same style, this isn't a problem, because IE effectively resolves them both down to a:hover. The same goes for :active. IE may behave unpredictably, however, when you want to style chained pseudo-classes differently, or when you want to style one and not the other. Most authors don't bother with this level of specificity and use the simpler a:hover selector or a contextual selector. For more information, see http://www.meyerweb.com/eric/css/tests/css2/sec05-10.htm.

Vertical CSS2 Menus

At WebReference.com, we created a demonstration of vertical CSS2 rollovers that gracefully degrade for Netscape 4 (http://www.webreference.com/new/rollovers). They look nearly identical on Netscape 4, but without the rollover effect. On browsers that do support the hover pseudo-class—Opera 3.5, IE4+, Netscape 6+ (Mozilla)—they roll over.

After extensive testing, we've arrived at a solution that works for all the browsers we tested, using the link tag for style sheets. Figure 8.2 shows the result, and Listing 8.3 shows the CSS.

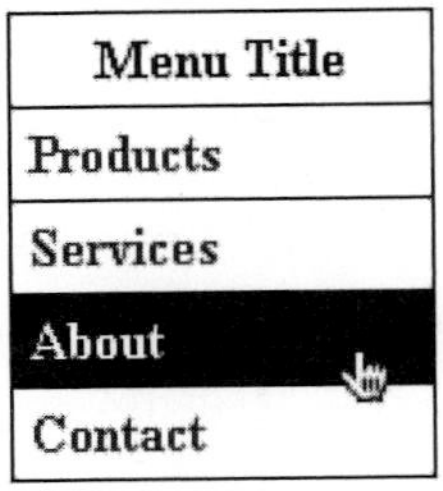

Figure 8.2
Pure CSS2 vertical rollovers.

Menu Title
Products
Services
About
Contact

Listing 8.3   CSS2 Vertical Rollovers: CSS

```
body {background:#fff;}

h4 {margin:0;padding:0.3em;text-align:center;}

div.menu {
       width:125px;
       background:#fff;
       padding:0;
       margin:1em;
       border:1px solid #000;
}

div.menu a {
       display:block;
       margin:0;
       width:100%;
       padding:0.3em;
       font-weight:bold;
       border-top:1px solid #000;
       color:#00f;
       text-decoration:none;
}

html>body div.menu a {width:auto;}

div.menu a:hover {background:#000;color:#fff;}
```

Note that in order to get the rollovers to work for the entire width of the menu, we used the "Tantek hack" (www.tantek.com) to reset non-IE6 browsers to auto for the link width:

```
html>body div.menu a {width:auto;}
```

Authors who want to avoid this hack can just use width:auto; for the block-level links and omit the hack. IE6 will then rollover only on the links. All the other CSS2-aware browsers will rollover on the entire box, and the link will be active.

The menu code in Listing 8.4 looks like garden-variety HTML with some breaks thrown in to make the links behave for older browsers. Outside the links, the
's tend to leave vertical gaps. Another option that allows you to avoid the gaps is to put them outside the links and style them to not display for CSS-aware browsers:

```
div.menu br {display:none;}
```

Listing 8.4   CSS2 Vertical Rollovers: HTML

```
<!DOCTYPE HTML PUBLIC "-//W3C//DTD HTML 4.01//EN" "http://www.w3.org/TR/html4/strict.dtd">
<html>
<head>
<title>Pure CSS2 Rollovers</title>
<link rel="stylesheet" href="vertical.css" type="text/css">

</head>
<body>

<div class="menu">
<h4>Menu Title</h4>
<a href="/products/">Products <br></a>
<a href="/services/">Services <br></a>
<a href="/about/">About <br></a>
<a href="/contact/">Contact <br></a>
</div>

</body>
</html>
```

To make the top menu item live, you can change the header into a styled link like the other menu items:

```
<div class="menu">
<a href="/home/">Home <br></a>
<a href="/products/">Products <br></a>
```

The problem is that you'll get a double border above the top menu item, because the outer div and home link both have top borders (see Figure 8.3).

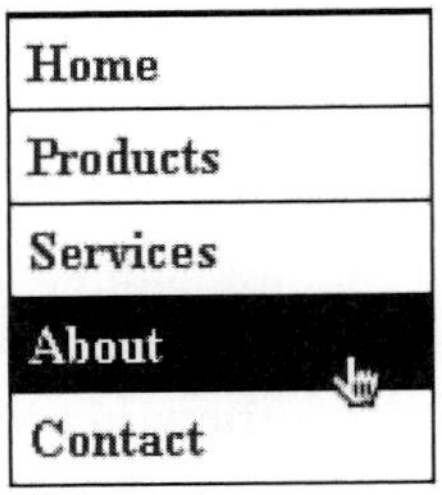

Figure 8.3
Pure CSS2 vertical rollovers—
seeing double.

To get rid of this extra border, simply eliminate it for the top of the surrounding div, like this (see the result in Figure 8.4):

```
div.menu {
        width:125px;
        background:#fff;
        padding:0;
        margin:1em;
        border:1px solid #000;
        border-top:0px; /* eliminate the double line */
}
```

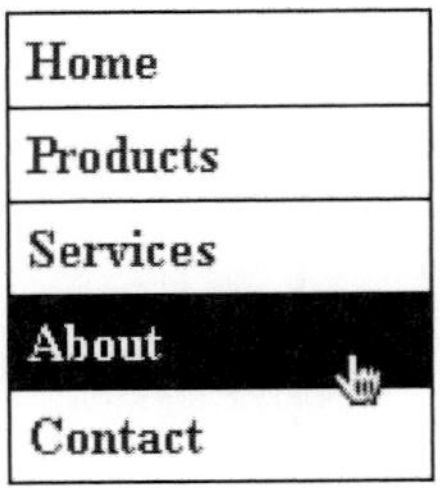

Figure 8.4
Pure CSS2 vertical rollovers—
back to normal.

If you add problematic CSS2 commands, for Netscape 4 safety you can optionally use the @import directive to read in the external style sheet. This demonstration was designed for a black and white book, although normally I don't recommend using black links. Even in menus, users expect the default of blue for links or at least something easily discerned from the text color.

Real-World Examples of CSS2 Rollovers

Designers are substituting these lightweight menus for old-style JavaScript/graphics rollovers. Let's look at some real-world examples of CSS2 rollovers. First up, Designmeme.com.

Designmeme.com

Stuart Robinson, webmaster at University of Guelph in Canada, uses both types of CSS2 rollovers at his own site, which is shown in Figure 8.5. On the left of his home page, he uses transparent GIFs and the hover pseudo-class to create JavaScript-free image rollovers. On the right, he uses pure CSS2 rollovers to create an interactive vertical menu bar without images.

Stuart is a pioneer who has been using CSS image rollovers since May 2001.

Figure 8.5
Designmeme.com.

http://www.designmeme.com/

Eric Meyer's CSS Edge

Eric Meyer, author of *Cascading Style Sheets: The Definitive Guide* (O'Reilly, 2000) and *Eric Meyer on CSS* (New Riders, 2002), demonstrates many of the CSS techniques he discusses in his books and then some. His CSS Edge site is a proving ground for valid, standards-based CSS techniques that work in modern browsers (see Figure 8.6).

Figure 8.6
Eric Meyer's CSS Edge.

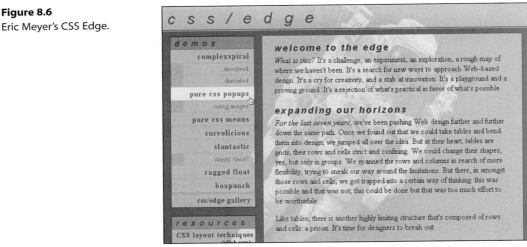

http://www.meyerweb.com/

Horizontal CSS2 Rollovers

You can use a similar technique without the `display:block` trick to create horizontal CSS2 rollovers. Mike Hall has a nice demonstration of horizontal menu bars using pure CSS2 rollovers at BrainJar.com (see Figure 8.7). Mike adds a 3D look to his menu buttons by using an offset and "light-sourced" border colors.

Figure 8.7
Mike Hall's BrainJar.

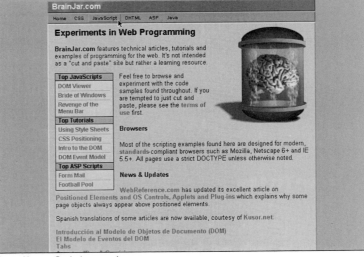

http://www.BrainJar.com/

He's taken it one step further by adding hierarchical drop-down menus using hidden `divs` and a dash of JavaScript. These menus work on Netscape 6 and IE5.5, but not on IE5 Mac or Opera (see Figure 8.8).

Figure 8.8
BrainJar.com's DOM-based hierarchical menus.

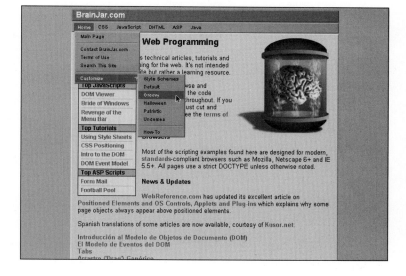

Thanks to Kwon Ekstrom and with Mike's permission, we "reverse engineered" the 3D menus to distill them down to the essentials. First, the HTML:

```
<div class="menubar" width="100%">
<a class="button active" href="/">Home</a>
<a class="button" href="/products/">Products</a>
<a class="button" href="/services/">Services</a>
<a class="button" href="/contact/">Contact</a>
</div>
...
```

The only thing unusual here is the extra "active" `class`. The optimized style sheet in Listing 8.5 sets up the nav bar and gives the active button a depressed look.

Listing 8.5   3D CSS2 Horizontal Menus

```
body {
     background:#fff;
     color:#000;
}
```

continues

Listing 8.5   3D CSS2 Horizontal Menus   *continued*

```css
div.menubar, div.menubar a:button {
      font: bold .9em arial,helvetica,sans-serif;
      text-decoration: none;
      color: blue;
}

div.menubar {
      background: #fd0;
      padding: 4px 2px;
      border: 2px solid;
      border-color: #ff9 #777 #777 #ff9;
      text-align: left; /* for ie when centering */
}

div.menubar a.button {
      background: transparent;
      border: 1px solid #fd0;
      cursor: default;
      left: 0px;
      top: 0px;
      margin: 1px;
      padding: 1px 4px;
      position: relative;
      z-index: 100;
}


div.menubar a.button:hover {
      background: transparent;
      border-color: #ff9 #993 #993 #ff9;
      color: blue;
}

div.menubar a.active,
div.menuBar a.active:hover {
      background: #777;
      border-color: #333 #ff9 #ff9 #333;
      color: #fff;
      left: 1px;
      top: 1px;
}
```

The key rules are the a.button rule and the corresponding hover styles. The button is defined with the same background color (transparent) as the surrounding div, so it blends into the nav bar. By setting a relative position for each button, you can offset and shade it to simulate a depressed look (see Figure 8.9). The a.button:hover style changes all four of the border colors to simulate a raised 3D look. On the active page (home, in this case), the active hover style moves the button 1 pixel down and to the right, flipping the border colors and darkening the background. For more details, see Hall's "Revenge of the Menu Bar" tutorial at BrainJar.com.

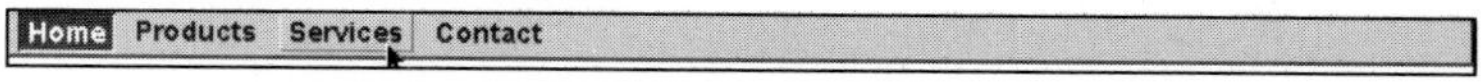

Figure 8.9
CSS2 menu bar.

Dynamic CSS2 Menu Bar

You can combine this 3D interactive button idea with conditional SSI to create a dynamic CSS2-based menu bar. Begin by abstracting both the menu bar HTML code and the corresponding CSS (see Listing 8.6).

Listing 8.6 CSS2 Menu Bar HTML Template

```
<html>
<head><title>CSS Menu Bar Demo</title>
<style type="text/css">
<!--
@import "/css/menubar.css";
-->
</style>
</head>
<body>
<!--#include virtual="/css/menubar2.html" -->
</body>
</html>
```

This allows you to include the menu bar site-wide and sets things up so that updates require that you edit only two files. Note that you're including an HTML file, not a text file. By setting a flag in your server configuration file (see Chapter 17, "Server-Side Techniques"), you can include conditional SSI in any included HTML files (see Listing 8.7).

Listing 8.7   Conditional Menu Bar SSI

```
<!--#if expr="(${DOCUMENT_URI} = /^\/products\/.*/)" -->
<div class="menubar" width="100%">
<a class="button" href="/">Home</a>
<a class="button active" href="/products/">Products</a>
<a class="button" href="/services/">Services</a>
<a class="button" href="/contact/">Contact</a>
</div>

<!--#elif expr="(${DOCUMENT_URI} = /^\/services\/.*/)" -->
<div class="menubar" width="100%">
<a class="button" href="/">Home</a>
<a class="button" href="/products/">Products</a>
<a class="button active" href="/services/">Services</a>
<a class="button" href="/contact/">Contact</a>
</div>

<!--#elif expr="(${DOCUMENT_URI} = /^\/contact\/.*/)" -->
<div class="menubar" width="100%">
<a class="button" href="/">Home</a>
<a class="button" href="/products/">Products</a>
<a class="button" href="/services/">Services</a>
<a class="button active" href="/contact/">Contact</a>
</div>

<!--#elif expr="((${DOCUMENT_URI} = /^\/$/) || (${DOCUMENT_URI} = /^\/index\.html/))" -->
<div class="menubar" width="100%">
<a class="button active" href="/">Home</a>
<a class="button" href="/products/">Products</a>
<a class="button" href="/services/">Services</a>
<a class="button" href="/contact/">Contact</a>
</div>
<!--#else -->
<div class="menubar" width="100%">
<a class="button" href="/">Home</a>
<a class="button" href="/products/">Products</a>
<a class="button" href="/services/">Services</a>
<a class="button" href="/contact/">Contact</a>
</div>
<!--#endif -->
```

Now the rollover menu bar changes which button is active depending on where you are in the site's hierarchy. With the Listing 8.5 style sheet, all you have to change is the location of the "active" class in your HTML. For example, when you go to the "contact" directory, the Listing 8.7 conditional SSI looks at the current URL and finds a match for this statement:

```
<!--#if expr="(${DOCUMENT_URI} = /^\/contact\/.*/)" -->
```

This expression matches any URL beginning with /contact/, such as /contact/staff.html (see Figure 8.10).

Figure 8.10
Dynamic CSS2 menu bar.

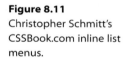

You could do this class assignment with JavaScript, but this method works with JavaScript turned off.

List-Based Menus

Christopher Schmitt, founder of BabbleList.com, is reportedly the first to publish the trick of using display:inline on list elements to get a horizontal rollover menu bar effect. See Figure 8.11 for an example.

Figure 8.11
Christopher Schmitt's
CSSBook.com inline list
menus.

http://www.cssbook.com/cssnav/css2.html

The difference between this method and the previous one is that you're using inline list elements to separate the menu items, not straight links. The advantage to this method is that the entire box is active, because the entire box *is* the link. Any padding around the links creates space around the text. You don't have to resort to block element links with this method. Here's the HTML:

```
<div id="nav"><p>Navigation:</p><ul><li><a href="/ankle">Ankle</a></li><li><a
href="/boat">Boat</a></li><li><a href="/cupcake">Cupcake</a></li><li><a
href="/double">Double</a></li><li><a href="/eatery">Eatery</a></li></ul></div>
```

Pretty straightforward; a "nav" div surrounding an unordered list, without spaces. Next, you style the list display to be `inline`, rather than the default, `list-item`:

```
#nav li {
    padding: 0;
    margin: 0;
    display: inline; /* turns li from block to inline element */
    font-size: 0.9em;
    font-family: Verdana, Arial, Helvetica, sans-serif;
}
```

Now add in some padding for the links and a `hover` effect as before:

```
#nav li a {
    display: inline;
    padding: 7px;
    margin: 0;
    color: #333;
    background-color: #ccc;
    font-size: 0.9em;
    font-family: Verdana, Arial, Helvetica, sans-serif;
    text-decoration: none;
}

#nav li a:hover {
    color: #fff;
    background-color: #666;
    font-size: 0.9em;
    font-family: Verdana, Arial, Helvetica, sans-serif;
    text-decoration: none;
}
```

Note that you could optimize this code using shorthand properties and eliminate some redundancy. Listing 8.8 shows the final optimized style sheet.

Listing 8.8   Optimized Inline List Menus

```
#nav {
    position:absolute;
    top: 12px;
    left: 12px;
    color: #fff;
    background: transparent;
    font: 0.9em verdana, arial, helvetica, sans-serif;
}
```

```
#nav ul, ul {
      margin: 0;
      padding: 0;
}

#nav li {
      padding: 0;
      margin: 0;
      display: inline;
      font: 0.9em verdana, arial, helvetica, sans-serif;
}

#nav li a {
      display: inline;
      padding: 7px;
      margin: 0;
      color: #333;
      background: #ccc;
      font: 0.9em verdana, arial, helvetica, sans-serif;
      text-decoration: none;
}

#nav li a:hover {
      color: #fff;
      background: #666;
}

#nav li a:active {
      color: #ccc;
      background: #333;
}
```

For More Information

You can learn more about inline list menus at Christopher Schmitt's CSSBook.com site, or in his book *Designing CSS Web Pages* (New Riders, 2002). See also Dave Lindquist's list-based DHTML menus for drop-down and expandable menus in under 6K at `http://www.gazingus.org/dhtml/?id=109`.

Tables and CSS

In Chapter 4, "Advanced HTML Optimization," you learned how to speed up tables with the CSS2 `table-layout:fixed;` property and `colgroup` and `col` elements. Another technique you can use for tiny tables is to use CSS to style table cell background colors instead of embedding `bgcolors` everywhere. So instead of this:

```
<table bgcolor="#ffcc00">
<tr bgcolor="somecolor">
<td>...</td>
<td bgcolor"anothercolor">...</td>
```

do this:

```
.x{background:#fc0}.y{background:#ffed9a}.z{background:#fff3ac}

<table class="x">
<tr class="y">
<td>...</td>
<td class="z">...</td>
```

All version 4 browsers and higher support this technique.

CSS Layout Control

CSS positioning can transform old table-based designs into elegant CSS-based layouts. Authors have found that transforming their pixel-perfect tables into CSS layouts can mean big savings in bandwidth and maintenance costs. By breaking out of the fixed-grid tyranny of tables, you also gain the flexibility to repurpose your content. By shunting your presentation into style sheets, your code becomes pure structure surrounding content. Changing layouts site-wide is as easy as changing one style sheet. Transforming your content into media- or platform-specific versions takes only a different style sheet, not painful recoding.

Two and three-column layouts are popular choices, with Netscape 4 compliance a plus (and a challenge). Let's take a look at the sample three-panel layout in Listing 8.9.

Listing 8.9   Three-Column Layout: The Old Way

```
<table>
      <tr>
            <td colspan="2">
                  <p>top navigation bar (branding and advertising) </p>
            </td>
      </tr>
      <tr>
            <td>
                  <p>left navigation bar</p>
            </td>
            <td>
                  <p>main content area</p>
            </td>
      </tr>
<table>
```

In CSS, you use `divs` instead of table cells, as shown in Listing 8.10.

Listing 8.10   Three-Column Layout: The New Way

```
<div id="adv">
      <p>top navigation bar (branding and advertising)</p>
</div>
<div id="nav">
      <p>left navigation bar</p>
</div>
<div id="main">
      <p>main content area</p>
</div>
```

This is much cleaner code. Notice that the `divs` are named by function, not by location. Now let's add some CSS to position these elements (see Listing 8.11).

Listing 8.11   Three-Column Layout: CSS

```
<style type="text/css">
<!--
div#adv {
      background:#ccc;
      width:auto;
      margin:0;
      padding:0.5em;
```

continues

Listing 8.11   Three-Column Layout: CSS   *continued*

```
}
div#nav {
        background:#ddd;
        float:left;
        width:25%;
        margin-right:0.5em;
        padding:0.5em;
}
div#main {
        background:#0fc;
        margin-left:25%;
        padding:0.5em;
}
-->
</style>
```

The key elements for two and three-column layouts in CSS are `float`, `margin-left`, and `right`. The `float` moves an element to the left or right, and the other content "flows" around it. In this case, you float the navigation `div` to the left, set a width and some padding, and add a margin to the right for whitespace. For the main content `div`, you set its left margin to correspond to the width of the left floated element. That's all there is to it.

Raising Relevance

The higher your main content is in your HTML code, the better for search engine relevance. You can use CSS to replicate the table trick you learned in Chapter 4. In Listing 8.12, you see that instead of floating the navigation bar to the left, you float the main content `div` to the right and reverse the procedure.

Listing 8.12   Improved Three-Column Layout: CSS

```
<style type="text/css">
<!--
div#adv {
        background:#ccc;
        width:auto;
        margin:0;
```

```
        padding:0.5em;
}
div#main {
        float:right;
        width:75%;
        background:#0fc;
        margin-left:0.5em;
        padding:0.5em;
}
div#nav {
        background:#ddd;
        margin-right:75%;
        padding:0.5em;
}
-->
</style>
```

Now you can flip the `main` and `nav` `div`s in the HTML, pushing the main content earlier in the page (see Listing 8.13).

Listing 8.13   Improved Three-Column Layout: HTML

```
<div id="adv">
        <p>top navigation bar (branding and advertising)</p>
</div>
<div id="main">
        <p>main content area</p>
</div>
<div id="nav">
        <p>left navigation bar</p>
</div>
```

The page looks identical, but the main content area appears earlier in the code and also displays faster. If you want, you can take this to an extreme and absolutely position the main content area first; then include the advertising and navigation `div`s as before.

> ## For More Information
>
> See the following sites for more demonstrations of CSS layout techniques:
>
> - `http://www.alistapart.com`—A List Apart uses CSS-based layouts and teaches developers how to use them.
> - `http://www.meyerweb.com/eric/css/edge/`—CSS Edge is Eric Meyer's standards-based CSS playground.
> - `http://developer.apple.com/internet/css/introcsslayout.html`—Introduction to CSS Layouts by Eric Costello.

Summary

To fully utilize CSS as it was intended, you've got to transform your code. Use abbreviated `class` and `id` names, and shorthand properties and grouping to minimize style sheets. Substitute CSS-based layout and rollover techniques for old table-based layout and JavaScript/image rollovers. For smaller tables, style table, row, and cell backgrounds with CSS instead of `bgcolor` for speed and flexibility. While you are at it, raise your content's relevance by pushing your main content higher in your code, with the table trick or CSS layout techniques. Here's a brief list of what you learned in this chapter:

- Use shorthand properties, grouping, and abbreviation to optimize your CSS.
- Substitute CSS-based effects for JavaScript and images (rollovers).
- Use the `hover` pseudo-class and styled links or lists to create CSS2 rollovers.
- Use `table-layout:fixed` for tables when possible and `colgroup` and `col` for speed.
- Use CSS to color data cells in tables (works in version 4+ browsers).
- Use CSS layout and positioning control and XHTML to separate presentation from structure to shrink your code, make your layout flexible, and raise search engine relevance.

Further Reading

- *Cascading Style Sheets: The Definitive Guide* by Eric Meyer (O'Reilly, 2000)—A great introduction to CSS.

- *Eric Meyer on CSS* by Eric Meyer (New Riders, 2002)—Meyer demonstrates real-world CSS with 13 conversion projects.

- A List Apart by Jeffery Zeldman, et al. (http://www.alistapart.com)—A good source of standards-based how-to advice, including CSS.

- Cascading Style Sheets, 1, 2, and 3, World Wide Web Consortium (http://www.w3.org/Style/CSS/)—The official CSS specifications.

- The Web Standards Project by Jeffery Zeldman, et al. (http://www.webstandards.org)—Now that they've convinced the browser manufacturers on standards, Zeldman and company have relaunched WaSP to sting the development tool makers.

Optimizing JavaScript for Download Speed

A lightweight interpreted language, JavaScript is ideally suited to data validation, interactive forms, and enhancing navigation. Presented with such a broad toolset to play with, many authors have gone overboard with JavaScript, bulking up their sites at an alarming rate. Fortunately, JavaScript offers rich opportunities for file-size and execution-speed optimization. By using techniques like packing, compression, and obfuscation, you can realize 50 to 90 percent savings off the size of your JavaScript files. This chapter shows you how to put your JavaScripts on a low-char diet. In Chapter 10, "Optimizing JavaScript for Execution Speed," you will learn how to speed up the execution speed of your code.

Because JavaScript is part of web page content and not a standalone application, making your JavaScripts load quickly is important. The challenge is to find the right balance between size and speed, or between features and responsiveness.

When to Opt for Optimization

"The first principle of optimization is don't."[1]

Most JavaScripts are so fast and many are so small that they don't need to be optimized. First, code your scripts to work correctly and be self-describing by using the best algorithms and data structures you can. Then, if users start to notice a delay in loading or execution time, it's time to start thinking about optimization.

Larger, more complex scripts, such as cascading menus and expandable outlines, can benefit more from download speed than from execution speed optimization. Realistic interactive games and simulations can benefit more from execution speed than from file size optimization. As you'll discover in Chapter 10, you can trade size for speed complexity and vice versa. Optimizing both size and speed while maintaining legible code takes a combination of techniques.

Trim the Fat

JavaScript can benefit from many of the same optimization techniques used with HTML and CSS. Whitespace removal, crunching and obfuscation, file consolidation, and compression can all be used singly or in combination to shrink your scripts. Scripts can typically be reduced by 50 to 70 percent, while combining techniques on amenable files can yield savings of 80 to 90 percent, or a factor of 5 to 10 times smaller.

JavaScript offers more opportunities for optimization than (X)HTML and CSS because you can name your own variables, functions, and objects. The only names you can't abbreviate are the built-in statements and methods like `document.getElementById()`.

As you've no doubt discovered, JavaScripts can become quite large, which can slow down the display of web pages. Any external scripts referenced in the `head` of your document must load before any `body` content displays. Even with smaller `.css` and `.js` files,

---

1. Brian W. Kernighan and Rob Pike, *The Practice of Programming* (Boston, MA: Addison-Wesley, 1999), 165.

it is important to minimize the number of HTTP requests as each one adds an indeterminate delay. The easiest way to optimize JavaScript is to trim the fat in the first place. Strive to add only features that will benefit users and save them time.

What About Legibility?

The knock against optimized scripts is that they are hard to read. This can be a good thing, because some authors want to obfuscate their code to make it difficult to copy and reverse engineer. However, optimized code is difficult to maintain and update. I recommend adopting a parallel strategy like the one you used for optimized HTML files. After you debug your code (which is fully commented and self-describing, right?), optimize it by hand or automatically optimize it to another file, like this:

```
script.js
script_c.js
```

Link to `script_c.js` for the added speed, and perform any edits on the original `script.js`, which you can then reoptimize.

Remove Whitespace

Well-written JavaScripts tend to have a lot of whitespace for better legibility. Indents, spaces, and returns make your code easier for you and others to read and modify; however, your browser doesn't care how pretty your code is. With a couple of exceptions, the JavaScript parser scans your script looking for tokens and ignores excess whitespace. So instead of this:

```
function printArray(a) {
    if (a.length == 0)
        document.write(" Array is empty");
    else {
        for (var i = 0; i < a.length; i++) {
            document.write(a[i] + " <br>");
        }
    }
}
```

Do this:

```
function printArray(a){
if(a.length==0)
document.write("Array is empty");
else{
for(var i=0;i<a.length;i++){
document.write(a[i]+"<br>");
}
}
}
```

Automatic Semicolon Insertion

The ECMAScript specification requires browsers to automatically insert semicolons where they are needed.[2] Although they are optional, ending your lines with semicolons is good defensive programming practice. Semicolons are also required by most optimization strategies that remove excess whitespace. Without semicolons, removing whitespace can cause unintended consequences, such as running lines together. They also help programmers avoid errors. (Let's save programmers some time, too.)

Cut the Comments

Commenting your code is good programming practice, but comments take up valuable space. What's a programmer to do? There are two approaches to cutting comments: abbreviate your comments or remove them entirely. So instead of this (from PopularMechanics.com):

```
function gotoFinList() {

//  "SAVE & FINISH"
//  this changes the bottom frameset to include a button to return to the homepage
//  it also submits the form in the main frame that will then generate a list of pages
//  added during content editing.
```

---

2. ECMA, "ECMAScript Language Specification, Standard ECMA-262," 3d ed. [online], (Geneva, SZ: ECMA, 1999), available from the Internet at http://www.ecma.ch/ecma1/STAND/ECMA-262.HTM. Defines the ECMAScript language (otherwise known as JavaScript).

Do this:

```
function gotoFinList() {

// chgs bottom frameset 2 incl button 2 ret 2 home
// also submits form in main form and gen list of pgs
// added during content editg
```

Or even better:

```
function gotoFinList() {
```

You can use the parallel approach mentioned previously to keep a fully commented version for future updates.

Apply JavaScripts Wisely

JavaScripts can be included in an (X)HTML document in any of four ways:

- In an external file

- Between a pair of `<script>`...`</script>` tags

- In an event handler

- After the `javascript:` pseudo-protocol in an URL

Let's use our minimal Mondrian to demonstrate them all:

```
<!DOCTYPE html
    PUBLIC "-//W3C//DTD XHTML 1.0 Strict//EN"
    "http://www.w3.org/TR/xhtml1/DTD/xhtml1-strict.dtd ">
<html xmlns="http://www.w3.org/1999/xhtml" xml:lang="en" lang="en">
<head>
<title>Piet Mondrian's Home Page</title>
<script src="/scripts/foo.js" defer="defer" type="text/javascript"></script>
<script type="text/javascript">
    var foo = 1;
</script>
</head>
<body>
    <h1>Piet Mondrian: Abstract Impressionist</h1>
    <p>Mondrian was one of the great abstract masters...</p>
    <p><a onmouseover="window.status='Mondrian Home Page'; return true;";
href="http://www.mondrian.com">Mondrian.com</a></p>
```

```
<p><a href="javascript:window.open('http://www.mondrian.com/')">Mondrian.com</a></p>
</body>
</html>
```

In honor of Mondrian and expediency, let's focus squarely on the first two options. Event handlers can be used to link behavior to elements (ideally with functions), but the `javascript:` pseudo-protocol should be avoided as the only reference of a link. The 11 percent of people without JavaScript won't be able to access this content.[3] This is not exactly user friendly.[4] A number of sites rely on JavaScript—even government sites that should be easily accessible like `http://www.canadapost.ca/`.

Here's the syntax of the `script` element:

\<script\>	
Function:	Defines an executable script
Attributes:	CHARSET, DEFER, LANGUAGE (deprecated), SRC, TYPE
Examples:	`<script type="text/javascript" src="/scripts/foo.js"></script>`
	`<script type="text/javascript" src="/f.js" defer="defer"></script>` `/* optimized */`
End tag:	`</script>`, not optional
Alternate:	`<noscript>alternate content</noscript>`
Used in:	`<head>`, `<body>`

Minimize HTTP Requests

Like CSS, your JavaScripts should be designed to maximize speed by minimizing the number of HTTP requests they require. You can embed smaller JavaScripts within high-traffic pages to avoid an extra HTTP request (with caveats for XHTML, discussed in

---

3. TheCounter.com, "JavaScript Stats," in Global Statistics 2002 [online], (Darien, CT: Jupitermedia Corporation, October, 2002), available from the Internet at `http://www.thecounter.com/stats/`.
4. Pamela L. O'Connell, "Site Unseen?," *New York Times*, 14 February 2002, Circuits section, D3. Shirley Kaiser of WebStandards.org and I were quoted in this story about Olympics.com, a site that required JavaScript.

Chapter 5, "Extreme XHTML"), and for site-wide bandwidth savings, use external files. Group files where possible to minimize the overhead of additional file requests.

Upon first encounter, external scripts take one HTTP request per file. I've found CSS files are cached more reliably than JavaScript files, however. External JavaScripts can continue to spawn HTTP requests even after their first encounter.[5] Unlike HTML objects (like images, Flash, and Java), which can be requested in parallel, the HTML parser must wait for the JavaScript interpreter to load and execute any JavaScript files before it can continue.

Defer or Delay Loading

Scripts are executed as they are loaded. You can have multiple non-overlapping `script` elements within an HTML document, both in the `head` and `body`. To maximize page-display speed, try to defer or delay loading your JavaScripts where possible. Every byte and HTTP request you put before your viewable content delays its display.

First introduced by Microsoft Internet Explorer 4, the `defer` attribute of the `script` element is now part of the HTML 4 and XHTML specifications. If your script does not produce any output, such as a function or array definition, you can use the `defer` attribute to give browsers a hint that they can defer execution until the rest of your HTML page loads. Here's an example:

```
<script src="/later.js" defer="defer" type="text/javascript"></script>
</head>
```

Try to design or rewrite your scripts to encapsulate code in functions that will execute `onload`. Then you can defer their execution and still include them in the `head` of your document. This technique has the added benefit of allowing external files to be compressed, because they are included within the `head`. You can execute defined functions `onload`, like this:

```
<body onload="later();">
```

---

5. Netscape Communications, "Problems caching .js source files?," in DevEdge Newsgroup FAQ [online], (Mountain View, CA: Netscape Communications, 1999), available from the Internet at http://developer.netscape.com/ support/faqs/champions/javascript.html#2-9. Add the following line to the mime types file to force Netscape to cache .js files properly: application/x-javascript exts=js.

Or you can avoid JavaScript errors in non-critical scripts that are triggered immediately (such as email validation or overlaid menus) by defining empty "stub" functions to be replaced by scripts that are redefined later:

```
<script>
<!--
function stub{};
// -->
</script>
</head>
<body>
...
<script src="/scripts/stub.js" type="text/javascript"></script>
</body>
```

Be careful with this approach because larger or multiple external scripts can bog down the response of your page after it displays. As you learned in Chapter 1, "Response Time: Eight Seconds, Plus or Minus Two," you want to avoid slow response times after a page loads. This technique works for HTML, but for XHTML you'll need to eliminate the surrounding SGML comments through conditional logic for post-HTML-3.2 browsers.

Even better, for high-traffic pages, SSI or merge them into the page to save an HTTP request. Here's an example of merging a script at the end of a page:

```
<script type="text/javascript">
<!--#include virtual="newsticker.js" -->
</script>
</body>
```

We use this approach on WebReference.com's front page news flipper. We first embed a couple HTML news headlines within the flipper `table`, and then overlay these links with other stories with the delayed DHTML include. The main content displays first, and then the script loads—not vice versa. This technique gracefully degrades for folks without JavaScript. For more details, see `http://www.webreference.com/headlines/nh/`.

Delay Gotchas

There are some downsides to delaying external loading of JavaScript files. Moving larger or multiple external scripts to the end of the `body` just postpones the pain. Although your content may display faster, leaving your page can become slow and sticky.

Functions called earlier in the page will not be available until the external file loads. You can include empty functions in the `head`, or better yet, check to be sure that external files have loaded or a flag has been defined to avoid calling nonexistent functions.

Finally, compressed JavaScripts located outside the `head` are not reliably decompressed by modern browsers. Instead, move compressed scripts inside the `head` and use the `defer` attribute where possible.

Place Compressed *.js* Files in the *head*

Because of the way the original Sun JavaScript parser worked, decompression of compressed external JavaScript files works only when they are embedded in the `head` of (X)HTML documents. We'll unravel that mystery in Chapter 18, "Compressing the Web."

Conditionally Load External JavaScripts

You can conditionally load external JavaScripts into your (X)HTML files with languages like JavaScript, XSSI, and PHP. Rather than create one large monolithic file, some authors split their JavaScript code into separate files. A common technique is to use separate libraries for Internet Explorer 4+, Netscape 4+, and DOM-based browsers (`ie4.js`, `ns4.js`, and `dom.js`, respectively). Depending on what type of browser loads the page, the following JavaScript loads only the necessary code:

```
dom = (document.getElementById) ? true : false;
ns4 = (document.layers) ? true : false;
```

```
ie  = (document.all) ? true : false;
ie4 = ie && !dom;

var src = '';
if (dom) src = '/dom.js';
else if (ie4) src = '/ie4.js';
else if (ns4) src = '/ns4.js';
document.write("<scr" + "ipt src=" + src + "><\/scr" + "ipt>");
```

This simple browser sniffer classifies browsers into four categories:

- `document.getElementById` (~ DOM)
- `document.layers` (Netscape 4)
- `document.all` (Internet Explorer 4+)
- Everything else

You'll learn more advanced compatibility techniques that can save HTTP requests in Chapter 17, "Server-Side Techniques."

Abbreviate and Map

Another JavaScript optimization technique you can use to crunch your code is abbreviation and mapping. Abbreviation in JavaScript is more flexible than in HTML. In JavaScript, you can name your variables, functions, and objects anything you want, but HTML requires a fixed set of tag names, although `class` and `id` names can be abbreviated.

So instead of this:

```
function validateParseAndEmail()
var firstButton
```

Do this:

```
function email()
var button1
```

Or even better:

```
function e()
var b
```

Here's an example from WebReference.com's home page. Peter Belesis' original dual "news flipper" was self-describing (`http://www.webreference.com/headlines/nh/`). It was also over 6.7K and slowed down our home page.

So instead of this (single-feed version):

```
<script src="/scripts/newsflipper.js">
</head>

...(newsflipper.js file below)
arTopNews=[];

for(i=0;i<arTXT.length;i++) {
    arTopNews[arTopNews.length] = arTXT[i];
    arTopNews[arTopNews.length] = arURL[i];
}

TopPrefix=prefix;

function NSinit() {
    fad1 = new Layer(119);
    pos1 = document.anchors['pht1'];
    pos1E = document.images['phb1'];
    fad1.left = pos1.x;
    fad1.top  = pos1.y;
    fad1.clip.width  = 119;
    fad1.clip.height = pos1E.y-fad1.top;
    fad1.bgColor = "#ffed9a";
    fad1.onmouseover = FDRmouseover;
    fad1.onmouseout  = FDRmouseout;
}
if (IE4) {
    IEfad1.style.pixelHeight=IEfad1.offsetHeight;
    IEfad1.onmouseover=FDRmouseover;
    IEfad1.onmouseout=FDRmouseout;
}

function FDRmouseover() {
    clearInterval(blendTimer);
}...
```

We manually abbreviated and optimized the code by over 50 percent to less than 3K and used SSI to add it to the end of the page, like this:

```
<!--#include virtual="/f.js" -->
</body>

... (f.js file below)
```

```
aTN=[];for(i=0;i<arTXT.length;i++){aTN[aTN.length]=arTXT[i];aTN[aTN.length]=arURL[i];}
tP=prefix;
function Ni(){fad1=new Layer(119);
dI=document.images;dA=document.anchors;
pos1=dA['pht1'];pos1E=dI['phb1'];fad1.left=pos1.x;fad1.top=pos1.y;fad1.clip.width=119;
fad1.clip.height=pos1E.y-fad1.top;fad1.bgColor="#ffed9a";
fad1.onmouseover=Fmv;fad1.onmouseout=Fmo;}
function Fmv(){clearInterval(bT);}...
```

Moving the script from an external file in the head to an SSI at the end of the page saves one HTTP request, displays the body content sooner, and raises relevance. Of course, these terse abbreviations can be hard to read. One solution is to create a map of names and their abbreviated counterparts either manually or automatically with an optimization program (such as index.jsmap). Here's an example:

```
email    e
button1  b
```

I have yet to see an optimizer that can abbreviate to user-defined maps (although I'm told some are in development). Some optimizers abbreviate variables and objects automatically, but you're stuck with what the program chooses.

Crunching and Obfuscation

Not to be confused with compression, *crunching* (or crushing or packing) is a term programmers have adopted to describe removing excess to reduce code to a minimum size. Although you can manually crunch by removing whitespace, comments, and abbreviating, automated programs are a more practical option for larger projects. There are several JavaScript crunchers available, including these:

- **JavaScript Crunchinator from BrainJar's Mike Hall** (http://www.brainjar.com/ js/crunch/)—Removes whitespace and comments from JavaScript files and combines literal strings.
- **ESC (ECMAScript Cruncher) from Saltstorm** (http://www.saltstorm.net/ depo/esc/)—This free Windows program is an ECMAScript pre-processor written in JScript. In addition to removing whitespace and comments from JavaScript, it can optionally rename variables in JavaScript. For IE5.5+ Win.

- **JSCruncher from Hoard's DOMAPI project** (`http://www.domapi.com/`)—Based on BrainJar's specifications, this free Windows application packs CSS and JavaScript files. Requires semicolons.

- **Script Squisher by Darren Semotiuk** (`http://batman.getmyip.com/projects/scriptsquisher/`)—This updated 5K entry squishes JavaScript by removing whitespace and comments. Does not require semicolons.

- **SpaceAgent from Insider Software, Inc.** (`http://www.insidersoftware.com/`)—This powerful Windows/Mac web site optimizer optimizes (X)HTML, XML, JavaScript, GIFs, and JPEGs. Server version also available.

- **VSE HTML Turbo from VSE Online** (`http://www.vse-online.com/`)—Like SpaceAgent, this Mac application optimizes (X)HTML, JavaScript, GIFs, and JPEGs.

These programs all work the same way, removing whitespace and comments to compact your code. Some, like ESC, optionally abbreviate object and variable names.

Obfuscation Anyone?

Because JavaScript is an interpreted language, hiding your scripts is impossible. You can, however, make them more difficult to decipher. Crunching certainly makes your code more difficult to read. But for some this is not enough. That's where obfuscators come in. Code obfuscators substitute cryptic string tokens and scramble names to make your code virtually unintelligible but still functional.

Blue Clam: JavaScript Obfuscator

By the time you read this, Solmar Solutions, Inc., will have released Blue Clam, a Java-based JavaScript obfuscator designed to protect your intellectual property and optimize JavaScript files. In development for two years, Blue Clam includes features not found in other JavaScript obfuscators, including recursive directory tree parsing, a user-defined keyword dictionary, variable-length obfuscated keyword support, extended file types (such as `.js`, `.jsp`, and `.asp`), and a graphical environment. For more information, see `http://www.solmar.ca`.

All obfuscators work in a similar way to transform your program internally while preserving the same external functionality. One common obfuscation is to substitute short
meaningless sequences like "cq" for longer descriptive names like "setAvatarMood." Let's
look at some real-world obfuscated code. So this:

```
function setAvatarMood(theMood) {
  try {
    //see if we have to reset the mood's duration
    var resetMoodDuration = ((theMood != null) && (theMood != 'anim'));

    //make sure there is a mood
    if (!theMood) theMood = avatar.data.mood;

    //store the new mood in the avatar
    if (theMood != 'anim') avatar.data.mood = theMood;

    //see if the mood exists
    if (!globals.moods[theMood]) theMood = globals.defaultMood;

    //set the appropriate mood-image to visible and all others to invisible
    //by moving them in or out of view
    for (var aMood in globals.moods) {
      avatar.labeledElements['avatar' + globals.moods[aMood] + 'Image'].style.top =
((aMood == theMood)?0:-10000) + 'px';

    }

    //let the mood expire if it is not equal to the default mood
    if (resetMoodDuration && (theMood != globals.defaultMood)) {
      if (theMood != 'anim') delayedEval(avatar.id + ".setMood", null);
      delayedEval(avatar.id + ".setMood", "try { engine.getAvatarByID('Quek', '" +
avatar.id + "').setMood('" + globals.defaultMood + "'); } catch(e){;}",
avatar.MOODDURATION);
    }
  } catch(e){}
}
```

Becomes this (without whitespace removal):

```
function cq(de) {
  try {
    var ch = ((de != null) && (de != 'anim'));
    if (!de) de = kj.data.hu;
    if (de != 'anim') kj.data.hu = de;
    if (!io.uy[de]) de = io.we;
    for (var ty in io.uy) {
      kj.op['avatar' + io.uy[ty] + 'Image'].style.top = ((ty == de)?0:-10000) + 'px';
```

```
      }
    if (ch && (de != io.we)) {
       if (de != 'anim') qw(kj.id + ".pw", null);
       qw(kj.id + ".setMood", "try { po.pp('Quek', '" + kj.id + "').pw('" + io.we + "'); }
catch(e){;}", kj.ua);
       }
   } catch(e){}
}
```

Even better (with whitespace removed):

```
function cq(de){try{var ch=((de!=null)&&(de!='anim'));if(!de)de=kj.data.hu;
if(de!='anim')kj.data.hu=de;if(!io.uy[de])de=io.we;for(var ty in io.uy){
kj.op['avatar'+io.uy[ty]+'Image'].style.top=((ty==de)?0:-10000)+'px';}
if(ch&&(de!=io.we)){if(de!='anim')qw(kj.id+".pw",null);
qw(kj.id+".setMood","try{po.pp('Quek', '" +kj.id+"').pw('"+io.we+"');}
catch(e){;}",kj.ua);}}catch(e){}}
```

Without a map, these internal transformations make your program extremely difficult to reverse engineer, plus it's 65 percent smaller (from 1,091 to 376 characters). The code is part of Quek (http://www.quek.nl), a browser-based surf/animate/chat application written in JavaScript. This function changes the mood of an avatar. Lon Boonen of Q42 (http://www.q42.nl) obfuscates his JavaScripts to prevent prying eyes with a home-grown script and some manual tweaking. Thanks to Lon Boonen for these snippets.

JavaScript Obfuscators

JavaScript obfuscators are few and far between. Here are some examples:

- JavaScript Scrambler (http://www.quadhead.de/jss.html)
- Jmyth (http://www.geocities.com/SiliconValley/Vista/5233/jmyth.htm)

You can go further and substitute extended ASCII characters to obfuscate and tokenize your code even more. For maximum confusion, obfuscate reserved words by breaking them up into strings and use a concatenated variable. So instead of this:

```
bc.getElementById = kj;
```

Do this:

```
jh='ge';kl='tEleme';oi='ntB';zy='yID';ui=jh+kl+oi+zy;
bc[ui]=kj;
```

Self-Extracting Archives

Some extreme programmers have gone so far as to create their own self-extracting archives. Trading time for space, they store their encoded script into one long string by substituting shorter tokens for longer repeated strings. Tack on a small decompressor at the end to replace the tokens with the original strings and eval the decompressed code and voilá!—a self-extracting script.

These self-extracting archives take longer to decompress and execute, but download much faster. Some 5K contestants (`http://www.the5k.org/`) have adopted this approach to squeeze the maximum functionality into as little space as possible.

Fans of Chris Nott's 1K DOM API used a similar technique to reduce his tiny API to 634 bytes. Chris has automated the process with his compression utilities at `http://www.dithered.com/experiments/compression/`.

Compression ratios average about 25 percent for 5K files and higher for larger files. Because the decompressor adds about 130 bytes, smaller files actually can become larger. Nott recommends using files over 500 bytes for his client-side compression scheme.

Chris Johnson's Extended ASCII JavaScript Packer substitutes single byte-token extended ASCII characters for longer strings for efficient packing of JavaScripts (`http://members.optusnet.com.au/~kris_j/javacomp.html`).

With both of these programs, there are reserved letters and techniques that you must avoid to make them work. For the 5K contest, only client-side techniques are allowed. For most sites, server-side compression is a more practical solution.

JavaScript and Compression

JavaScript files are highly compressible, in some cases by as much as 60 to 80 percent. Modern browsers can decompress JavaScripts either in external files or embedded within (X)HTML files. As Chapter 11, "Case Study: DHTML.com," shows, the difference in size and speed can be dramatic. You can compress JavaScript files in two different ways: proprietary and standards-based.

Each browser has its own proprietary way of compressing JavaScripts, related to signed scripts, Java archives, or help file systems. In theory, you could create a sophisticated sniffer to load the appropriate file for the visiting browser, but you'd have to maintain four separate files. A cleaner way is to use standards-based gzip content encoding.

Like HTML, external JavaScripts can be delivered compressed from the server and automatically decompressed by HTTP 1.1-compliant browsers. The only gotchas to watch out for are that external compressed JavaScript files must be referenced within the head element to be reliably decompressed by modern browsers, and Explorer 5 has a subtle onload bug with compressed scripts. You can work around both gotchas, however. You'll learn all the details in Chapter 18, "Compressing the Web."

By grouping external JavaScripts and using compression, you can dramatically reduce their impact on page display speed and bandwidth usage.

Summary

The easiest way to optimize JavaScript is to avoid the need for it in the first place. First, trim the fat by deleting unnecessary scripts and features. To avoid being featured in an accessibility story, use JavaScript only to enhance the user experience, not to create it. Email validation, responsive pop-up menus, and more can be created without the need for optimization. For larger projects where size or speed is an issue, optimization makes more sense.

Because JavaScript must be downloaded, make sure that your code is optimized for size and grouped to minimize HTTP requests. Many a site has added fancy navigational gizmos that are slow to load, because of many small (and not so small) files, each taking an indeterminate amount of time to download. Embed shorter scripts on high-traffic pages for maximum speed.

Automated packing programs can remove white space and comments, and some can abbreviate names. For maximum control, however, abbreviate your object and variable names manually. Where possible, defer program execution and loading, and compress larger scripts located in the `head`. Here's a list of the techniques you learned in this chapter:

- Trim the fat by removing excess whitespace and comments, and using semicolons to avoid any misunderstandings.
- Minimize HTTP requests by combining files and merging or embedding scripts on high traffic pages.
- Defer or delay loading where possible (but avoid sticky pages).
- Load only what's necessary—segment API code (NS4, IE5, DOM, and so on).
- Compress larger external files located in the `head`.
- Gracefully degrade—avoid JavaScript-only techniques.
- Abbreviate and map names automatically or manually to make your optimization reversible.
- Crunch and obfuscate your code to shrink scripts and deter prying eyes.
- Create self-extracting archives if entering the 5K competition.
- Use ESC or Blue Clam to abbreviate variable and object names for maximum packing.

Further Reading

- *JavaScript: The Definitive Guide, 4th ed.* by David Flanagan (O'Reilly, 2001).
- *Programming Pearls, 2nd ed.* by Jon Bentley (Addison-Wesley, 1999)— See Column 10: "Squeezing Space."
- `http://www.ecma.ch`—The ECMAScript Standards.
- `http://www.javascript.com`—The definitive JavaScript resource. News, views, and how-tos.
- `http://directory.google.com/Top/Computers/Programming/Languages/ JavaScript/`—Open Directory JavaScript Resources.

10

Optimizing JavaScript for Execution Speed

JavaScript can benefit from many of the same speed-optimization techniques that are used in other languages, like C[1,2] and Java. Algorithms and data structures, caching frequently used values, loop unrolling and hoisting, removing tail recursion, and strength-reduction techniques all have a place in your JavaScript optimization toolbox. However, how you interact with the Document Object Model (DOM) in large part determines how efficiently your code executes.

Unlike other programming languages, JavaScript manipulates web pages through a relatively sluggish API, the DOM. Interacting with the DOM is almost always more expensive than straight computations. After choosing the right algorithm and data structure and refactoring, your next consideration should be minimizing DOM interaction and I/O operations.

With most programming languages, you can trade space for time complexity and vice versa.[3] But on the web, JavaScripts must be downloaded. Unlike desktop applications

1. Jon Bentley, *Programming Pearls*, 2d ed. (Boston, MA: Addison-Wesley, 1999).
2. Brian W. Kernighan and Rob Pike, *The Practice of Programming* (Boston, MA: Addison-Wesley, 1999). See the "Performance" chapter, 165-188.
3. Bentley, *Programming Pearls*, 7. The space-time tradeoff does not always hold. The ideal situation is mutual improvement. Bentley found that often "reducing a program's space requirements also reduces its run time."

where you can trade another kilobyte or two for speed, with JavaScript you have to balance execution speed versus file size.

How Fast Is JavaScript?

Unlike C, with its optimizing compilers that increase execution speed and decrease file size, JavaScript is an interpreted language that usually is run over a network connection (unless you count Netscape's Rhino, which can compile and optimize JavaScript into Java byte code for embedded applications[4]). This makes JavaScript relatively slow compared to compiled languages.[5] However, most scripts are usually so small and fast that users won't notice any speed degradation. Longer, more complex scripts are where this chapter can help jumpstart your JavaScript.

4. Mozilla.org, "Rhino: JavaScript for Java" [online], (Mountain View, CA: The Mozilla Organization, 1998), available from the Internet at `http://www.mozilla.org/rhino/`.
5. Geoffrey Fox, "JavaScript Performance Issues," Online Seminar, Northeast Parallel Architectures Center [online], (Syracuse, NY: Syracuse University, 1999), available from the Internet at `http://www.npac.syr.edu/users/ gcf/forcps616javascript/msrcobjectsapril99/tsld022.htm`. According to Fox, JavaScript is about 5,000 times slower than C, 100 times slower than interpreted Java, and 10 times slower than Perl.

Design Levels

A hierarchy of optimization levels exists for JavaScript, what Bentley and others call *design levels*.[6] First comes the global changes like using the right algorithms and data structures that can speed up your code by orders of magnitude. Next comes refactoring that restructures code in a disciplined way into a simpler, more efficient form[7]). Then comes minimizing DOM interaction and I/O or HTTP requests. Finally, if performance is still a problem, use local optimizations like caching frequently used values to save on recalculation costs. Here is a summary of the optimization process:

6. Bentley, *Programming Pearls*.
7. Martin Fowler, *Refactoring: Improving the Design of Existing Code* (Boston, MA: Addison-Wesley, 1999).

1. Choose the right algorithm and data structure.

2. Refactor to simplify code.

3. Minimize DOM and I/O interaction.

4. Use local optimizations last.

When optimizing your code, start at the highest level and work your way down until the code executes fast enough. For maximum speed, work at multiple levels.

Measure Your Changes

Measurement is a key part of the optimization process. Use the simplest algorithms and data structures you can, and measure your code's performance to see whether you need to make any changes. Use timing commands or profilers to locate any bottlenecks. Optimize these hot spots one at a time, and measure any improvement. You can use the date object to time individual snippets:

```
<script type="text/javascript">
function DoBench(x){
    var startTime,endTime,gORl='local';
    if(x==1){
        startTime=new Date().getTime();
        Bench1();
        endTime=new Date().getTime();
    }else{
        gORl='global';
        startTime=new Date().getTime();
        Bench2();
        endTime=new Date().getTime();
    }
alert('Elapsed time using '+gORl+' variable: '+((endTime-startTime)/1000)+' seconds.');
}
...
</script>
```

This is useful when comparing one technique to another. But for larger projects, only a profiler will do. Mozilla.org includes the Venkman profiler in the Mozilla browser distribution to help optimize your JavaScript.

The Venkman JavaScript Profiler

For more information on the Venkman profiler, see the following web sites:

- `http://mozilla.org/performance/jsprofiler.html`
- `http://www.hacksrus.com/~ginda/venkman/profiles/`

The Pareto Principle

Economist Vilfredo Pareto found in 1897 that about 80 percent of Italy's wealth was owned by about 20 percent of the population.[8] This has become the 80/20 rule or the Pareto principle, which is often applied to a variety of disciplines. Although some say it should be adjusted to a 90/10 rule, this rule of thumb applies to everything from employee productivity and quality control to programming.

Barry Boehm found that 20 percent of a program consumes 80 percent of the execution time.[9] He also found that 20 percent of software modules are responsible for 80 percent of the errors.[10] Donald Knuth found that more than 50 percent of a program's run time is usually due to less than 4 percent of the code.[11] Clearly, a small portion of code accounts for the majority of program execution time. Concentrate your efforts on these hot areas.

---

8. Vilfredo Pareto, *Cours d'économie politique professé à l'Université de Lausanne*, 2 vols. (Lausanne, Switzerland: F. Rouge, 1896-97).

9. Barry W. Boehm, "Improving Software Productivity," *IEEE Computer* 20, no. 9 (1987): 43-57.

10. Barry W. Boehm and Philip N. Papaccio, "Understanding and Controlling Software Costs," *IEEE Transactions on Software Engineering* 14, no. 10 (1988): 1462-1477.

11. Donald E. Knuth, "An Empirical Study of FORTRAN Programs," *Software—Practice and Experience* 1, no. 2 (1971): 105-133. Knuth analyzed programs found by sifting through wastebaskets and directories on the computer center's machines.

Algorithms and Data Structures

As we learn in computer science classes, global optimizations (such as algorithm and data structure choices) determine in large part the overall performance of our programs. For larger values of "n," or the number of input elements, the complexity of running time can dominate any local optimization concerns. This complexity is expressed in O-notation, where complexity or "order" is expressed as a function of n. Table 10.1 shows some examples.

Table 10.1   Run-Time Complexity of Classic Algorithms[12,13]

Notation	Name	Example
$O(1)$	constant	array index, simple statements
$O(\log n)$	logarithmic	binary search
$O(n)$	linear	string comparison, sequential search
$O(n\log n)$	$n\log n$	quicksort and heapsort
$O(n^2)$	quadratic	simple selection and insertion sorting methods (two loops)
$O(n^3)$	cubic	matrix multiplication of n×n matrices
$O(2^n)$	exponential	set partitioning (traveling salesman)

12. Kernighan and Pike, *The Practice of Programming*, 41.

13. Andrew Hunt and David Thomas, *The Pragmatic Programmer: From Journeyman to Master* (Boston, MA: Addison-Wesley, 1999), 179.

Array access or simple statements are constant-time operations, or $O(1)$. Well-crafted quicksorts run in *n*log*n* time or $O(n\log n)$. Two nested for loops take on the order of n×n or $O(n^2)$ time. For low values of n, choose simple data structures and algorithms. As your data grows, use lower-order algorithms and data structures that will scale for larger inputs.

Use built-in functions whenever possible (like the Math object), because these are generally faster than custom replacements. For critical inner loops, measure your changes because performance can vary among different browsers.

Refactor to Simplify Code

Refactoring is the art of reworking your code to a more simplified or efficient form in a disciplined way. Refactoring is an iterative process:

1. Write correct, well-commented code that works.

2. Get it debugged.

3. Streamline and refine by refactoring the code to replace complex sections with shorter, more efficient code.

4. Mix well, and repeat.

Refactoring clarifies, refines, and in many cases speeds up your code. Here's a simple example that replaces an assignment with an initialization. So instead of this:

```
function foo() {
    var i;
    // ....
    i = 5;
}
```

Do this:

```
function foo() {
    var i = 5;
    // ....
}
```

For More Information

Refactoring is a discipline unto itself. In fact, entire books have been written on the subject. See Martin Fowler's book, *Refactoring: Improving the Design of Existing Code* (Addison-Wesley, 1999). See also his catalog of refactorings at

```
http://www.refactoring.com/.
```

Minimize DOM Interaction and I/O

Interacting with the DOM is significantly more complicated than arithmetic computations, which makes it slower. When the JavaScript interpreter encounters a scoped object, the engine resolves the reference by looking up the first object in the chain and working its way through the next object until it finds the referenced property. To maximize object resolution speed, minimize the scope chain of objects. Each node reference within an element's scope chain means more lookups for the browser. Keep in mind that there are exceptions, like the window object, which is faster to fully reference. So instead of this:

```
var link = location.href;
```

Do this:

```
var link = window.location.href;
```

Minimize Object and Property Lookups

Object-oriented techniques encourage encapsulation by tacking sub-nodes and methods onto objects. However, object-property lookups are slow, especially if there is an evaluation. So instead of this:

```
for(var i = 0; i < 1000; i++)
    a.b.c.d(i);
```

Do this:

```
var e = a.b.c.d;
for(var i = 0; i < 1000; i++)
    e(i);
```

Reduce the number of dots (object.property) and brackets (object["property"]) in your program by caching frequently used objects and properties. Nested properties are the worst offenders (object.property.property.property).

Here is an example of minimizing lookups in a loop. Instead of this:

```
for (i=0; i<someArrayOrObject.length; i++)
```

Do this:

```
for (i=0, var n=someArrayOrObject.length; i<n; i++)
```

Also, accessing a named property or object requires a lookup. When possible, refer to the object or property directly by using an index into an object array. So instead of this:

```
var form = document.f2; // refer to form by name
```

Do this:

```
var form = document.forms[1]; // refer to form by position
```

Shorten Scope Chains

Every time a function executes, JavaScript creates an *execution context* that defines its own little world for local variables. Each execution context has an associated *scope chain* object that defines the object's place in the document's hierarchy. The scope chain lists the objects within the global namespace that are searched when evaluating an object or property. Each time a JavaScript program begins executing, certain built-in objects are created.

The *global object* lists the properties (global variables) and predefined values and functions (Math, parseInt(), etc.) that are available to all JavaScript programs.

Each time a function executes, a temporary *call object* is created. The function's arguments and variables are stored as properties of its call object. Local variables are properties of the call object.

Within each call object is the *calling scope*. Each set of brackets recursively defines a new child of that scope. When JavaScript looks up a variable (called *variable name resolution*), the JavaScript interpreter looks first in the local scope, then in its parent, then in the parent of that scope, and so on until it hits the global scope. In other words, JavaScript looks at the first item in the scope chain, and if it doesn't find the variable, it bubbles up the chain until it hits the global object.

That's why global scopes are slow. They are worst-case scenarios for object lookups.

During execution, only with statements and catch clauses affect the scope chain.

Avoid *with* Statements

The `with` statement extends the scope chain temporarily with a computed object, executes a statement with this longer scope chain, and then restores the original scope chain. This can save you typing time, but cost you execution time. Each additional child node you refer to means more work for the browser in scanning the global namespace of your document. So instead of this:

```
with (document.formname) {
field1.value =  "one";
field2.value = "two";...
}
```

Do this:

```
var form = document.formname;
form.field1.value = "one";
form.field2.value = "two;
```

Cache the object or property reference instead of using `with`, and use this variable for repeated references. `with` also has been deprecated, so it is best avoided.

Add Complex Subtrees Offline

When you are adding complex content to your page (like a table), you will find it is faster to build your DOM node and all its sub-nodes offline before adding it to the document. So instead of this (see Listing 10.1):

Listing 10.1   Adding Complex Subtrees Online

```
var tableEl, rowEl, cellEl;
var numRows = 10;
var numCells = 5;

tableEl = document.createElement("TABLE");
tableEl = document.body.appendChild(tableEl);
for (i = 0; i < numRows; i++) {
    rowEl = document.createElement("TR");
    for (j = 0; j < numCells;j++) {
        cellEl = document.createElement("TD");
```

continues

Listing 10.1   Adding Complex Subtrees Online   *continued*

```
            cellEl.appendChild(document.createTextNode("[row "+i+" cell "+j+ "]"));
            rowEl.appendChild(cellEl);
        }
        tableEl.appendChild(rowEl);
}
```

Do this (see Listing 10.2):

Listing 10.2   Adding Complex Subtrees Offline

```
var tableEl, rowEl, cellEl;
var numRows = 10;
var numCells = 5;

tableEl = document.createElement("TABLE");
for (i = 0; i < numRows; i++) {
    rowEl = document.createElement("TR");
    for (j = 0; j < numCells;j++) {
        cellEl = document.createElement("TD");
        cellEl.appendChild(document.createTextNode("[row " +i+ " cell "+j+"]"));
        rowEl.appendChild(cellEl);
    }
    tableEl.appendChild(rowEl);
  }
document.body.appendChild(tableEl);
```

Listing 10.1 adds the table object to the page immediately after it is created and adds the rows afterward. This runs much slower because the browser must update the page display every time a new row is added. Listing 10.2 runs faster because it adds the resulting table object last, via document.body.appendChild().

Edit Subtrees Offline

In a similar fashion, when you are manipulating subtrees of a document, first remove the subtree, modify it, and then re-add it. DOM manipulation causes large parts of the tree to recalculate the display, slowing things down. Also, createElement() is slow compared to cloneNode(). When possible, create a template subtree, and then clone it to create others, only changing what is necessary. Let's combine these two optimizations into one example. So instead of this (see Listing 10.3):

Listing 10.3   Editing Subtrees Online

```
var ul = document.getElementById("myUL");
for (var i = 0; i < 200; i++) {
    ul.appendChild(document.createElement("LI"));
}
```

Do this (see Listing 10.4):

Listing 10.4   Editing Subtrees Offline

```
var ul = document.getElementById("myUL");
var li = document.createElement("LI");
var parent = ul.parentNode;

parent.removeChild(ul);

for (var i = 0; i < 200; i++) {
    ul.appendChild(li.cloneNode(true));
}

parent.appendChild(ul);
```

By editing your subtrees offline, you'll realize significant performance gains. The more complex the source document, the better the gain. Substituting `cloneNode` instead of `createElement` adds an extra boost.

Concatenate Long Strings

By the same token, avoid multiple `document.writes` in favor of one `document.write` of a concatenated string. So instead of this:

```
document.write(' string 1');
document.write(' string 2');
document.write(' string 3');
document.write(' string 4');
```

Do this:

```
var txt = ' string 1' +
' string 2' +
' string 3' +
' string 4';
document.write(txt);
```

Access NodeLists Directly

NodeLists are lists of elements from object properties like `.childNodes` and methods like `getElementsByTagName()`. Because these objects are live (updated immediately when the underlying document changes), they are memory intensive and can take up many CPU cycles. If you need a NodeList for only a moment, it is faster to index directly into the list. Browsers are optimized to access node lists this way. So instead of this:

```
nl = document.getElementsByTagName("P");
for (var i = 0; i < nl.length; i++) {
    p = nl[i];
}
```

Do this:

```
for (var i = 0; (p = document.getElementsByTagName("P")[i]); i++)
```

In most cases, this is faster than caching the NodeList. In the second example, the browser doesn't need to create the node list object. It needs only to find the element at index i at that exact moment.

Use Object Literals

Object literals work like array literals by assigning entire complex data types to objects with just one command. So instead of this:

```
car = new Object();
car.make = "Honda";
car.model = "Civic";
car.transmission = "manual";
car.miles = 1000000;
car.condition = "needs work";
```

Do this:

```
car = {
    make: "Honda",
    model: "Civic",
    transmission: "manual",
    miles: 1000000,
    condition: "needs work"
}
```

This saves space and unnecessary DOM references.

Local Optimizations

Okay, you've switched to a better algorithm and revamped your data structure. You've refactored your code and minimized DOM interaction, but speed is still an issue. It is time to tune your code by tweaking loops and expressions to speed up hot spots. In his classic book, *Writing Efficient Programs* (Prentice Hall, 1982), Jon Bentley revealed 27 optimization guidelines for writing efficient programs. These code-tuning rules are actually low-level refactorings that fall into five categories: space for time and vice versa, loops, logic, expressions, and procedures. In this section, I touch on some highlights.

Trade Space for Time

Many of the optimization techniques you can read about in Bentley's book and elsewhere trade space (more code) for time (more speed). You can add more code to your scripts to achieve higher speed by "defactoring" hot spots to run faster. By augmenting objects to store additional data or making it more easily accessible, you can reduce the time required for common operations.

In JavaScript, however, any additional speed should be balanced against any additional program size. Optimize hot spots, not your entire program. You can compensate for this tradeoff by packing and compressing your scripts.

Augment Data Structures

Douglas Bagnall employed data structure augmentation in the miniscule 5K chess game that he created for the 2002 5K contest (`http://www.the5k.org/`). Bagnall used augmented data structures and binary arithmetic to make his game fast and small. The board consists of a 120-element array, containing numbers representing either pieces, empty squares, or "off-the-board" squares. The off-the-board squares speed up the testing of the sides—preventing bishops, etc., from wrapping from one edge to the other while they're moving, without expensive positional tests.

Each element in his 120-item linear array contains a single number that represents the status of each square. So instead of this:

```
board=[16,16,16,16,16,16,16,16,16,16,16,16,16,16,16,16,16,16,2,3,4,5,6,2,3,4,5,16,....]
```

He did this:

```
bstring="gggggggggggggggggggggg23456432gg11111111gg0000 ... g";
for (z=0;z<120;z++){
     board[z]=parseInt(bstring.charAt(z),35);
}
```

This base-35 value represents the squares on the board (parseInt using a radix of 35). As alpha "g" corresponds to 16 (the 5th bit; that is, bit 4), Bagnall says he actually could have used base-17 instead of 35. Perhaps this will leave room for future enhancements.

Each position on the board is encoded like this:

```
bit 4   (16): 0 = on board, 1 = off board.
bit 3    (8): 0 = white, 1 = black.
bits 0-2(7): 0 = empty, non-zero = the piece type:
```

```
1 - pawn
2 - rook
3 - knight
4 - bishop
5 - queen
6 - king
```

So to test the color of a piece, movingPiece, you'd use the following:

```
ourCol=movingPiece & 8;     // what color is it? 8=black, 0=white
      movingPiece &= 7;     // now we have the color info, dump it.
    if(movingPiece > 1){    // If it is not a pawn.
```

Bagnall also checks that the piece exists (because the preceding code will return white for an empty square), so he checks that movingPiece is non-empty. To see his code and the game in action, visit the following sites:

- http://halo.gen.nz/chess/

- http://halo.gen.nz/chess/main-branch/ (the actual code)

Cache Frequently Used Values

One of the most effective techniques you can use to speed up your JavaScripts is to cache frequently used values. When you cache frequently used expressions and objects, you do not need to recompute them. So instead of this (see Listing 10.5):

Listing 10.5 A Loop That Needs Caching and Fewer Evaluations

```
var d=35;
for (var i=0; i<1000; i++) {
    y += Math.sin(d)*10;
}
```

Do this (see Listing 10.6):

Listing 10.6 Caching Complex Calculations Out of a Loop

```
var d=35;
var math_sind = Math.sin(d)*10;

for (var i=0; i<1000; i++) {
    y += math_sind;
}
```

Because Math is a global object, declaring the math_sind variable also avoids resolving to a global object for each iteration. You can combine this technique with minimizing DOM interaction by caching frequently used object or property references. Simplify the calculations within your loops and their conditionals.

Store Precomputed Results

For expensive functions (like sin()), you can precompute values and store the results. You can use a lookup table (O(1)) to handle any subsequent function calls instead of recomputing the function (which is expensive). So instead of this:

```
function foo(i) {
    if (i < 10) {return i * i - i;}
}
```

Do this:

```
values = [0*0-0, 1*1-1, 2*2-2, ..., 9*9-9];

function foo(i) {
    if (i < 10) {return values[i];}
}
```

This technique is often used with trigonometric functions for animation purposes. A sine wave makes an excellent approximation of the acceleration and deceleration of a body in motion:

```
for (var i=1; i<=360; i++) {
    sin[i] = Math.sin(i);
}
```

In JavaScript, this technique is less effective than it is in a compiled language like C. Unchanging values are computed at compile time in C, while in an interpreted language like JavaScript, they are computed at runtime.

Use Local versus Global Variables

Reducing the scope of your variables is not only good programming practice, it is faster. So instead of this (see Listing 10.7):

Listing 10.7   Loop with Global Variable

```
function MyInnerLoop(){
    for(i=0;i<1000;i++);
}
```

Do this (see Listing 10.8):

Listing 10.8   Loop with Local Variable

```
function MyInnerLoop(){
    for(var i=0;i<1000;i++);
}
```

Local variables are 60 percent to 26 times faster than global variables for tight inner loops. This is due in part to the fact that global variables require more time to search up the function's scope chain. Local variables are properties of the function's call object and are searched first. Netscape 6 in particular is slow in using global variables. Mozilla 1.1 has improved speed, but this technique is relevant to all browsers. See Scott Porter's local versus global test at http://javascript-games.org/articles/local_global_bench.html.

Trade Time for Space

Conversely, you can trade time for space complexity by densely packing your data and code into a more compact form. By recomputing information, you can decrease the space requirements of a program at the cost of increased execution time.

Packing

Packing decreases storage and transmission costs by increasing the time to compact and retrieve the data. Sparse arrays and overlaying data into the same space at different times are two examples of packing. Removing spaces and comments are two more examples of packing. Substituting shorter strings for longer ones can also help pack data into a more compact form.

Interpreters

Interpreters reduce program space requirements by replacing common sequences with more compact representations.

Some 5K competitors (http://www.the5k.org/) combine these two techniques to create self-extracting archives of their JavaScript pages, trading startup speed for smaller file sizes (http://www.dithered.com/experiments/compression/). See Chapter 9, "Optimizing JavaScript for Download Speed," for more details.

Optimize Loops

Most hot spots are inner loops, which are commonly used for searching and sorting. There are a number of ways to optimize the speed of loops: removing or simplifying unnecessary calculations, simplifying test conditions, loop flipping and unrolling, and loop fusion. The idea is to reduce the cost of loop overhead and to include only repeated calculations within the loop.

Combine Tests to Avoid Compound Conditions

"An efficient inner loop should contain as few tests as possible, and preferably only one."[14] Try to simulate exit conditions of the loop by other means. One technique is to

---

14. Bentley, *Programming Pearls*, 192.

embed sentinels at the boundary of data structures to reduce the cost of testing searches. Sentinels are commonly used for arrays, linked lists, and binary search trees. In JavaScript, however, arrays have the length property built-in, at least after version 1.2, so array boundary sentinels are more useful for arrays in languages like C.

One example from Scott Porter of JavaScript-Games.org is splitting an array of numeric values into separate arrays for extracting the data for a background collision map in a game. The following example of using sentinels also demonstrates the efficiency of the switch statement:

```
var serialData=new;
Array(-1,10,23,53,223,-1,32,98,45,32,32,25,-1,438,54,26,84,-1,487,43,11);
var splitData=new Array();
function init(){
    var ix=-1,n=0,s,l=serialData.length;
    for(;n<l;n++){
        s=serialData[n];
        switch(s){  // switch blocks are much more efficient
            case -1 : // than if... else if... else if...
                splitData[++ix]=new Array();
                break;
            default :
                splitData[ix].push(s);
        }
    }
    alert(splitData.length);
}
```

Scott Porter explains the preceding code using some assembly language and the advantage of using the switch statement:

> "Here, -1 is the sentinel value used to split the data blocks. Switch blocks should always be used where possible, as it's so much faster than an if—else series. This is because with the if else statements, a test must be made for each "if" statement, whereas switch blocks generate vector jump tables at compile time so NO test is actually required in the underlying code! It's easier to show with a bit of assembly language code. So an if/else statement:
>
> ```
> if(n==12)
>     someBlock();
> else if(n==26)
>     someOtherBlock();
> ```

becomes something like this in assembly:

```
cmp eax,12;
jz     someBlock;
cmp eax,26;
jz     someOtherBlock;
```

Whereas a switch statement:

```
switch(a){
    case 12 :
        someBlock();
        break;
    case 26 :
        someOtherBlock();
        break;
}
```

becomes something like this in assembly:

```
jmp [VECTOR_LIST+eax];
```

where VECTOR_LIST would be a list of pointers to the address of the start of the someBlock and someOtherBlock functions. At least this would be the method if the switch were based on a numeric value. For string values I'd imagine eax would be replaced by a pointer to the location of a string for the comparison.

As you can see, the longer the if...else if... block became, the more efficient the switch block would become in comparison."[15]

Next, let's look at some ways to minimize loop overhead. Using the right techniques, you can speed up a for loop by two or even three times.

Hoist Loop-Invariant Code

Move loop-invariant code out of loops (otherwise called *coding motion out of loops*) to speed their execution. Rather than recomputing the same value in each iteration, move it outside the loop and compute it only once. So instead of this:

```
for (i=0;i<iter;i++) {
    d=Math.sqrt(y);
```

---

15. Scott Porter, email to author, 16 July 2002.

```
    j+=i*d;
}
```

Do this:

```
d=Math.sqrt(y);
for (i=0;i<iter;i++) {
    j+=i*d;
}
```

Reverse Loops

Reversing loop conditions so that they count down instead of up can double the speed of loops. Counting down to zero with the decrement operator (i--) is faster than counting up to a number of iterations with the increment operator (i++). So instead of this (see Listing 10.9):

Listing 10.9   A Normal for Loop Counts Up

```
function loopNormal() {
    for (var i=0;i<iter;i++) {
        // do something here
    }
}
```

Do this (see Listing 10.10):

Listing 10.10   A Reversed for Loop Counts Down

```
function loopReverse() {
    for (var i=iter;i>0;i--) {
        // do something here
    }
}
```

Flip Loops

Loop flipping moves the loop conditional from the top to the bottom of the loop. The theory is that the do while construct is faster than a for loop. So a normal loop (see Listing 10.9) would look like this flipped (see Listing 10.11):

Listing 10.11 A Flipped Loop Using do while

```
function loopDoWhile() {
var i=0;
do
{
    i++;
}
while (i<iter);
}
```

In JavaScript, however, this technique gives poor results. IE 5 Mac gives inconsistent results, while IE and Netscape for Windows are 3.7 to 4 times slower. The problem is the complexity of the conditional and the increment operator. Remember that we're measuring loop overhead here, so small changes in structure and conditional strength can make a big difference. Instead, combine the flip with a reverse count (see Listing 10.12):

Listing 10.12 Flipped Loop with Reversed Count

```
function loopDoWhileReverse() {
var i=iter;
do
{
    i--;
}
while (i>0);
}
```

This technique is more than twice as fast as a normal loop and slightly faster than a flipped loop in IE5 Mac. Even better, simplify the conditional even more by using the decrement as a conditional like this (see Listing 10.13):

Listing 10.13 Flipped Loop with Improved Reverse Count

```
function loopDoWhileReverse2() {
var i=iter-1;
do
{
    // do something here
}
while (i--);
}
```

This technique is over three times faster than a normal `for` loop. Note the decrement operator doubles as a conditional; when it gets to zero, it evaluates as false. One final optimization is to substitute the pre-decrement operator for the post-decrement operator for the conditional (see Listing 10.14).

Listing 10.14   Flipped Loop with Optimized Reverse Count

```
function loopDoWhileReverse3() {
var i=iter;
do
{
    // do something here
}
while (--i);
}
```

This technique is over four times faster than a normal `for` loop. This last condition assumes that i is greater than zero. Table 10.2 shows the results for each loop type listed previously for IE5 on my Mac PowerBook.

Table 10.2   Loop Optimizations Compared

	Normal	Do While	Reverse	Do While Reverse	Do While Reverse2	Do While Reverse3
Total time (ms)	2022	1958	1018	932	609	504
Cycle time (ms)	0.0040	0.0039	0.0020	0.0018	0.0012	0.0010

Unroll or Eliminate Loops

Unrolling a loop reduces the cost of loop overhead by decreasing the number of times you check the loop condition. Essentially, loop unrolling increases the number of computations per iteration. To unroll a loop, you perform two or more of the same statements for each iteration, and increment the counter accordingly. So instead of this:

```
var iter = number_of_iterations;

for (var i=0;i<iter;i++) {
    foo();
}
```

Do this:

```
var iter = multiple_of_number_of_unroll_statements;

for (var i=0;i<iter;) {
    foo();i++;
    foo();i++;
    foo();i++;
    foo();i++;
    foo();i++;
    foo();i++;
}
```

I've unrolled this loop six times, so the number of iterations must be a multiple of six. The effectiveness of loop unrolling depends on the number of operations per iteration. Again, the simpler, the better. For simple statements, loop unrolling in JavaScript can speed inner loops by as much as 50 to 65 percent. But what if the number of iterations is not known beforehand? That's where techniques like Duff's Device come in handy.

Duff's Device

Invented by programmer Tom Duff while he was at Lucasfilm Ltd. in 1983,[16] Duff's Device generalizes the loop unrolling process. Using this technique, you can unroll loops to your heart's content without knowing the number of iterations beforehand. The original algorithm combined a do-while and a switch statement. The technique combines loop unrolling, loop reversal, and loop flipping. So instead of this (see Listing 10.15):

Listing 10.15 Normal for Loop

```
testVal=0;
iterations=500125;

for (var i=0;i<iterations;i++) {
    // modify testVal here
}
```

---

16. Tom Duff, "Tom Duff on Duff's Device" [electronic mailing list], (Linköping, Sweden: Lysator Academic Computer Society, 10 November 1983 [archived reproduction]), available from the Internet at http://www.lysator.liu.se/ c/duffs-device.html. Duff describes the loop unrolling technique he developed while at Lucasfilm Ltd.

Do this (see Listing 10.16):

Listing 10.16   Duff's Device

```
function duffLoop(iterations) {

    var testVal=0;

    // Begin actual Duff's Device
    // Original JS Implementation by Jeff Greenberg 2/2001

    var n = iterations / 8;
    var caseTest = iterations % 8;

    do {
        switch (caseTest)
        {
        case 0: [modify testVal here];
        case 7: [ditto];
        case 6: [ditto];
        case 5: [ditto];
        case 4: [ditto];
        case 3: [ditto];
        case 2: [ditto];
        case 1: [ditto];
        }
        caseTest=0;
    }
    while (--n > 0);
}
```

Like a normal unrolled loop, the number of loop iterations (n = iterations/8) is a multiple of the degree of unrolling (8, in this example). Unlike a normal unrolled loop, the modulus (caseTest = iterations % 8) handles the remainder of any leftover iterations through the switch/case logic. This technique is 8 to 44 percent faster in IE5+, and it is 94 percent faster in NS 4.7.

Fast Duff's Device

You can avoid the complex do/switch logic by unrolling Duff's Device into two loops. So instead of the original, do this (see Listing 10.17):

Listing 10.17 Fast Duff's Device

```
function duffFastLoop8(iterations) {

// from an anonymous donor to Jeff Greenberg's site

    var testVal=0;
    var n = iterations % 8;
    while (n--)
    {
        testVal++;
    }

    n = parseInt(iterations / 8);
    while (n--)
    {
        testVal++;
        testVal++;
        testVal++;
        testVal++;
        testVal++;
        testVal++;
        testVal++;
        testVal++;
    }
}
```

This technique is about 36 percent faster than the original Duff's Device on IE5 Mac. Even better, optimize the loop constructs by converting the while decrement to a do while pre-decrement like this (see Listing 10.18):

Listing 10.18 Faster Duff's Device

```
function duffFasterLoop8(iterations) {

    var testVal=0;
    var n = iterations % 8;

    if (n>0) {
        do
        {
            testVal++;
        }
        while (--n); // n must be greater than 0 here
    }
```

continues

Listing 10.18   Faster Duff's Device   *continued*

```
    n = parseInt(iterations / 8);
    do
    {
        testVal++;
        testVal++;
        testVal++;
        testVal++;
        testVal++;
        testVal++;
        testVal++;
        testVal++;
    }
    while (--n);
}
```

This optimized Duff's Device is 39 percent faster than the original and 67 percent faster than a normal for loop (see Table 10.3).

Table 10.3   Duff's Device Improved

500,125 Iterations	Normal for Loop	Duff's Device	Duff's Fast	Duff's Faster
Total time (ms)	1437	775	493	469
Cycle time (ms)	0.00287	0.00155	0.00099	0.00094

How Much to Unroll?

To test the effect of different degrees of loop unrolling, I tested large iteration loops with between 1 and 15 identical statements for the Faster Duff's Device. Table 10.4 shows the results.

Table 10.4   Faster Duff's Device Unrolled

Duff's Faster	1 Degree	2	3	4	5	6	7
Total time (ms)	925	661	576	533	509	490	482
Cycle time (ms)	0.00184	0.00132	0.00115	0.00106	0.00101	0.00097	0.00096

Duff's Faster	8	9	10	11	12	13	14	15
Total time (ms)	469	467	457	453	439	437	433	433
Cycle time (ms)	0.00093	0.00093	0.00091	0.00090	0.00087	0.00087	0.00086	0.00086

As you can see in Table 10.4, the effect diminishes as the degree of loop unrolling increases. Even after two statements, the time to loop through many iterations is less than 50 percent of a normal for loop. Around seven statements, the time is cut by two-thirds. Anything over eight reaches a point of diminishing returns. Depending on your requirements, I recommend that you choose to unroll critical loops by between four and eight statements for Duff's Device.

Fuse Loops

If you have two loops in close proximity that use the same number of iterations (and don't affect each other), you can combine them into one loop. So instead of this:

```
for (i=0; i<j; i++) {
    sumserv += serv(i);
}

for (i=0; i<j; i++) {
    prodfoo *= foo(i);
}
```

Do this:

```
for (i=0; i<j; i++) {
    sumserv  += serv(i);
    prodfoo *= foo(i);
}
```

Fusing loops avoids the additional overhead of another loop control structure and is more compact.

Expression Tuning

As regular expression connoisseurs can attest, tuning expressions themselves can speed up things considerably. Count the number of operations within critical loops and try to reduce their number and strength.

If the evaluation of an expression is costly, replace it with a less-expensive operation. Assuming that a is greater than 0, instead of this:

```
a > Math.sqrt(b);
```

Do this:

```
a*a > b;
```

Or even better:

```
var c = a*a;
c>b;
```

Strength reduction is the process of simplifying expensive operations like multiplication, division, and modulus into cheap operations like addition, OR, AND, and shifting. Loop conditions and statements should be as simple as possible to minimize loop overhead. Here's an example from Listing 10.10. So instead of this:

```
for (var i=iter;i>0;i--)
```

Do this:

```
var i=iter-1;
do {} while (i--);
```

This technique simplifies the test condition from an inequality to a decrement, which also doubles as an exit condition once it reaches zero.

Miscellaneous Tuning Tips

You can use many techniques to "bum" CPU cycles from your code to cool down hot spots. Logic rules include short-circuiting monotone functions, reordering tests to place the least-expensive one first, and eliminating Boolean variables with if/else logic. You also can shift bits to reduce operator strength, but the speed-up is minimal and not consistent in JavaScript.

Be sure to pass arrays by reference because this method is faster in JavaScript. If a routine calls itself last, you can adjust the arguments and branch back to the top, saving the overhead of another procedure call. This is called *removing tail recursion.*

For More Information

For more tuning tips, see the following sites:

- `http://www.cs.bell-labs.com/cm/cs/pearls/apprules.html`—Jon Bentley's rules for code tuning.

- `http://www.refactoring.com/catalog/`—Martin Fowler's catalog of refactoring techniques.

- `http://home.earthlink.net/~kendrasg/info/js_opt/`—Jeff Greenburg's JavaScript speed-optimization tests.

- `http://www.xp123.com/xplor/xp0002d/`—William Wake's refactorings from Bentley's *Writing Efficient Programs.*

Flash ActionScript Optimization

Like JavaScript, ActionScript is based on the ECMAScript standard. Unlike JavaScript, the ActionScript interpreter is embedded within Macromedia's popular Flash plug-in and has different performance characteristics than JavaScript. Although the techniques used in this chapter will work for Flash, two additional approaches are available to Flash programmers. You can speed up Flash performance by replacing slower methods with the prototype command and hand-tune your code with Flasm.

continues

continued

Flasm is a command-line assembler/disassembler of Flash ActionScript bytecode. It disassembles your entire SWF file, allowing you to perform optimizations by hand and replace all actions in the original SWF with your optimized routines. See `http://flasm.sourceforge.net/#optimization` for more information.

You can replace slower methods in ActionScript by rewriting these routines and replacing the originals with the prototype method. The Prototype site (`http://www.layer51.com/proto/`) provides free Flash functions redefined for speed or flexibility. These functions boost performance for versions up to Flash 5. Flash MX has improved performance, but these redefined functions can still help.

Summary

To speed execution, optimize your code at the right design level or combination of levels. Start with global optimizations first (for example, algorithm and data structure choices), and then move down toward more local optimizations until your program is fast enough. Refactor to simplify your code, and then minimize DOM interaction and I/O requests. Finally, if all else fails, tune your code locally with the techniques outlined in this chapter. Measure each change, and cool hot spots one at a time. Here is a summary of the optimization techniques discussed in this chapter:

- Avoid optimization if at all possible.
- Optimize globally to locally until the code is fast enough.
- Measure your changes.
- Keep Pareto in mind.
- Cool hot spots one at a time.
- Minimize DOM and I/O interaction (object and property lookups, create and edit subtrees offline).
- Shorten scope chains to maximize lookup speed. Avoid `with` statements because they extend scope chains.

- Cache frequently used values.
- Simplify loop conditions, hoist loop-invariant code, flip and reverse, and unroll loops with an optimized Duff's Device.
- Use local optimizations last.
- Tune expressions for speed.

Recommended Reading

If you want to learn more about optimizing JavaScript, I recommend these sources:

- Jon Bentley's *Programming Pearls, 2nd ed.* (Addison-Wesley, 1999) and *More Programming Pearls: Confessions of a Coder* (Addison-Wesley, 1988). These books include many examples of code tuning and recap the 27 code-tuning rules in his out-of-print classic, *Writing Efficient Programs.*
- Brian Kernighan and Rob Pike's *The Practice of Programming* (Addison-Wesley, 1999) describes best programming practices, including Chapter 7 on performance.
- Donald Knuth's *The Art of Computer Programming* series (Addison-Wesley, 1998).
- Steve C. McConnell's *Code Complete: A Practical Handbook of Software Construction* (Microsoft Press, 1993), especially Chapters 28 and 29.

11

Case Study: DHTML.com

Now you can take what you learned in Chapter 9, "Optimizing JavaScript for Download Speed," and apply these techniques to a real-world example. To show you how effective JavaScript packing and compression can be, we'll crunch and compress an actual script from WebReference.com. Peter Belesis' popular hierarchical menus are available at WebReference.com, the site I founded (`http://www.webreference.com/dhtml/hiermenus/`). His menus use five files to account for different browsers (see Table 11.1).

Table 11.1   Original JavaScript Files

Filename	Size in Bytes
HM_Loader.js	3564
HM_Arrays.js	9950
HM_ScriptDOM.js	45623
HM_ScriptIE4.js	40014
HM_ScriptNS4.js	36956

The loader file loads two files, the menu arrays, and the appropriate browser API for a total of three HTTP requests. One quick optimization you can do is combine the arrays file with each browser file to save an HTTP request, like this (see Table 11.2).

Table 11.2   Combined JavaScript Files

Filename	Size in Bytes
HM_Loader.js	3564
HM_ScriptDOM_arrays.js	55573
HM_ScriptIE4_arrays.js	49964
HM_ScriptNS4_arrays.js	46906

Combining the menu arrays with each file trades maintenance costs for speed. If your site's navigation won't change very often, you can do this manually; otherwise, you could merge these programmatically on the server. To give you an idea of how effective packing and compression can be, let's optimize the size of the largest DOM file.

> **NOTE**
>
> Note that these files are well-commented and self-describing to make maintenance and teaching easier. This example shows you the kind of savings you can expect by optimizing well-written JavaScripts. Because of the way the loader.js file works, any compressed version of this file must be directly referenced in the page with the appropriate script API, using conditional logic. See Chapter 17, "Server-Side Techniques," for details.

Here's an excerpt of HM_ScriptDOM_arrays.hs before packing:

```
HM_Array1 = [

[150,,,

,,,,,,,,,,,,,,,

1,true],

["Experts","http://www.webreference.com/experts/",1,0,1],

["Contents","http://www.webreference.com/index2.html",1,0,0],
...
HM_MenuIDPrefix = "HM_Menu";

HM_ItemIDPrefix = "HM_Item";

HM_ArrayIDPrefix = "HM_Array";

Function.prototype.isFunction = true;

Function.prototype.isString = false;
```

```
String.prototype.isFunction = false;

String.prototype.isString = true;

String.prototype.isBoolean = false;

String.prototype.isNumber = false;

Number.prototype.isString = false;
...
if(HM_IE) {

        HM_a_ElementsCreated = [];

        function HM_f_StoreElement(el){

                HM_a_ElementsCreated[HM_a_ElementsCreated.length] = el;

        }

}
```

Here's that same excerpt after packing and manual abbreviation:

```
Array1=[
[150,,,
,,,,,,,,,,,,,,,
1,true],
["Experts","/experts/",1,0,1],
["Contents","/index2.html",1,0,0],
...
mp="Menu";ip="Item";ap="Array";Function.prototype.isf=true;Function.prototype.iss=false;
String.prototype.isf=false;String.prototype.iss=true;String.prototype.isb=false;
String.prototype.isn=false;Number.prototype.iss=false;...if(IE){a_ec=[];function
f_s(el){a_ec[a_ec.length]=el;}}
```

Packing the file to remove comments and whitespace saves 17 percent, reducing the file to 46,051 bytes. Manually packing to abbreviate variable and function names saves 52 percent, reducing from 55,573 to 26,870 bytes. Table 11.3 shows a summary of the packing and compressed file sizes.

Table 11.3 Packing and Compressed File Size Summary

File	Size	PACK	GZIP –9	PACK+GZIP
HM_ScriptDOM_arrays.js	55,573	26,870	10,655	7,808

Of course the file is all but indecipherable now, but it is less than half the size. GZIP compressing the original file saves over 80 percent in file size (from 55,573 to 10,655 bytes). Packing plus GZIP compression saves 86 percent, reducing from 55,573 to 7,808 bytes. By combining two files, and packing and compressing the combined file, you save one HTTP request and over 46K (86 percent) for the DOM-based code, a savings of over 10 seconds at 56Kbps.

Instead of loading two files totaling over 54K, you can send one 26K packed file or one 7,808 byte file by serving a combined, packed, gzipped file, which gives you a six-fold improvement in speed. Even without compression, you save over 50 percent in file size. These savings of 50 to 90 percent are typical for JavaScript files. Ideally, you'd eliminate the loading file by using either server-side sniffing or a client-side `document.write`. Packing with an automated program like ESC and compressing with mod_gzip would achieve similar results, but with less naming control.

IV

Graphics and Multimedia Optimization

12

Optimizing Web Graphics

This chapter shows you how to optimize your images to maximize visual quality and download speed. Images give the web pizzazz. They blink, they're bright, and they sometimes take flight (with the help of some DHTML). In fact, images are so popular, they make up the bulk of web page downloads, and determine a large part of the total download time of your pages.[1]

This chapter shows you how web graphics formats work and how you can take advantage of their compression algorithms to minimize file size. Graphics programs optimize the file size and quality of GIFs, JPEGs, and PNGs to varying degrees. Each has its own strengths and weaknesses. You'll realize the most savings in eliminating and replacing them with text and CSS, combining neighboring graphics, and reusing graphics with the same URLs.

Excluding network performance and hardware and software configurations, the size of your HTML "base" page and the number and size of your images and multimedia

---

1. Eric Siegel of Keynote Systems, email to author, 25 September 2002. The median KB40 site has over 50 percent graphics, and without JavaScript, over 60 percent. The average KB40 page size is over 93KB with the HTML portion averaging 33KB. The average page has a total of 24 embedded objects.

objects determines the display speed of your pages.[2] The base page size determines the initial download speed of your pages, while the embedded content determines the total download time. Because images and multimedia make up over 50 percent of the average web page, it is important to pay careful attention to the number and size of your images.

This chapter assumes that you already have some familiarity with web graphics formats. For more information, see *Designing Web Graphics 4* by Lynda Weinman (New Riders, 2003), and *Web Style Guide, 2nd ed.* by Patrick Lynch and Sarah Horton (Yale University Press, 2002) for an excellent introduction to web graphics. See also `http://www.webstyleguide.com/graphics/` for an online version of the graphics chapter of their book.

Capturing and Preparing Images

This section gives some guidelines that work with all types of images. The key to reducing image file size is to reduce the number of colors, resolution, dimension, and quality of your web-bound images. The art in graphics optimization is in balancing this size-versus-quality tradeoff. On the web, you can err on the low side of the quality scale. Here are a few general guidelines for preparing your graphics for the web:

- **When taking photographs**, minimize smear and maximize sharpness by using a stable platform, such as a tripod, image stabilizer, or gyroscopic stabilizer (`http://www.ken-lab.com`).

- **Simplify your designs** to remove extraneous detail, minimize colors, or work in grayscale for smaller images (see `http://www.the5k.org`).

- **Creatively crop** your images to reduce their size, or eliminate them altogether and replace them with text and CSS.

- **Minimize HTTP requests** by combining, reusing, and eliminating images where possible. Convert graphic text to styled text. Substitute styled backgrounds or table cells for graphic backgrounds.

- **Use thumbnails** to point to larger images to save bandwidth.

---

2. Jing Zhi, "Web Page Design and Download Time," *CMG Journal of Computer Resource Management*, no.102 (2001): 40–55.

Clean Up Your Image

Digital images that you capture with a digital camera or scan often need corrections. PhotoCD scans have their own characteristics (generally they are too dark, have a magenta cast, and don't use the entire tonal range), as do drum scans. To improve your photographs, you can manually tweak levels, saturation and contrast, and curves (see Figure 12.1).

Figure 12.1
Original scan before adjusting levels.

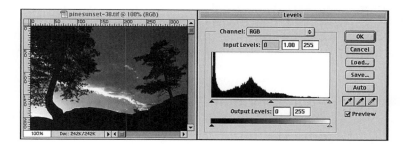

Notice that in the Levels dialog box of this PhotoCD slide scan, the full tonal range of the image is not being used. Adjust the dark, light, and mid-point of your image's levels (automatically or manually—see Figure 12.2), boost up the contrast and saturation, and crop maximally.

Figure 12.2
Final image after adjusting levels.

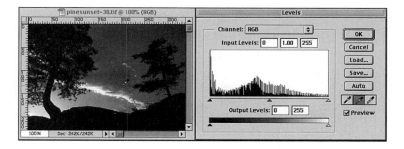

Make sure that your image is as clean and noise-free as possible before you compress it. Despeckle and remove dust and scratches if necessary and clean up any rough areas.

Or you can use tools like Intellihance (http://www.extensis.com) to automatically improve your digital images with predefined enhancements and input devices. In Intellihance, the PhotoCD and Digital Camera settings make quick work of correcting digitally captured images for the web.

> ### For More Information
>
> For more details on enhancing digital images for the web, see Wendy Peck's "Web Images that Pop" at `http://www.webreference.com/graphics/column49/`.

JPEG Optimization

JPEG is the compression algorithm used in JFIF (JPEG File Interchange Format) files, commonly known as JPEG. JPEG was designed by the Joint Photographic Experts Group to compress realistic true-color or grayscale images, such as photographs or fine artwork. It does not work well on scanned text, comic strip art, or line art because these have hard edges and areas of flat color, which are better suited for GIFs or PNGs.

JPEG supports 256 color grades (8 bit) per color channel. This equals 24 bits per pixel in color mode (16 million colors) and 8 bits per pixel in grayscale. Grayscale images are thus smaller than their full-color counterparts.

The JPEG format we use on the Internet is lossy. *Lossy* means that the compression algorithm discards data when compressing your image. After decompression, lossy formats are slightly different from the original. This is the price you pay for high compression ratios. JPEGs can compress the average color image about 20 times without visual quality loss. The exact savings depends on the complexity of the image. As the compression ratio approaches 50, it becomes more and more "defected."[3] Images compressed 100 times usually look pretty ugly, but the scene usually will still be recognizable. Compare this with lossless algorithms, which usually compress at 2:1 for these types of images.

JPEGs exploit several limitations of the human eye. First, our eyes are much more sensitive to small differences of brightness than to small differences in color, especially at higher frequencies. Second, larger image details are more important to us than smaller ones. The eye also ignores a little noise, which means that it can be added or removed.

---

3. Tom Lane, "The JPEG FAQ" [online], (1999), available from the Internet at `http://www.faqs.org/faqs/jpeg-faq/`.

The JPEG Compression Algorithm

JPEGs compress images based on their *spatial frequency,* or level of detail in the image. Areas with low levels of detail (smooth areas of color like clear sky or calm water) compress better than areas with high levels of detail (like sharp-edged leaves or grass). Hard-edged lines and abrupt color changes pose a challenge for JPEGs.

First, to take advantage of our lower sensitivity to higher chrominance frequencies versus higher luminance frequencies, the JPEG algorithm transforms the image from an RGB color space into the luminance/chrominance (Y-Cb-Cr) color space (see Figure 12.3). In other words, JPEG separates brightness or grayscale (Y) from the two hue or color components (Cb and Cr).

Figure 12.3
The JPEG compression
algorithm.

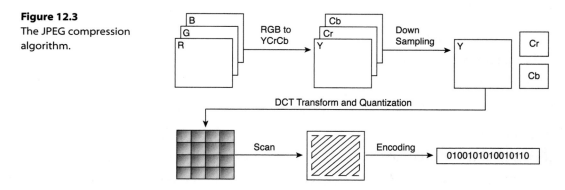

Then the algorithm leaves luminance alone and "downsamples" the chroma components 2:1 horizontally (either by discarding every second horizontal sample or averaging the two hue values into one) and 2:1 or 1:1 vertically, saving about one-half to one-third off the image data. This is often abbreviated as 4:2:2 or 4:1:1 sampling.

Next, the pixel values for each component are grouped into 8×8 blocks. These blocks then are transformed from the spatial domain to the frequency domain with a Discrete Cosine Transform (DCT), performed separately for brightness and both color parts. This step converts the image into a two-dimensional array of frequency coefficients. Coefficients in the top-left corner of each block represent the average of the block. Coefficients in the other corners represent higher frequencies (small details and noise). Higher frequencies can now be discarded without affecting lower ones.

Quantization occurs when the DCT coefficients are downsampled, and most coefficients become zero. This is the main source of information loss for JPEGs, and what makes compression more efficient. Each block of 64 frequency components is divided by a separate quantization coefficient and rounded to integer values. Higher frequencies and chroma are quantized by larger coefficients than lower frequencies and luminance. This is what you control with JPEG quality sliders—how much these blocks of frequencies are downsampled. Quantization tables can range from simple linear scaling from the JPEG standard to highly tuned, closely guarded secrets.

The last step is a zigzag scanning of each block starting from the top-left corner and lossless compression of non-zero coefficients with arithmetic or Huffman coding.

▷ **For More Information**

For more details on the JPEG algorithm, see `http://www.faqs.org/faqs/compression-faq/part2/section-6.html`.

Baseline and Progressive JPEG

In standard baseline mode, JPEGs store images as a single top-to-bottom scan. Browsers cannot show the image unless it has completely loaded. Progressive JPEG divides the image into a series of three to five scans. The first scan quickly displays a low-quality version of the image. Subsequent scans build up the image quality until the final image appears at full resolution.

Progressive JPEGs can become 1 to 4 percent larger than baseline files. They actually can become slightly smaller with Huffman encoding, however, because they allow different Huffman tables for each scan, which can make up for the overhead of the additional scans. For larger JPEGs, consider using progressive mode.

Note that current graphics programs are tuned for quality settings around 50 to 75 for progressive JPEGs.[4] At quality settings higher than 75 (or the equivalent), later scans

---

4. Lane, "The JPEG FAQ" [online].

add no appreciable quality to the image. Also keep in mind that JPEGs trade time for space. Progressive JPEGs add an additional load to the CPUs of your users. Each scan is like decoding a separate JPEG, so the overhead is a multiple of the number of scans. Over a network like the Internet, however, CPU speed is cheap compared to bandwidth.

Arithmetic Coding versus Huffman Coding

IBM, AT&T, and Mitsubishi hold a patent on the variant of arithmetic coding implemented in JPEG. Don't use arithmetic coding unless you have a license from these companies. Arithmetic coding provides 5 to 10 percent better compression than Huffman coding, but it is not worth the legal problems. Pegasus Imaging has a patented version of arithmetic coding, but it requires a plug-in.

Preparing JPEGs for Better Compression

Anything that smoothes, smears, lowers contrast, and blurs edges will increase compression for JPEGs. Try to minimize background details by using large apertures, telephoto lenses, panning, or blurring in your favorite graphics program.

Digital Cameras and JPEGs

Most digital cameras allow you to set the pixel resolution of your images. Some allow you to set the JPEG compression level, or use the EXIF format (JPEG with additional information like a thumbnail) or a lossless archive format like TIFF. Many authors simply upload JPEGs directly to the web from their digital cameras, however. The default settings are designed for creating prints, not for web pages. Be sure to optimize your digital images with the web in mind. The image resolution should be set to 72 dpi, with the lowest acceptable JPEG quality.

Scanners and PhotoCDs

Digital cameras provide higher-quality images than most scanners, even from good camera prints. Every generation you remove an image from the original loses definition and color saturation. High-quality scans from slides or negatives are an exception, however—especially drum scans. Drum scans give you the highest possible resolution and tonal range for larger prints. I had some 6×7cm slides drum scanned for some 30×40-inch prints. The resulting files approached 200MB. This is how some glossy magazines like *National Geographic Adventure* input their photographs.

PhotoCDs provide multi-resolution scans up to 2048×3072 pixels (18MB) for prints up to 20×30 inches in size. Pro PhotoCDs provide deeper shadow details plus a 4096×6144 (72MB) pixel scan. Photographers using 35mm cameras often choose PhotoCDs, while photographers using 120mm and 4×5 in cameras often scan their slides to Pro PhotoCDs. Unless you are running an art gallery, use the lower-resolution scans from PhotoCDs for the web. Choose a resolution about twice as large than you need, and reduce, correct, and sharpen it. See the "Capturing and Preparing Images" section in this chapter for more details on image correction.

Kodak's Picture CD provides a convenient way to process film and get a CD with your digitized images. Their Picture CD Select allows Kodak, AOL's "You've Got Pictures," or other photo site members to save selectively up to 200 images per CD. Services like Snapfish.com and Ofoto.com will develop your film, and create up to 1024×1536 pixel scans. This resolution is optimized to print on 8.5" × 11" paper. The lower-resolution scans (600×900, 280×420) usually are adequate for web use.

For More Information

For more information on scanning slides to PhotoCD and correcting images in Photoshop, see Philip Greenspun's "Adding Images to Your Site" at `http://philip.greenspun.com/panda/images.html`. See also Cornell's evaluation of PhotoCDs at `http://www.library.cornell.edu/preservation/kodak/kodak-htm.htm`.

Improving Compression and Apparent Resolution

Before you save the image, if you have a foreground feature like a human face or product and a less important background, blur the background. The fewer hard edges JPEGs have to deal with, the more efficient the compression. Some JPEG optimizers offer a "smoothing" or softening feature that also can improve compression by averaging nearby pixels.

For maximum quality, crop any borders around photographs. Borders can create visible artifacts in JPEGs and reduce display quality on older video cards.

Set the resolution to 72 dpi for the web. Then reduce its dimensions while maintaining the resolution and sharpen with an unsharp mask. Sharpening should be the last step in the correction process. Now you are ready to compress.

Saving JPEGs

Now that you've prepared your image for maximum compressibility, and cropped it down, it is time to compress. "Save for Web" in Photoshop brings up the dialog box shown in Figure 12.4.

Figure 12.4
Saving to a JPEG in Photoshop.

Do not use higher-quality values for the web. Usually raising quality above 80 percent of the quality range doesn't make any difference to our eyes, but it increases file size dramatically. There is no standard on the JPEG quality scale. Even though most tools today have a scale from 0 to 100 percent, when you set the same percent quality in different tools, you can expect very different file sizes.

If there are sharp color edges, it sometimes makes sense to turn downsampling off if you need the best quality (see Figure 12.5). Note that if you applied subsampling to the image in the figure, the sharp edges between colors in the lower part of the balloon would blur. The image is 28 percent larger, but it appears much sharper (6,824 versus 4,901 bytes).

Figure 12.5
Better image sampling
defines sharp edges in
ProJPEG.

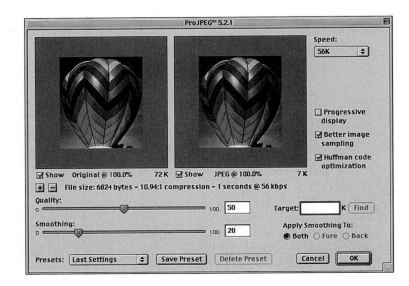

If you have sharp edges between colors and they are getting blurred, try turning off downsampling and see whether it helps. Be prepared for your file size to increase by about 50 percent, however. In most cases, you can turn subsampling off and boost quality and still have a smaller image. Your web page visitors would rather have smaller file sizes with slightly blurred edges than crystal-clear images that take longer to download.

If you have the original image at a high resolution and a scaled copy on your web site and you need to rescale the image, make it from the original. Remember that every time you recompress a JPEG, it accumulates quality loss. You can minimize this information loss by recompressing to the same quality first used.

In some situations, however, you can manipulate JPEGs losslessly. Lossless transforms (like 90-degree rotations and flips) require the dimensions of the JPEG to be a multiple of the block size (16×16, 16×8, or 8×8 pixels for color JPEGs). Lossless crops are also possible by cropping to block boundaries with specialized software. JPEG Wizard and others allow lossless JPEG transformations without losing image quality because they operate directly on the JPEG data without having to uncompress to do any editing (see Figure 12.6).

Figure 12.6
JPEG Wizard, a power tool for Windows.

Photoshop and Fireworks do a good job of compressing JPEGs; however, third-party tools often can give you higher-quality results and more options. There are a number of tools available, but JPEG Cruncher (`http://www.spinwave.com`), JPEG Wizard (`http://www.jpg.com`), ProJPEG (`http://www.boxtopsoft.com`), and Web Image Guru (`http://www.vimas.com`) in particular are good choices for JPEG compression. The first two offer online versions. All offer standalone applications or Photoshop plug-ins for convenience.

JPEG Wizard, ProJPEG, and Web Image Guru also offer regional compression to apply different degrees of compression to different areas. Web Image Guru allows finer control than the others with Color Tuning for controlling chrominance compression, Sharpness for artifacts and edges, and Subsampling controls.

Use Weighted Optimization

You can use the "regional" or "weighted" compression that Photoshop, Fireworks, and other products have by using an alpha channel mask to apply different compression settings to different areas of your image. This actually is a fudge that essentially discards the highest-frequency detail in the regions of the image that are less important. JPEGs produced using this technique are still compliant. JPEG2000 includes regional compression as part of the specification.

Text and JPEGs

Including text within JPEGs can be tricky. At higher-quality settings, this usually isn't a problem. But once you use more realistic settings for the web, artifacts can begin to show around sharp-edged text. One solution is to use a JPEG as a background image (say in a table cell) and a transparent aliased GIF in the foreground (see Figure 12.7).

By removing the text from this peaceful scene, I was able to bump up the JPEG quality, while still making the combined image smaller than the original (7,368 bytes versus 7,387 bytes for the original with embedded text). Of course, the tradeoff is another HTTP request for the GIF image. Here's the code to accomplish this overlay:

```
<td background="background.jpg" valign="top" width="300" height="240"><img src="label.gif"
width="300" height="26"></td>
```

Note that you can crop the GIF vertically and horizontally, but I used a full-width transparent GIF cropped vertically to ensure the cell width behaved. A faster way is to overlay styled text instead of a transparent GIF to avoid an HTTP request (see Figure 12.8). This looks nearly identical to Figure 12.7 and saves one HTTP request:

```
<td background="background25.jpg" valign="top" width="300" height="240" class="text">The
St. Lawrence</td>
```

Even better, use CSS to set the background image:

```
<style type="text/css">
    div#b {background-image: url(background25.jpg);
    width:300;height:240;
    font: 1.2em...}
</style></head><body>
<div id="b">The St. Lawrence</div>
```

Figure 12.7
GIF overlaid background JPEG—
6,985(JPEG)+383(GIF)=7,368
bytes.

Figure 12.8
Text overlaid JPEG—
7,233(JPEG)+16(Text)=7,249
bytes.

Each step in this process allows you to increase JPEG quality without increasing total file size.

> **NOTE**
>
> You can see all of these examples in full-color on the companion web site at WebSiteOptimization.com.

JPEG Optimization Summary

Optimizing JPEGs is a multi-step process. First, make sure that you capture the sharpest image possible at a higher resolution than you need. Blur the background and remove any borders for the highest possible quality. Correct and enhance the image, reduce by 50 percent, and sharpen to increase the apparent resolution. Set the resolution to 72 dpi for the web and compress with the right tools. Experiment with different settings, and use weighted optimization. In summary, to create the smallest possible JPEGs, do the following:

- Capture your photographs with high-quality digital or film-based cameras.

- Use a solid platform (tripod, image stabilization, or gyroscopic stabilizer) to minimize image smear and maximize sharpness.

- Blur backgrounds with large apertures, telephoto lenses, panning, or your favorite graphics program to minimize noise.

- Capture and scan at a higher resolution than you need, correct and enhance, halve its dimensions, and then unsharp mask to increase apparent resolution.

- To improve compression, smooth, smear, lower contrast, and blur edges. Remove any borders.

- Maximize crop and minimize dimensions.

- Avoid hard edges and lines. These are better suited to palette-based formats like GIF or PNG. Alternatively, you can overlay text or transparent images over background JPEGs.

- Maximize compression with the lowest acceptable quality.

- Use weighted optimization to apply compression selectively.

- Use the right tool and experiment—try subsampling, sharpening, smoothing, and optimized Huffman encoding.

- Save grayscale images to grayscale JPEGs.

- Minimize unnecessary information (comments and thumbnails).

GIF Optimization

GIF, or Graphics Interchange Format, is an indexed color image format created by CompuServe in 1987 (GIF87) and modified to support animation, transparency, and interlacing in 1989 (GIF89a).[5] GIFs have a maximum color bit-depth of 8, which stores

---

5. CompuServe, "Graphics Interchange Format—Version 89a," (GIF89a) [online], (1990), available from the Internet at http://www.w3.org/Graphics/GIF/spec-gif89a.txt.

a maximum of 256 colors. Indexed color images work well for buttons, bullet points, arrows, borders, and logos. They are not a good choice for photographs and 3D artwork.

Indexed color images consist of a palette table and matrix of palette indexes instead of RGB color values. The maximum palette size is 256 colors. There are several advantages of this approach:

- **File size**—The index is 8 bits per pixel while RGB values are 24 bits, so the image file becomes three times smaller.

- **Transparency**—In palette-based formats, one color can be declared as transparent. All the areas filled with this color will be transparent.

- **Better compression**—LZW- and deflate-based algorithms compress indexes much better than RGB values.

Palette-based images also have some disadvantages, however:

- RGB to indexed color conversion requires "color quantization." This process is lossy, because there is no way to convert 16 million colors to 256 without some loss.

- GIFs and PNGs use lossless compression algorithms. There is no way to sacrifice quality for the sake of file size besides palette reduction and raising redundancy along scanlines in programs like Photoshop (http://www.adobe.com) and Fireworks (http://www.macromedia.com) with their "lossy" GIF sliders.

LZW Compression

GIFs use LZW compression that looks for repeated pixel patterns along rows.[6] LZW is a member of the LZ78 class of algorithms, which substitute dictionary indexes for existing byte phrases.[7] The actual algorithm is a variable-length variant of the Lempel-Ziv (LZ)

---

6. Terry A. Welch, "A Technique for High-Performance Data Compression," *IEEE Computer* 17, no. 6 (1984): 8–19. The LZW algorithm described.

7. Jacob Ziv and Abraham Lempel. "Compression of Individual Sequences via Variable Rate Coding," *IEEE Transactions on Information Theory* 24, no. 5 (1978): 530–536. LZ78 described.

algorithm that substitutes variable-length codes (or tokens) for patterns detected in the data stream. The algorithm builds a translation table of patterns detected in the data stream. Each time a new pattern is found, it is entered into the table. Identical patterns are replaced by a table index. When these tokens are smaller than the phrase they replace, the file is compressed.

The initial size of each code or token is usually determined by the bit-depth of the image. Variable-length codes range from 3 to 12 bits each. This is one reason why smaller bit-depths result in smaller GIFs.

Minimize Bit-Depth

Being a palette-based format, the size of a GIF is directly related to the size of its palette, or the number of colors in the image. File size jumps each time you cross over a factor of 2, or 1 additional bit. A 65-color image must use a seven-bit palette, while a 64-color image can use a six-bit palette. Minimize the number of colors you use within GIFs to minimize file size.

Avoid antialiasing of text where possible because this adds more colors. Design your images with orthogonal and 45-degree lines.

For More Information

See the "Text and JPEGs" section and *Web Style Guide, 2ⁿᵈ ed.* for more details (http://www.webstyleguide.com). For some fonts specifically designed for monitor display, see http://www.minifonts.com.

Color Quantization

Color quantization is a fancy name for converting RGB images into indexed colors. There are several quantization algorithms. The first ones did not always work well, so graphics programs gave you a choice. Nowadays, they've figured out how to do it right, so programs don't ask you to choose anymore.

They do ask you, however, which palette to quantize to. Usually they offer standard palettes (Windows System, Mac System, and Web Safe), Selective, Adaptive, or "Web-snap Adaptive." Some tools also offer a Perceptual palette. This is a variation of the Selective palette adapted to the human eye. In some cases, the Perceptive palette works slightly better than the Selective or Adaptive palettes.

Influence Histograms

For smooth-toned images, you can influence the color palette Photoshop creates by first creating selection(s) over troublesome areas likely to create banding. When you convert from RGB to indexed color, these selections influence the color palettes produced by Photoshop. This makes it possible to optimize the color palette of images more precisely to minimize banding for GIFs and PNGs.

Minimize Dithering to Smooth Things Over

Color quantization can convert smooth color gradients into discernible bands of color. *Dithering* is the process of strategically mixing pixels to smooth out these edges. Dithering blends pixels of available colors to emulate colors eliminated from the original image by the color quantization process. Images with dithering usually look better, but dithering makes files bigger.

The LZW algorithm used in the GIF format looks for repeated patterns in pixels along horizontal scanlines. Anything that disturbs this regularity will increase file size. Certain types of dithering (such as pattern dithering) are more "regular" than others and therefore compress better in LZW. However, diffusion dithering usually looks better than pattern dithering.

A 32-color image with 100 percent dithering often has the same size as 64 colors image with no dithering. However, dithering allows you to use lower bit-depth images that can be smaller. Experiment with different settings. If an image looks bad without dithering, consider converting it to JPEG. Try to use as little dithering as possible to minimize file size (see Figure 12.9).

Figure 12.9
Full-color balloon quantized
to 64 colors in PhotoGIF (with
a dash of dithering).

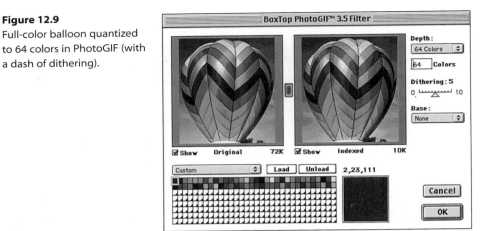

Dithered Transparency

First seen in Ulead's SmartSaver, dithered transparency allows you to simulate an alpha channel's partial opaqueness in GIFs. Dithered transparency disperses transparent pixels in the image so that the underlying image shines through. In ImageReady 7 and Web Image Guru 5, you can use dithered transparency to help blend GIFs seamlessly over background images.

Maximize Horizontal Redundancy and Flat Color Areas

To minimize the size of your GIFs, design them with the LZW algorithm in mind. LZW likes row upon row of large areas of flat color or the same pixel pattern. Avoid gradients (especially horizontal) and continuous-tone areas of color. Think horizontally when designing GIFs. IBM's logo is an excellent example of a compressible image. It has few colors and uses horizontal features.

The so-called "lossy" sliders in Photoshop and Fireworks increase horizontal redundancy by changing similar patterns into identical patterns and strategically rearranging and replacing pixels. This improves the compression efficiency of the LZW algorithm because there are fewer patterns to store. Low levels of lossy are hardly noticeable, but higher values can cause noticeable horizontal artifacts.

Consider Interlacing to Improve Perceived Speed

The GIF89a format supports interlacing. This feature quickly shows a lower-resolution version of the image and then gradually improves the resolution until the image is fully downloaded.

GIFs use a four-pass one-dimensional interlacing scheme, with the first pass displaying 1/8 (12.5 percent) of the image. Subsequent passes display 25, 50, and 100 percent of the image. The first pass stretches the pixels by a factor of 8, the second by a factor of 4, and so on.

Interlacing can increase the file size of GIFs by 5 to 15 percent. Interlacing doesn't make sense for smaller images. For larger GIFs, consider interlacing for imagemaps and the like to give users something to interact with quickly. Don't interlace animated GIFs, unless you want to annoy your users. For minimum file size, avoid interlacing indexed formats.

Use Weighted Optimization

Like JPEGs, you can use alpha masks to apply different degrees of optimization to different parts of your image. In Photoshop or Fireworks, create an alpha channel mask to select areas where you want to apply different optimization levels. You can selectively reduce colors, apply dithering, and impart lossiness to fine-tune your optimization for different areas of your image.

Browser Issues

A few older PCs still work in 256-color mode.[8] In these older machines, the browser converts all the images to the local palette. If an image contains colors not in the local palette, the browser may apply dithering. For large areas filled with the same color, dithering can be pretty noticeable. To avoid this problem, fill large areas of flat color with non-dithering colors that will be in the browser's local palette.

---

8. Only three percent of client PCs have 256 colors or less as of September 2002.
   Source: http://thecounter.com/stats/

There are 216 so-called "web-safe" colors that are always present in the palette of most web browsers. The R, G, and B values happen to be multiples of 20 percent, or 51 in decimal, and 33 in hex. So any combination of 00, 33, 66, 99, cc, and ff are web-safe colors. 216 colors (a 6×6×6 color cube) cover all the possible combinations. In the past, I would have recommended using this restricted set of colors for palette-based images. However, because most client PCs (97 percent and growing) now have 65,000 colors or higher, the non-dithering palette may go the way of the dinosaur.

There is one caveat, however. A client PC can display its bit-depth only for the entire screen, including all the windows and images it displays. If you have a full-color image in one window and an image with a different palette in another window, the second image can still experience some color shifting or dithering. If you want to avoid any possibility of dithering—either for the three percent of users with 8-bit displays or for those times you're working with images that have different palettes—coordinate your palettes and use web-safe colors where possible.

JPEGs are true-color images, so many authors adopt a hybrid approach letting JPEGs dither for the few users with older machines, and using non-dithering colors for GIFs, PNGs, and background colors. For more information on color palettes, see Chapter 7, "CSS Optimization."

GIF Optimization Summary

The best way to optimize GIFs is to design them to make the LZW algorithm happy. You can help LZW along by designing your GIFs to include horizontal features that repeat and maximizing flat areas of color. Reduce bit depth, use the appropriate palette, and limit the amount of dithering you use. Avoid antialiased text because it increases the number of necessary colors. In summary, to optimize GIFs, do the following:

- Minimize bit depth and maximize cropping.

- Maximize flat areas and similar row patterns (use "lossy" and "smoothing" sliders).

- Consider interlacing larger GIFs, to give a preview (but don't interlace animated GIFs!).

- Avoid antialiased text and convert graphic text to styled text wherever possible.

- Use 72 dpi resolution.

- Use a high-quality quantizer to minimize banding and minimal dithering to smooth things over.

- Influence histograms where possible to optimize custom palettes and minimize banding.

- Remove embedded comments.

- Use short, descriptive alt attributes for functional images, and blanks for spacer images.

Optimizing Animated GIFs

An animated GIF (or the GIF89a format) is just a set of indexed-color GIFs with embedded timing and looping information. This means that everything applicable to GIF optimization also applies to animated GIFs.

Working with animation gives you some animation-specific tricks because of the multiple frames and various disposal methods that you can choose. As far as timing goes, avoid infinite loops and short cycle times because they strain CPUs and can distract and annoy your users.

First, you don't have to make all the frames as big as the image size. The first one can become a "key" frame, and the others can be smaller and offset within the "logical screen."[9] This allows the image to be composited onto the screen, leaving non-image pixels alone. Resizing them down to the size of the area that has actually changed is an inter-frame technique that improves compressibility because there are fewer pixels to compress.

Second, if part of the frame is identical to the background, make it transparent. Because more pixels have the same color, the odds of longer runs of that color improve; hence, it tends to be more compressible.

---

9. CompuServe, "Graphics Interchange Format" [online].

The GIF89a format supports multiple palettes. You can have an individual palette for each frame. Sometimes it makes sense to use a global palette, and sometimes it is better to create a local one. Smaller palettes provide better compression for two reasons:

- The palette itself consumes less space.
- Fewer bits are needed to represent the image color indices so the GIF codes start out at a smaller bit length.

Because they are built with multiple GIFs, animated GIFs allow *inter-frame* optimization. Some older programs use minimum bounding box inter-frame optimization that offsets a smaller box surrounding the pixels that change within the "logical screen" of the image. Many graphics programs use *frame differencing*, in which only the pixels that change from frame to frame are preserved. The pixels identical to the previous frame are set to the transparent color within the bounding box, leaving only the pixels that change.

Finally, the best optimization programs take frame differencing one step further. They perform run-length *intra-frame* optimization by equalizing run-lengths of some differenced lines to help the LZW algorithm better optimize the composite GIF89a. Intra-frame optimization provides up to two percent better compression than frame differencing.

Many tools optimize GIF animations automatically. Look for tools that provide intra-frame optimization for better compression. GIFMation and SuperGIF (`http://www.boxtopsoft.com`), GIFWizard.com, Fireworks (`http://www.macromedia.com`), and WebPainter (`http://www.totallyhip.com`) provide intra-frame optimization.

For More Information

For more details, see Andy King's "Optimizing Animated GIFs" article at `http://www.webreference.com/dev/gifanim/`.

Optimizing Animated GIFs Summary

In summary, for the smallest animated GIFs, do the following:

- Use the same techniques you use for GIFs (minimize bit depth, maximize cropping).
- Minimize the number and size of frames.
- Use intra-frame optimizers and horizontal movements.
- Use regional bit-depth reduction (be selective by surrounding flatter areas).
- Use lossy GIF sliders (Fireworks MX).
- Remove comments.

PNG Optimization

PNG, or Portable Network Graphics, supports indexed, true-color up to 48-bit RGB, and grayscale modes.[10] I don't recommend using true-color PNGs on web pages, although they are excellent for archiving original images, and some programs (such as Fireworks) use them as their main file format.

Because most PNGs used on the web are in index-color mode, many of the same techniques you learned in the "GIF Optimization" section apply to optimizing PNGs. Influencing histograms, weighted optimization, and minimizing bit depth all work on PNGs as well as GIFs.

Deflate Compression for PNGs

PNGs use the "deflate" compression algorithm typically with a 32KB sliding window (PNG decoders can handle window sizes as small as 512 bytes). Deflate is a newer, more efficient cousin of LZW, which is designed to be free of patent problems.

---

10. Thomas Boutell, ed., "PNG (Portable Network Graphics) Specification, Version 1.0," [online], (1996), available from the Internet at http://www.w3.org/TR/REC-png.

Deflate is a variant of the LZ77 algorithm used in zip programs like WinZip, PKZip, ZipIt, and gzip.[11,12] Originally created by Phil Katz for version 2 of his PKZip tool, Deflate combines LZ77 with Huffman coding. Deflate typically compresses files 20 to 30 percent more than LZW, which is the same difference you'll find between gzip and compress on Unix systems, and PKZip 1 and PKZip 2 on Windows.

Some PNG compression tools have an optional "compression ratio" with values ranging from one to nine. Six is the default. Nine is almost always the best setting; it will save you a few percent off your file size. This is similar to the compression settings for gzip compression you will read about in Chapter 18, "Compressing the Web." Pngcrush can help you find near-optimal settings for PNGs and outputs somewhat cryptic diagnostics on which settings work best (http://pmt.sourceforge.net/pngcrush).

Minimize Bit-Depth

Like GIFs, PNGs are a palette-based format. The size of PNGs is directly related to the size of the color palette. Try to stay under powers of two when reducing colors. PNG palettes also can be truncated, although GIF palettes are always a factor of two.

Avoid Interlaced PNGs

PNGs use a seven-pass two-dimensional interlacing scheme, with the first pass displaying 1/64 of the image data. PNG's superior two-dimensional interlacing scheme only stretches pixels by 2 on the first pass. Greg Roelofs estimates that embedded text is readable approximately twice as fast in an interlaced PNG versus a GIF (see http://www.libpng.org/pub/png/pngintro.html).

PNG's creators claim that interlacing "slightly expands the file size on average,"[13] although the increase can be as large as 20 to 35 percent. For this reason, I don't recommend interlacing PNGs unless the increase in file size is small.

---

11. L. Peter Deutsch, "DEFLATE Compressed Data Format Specification Version 1.3," RFC 1951 [online], (Alladin Enterprises, 1996), available from the Internet at http://www.ietf.org/rfc/rfc1951.txt.

12. Jacob Ziv and Abraham Lempel, "A Universal Algorithm for Sequential Data Compression," *IEEE Transactions on Information Theory* 23, no. 3 (1977): 337–343.

13. Boutell, "PNG Specification" [online].

Transparency Gotchas

Transparency is often essential to make web sites look professional. There are two types of transparency:

- Transparent color-based, for indexed color images
- Alpha channel-based, for full-color images

GIF supports the first type—every pixel can be either transparent or not. PNG supports transparent color-based transparency for indexed color mode and alpha channel for true-color mode. With alpha channel, every pixel can have an individual level of opaqueness. Alpha channels can make a web designer's life easier, but what about file size and browser compatibility?

File size is not an issue; alpha channels usually don't make the file much larger.

Browser compatibility is an issue, however. Mozilla and Netscape support PNGs with alpha channels (see Figure 12.10), but Internet Explorer 6 does not (see Figure 12.11). That is why I do not yet recommend using transparent PNG images on web pages.

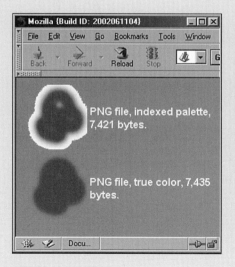

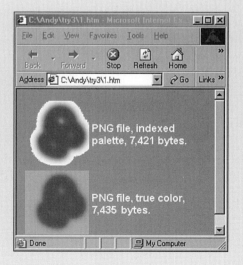

Figure 12.10
Transparent PNG in Mozilla 1.1.

Figure 12.11
Transparent PNG in Internet Explorer 6.

Use Filters for Better Compression

PNGs can run image data through a series of filters to make them more compressible. PNG runs your image data, scanline by scanline, through one of five filters (Sub, Up, Average, Paeth, and Adaptive). Each scanline can begin with a different filter type byte, allowing adaptive filtering. Up, Average, and Paeth filters work in two dimensions, and the others work in one dimension. Indexed color PNGs (8 bits or less) usually do not benefit from filtering, so use "none" when there is a choice. For true-color or grayscale images, use Adaptive.

For all formats, make sure that your original is as clean as possible. Run any necessary filters (despeckle, dust, and scratches), and manually remove any remaining stray pixels with cloning tools.

PNG versus GIF

An image with the same palette and dithering will usually have a similar size as a GIF or a PNG. Many times PNGs will be 5 to 25 percent smaller, but sometimes they can be larger. Table 12.1 shows file sizes created by different tools using the same image (see Figure 12.12). All the files are in non-interlace mode and have the same 16-color palette.

Figure 12.12
Optimizing a sample web image—a toolbar.

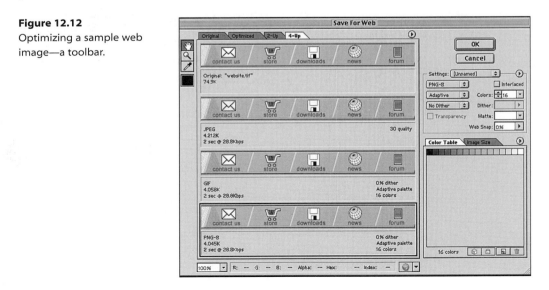

Table 12.1 Comparing GIF and PNG: Tools and File Sizes (Bytes)

Tool	GIF	PNG
ImageReady 7	4,155	4,142
Fireworks MX	3,932	3,246
Web Image Guru 4	3,973	3,076
IrfanView 3.75	4,540	3,635
Pngcrush	N/A	3,076 (from WIG)

As you can see, different programs create different file sizes for GIFs and PNGs. PNGs are usually smaller than GIFs, but this is true only when they are created with the proper tool. Table 12.2 shows how the first three programs fare with our worst-case quantization scenario test balloon for both Perceptive and Adaptive palettes.

Table 12.2 Quantizing a Full-Color Balloon into GIF and PNG (in Bytes)

Tool	GIF (Perceptive/Adaptive)	PNG (Perceptive/Adaptive)
ImageReady 7	9,121/9,301	9,740/9,934
Fireworks MX	N/A /9,584	N/A /8,085
Web Image Guru 4	10,152/9,878	8,371/8,210
Pngcrush	N/A	8,094 (from FWMX)

> **NOTE**
>
> Note that the Perceptive palette gave better results, but only Adaptive was available on all programs. Note also that Pngcrush, which can reduce existing PNGs, could not reduce Web Image Guru's PNG any further, and actually made the PNG created by Fireworks MX slightly larger than our test balloon.

Fireworks and Web Image Guru created smaller PNGs than ImageReady, and ImageReady actually created larger PNGs than GIFs. The Perceptual palette created the least banding for this smooth-toned image. ImageReady and Web Image Guru created the best-quantized GIFs, although ImageReady's version was smaller. Guru's unique smoothing feature (available for GIFs, JPEGs, and PNGs) improved the image even further (see Figure 12.13). Web Image Guru from VIMAS combines all web formats into one filter. It offers fine-grained control, including seven filters for GIFs, JPEGs, and PNGs.

Figure 12.13
Web Image Guru in action—
smoothing a GIF in Windows.

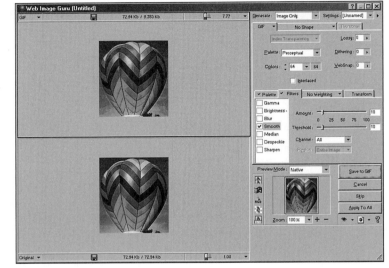

PNG Optimization Summary

Because GIF and PNG are both palette-based formats, many of the same techniques you learned in the "GIF Optimization" section also work on PNGs. Because PNGs use a similar dictionary-based algorithm with one- and two-dimensional filters, the strategy for PNGs is a little different. Maximize horizontal and vertical pixel pattern redundancy, remove noise (common after resizing), and use 8-bit or smaller PNGs for web use. Here's a summary of PNG optimization tips:

- Maximize horizontal redundancy (and vertical redundancy, for full-color PNGs).

- Remove any noise, and remove stray pixels in flat areas.

- Use 8-bit PNGs (or lower), not 24-bit PNGs.

- Reduce bit-depth and maximize cropping.

- Avoid interlaced PNGs—use only for larger PNGs with similar file sizes.

- Use the maximum compression available (9).

- Use grayscale where possible.

- Use Pngcrush for maximum compression.

Download Time: Packet Count versus Page Size

After you've optimized your images for size and grouped them (or better yet, replaced them with text and CSS), there is one more thing you can do: Fit them into packet-sized chunks. Keep in mind that this is an extreme technique to be used only if you want to achieve the absolute maximum speed for your pages.

As a packet-based network, the Internet is designed for redundancy and reliability. Resources are divided into packets and routed to their destination, where they are reassembled. If a backhoe severs a fiber-optic line somewhere in New Jersey, the packets happily reroute themselves around the problem.

Packet sizes are negotiated between browser and server at connection time. The maximum transmission unit (MTU), or the size of a packet, is typically between 576 and 1,500 bytes depending on connection speed. On low-speed connections (less than 56Kbps) in older machines, packet sizes can be 576 bytes and higher. For low-speed connections, multithreading is a minor factor for performance tuning. In this case, total page size and the number and size of external objects (including graphics) determines download speed.

On faster connections (more than 128Kbps), it is the total number of TCP/IP packets (typically 1,500 bytes) that your content takes to send that directly affects download time. With low-speed connections, the pipe usually is filled and browser threads are few. For higher-speed connections, the pipe usually is not fully utilized, and you can keep more browser threads active. The limit then becomes not the pipe, but how many packets you can send with how many threads. However, even on unrestricted lines, "the benefits of multithreading are eventually outweighed as the number of images—and thus the likelihood of complications—increases."[14]

---

14. Jing Zhi, "Web Page Design and Download Time," *CMG Journal of Computer Resource Management*, no. 102 (2001): 40–55. Available from the Internet at http://www.keynote.com/solutions/assets/applets/Web_Page_Design_and_Download_Time.pdf. Zhi, of Keynote Systems, found that for fast connections (> 128Kbps) after TCP slow start, download time is nearly linearly related to the number of packets sent, which is determined by the size of each file and packet size. Four or more equal-sized images downloaded faster than one large image due to browser multithreading. For slower connections, download time was dependent on total content size and the number of objects.

With a TCP/IP overhead of 40 bytes, this gives an effective payload of 1,460 bytes for each packet for faster connections. When a server first answers a client request, the HTTP response header adds another 250 to 300 bytes. So the first packet sent for each object is around 1,160 to 1,210 bytes, while subsequent packets are 1,460 bytes in size. Zhi found that for higher-speed connections, it is the number of packets sent—not content size—that is a better determinant of download speed.

Try to reduce each graphic (or external file) to fit into one or more packet multiples. On higher-speed connections, files larger than around 1,160 bytes will "spill over" into the next packet, requiring twice the time to send, even though they may be only a few percent larger. So keep packet size in mind while you are designing graphics and external objects like .js and .css files. This dependence on packet count versus page size will become more important as bandwidth inevitably increases.

The best strategy is to minimize HTTP overhead (which can be substantial) by minimizing the overall size of your page and the number and size of embedded external objects.

On the Horizon: JPEG2000 and Vector-Based Graphics

Two types of graphic formats on the horizon look promising: JPEG2000 and vector-based graphics.

The new JPEG2000 format is designed to be a superior replacement for the popular JPEG format. The JPEG2000 format uses wavelet technology to achieve higher compression ratios with radically reduced artifacts. The JPEG2000 format can compress images to 100:1 ratios or higher with much less image degradation than JPEGs. JPEG2000 also has a lossless compression option that typically achieves 3:1 to 4:1 compression. The JPEG2000 specification has been approved, but we won't see widespread use of this image format until browsers embed a JPEG2000 decompressor within their code.

Vector-based formats are much more efficient for displaying graphics on the web. Flash is ubiquitous, and it typically creates animations 10 times smaller than animated GIFs. Scalable Vector Graphics is the W3C's standards-based answer to Flash. These vector-based graphical formats can help reduce the footprint of images on the web, but can require plug-ins. For Flash optimization techniques, see Chapter 13, "Minimizing Multimedia," and Chapter 10, "Optimizing JavaScript for Execution Speed."

Graphics Tools

There are too many tools to list them all here. The following list includes only tools with PNG support. Most of them support GIF and JPEG as well.

- Viewers: http://www.libpng.org/pub/png/pngapvw.html
- Editors: http://www.libpng.org/pub/png/pngaped.html
- Converters: http://www.libpng.org/pub/png/pngapcv.html

The most popular of these are listed here:

- ACDSEE: http://www.acdsystems.com
- Macromedia Fireworks: http://www.macromedia.com
- Adobe Photoshop and ImageReady: http://www.adobe.com
- IrfanView: http://www.irfanview.com/
- JPEG Cruncher and GIF Cruncher from Spinwave: http://www.spinwave.com/
- JPEG Wizard etc. from Pegasus Imaging: http://www.jpg.com
- ProJPEG, PhotoGIF, GIFMation, SuperGIF, and other tools from BoxTop Software: http://www.boxtopsoft.com/
- Web Image Guru (GIF, JPEG, and PNG optimization) from VIMAS: http://www.vimas.com/

Summary

The key to optimizing web graphics is to minimize their size, number, and quality, and maximize cropping. Combine adjacent images and use client-side imagemaps instead. Substitute CSS-based rollovers for bandwidth-hungry image-based rollovers. Replace graphic text with styled text. Finally, to minimize HTTP requests, reuse images with the same URL.

For palette-based formats, each reduction in bit-depth gives an abrupt drop in file size. When reducing smooth-toned images, use a high-quality quantizer and a dash of dithering, influence histograms, or consider switching to a JPEG. Avoid antialiasing in GIFs and PNGs to minimize color palettes. Design GIFs and PNGs with the horizontal in mind. Maximize pixel patterns along scanlines and use the "lossy" slider in Photoshop and Fireworks for GIFs to increase redundancy to maximize LZW compression.

Design animated GIFs to have small horizontal motion areas with few frames and limited loops. Optimize animated GIFs with programs that offer intra-frame optimization for maximum compression.

With all graphics, you can't go wrong if you do the following:

- Eliminate and combine your images to minimize HTTP requests.
- Convert graphic text into styled text.
- Maximize cropping and minimize dimensions.
- Use the right image format (JPEGs for photographs).
- Use interlacing with care (avoid interlacing on smaller images and most PNGs).
- When capturing photographs, use a stable platform.
- Minimize noise, smear, and complexity.
- Use weighted optimization to reduce less important areas and blur backgrounds (for JPEGs).
- Minimize colors (bit-depth) for palette-based formats.
- Use a high-quality quantizer on true-color originals and limit dithering.
- Set your image resolution to 72 dpi.

- Specify the actual `height` and `width` of all images.
- Use grayscale where possible.
- Use thumbnails linked to larger images.
- Experiment with different settings and programs.

Further Reading

For more information on web graphics formats and optimization, see the following resources:

- Graphics.com (`http://www.graphics.com`)—News, reviews, and information on the graphics world.
- DeskTopPublishing.com (`http://www.desktoppublishing.com`)—One of the oldest and largest resources for artists and web designers.
- "Optimizing Web Graphics" by Andy King (`http://www.webreference.com/dev/graphics/`)—Tools and techniques you can use to shrink web graphics. Originally appeared in the December 1996 issue of *Web Techniques*.
- *Compressed Image File Formats: JPEG, PNG, GIF, XBM, BMP* by John Miano (Addison-Wesley, 1999)—Boils down the specifications into understandable language. Focuses on JPEG and includes C code.
- *PNG: The Definitive Guide* by Greg Roelofs (O'Reilly, 1999)—The ultimate reference for the PNG format, which includes some optimization tips for authors and programmers.
- *Web Designer's Guide to Graphics: PNG, GIF, & JPEG* by Timothy Webster, Paul Atzberger, and Andrew Zolli (Hayden Books, 1997)—Although somewhat dated, this full-color book shows you how to create quality graphics that download quickly.

13

Minimizing Multimedia

by Jason Wolf

In this chapter, you'll learn how to optimize both the size and the speed of your multimedia content to help deliver your message to your target audience. Multimedia combines audio, video, text, graphics, and animation into an interactive experience. According to recent studies, multimedia is playing a larger role in overall Internet traffic.

Multimedia Dominates Traffic, Film at 11

Most streaming-media files are low in bit-rate (less than 56Kbps), small in size (less than 1MB), and short in duration (under 10 minutes). However, a small fraction (3 percent) of streaming media is responsible for nearly half of this traffic.[1] P2P traffic is also on the rise. At a study at the University of Washington in May 2002, peer-to-peer traffic (mainly video) consumed three times the bandwidth of WWW traffic.[2]

---

1. Maureen Chesire, Alec Wolman, Geoffrey M. Voelker, and Henry M. Levy, "Measurement and Analysis of a Streaming-Media Workload," in *Proceedings of the Third USENIX Symposium on Internet Technologies and Systems* (Berkeley, CA: USENIX Association, 2001).
2. Stefan Saroiu et al., "An Analysis of Internet Content Delivery Systems," in *Proceedings of the 5th Symposium on Operating Systems Design and Implementation (OSDI)* (Berkeley, CA: USENIX Association, December 2002).

Multimedia applications allow you to create engaging interactive experiences. Remember, the tricky part is not creating your content but delivering your content efficiently.

Multimedia Basics

This section introduces you to some fundamental multimedia concepts. Learning these concepts is a necessary starting point from which to build. You can think of multimedia as a collection of many different forms of data types (file formats) that are all used together to give the audience a richer, potentially interactive experience.

Web Multimedia Datatypes

Before you can understand the process and procedures behind efficiently delivering your multimedia, you first need to understand the strengths and weaknesses of the various multimedia file types you will encounter on the web. Let's first take a look at audio files.

Audio Data Types

Effective audio can help deliver your message with impact. Audio is as important as visuals in your presentation. Audio can convey a sense of emotion much better than a photo. You should learn as much about audio and audio compression as possible so that you can make an accurate assessment of the audio needs of your project.

Audio can be contained in and delivered with different types of files. For example, you might digitize your audio and save the file in Sound Designer II format on your hard drive, but when it comes time to deliver that same audio file, you'll want to compress the data into something like the MP3 format. Compression saves storage space and speeds delivery.

Most of the audio files you'll find on the Internet are in one of the formats discussed in the next sections.

MP3

MP3 is a compressed audio format that sounds excellent. MP3 is designed for delivering music but can be used for voice as well. MP3 uses perceptual encoding, where the algorithm "listens" to the sound and removes frequencies you cannot hear. The MP3 format lets you choose a target bit-rate setting to encode to. A setting of 128K sounds just like a normal audio CD but is one tenth the size. A setting of 40K to 60K is perfect for a simple voiceover track. MP3 can also be used for archiving CDs or other audio samples. Because audio is sampled at 16-bit 44.1K takes up 44.1K of disk space for every second in length (88.2K for stereo files), a normal CD track takes about 10.5MB of hard disk space. MP3s, on the other hand, can save files in an archive format, and the same file is only about 2MB but sounds exactly the same. MP3 compression is lossy (see `http://www.mpeg.org` for more information).

Qdesign Music

Qdesign Music is a compressed audio format that comes in standard and pro versions. The psycho-acoustic parametric coding algorithm is designed for low data rate applications. This codec allows you to save compressed audio in different sampling rates (11, 22, or 44kHz), at different bit depths (8 or 16-bit), and in mono or stereo. When used with Cleaner, this codec allows you to adjust the track volume, change the dynamic range, add reverb, and apply other effects normally seen only on external hardware devices such as compressors.

The Qdesign Music codec also comes in a professional version—for more money, of course. It allows control over targeting a specific bit-rate, has a setting so you can tell it to lean more toward "quality" or "speed" (size), and features two pass variable bit-rate encoding for more precise data-rate targeting. See `http://www.qdesign.com` for more information.

Qualcomm PureVoice

Qualcomm PureVoice is a codec designed for encoding voice signals. It has some amazing compression capabilities that can be helpful when you are simply using voice as your source material. The codec allows you to change the sample rate, the bit rate, the number of channels, and the setting that determines whether to use the "full rate" or "half rate" settings. The full rate settings can compress your audio in a 9:1 ratio, and the half rate setting can achieve a 19:1 compression ratio. This is pretty heavy compression, but nonetheless the audio is more than acceptable—it sounds like a long-distance phone call.

IMA 4:1

IMA 4:1 is a compressed delivery format from the Interactive Multimedia Association. As its name implies, IMA compresses audio by 75 percent with high-quality sound. Eight- and 16-bit IMA has the same quality and file size. The limitation of IMA is that you cannot IMA-compress an AIFF file for playback on a Windows system. This codec was originally designed for audio that needs to be played off a CD-ROM in real time, and it does the job well. It is one of the oldest codecs, but it is still used today for CD-ROM work and backward compatibility.

MPEG-4 Audio

MP4 is the new audio standard replacing MP3. MP4 supports bit rate, sample rate, depth, channel, hinted streaming tracks, and more. What makes this the codec of choice is that its compression algorithms are better. MP4 uses the Advanced Audio Coding (AAC) method to produce smaller files and higher quality. In fact, AAC-compressed sounds deliver higher quality than uncompressed CD audio. A 20-second 16-bit, 22.5kHz audio file of 900K compresses to 128K in MP3 at 40kHz and sounds muddy. The same file compressed with MP4 is 108K and sounds nearly identical to the original. The trouble is that because this codec is so new, most people don't have the means to decode it (another thing to worry about!). See `http://www.apple.com/mpeg4/` and `http://mpeg.telecomitalialab.com/` for more information.

WAVE

This format is used extensively in Microsoft Windows to store and deliver audio, and is also used in wavetable synthesis, such as E-mu's SoundFont. Conversion tools can convert .wav files to other operating systems. See `http://www.microsoft.com/` for more information.

QuickTime Audio

QuickTime is both a file container and delivery format; that is, you can use QuickTime to embed MP3, AIFF, MP4, and video in your web pages and CD-ROMs. The QuickTime format is cross-platform for people with Macs and PCs. You can use QuickTime files to edit your audio and then compress them for distribution, making this a very versatile format.

The next section explains video formats for the web and their strengths and weaknesses.

Video Data Types

When video is digitized, it becomes "data" that needs to be contained inside some type of file format, such as QuickTime. Once video is stored in an electronic file, it can be edited (rearranged in a new order other than that in which it was shot), and then the video can be compressed and delivered to your target device, such as the web or a CD-ROM. Here are the different types of video formats you will encounter:

- **QuickTime (QT)**—QT is the king of video formats. Over 15 years old, QT is cross-platform, supports both progressive downloading and real-time streaming, and can get through firewalls. The professional version is for media creators, offering additional file translation and sampling capabilities that are well worth the cost. Nearly every video application supports QT. It can handle VR 3D fly-throughs, and supports scripting for interactive presentations. QuickTime requires a plug-in, which most modern browsers bundle, or you can download it from `http://www.apple.com/quicktime`.

- **RealMedia**—This is RealNetworks' cross-platform audio and video streaming delivery technology. It allows different target bandwidths and desktop or web playback. Unlike QuickTime, RealVideo files are only stored compressed, so there's no way to revert to raw video or audio for editing.

- **Windows Media Player**—Microsoft's answer to QuickTime. The Windows Media Player will play back either compressed or streaming WMP files in real time to all target bandwidths, such as a DSL or a 56Kbps modem. WMP can deliver compressed, downloadable files or stream a live signal. See `http://www.microsoft.com` for more information.

Because compression for QuickTime, RealPlayer, and Windows Media Player are all very similar, I explain the concepts further in the "Codecs" section, later in this chapter.

Animation

Animation on the Internet comes in two primary forms: the traditional 2D animation and the more recent 3D animation. 2D animation is the equivalent of cartoon-style frame-by-frame animation. Modern computers have made this process much easier by way of keyframes. Now artists need only to draw keyframes of the animation and let the computer interpret the motion between keyframes, a process with the delightful name of *tweening*. Applications such as Flash from Macromedia work this way.

There are currently three main data types for web-based animation:

- **Flash**—The most popular animation format on the web. Vector-based format files are generally small and bandwidth friendly. Flash files are compressed into SWF file format and delivered with Macromedia Shockwave technology. Flash is nearly ubiquitous on the web; 95 percent of all browsers are able to display Flash animations. For all its benefits, Flash has a clumsy professional development environment. Visit http://www.macromedia.com for more information.

- **Shockwave and Shockwave 3D**—Director allows the creation of vector or bitmapped-based content compressed into DCR (Director Compressed Resource) files that are played back on the web using Shockwave. Macromedia and Intel recently introduced Shockwave 3D, which also supports 3D data from applications like 3ds max or Maya for 3D experiences. Your audience can fly through online stores and examine items with HTTP links. However, creating 3D worlds with textures, lighting, and Lingo code takes a lot of skill. DCR files and the plug-in are much larger than their Flash counterparts. For more information, visit the Macromedia web site at http://www.macromedia.com.

- **Cult3d**—Cult3D tries to blend the simplicity of Flash with the capabilities of Director for web 3D. Cycore has a large installed base of Cult3D player downloads. Cult3D is designed with 3D e-commerce in mind, with XML database interaction and shopping cart functions built-in. For more information, visit their web site at http://www.cult3d.com.

Limitations to Multimedia

You didn't think there weren't going to be any limitations to multimedia, did you? Multimedia work requires cutting-edge technology. When you are developing multimedia, you are working in the latest video, audio, and image-editing applications, and there are always limitations and issues you face when you are trying to stay current with technology.

In short, when you're a multimedia developer, you always have to have the latest technology to impress your clients. That means constant upgrading of software, and thus operating systems. Unlike accountants, who can get away with using one version of Excel for years, multimedia developers are constantly upgrading their hardware and software.

Once you get used to continuously upgrading, your next limitation will be the raw speed of your connection to the Internet. You generally need the fastest connection you can get because you are going to not only be transferring large files, but you will also need to test regularly video and audio playback on the web.

Processing Speed

Get the fastest processor you can afford because compression often is time-consuming and editing video and/or audio is CPU-intensive. However, the real limitation here is going to be your customer's CPU speed. You will need to make a CPU cut-off point for some of your projects just to protect yourself in some cases. For full-blown multimedia projects with audio, video, text, and photos, you'll have to test your finished piece on many different computers to find the ones on which it plays well, those on which it plays adequately, and the ones on which it just doesn't work at all. Then you will either have to go back to your project and more tightly compress the audio and video or print a CPU requirement on your web site or CD-ROM package.

Bandwidth

The speed of your connection will always feel like a limiting factor, regardless of how fast it is. When I started using the Internet, 1200- and 2400-baud modems were the fastest modems you could use, but they felt slow to me. A few years later, everyone had 56,000 baud, but that speed felt faster only temporarily because larger sites made even that speed feel slow. Today I'm sitting at the opposite end of a 6Mb DSL (6,000,000 bits/second) connection at home, and it still feels slow to me. Remember:

- It's not your connection speed but your customers' speed that's important.
- Regardless of your speed, you need to learn to compress your files as much as possible.
- Considering that most people don't upgrade, you also need to make versions of your files backward compatible.

Codecs

When you have files on your hard drive and you plan on delivering them either over the Internet, via CD-ROM, or even by email, they need to be compressed. Compression actually has two parts to it: compression and decompression. This is where the term *codec* comes from: **co**mpression and **dec**ompression. *Compression* is what you do to a video or sound file to make it smaller, and *decompression* is how it plays the file back. You have control over both aspects of the process using different codecs.

You can actually purchase codecs for video or audio that are professional versions designed for multimedia professionals. For example, the Sorenson Pro Developer Codec is used by Industrial Light & Magic (ILM) to compress all the *Star Wars* trailers you see on the Internet (http://www.apple.com/trailers/).

Why Codecs Are Necessary

Without the use of compression, video and audio could not effectively be distributed over the Internet. Consider the *Star Wars* trailer, for example. The high-speed broadband version of that video clip on the Internet is about 25MB in size. That same clip uncompressed could easily be 250 to 500MB in size; this would take up the better part of an entire CD-ROM.

In addition to delivery, codecs make video playback possible. Video is a CPU-intensive medium simply because there is so much data involved. One second of NTSC video captured from the miniDV format is about 3.5MB of disk space. This means that every 60 seconds of video is 210MB of data, and every five minutes is a little over 1GB of data (or 9,000 frames of images). Now, even the latest computers could have trouble trying to process 1GB of data so fast that you don't see any jerky playback or pauses. This is why codecs are needed. You can easily reduce the size of your video 10:1, 20:1, 50:1, or even 100:1 using modern codecs. In order for your computer to play five minutes of video (210MB prior to compression), all it has to handle is about 2MB of data. Because 2MB is a smaller amount of data, older and slower computers can now play back video and see your creations.

How Codecs Work

Compression is an extremely complex operation that in some cases takes days for your computer to calculate. But remember that the compression you do prior to delivery creates smaller finished video, which plays smoother on more machines.

Compressing video works by removing redundant data in two ways: on a frame-per-frame (spatial) basis, and on an over-time (temporal) basis.

Spatial compression is where the compression application looks at every frame of your video and then groups every pixel in that one frame based on how close pixel colors are to one another. The algorithm then sets similar RGB color values to the same value. What this allows is instead of assigning every pixel three values between 0 and 255, you have big groups of pixels all with the same value, resulting in at least a 2:1 savings in compression. This is similar to how static image compression works, across a set of "images."

In addition to pixel compression, codecs can do something called *temporal compression*. Temporal is an over-time compression technique over which you really don't have too much control. The Sorenson codec, for example, creates natural keyframes when the video changes dramatically from one scene to the next. These keyframes are compressed more lightly than your entire video and are used by the codec as references on how to draw the frames around it.

Temporal compression smoothes pixels over time and tries to remove video noise. Temporal settings also can help you remove one-frame artifacts.

Streaming Media

Streaming content is multimedia content that is played on the user's computer while it is being downloaded from a server. Streaming media can protect content by preventing users from saving data directly on their hard drives. It also has the advantage of being able to stream very long pieces of data. Streams of 90 minutes or more are possible, provided your users have a stable connection. The stream quality, or bits per second, can depend on the user's connection speed.

QuickTime

Apple's QuickTime is the best solution for video delivery on the Macintosh and some would say on the PC as well. The streaming aspect of QuickTime is no less than awesome with its feature set, performance, and ease of use for both the developer and the client.

Apple provides two types of streaming technologies:

- Real-Time, for streaming video over the Internet during a live event.
- Progressive, for delivering video over the Internet with prerecorded material.

With real-time, you can hook up your video camera to your computer, which is running a copy of QuickTime's Broadcaster. This allows you to send live video over a streaming server out to thousands of viewers (see Figure 13.1). Broadcaster takes advantage of all of QuickTime's codecs such as MP3 streaming, MP4 streaming, and video streaming.

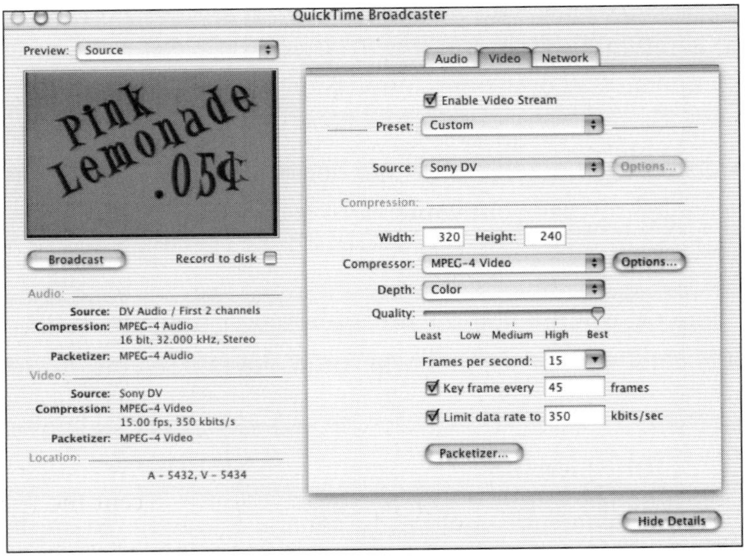

Figure 13.1
The QuickTime streaming server is powerful and simple to use.

NOTE

With the new ISO standards, MPEG4 is now starting to show up in cellphones and other PDA devices. The QuickTime streaming server will enable you to communicate with all of these devices.

In terms of compression for streaming QuickTime content, there is not much to do other than normal compression. Video compression is both spatial and temporal. With streaming content, you pick a target bandwidth, video size, and frame rate; enable "hinted tracks;" and let the file compress. Once it's done, you upload the file to your server and make a link to it on your web page. When a user clicks on this link, the video is requested, sent to the client, buffered for a moment, and then playback starts. Remember:

- Dial-up modems are almost useless for video.
- Your client should be able to handle a 256Kbps download or it's not worth it.
- Use QuickTime progressive for content below 256Kbps downloads.

QuickTime progressive downloads begin playing as soon as enough content is buffered to allow smooth playback for the duration of the clip.

For More Information

If you think you'll use QuickTime, go to `http://www.apple.com/quicktime/tools_tips/tutorials/activex.html` for instructions on making your QuickTime files viewable on all platforms and browsers. If you are using version 5.5 SP2 of Internet Explorer for Windows, you must view QuickTime as an ActiveX control because Microsoft has discontinued support for Netscape style plug-ins.

I've found that people are much more accepting of temporal compression (over-time) of the video than spatial (frame-per-frame) compression. By cutting the frame rate from 15fps to 10fps or even 8fps, each frame has 50 percent more data per frame for the same file size, which will increase the quality of the picture. The minimum size should be 320×240. If your clients have a fast Internet connection, 400×300 is better. Anything smaller than 320×240 is just too small. To maintain good quality, always up the data rate in proportion to the image size. Also remember that doubling image size (320×240 to 640×480) requires a 4X (not 2X) increase in data rate.

Use this data rate formula to help target your movie for the right delivery medium:

Date Rate = (frames per second) × (movie width) × (movie height) divided by 35000

This translates to DR = FPS * W * H / 35000.

Here is an example: A 320×240 movie with 15 frames per second needs to be compressed to about 32.9K of data per second. Realistically, I would round this up to 35K.

Gamma, or the relative brightness of computer displays, is another issue that you need to understand. Macs and PCs display images with different gamma levels. If you're working with a compression tool that supports gamma adjustment (Cleaner, for example), an image you create on a Mac and display on a PC will look too dark. Conversely, an image created on a PC and displayed on a Mac will look too bright. The cross-platform gamma adjustment with Cleaner is +25 to +30 when going from Mac to PC and −30 when going from PC to Mac. Positive numbers lighten the image, and negative numbers darken the image.

RealMedia

RealMedia is bigger on the Windows operating system than it is on the Macintosh, mainly because RealNetworks can't compete with a player that comes embedded into the operating system such as QuickTime.

There are three different type of streaming content distribution technologies:

- **Unicast**—Unicast streams are simple point-to-point streams, similar to a telephone call from the host server to a individual client computer. To reach many clients at once, the server must send many streams simultaneously, which is a less efficient use of bandwidth. However, viewers of a unicast stream can randomly access movies, playing only the parts they want to see. Typically, unicast is used to stream pre-recorded movies that are stored on a host computer.

- **Multicast**—Multicast streams are sent directly to a group address, which can then be simultaneously accessed by many client computers.

- **Reflected**—Reflected multicast streams take live media from another source, such as a radio or TV broadcast, and stream it out to viewers as a series of unicasts.

Because the RealMedia compression tool(s) save compression attributes, picking the same compression setting for many clips is easy. Remember that video on the web really isn't effective unless you can target a 256K user. This means that the best settings for the RealEncoder are these:

- 256K DSL/cable modem
- 2-pass encoding
- Variable bit rate encoding

Windows Media

Microsoft (and some web reviews) say that their new Media Player provides the best audio and video quality on the web. What they don't mention is that the quality is limited to the bandwidth of your user's connection speed. It's their connection speed that determines how high-quality a streaming file their computer can handle. The latest version of the player has incorporated many new features, including these:

- Windows Media Audio 8 (WMA8) encoding
- Smart Transcode support for the best quality transfer to portable devices
- Windows Media Audio and Video 8 decoding
- A new enterprise deployment pack for larger scale (ISP-sized) streaming solutions

Windows Media Player is more than a streaming application; it's truly a complete "media player."

Windows Media Player has an impressive set of features and is integrated into Windows; unlike Real, which often has issues with streaming video through firewalls. See www.WindowsMedia.com for more information.

Regardless of which technology you choose to use, the "Audio Compression and Optimization" and "Video Optimization" sections will give you a start on optimizing your audio and video for delivery over the Internet or other forms of media such as CD-ROMs.

Streaming versus Downloading

The three types of video delivery methods for playback are these:

- **Streaming**—Video that is played while it is being downloaded.

- **Progressive downloading**—The progressive format is a blending of streaming and simple downloading. With progressive video, you get the benefit of video starting right away (with a little buffer), and when the video has completely loaded, you have the ability to save it to your computer for offline playback.

- **Just plain downloading**—In order for downloaded video to work correctly, the entire video must download before it can start playing. The advantage, however, is that once the entire video has downloaded, it will play flawlessly, assuming the user's computer is up to the task.

Multimedia Production Tips

Media optimization projects of all sizes benefit from planning right from the beginning. To give your projects a better chance of success, keep these questions in mind while you are planning your projects:

- What are your goals, who defines them, and how will you know when you've met them?

- Who is your target audience, what kind of computers do they use, and how do they connect to the Internet?

- What are the limiting factors to delivering your media to your target audience? (This might be connection speed, CPU speed, server disk space, and so on.)

- What copyright restrictions apply to your source material if it's not original content?

Along with a project plan, you also may want to develop a storyboard and script. It is wise to consider, particularly with the bandwidth requirements of streamed audio and video, that your audience most likely will experience the end result in a small window on a computer screen.

Audio Compression and Optimization

Once you have sorted out all these issues surrounding your project, you should be ready to get started. There are three rules to follow:

- Reduce outside/background noise
- Use professional equipment
- Record digitally (DAT, Minidisc, miniDV)

Equipment

Depending on your location, you might need different equipment. If you are indoors, for example, you will have much better control over the quality of audio you can capture because you can control environmental noise factors. If you are outdoors, you might have to implement some additional hardware to better your chances of getting clean audio.

Equipment Quality Matters

Whenever you capture audio or video, use the highest-quality equipment you can afford for the job. Nothing is worse than recording bad audio or video only to find this out after the shooting or recording session is over.

For starters, you will want to record at least at CD quality using a Digital Audio Tape (DAT), Minidisk, or miniDV device. *CD quality* is defined as audio that is captured at 16-bits and 44,100 samples per second in stereo. If you are recording outside, you will want some type of field recording unit, such as a Sony TCD-D10PRO2 Professional DAT Recorder with XLR inputs for attaching a professional-quality microphone. If you are in a studio, you will want a professional TASCAM DA-60MKII. Both of these are top-of-the-line DAT players.

Microphones also are available in indoor and outdoor models, and you have many choices, from shotgun (for focused recording) to lavalier (clip-on mics). For outdoor options, look at brands such as Sennheiser or Beyerdynamic.

In addition to recorders and microphones, you will need audio patch cables. When you are working with professional audio equipment, you will be working with balanced XLR patch cables. Balanced audio interconnects utilize two conductors, while standard RCA audio interconnects use only a single "unbalanced" conductor. This enhanced design gives balanced audio interconnects the power to provide greater resistance against sources of noise. This results in purer signal transfer.

Level Matching

One important thing to know is that your audio's volume is referred to as *levels*. The levels (the term is plural because there are two sound channels: left and right) basically tell you how loud your sound clips are recorded. If you digitize your audio with the same computer all in one continuous block, you shouldn't have to worry about the levels too much.

In some cases, you will need to adjust your audio clips so that they sound either louder or quieter than each other. This is when you need to make a levels adjustment. The best way to understand the levels adjustment process is to imagine wearing headphones with the volume (or levels) set to 8. You hear the audio at a specific decibel level when it is set at 8 as opposed to 4.

When your audio source is plugged into your computer and you are digitizing your audio, your computer is "listening" to the sound much in the same way that your ears listen to sound. This means that if you record 30 seconds at a volume of 8 and then record 30 seconds at a volume of 4, your second clip is going to be half as loud. This is bad, because your audio will instantly get louder or quieter.

If you are planning on playing back your digitized audio clips together, you are going to have to make some adjustment to the levels either before you digitize (by making sure they are all the same) or after you have digitized (by adjusting the normalization settings). You learn more about this in the "Normalization" section that follows.

In addition to making sure that your levels are consistent, you also need to worry about the levels for each independent stereo track. If you are recording with two mics, this could be an issue.

When you record with two microphones, you have two separate audio streams and each has its own levels setting during recording. Under normal situations, you want the levels setting of the right and left channels to be exactly the same. However, you might run into a situation in which the left channel after digitizing sounds is lower than the right. In this case, you will have to adjust the levels of the left channel. By boosting the left channel level setting, you can better balance the stereo between both channels (see Figure 13.2).

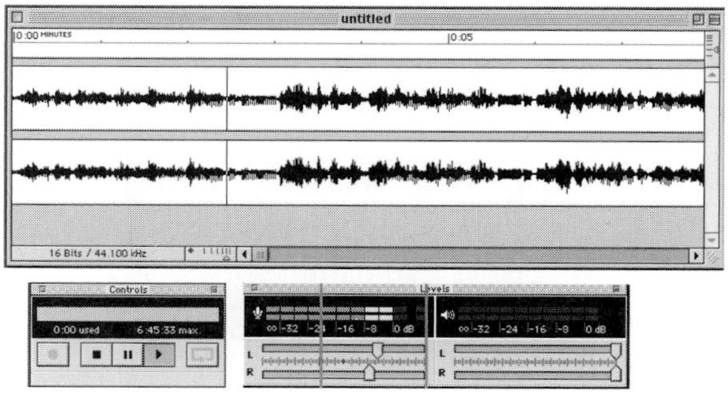

Figure 13.2
Use the Levels window to "see" the volume at which your incoming recorded audio is set. Lower the volume if the levels meter starts hitting the red.

Normalization

What do you do when you are recording your audio subject and either the sound that is being recorded changes volume or the person you are recording begins to speak more loudly? Don't you hate that? Unless there is some contextual reason for the change in volume, you normalize your audio.

Normalization is the process of "looking" at your audio and finding the loudest point; then resetting that point to be (for example) 90 percent of maximum loudness.

Take a look at Figure 13.3. This figure shows the waveform of a digitized audio clip, set at approximately 20 percent of its maximum level.

Figure 13.3
This audio clip is only at about 20 percent of its maximum level.

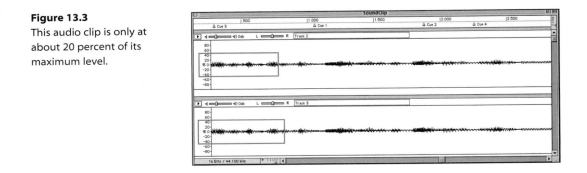

The fact that the audio clip is set to 20 percent of maximum could be caused by recording it at a lower level. This means that for any given volume setting on the playback device, this piece of audio will be playing only at 20 percent of its loudness. You can fix the loudness problem by adjusting the levels of the clip. The simplest way to do this is to use a Normalize command (see Figure 13.4).

Figure 13.4
Using the Normalize command, you can boost your level to a specific point.

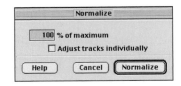

Normalization looks at your audio sample, finds the loudest segment, and pulls it up to 100-percent capacity for that given volume. After your normalization setting is applied, you will see your audio waveform fill more of the amplitude. In Figure 13.5, you can see that the audio is now playing at or close to 100 percent of its volume level. This means that when someone turns the volume up to 5, for example, the audio will sound like audio that is set to a volume level of 5, instead of 20 percent of a 5 level. Keep in mind that normalization also amplifies any noise in your audio tracks, so make sure that you have a clean signal.

The most important thing about this entire lesson is that you *must* apply the same normalization setting to all your clips that will be playing together! If you don't, your customer will hear audio that is quiet one moment and too loud then next. This is the biggest mistake a novice audio developer can make.

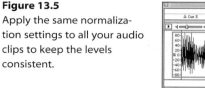

Figure 13.5
Apply the same normaliza-
tion settings to all your audio
clips to keep the levels
consistent.

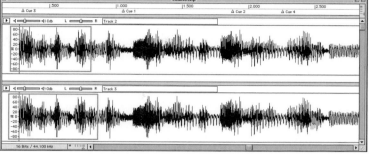

Audio Compressors

Not to be confused with file compression, audio compressors compress an audio signal
to smooth out any extremes. A compressor alters the dynamics or difference between
low and high volume within an audio signal. Compressors are useful for taking out the
sharp peaks in the audio and maximizing the volume going to the recorder, without
adding any distortion caused by having the levels turned up too loud.

Compressors also can be used as an effect to make voices sound bigger and fuller,
increase loudness, and smooth out mixes. Have you ever wondered why ads on TV
sound louder than the programs and why DJ's voices on the radio sound so full? These
are effects produced by compressors.

Here are some common functions on a compressor that you need to know:

- **Threshold**—This is the volume level above which the compressor begins compressing. Everything above the threshold will be brought down in volume.

- **Ratio**—This setting controls how much the volume above the threshold will be
  reduced. For example, at a setting of 1:1, the signal will not be compressed; at 3:1,
  the volume will be brought partly down; and at Infinity:1, the volume will be
  brought down to match the threshold.

- **Attack & Release**—Attack controls how fast the compressor reacts to signals pass-
  ing over the threshold point. Release is how quickly it stops reacting once the signal moves under the threshold.

- **Output Gain**—This setting amplifies the signal after it has been compressed to
  compensate for the reduction in high volumes.

- **Over Easy or Soft Knee**—This functions smoothes out the threshold point and moves it around, rather than placing it exactly at a particular point.

- **Contour**—This function is less sensitive to low frequencies and comes in handy when you are compressing an entire mix.

- **Limiter**—A limiter is built into many compressors to catch any extra volume peaks that escape compression. This stops the signal from going over a particular volume and distorting.

- **Gate**—This function fades your audio to silence if the volume passes under the gate threshold point. This is useful for removing hiss from the quiet sections.

Useful Compressor Settings

The compressor is a creative tool. There is no one right way to use it. The best way to work out what to do is to use your ears (using headphones is best, of course). Keeping this in mind, this section provides some settings I have found useful.

To correctly install a compressor, you need to put it in-between your input device (such as a microphone or DAT player) and your computer. That is, when you would normally run a wire from your DAT to the input of your computer, you would now run the wire from your DAT to the compressor, and then run a wire from the compressor into the computer.

The following lists give you the best general use settings for cleaning up your audio before it goes into your computer for recording.

Best compression:

    GATE: OFF
    THRESHOLD: –15dB
    RATIO: 3:1
    OVEREASY: ON
    ATTACK: FAST
    RELEASE: MEDIUM SLOW

LIMITER: +5DB

OUTPUT: +6dB

Or try the deep radio voice settings:

GATE: OFF

THRESHOLD: –20dB

RATIO: 6:1

OVEREASY: ON

ATTACK: FAST

RELEASE: SLOW

LIMITER: +5dB

OUTPUT: +10dB

Encoding

In order to deliver your audio content, you must compress its size so that it can be successfully streamed (or downloaded) to your target audience. Encoding is the process by which this compression happens, and it is full of tough, interdependent decisions. Some of these decisions include:

- **Streaming media format**—QuickTime versus RealMedia versus Windows Media.
- **Supported playback platforms**—Microsoft Windows versus Macintosh, or both.
- **Delivery method**—True real-time streaming versus HTTP streaming.
- **Overall data rate**—Compression versus quality versus bandwidth required.
- **Audio quality**—Mono versus stereo.

To meet your goals, you may end up encoding multiple versions in different formats and data rates.

Figure 13.6 shows the current king of encoders, Cleaner, which is made by Discreet (http://www.discreet.com).

Figure 13.6
Use an application like
Cleaner to compress your
audio and help you manage
the range of available
options.

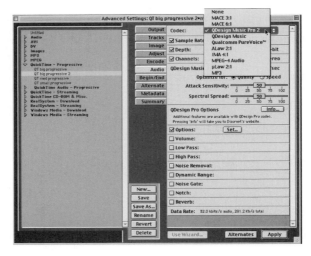

With audio encoding, you have to make a basic tradeoff: Quality versus file size. This tradeoff is often very hard to make because you always want your finished piece to look and sound as good as possible but also be as small as possible. Unfortunately, there isn't a magic setting for this; each audio and/or video clip is different.

To get an idea of the capabilities of these audio formats, see Table 13.1.

Table 13.1   Sound Quality and File Size versus Audio Format

	Raw Audio	MP3	MP4	QPV	QDX
File Size	900K	128K	108K	47 to 100K	9K
Quality	High	Medium	High	Low-Med	Medium

Video Optimization

Before you decide to shoot some video that you intend to use on the computer, there are some things you should know that will help you make your video look as good as possible.

Media creation can be described as a war against unnecessary noise in your content. The more noise, the less your content can be compressed, the harder it is to stream to an audience. Follow these tips to produce high-quality video:

- Minimize camera motion with a tripod
- Minimize subject motion
- Use a lot of light
- Use a simple background
- Avoid camera pans and zooms
- Use professional equipment
- Use a digital format

Carefully shooting and editing video for streaming or downloading can substantially improve the final quality of your video. Remember that the overall goal in producing video that encodes well is to create the highest-quality video with the least amount of noise, camera movement, and fine detail. This helps the source encode as efficiently as possible and look good at smaller image sizes. In order to create a good video source, you should use a high-quality camera, light the subjects well, and stabilize the camera with a tripod as much as possible.

Avoid handheld shooting whenever you can. If you need to film a handheld shot, a motion stabilizer such as a Steadi-cam or gyroscopic system like Kenyon Lab's (`http://www.ken-lab.com`) will help your results. If your camera has an image stabilization option (either optical or digital), use it to reduce subtle changes between frames caused by camera motion.

Keeping the detail within the scene to a minimum will help the individual frames of video compress more easily, giving you better results than video with lots of detail. It will also make the video easier to see when the movie is reduced in size for delivery. Trees often are used as backdrops for interviews filmed outside. The detail of the leaves poses a challenge for encoding and should always be avoided. If you must shoot against a background that uses trees, using a shallow depth of field to blur the leaves will often improve the final movie. Beware of trees moving in a breeze—the high detail and subtle changes between frames make both temporal and spatial compression difficult. Ask your subjects to wear clothes that don't have high contrast patterns or lots of detail. Plain colors are best.

Equipment

A common misconception is that because the final movie will end up as a small part of the computer screen, a cheaper camera won't make a difference in the process. This is completely wrong. Video noise substantially degrades the encoding process, which means that a clean video signal produced by a high-quality camera will encode much better than a noisy signal produced by a low-quality camera. Also, the resolution and sharpness of the camera has a significant effect on the final stream quality.

Some miniDV cameras offer a progressive scan feature. This records each frame as a single "non-interlaced" image instead of two separate interlaced fields. Progressive scan source material may not play as smoothly on a television monitor as interlaced material, but it is superior for streaming because it contains no interlacing artifacts. You should look for this feature when buying a miniDV camera and use it when creating streaming content.

You can find a wide range of available miniDV cameras. Lower-priced cameras generally have a single CCD, smaller optics, and fewer features. Higher-quality miniDV cameras offer as many as three CCDs, higher-quality optics, image stabilization, and many other features to deliver superior image quality. If you don't currently own a camera, I would recommend you get a miniDV camera.

The analog formats (S-VHS, VHS, Hi8) produce noisier signals and lower-resolution video than miniDV. Because these formats are analog, you need either an analog-to-FireWire converter or an analog-compatible video capture system to make them work on your computer.

Professional formats generally produce the highest-quality results and often work with green- and blue-screen better than the other types of cameras. However, these professional formats are very expensive. In order to work with a pro format on your computer, you'll need to use a video system that is capable of handling the formats, such as a Media 100 or Avid system.

Lighting

Generally speaking, video that is well lit encodes better than under- or over-exposed material. Adequate lighting is critical to creating superior streaming movies because low light conditions also produce excessively noisy video signals that lack detail in the shadows. Overexposure is usually less of a problem but should also be avoided.

Don't shoot video that you know is exposed incorrectly and then plan on fixing it in your computer. Missing detail and excessive noise can never be fully corrected. Properly lighting your video is the only way to ensure the highest-quality results.

Because lighting is an art form all in its own, I recommend that you get a book or two on the subject of lighting for video or film. I recommend *Learning to Light* by Roger Hicks and Frances Schultz (Amphoto, 1998).

There are spotlights, umbrella lights, three point lighting, tungsten lights, and fluorescent, just to name a few. Each type of light has a different "temperature" and a different white-point associated to them. You will need to learn about this and many other aspects of proper lighting if you plan on doing this professionally.

Capturing

In order to edit video on your computer, you must first get it onto your hard drive. This is called *capturing* the video, or *digitizing*.

If you shot your video with a miniDV camera, you can simply transfer the video to your computer via the camera's IEEE 1394 port, also called FireWire or iLink. This results in very high-quality source video because there is no analog-to-digital conversion when capturing.

If you did not use a miniDV to capture your material, you have two options for digitizing it. You can use a converter to transform the analog signal to a digital signal and then capture. Or you can capture your analog video with an analog video capture card or a system that can handle analog signals such as a Media 100i, Avid, or other capable system. Both technologies provide the same quality level.

Analog

If you are using an analog video system, you can do several things to improve the quality of the video.

To get the highest-quality results, capture your analog video at full-screen resolution—that is, 640×480 (NTSC) or 720×486 (miniDV)—depending on the native resolution of your source. Even if you intend to deliver smaller final movies, a full-screen capture will generally give you better results for a number of reasons. For example, capturing at full screen and scaling down the image tends to reduce video noise and results in a smoother-looking image. Because the noise is reduced, the video clip tends to compress better than the non-scaled-down clip.

Most captured video has a black border around the perimeter. This is often called *over-scanning* or *edge blanking;* you must remove these edges. Starting from a larger image allows you to crop and then scale down the image. If you capture only at the final size you want to use to deliver your video, removing edge noise requires you to crop and then scale up the video, which degrades image quality.

The biggest problem while capturing video is missing or "dropped" frames. The most common cause of dropped frames is trying to capture your video at a higher data rate than your hard drive can support. As it falls behind, the capture starts to lose frames. Dropped frames often occur sporadically in the captured video, causing the video to randomly stutter or jerk.

For this reason, capture at the maximum quality your system can properly handle. (This should normally be at least 3 MB/sec.) If you can't capture at a very high-quality setting, consider buying a faster hard drive.

Configure your capture system to warn you of dropped frames and to stop capturing if they occur. To avoid dropped frames, you may need to defragment your hard drive, buy a faster hard drive or a RAID system, or lower the quality of your capture.

Digital (IEEE 1394)

Ah, the IEEE 1394 standard—by far the easiest way for you to get your content into the computer. The IEEE 1394 standard (or FireWire, as it's branded) is a connection that most newer Macintosh and Windows computers have. The connection allows you to simply plug in your miniDV camera or deck, and the computer will not only control the device from the cable but will also transfer high-quality audio and video to your computer.

An example of this is Final Cut Pro for the Macintosh (see Figure 13.7). Final Cut Pro allows you to connect to your deck or camera, control its functions from the screen, digitize the entire tape (or sections of it), and then edit that content and finally put it back out to tape.

Figure 13.7
Apple's Final Cut Pro software for the Macintosh is a one-stop solution to digitizing and editing your video.

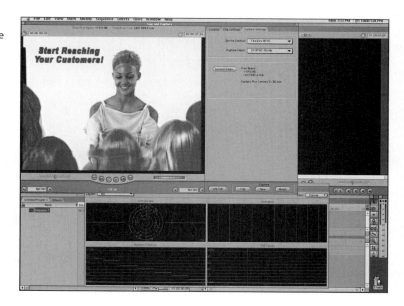

Optimizing Video After You Capture It

After capturing your source material, edit it as needed, adding any titles and effects you want to use. After that, you can, and probably should, optimize your source content. Here are some tips professionals use to create high-quality source content for encoding and streaming:

- Crop the fuzzy edges
- Reduce video noise (with filters)
- Adjust contrast

- Adjust gamma level (for cross-platform viewing)
- Restore black and white
- Deinterlace

Aspect Correction

Some formats, such as miniDV, do not have square pixels and must be corrected to look normal on a computer screen. In some cases, you may want to manually set a specific aspect ratio correction to compensate for unusual source material. Applications such as Cleaner will allow you to do this.

To produce the highest-quality file, you need to crop your video. Cropping allows you to specify which part of the image you want to keep in your file and is useful for eliminating the black edges around the video. For cropping details, consult your video program's manual.

Pixel Aspect Ratio

Normal pixels in the graphics world are square. A 50-pixel vertical line is the same length as a 50-pixel horizontal line on a computer monitor.

Pixels in some video signals are non-square. A 50-pixel vertical line may be longer or shorter than a 50-pixel horizontal line on a video monitor, depending on the video standard. The term that describes this is the *pixel aspect ratio*. It is specified as a fraction of vertical (y) pixel size divided by (x) horizontal pixel size. The pixel aspect ratio for square pixels is 1/1.

This term is different than *frame aspect ratio*, which is a fraction of total vertical (y) frame size over total horizontal (x) frame size, for a given definition of "frame." Typical frame aspect ratios for video are 4/3 and 16/9.

You may be wondering why this matters. Well, many image-processing operations assume a certain pixel aspect ratio. For example, a blur operation may look bad on non-square pixels. For this reason, any rendering of geometry-based graphics to an image must take the pixel aspect ratio into account.

The miniDV format is an example of a non-square pixel format. In general, this is just something that you need to be aware of; there is nothing you need to do to your video to make it non-square. Just understand that what you are looking at on your computer screen isn't the way it will look on a TV screen. Because of this, many professional video editors also have TV monitors hooked to their computers.

If you digitize video from a miniDV source but plan to show that video only on a computer or the Internet, you will need to compress the video by adjusting the pixel aspect ratio so that it is 1/1. The adjustment is done during the encoding process.

When you are using Cleaner to make a QuickTime, RealMedia, or Windows Media Player file, Cleaner can automatically make aspect ratio adjustments for you (see Figure 13.8). This is a great way to get an idea of what your video will look like after it's compressed.

Figure 13.8
Cleaner lets you make aspect ratio adjustments to your video.

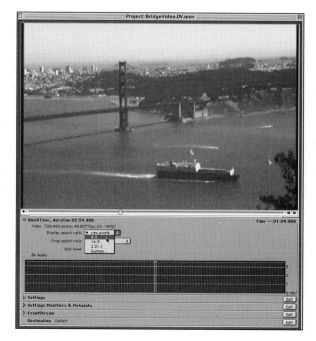

Video Compression

Now that your video has been edited, look at the file size of the clip. How will you ever be able to put it on the Internet, or even burn it onto a CD? This is where a compression tool like Cleaner comes in handy.

Compressing Video for the Web

Video files on a hard drive are usually enormous. For example, just one minute of uncompressed video takes up 1.5 GB of storage. Luckily, most video recorders automatically compress captured video at a ratio of about 5:1. However, this compression still leaves the video file too large to distribute over the Internet

Always keep your target audience in mind. Will your viewers be using 56K modems, or will they be using T-1 lines? Whichever you choose, don't forget these two concepts:

- The higher the data rate, the better quality the video.
- Choose your compression settings with the slowest connection in mind.

Another decision you have to make is whether to stream your video or make it available through progressive download.

Streaming keeps your computer in constant contact with the server running the movie. Video data is transferred, displayed, and then optionally discarded once it has been seen. If the end user's connection is too slow or the network experiences congestion, the data transfer rate may be reduced in order to preserve the best real-time playback possible. This type of media delivery is best suited to video clips more than a few minutes in length.

Compress Only Once

Video editing programs normally compress video by default during export. I recommend that you turn off any compression when exporting video by setting the compressor option to None. Although the file output will be larger to begin with, it will look much better when it is compressed only once.

Progressive download works by downloading the entire video to your hard disk. When you use the "fast start" option, after enough of the file has been transferred, the video starts playing automatically. Because of these limitations, progressive download is best for high-quality, relatively short video clips at a maximum of two to three minutes, and it offers better-quality video at low bandwidths than does streaming.

QuickTime Compression

In terms of compression, QuickTime has lots of options. When you double-click on any QuickTime movie (if you have the Pro version of QuickTime installed), you can compress your movie with many different choices. The video and/or audio data can be compressed (using codecs) into any format, but regardless of the compression codec that you use, you're still using the QuickTime format to "contain" and deliver the data.

Even though the Pro version of QuickTime allows you to compress your video right from the basic player application, if you are doing any serious work, you will need a compression application such as Discreet's Cleaner. You need Cleaner because some codecs have extended features that Cleaner allows you to access more easily. For example, the best video compression codec for web delivery is Sorenson Video 3 Pro; it has tons of features that Cleaner presents to you in a nice, easy-to-use interface (see Figure 13.9).

Figure 13.9
The Sorenson interface in Cleaner is simple and elegant.

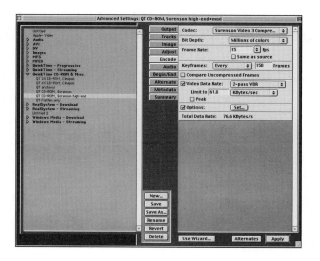

Here are the keys you need to remember when you use Sorenson:

- Sorenson is designed to make your video as small as possible, so when you are picking a data rate setting, start by using the `width * height * FPS / 35000` formula.

- Always use 2-pass VBR. It's the reason you buy Sorenson and what makes it work so well.

- Don't set a "peak." Trying to figure it out is a waste of time; besides, the video will be small anyway.

- Don't use "compare uncompressed frames." That setting is for computer animation type data.

- Start with a multiple of 10 times your FPS as your keyframe setting. For example, 15FPS = keyframes every 150 frames.

You can learn more about Sorenson at their web site `http://www.sorenson.com`.

RealMedia Compression

To compress RealMedia, you need either Cleaner or the RealMedia encoding software, which you can get from the real.com web site. Regardless of which application you choose to use, your thinking process will have to be the same. You need to compress your video so that it looks as good as possible but is also as small as possible. You also have the option to use a RealMedia Export plug-in, such as the one for Premiere. It can produce perfect results with very little effort on your part. Just make sure to use the two-pass VBR option so that the codec can analyze your video before attempting to compress it. Also, if you can get away with it, lower your frames per second from 15 (the default) to 10, and then use that extra file-size savings to increasing image quality.

This tricky compression-versus-quality tradeoff is something that you will have to play with on your own because every piece of video needs different compression settings.

Flash Optimization

Due to its vector format, Macromedia Flash can create rich movies while keeping file sizes reasonable. Flash movies can also stream over the web. You can choose to have parts of your movie, or the entire movie, preloaded into a user's machine for smoother playback. As you've discovered on the web, however, Flash movies can get pretty large.

Optimizing Flash is a matter of using the right primitives and design techniques, optimizing ActionScript, and having the right compression and optimization tools. However, compressing sound and images within Flash is not ideal. It is much better to do all of your sound/image optimization in external programs that specialize in compression, and then import them into Flash. Flash MX offers improved media compression features, however, so be sure to work with the latest version.

Like other technologies, you can trade off playback optimization (smoothness) with file-size optimization (bytes transferred). Designers will always struggle with the two in Flash because files that load quickly can take up a lot of processing power, so they playback slowly. Yet files that download more slowly can play quickly in Flash presentations.

The best aid for playback is, of course, keeping the file size small. Here are a few design tips to help you tune your movies to keep their file sizes as small as possible:

- **Audio**—For audio, the best overall compression codec within Flash is MP3. MP3 offers superb quality for both voice and music and allows you to set the bit rate.

- **Bit rates**—The bit rate setting is where you make that quality-versus-size decision. Generally, 32Kbps is fine for a person talking and 56Kbps is good for music. If you need excellent music quality, you can go as high as 80Kbps, but remember that this is 80K per second that needs to download. The higher the bit rate you choose, the larger the file size of the Flash movie. For best results, optimize any images and audio beforehand and import them into Flash.

- **Images versus symbols**—Most of the size reduction you'll realize in all versions of Flash come from drawing symbols within Flash. Importing bitmapped images is always larger than drawing within this vector-based program.

- **Reuse symbols**—When you create a movie with multiple instances of the same object, convert the object into a symbol. Ten instances of a symbol take up just a little more file size than one instance of the symbol. The file size would be increased for each object, if the objects were not symbols.

- **Compression**—With Flash 4 and 5, you can reduce the size of your SWFs by 50 percent, using Generator. With MX, however, Macromedia added a compression scheme to the version 6 plug-in that gives nearly a 50-percent reduction in file size.

- **Minimize fonts**—Keep the number of fonts to a minimum. As is true with most development programs, when you increase the number of fonts used, you increase the size of your file.

- **Test early and often**—The only way to be sure your movies are loading properly is to test them in different browsers and connection speeds.

- **Use your artwork efficiently**—Try to discard any redundant or superfluous artwork. Lines drawn with the pencil take up less space than brush strokes. Familiarize yourself with the smooth, straighten, and optimize curves options. By optimizing curves, you will reduce the size of the movie.

- **Don't go overboard on animation**—Animation eats up processing power and that can slow down the playback of your movie. Remember that tweened animations are computed, so keep to a minimum the number of computations the Flash movie has to do simultaneously. If you have to do animations, try to use tweens instead of frame-by-frame animations, because tweened animations take up far less file size than the same animation in a bunch of keyframes.

After optimizing your movie, you can have Flash generate a file size report for your movie. Before publishing the movie, choose File > Publish > Settings, click the Flash tab, and click Generate size report.

When you publish the movie, Flash will generate a separate text file that contains different information about the size of your file.

Programming and Optimization Tips

Regardless of the version of Flash you use, you can benefit from learning some simple programming tips to help you speed up your movies.

First, scripts are always executed from the beginning to the end, and no event or `gotoAndPlay()` script will interrupt execution of other code. This is why any large `for-loop` will cause the Flash player to crash or hang.

If you are serious about writing Flash applications that run as fast as possible, you might want to consider using Flash 4 instead of using Flash 5 or even MX. Flash 4's style of coding is faster, including math functions, algorithms, arrays, and movieclip methods. Use that version whenever possible.

Here are some additional tips to help speed up your movies:

- Keep all scripts less than 64KB (compiled) per frame.
- Use `tellTarget` instead of `with` where possible.
- Define local variables in functions with the `var` keyword. Local variables are faster (and using them is considered good practice).
- Choose short names for variables.
- Use `a[a.length] = 5` instead of `a.push(5)`.
- Replace suboptimal built-in functions with prototype.

> **NOTE**
>
> To help make your code faster, always work with objects using Flash 4 syntax—for example, `../:myVar` not `_parent.myVar`.

Figuring out all the things in Flash that can cause slowdowns isn't easy. Math functions, especially floating-point operations, perform well in general. There are cases, however, where simply using `tellTarget("themovie") gotoAndStop()` is considerably faster than `themovie.gotoAndStop()`.

Because identifier length matters, choose short names for variables. To try and save more space, you can extend this practice to functions also. Keep in mind that unlike JavaScript, some Flash functions are not optimal. You can replace slower functions with faster ones using the prototype method.

See Chapter 10, "Optimizing JavaScript for Execution Speed," for more details on Flash ActionScript optimization.

Flash Optimization Tools

Here are some excellent Flash optimization tools:

- **Flasm**—Free server application that allows fine-tuning of byte-level code. Also includes information on refactoring and Flash optimization (`http://flasm.sourceforge.net/`).

- **Optimaze**—Commercial application to optimize Flash movies (`http://www.optimaze.us`).

Shockwave Optimization

Optimization of a Shockwave file is done in the creation application Director. When Director imports bitmapped images, they are stored as cast members. These bitmapped cast members are where you can find the most file-size savings. Generally, Director will import your images in the bit depth to which your monitor is currently set. This isn't always the best solution, and you will have to re-adjust your images inside either the paint window or the cast window. Here's how:

- When you save an image from Photoshop and import it into Director, the image will come in as either 16- or 32-bit. In most cases, that is way too much data per pixel and will seriously inflate your final .DXR (Shockwave) file size.

- To reduce the size, reduce the number of colors. Either double-click on your cast-member to open the paint window or press Command+5 (Ctrl-5 on PC) on the keyboard.

- Notice the color depth indicator in the lower-left corner of the paint window. It should show 16 or 32 bits. Double-clicking on this indicator will bring up the Color Depth Setting window, and you can choose the desired color depth from a pop-up menu.

Here a few things to remember about adjusting your color depth. If you have a 32-bit image and you take it down to 16 and then decide to take it to 8, you should start over and go directly from 32 to 8. Each step from one bit-depth setting to the other can introduce noise in your image.

Remember that you have to do this for all of your bitmapped images. Multimedia work done well is a time-consuming process, but professionals can spot amateur work a mile away. A 500KB Shockwave movie with a few moving images and a "click" sound can easily be reduced to 50KB if you spend the time to do it right.

Now that I've scared you a bit, let me give you a little tip that will help speed up your bitmap conversion process. If you decide that all your images can be dithered to 8-bit, you can Shift+click all of them in your cast window and then go to the Modify menu and choose Transform Bitmap. This brings up the same transform bitmap window from the paint window; however, this time it will apply your bitmap changes to all your selected cast members. This a big timesaver when you are changing hundreds of images from 32-bit to 8-bit.

Shockwave Warning!

Director supports alpha channel masks from Photoshop. However, in order for alpha channels to work correctly, the specific image must stay at 32-bits. Changing the bitmap bit-depth setting of an image with an alpha channel to anything other than 32-bits will delete the alpha channel.

Cult3D Optimization

Optimization of Cult3D files involves altering the target delivery bandwidth and/or altering the number of polygons in your 3D model. However, Cult3D is a streaming technology that will alter the polygon data based on the connection speed. For example, if you have a 250KB 3D model, when users view it on the web, they don't have to wait for the full 250KB to download before the model starts to appear.

Cult3D, just like a progressive JPEG image, improves its quality over time. You can, however, decrease the time required to reach the maximum quality by reducing the number of polygons in your 3D model. In 3ds max, you can add an "optimize" modifier to your 3D model. This reduces the polygon count, making your model smaller. You also can use the poly count tool in 3ds max to teach yourself new ways of creating geometry that doesn't require so many polygons.

Next up for optimization are texture maps. If your textures are too big, your model will take much longer to download. Generally, textures of 512×512 are high resolution for 3D on the web, and 256 or even 128×128 are better.

PDF Optimization

Many PDFs are designed for high-quality print output and are not optimized for the web. PDF files are based on PostScript and contain binary data. PDFs use LZW, JPEG, Flate (ZIP), CCITT (the facsimile standard, Group 3 or 4), run-length, and JBIG2 compression (in PDF version 1.4). The last four are used for monochrome images. Like other multimedia formats, optimizing PDFs takes a two-step approach: creating the compound document, and saving it.

Creating Small PDFs

The main factors that increase the size of PDFs are image resolution, image type (bitmapped or vector), and PDF version. To create the smallest possible PDFs for the web, minimize the number embedded images and fonts, substitute vector-based graphics where possible, and capture and prepare the images you include for maximum compressibility. See Chapter 12, "Optimizing Web Graphics," for more information on preparing compressible images.

For graphics that must be inserted as bitmapped images, use the best-quality images that you can at the output resolution of the PDF. This way, Acrobat Distiller compresses them only once, rather than resampling and recompressing images. Inserting compressed JPEGs within PDFs and recompressing them in Distiller can create noticeable artifacts.

Use vector-based graphics when possible for images that you would make into GIFs. Vector images are compact, scale perfectly, and look great at any resolution, even when printed. You also can compress vector image data in your PDF using ZIP compression, which is built into the PDF format. Acrobat Reader version 4 and higher also supports SVG.

Minimize the number of fonts that you use in your PDFs, or use one of the 14 built-in "base" fonts for maximum download speed.

Dynamic PDF Creation

You can create PDFs on the fly in a number of ways. Both open source and commercial products are available. For XML source files, you can use the Formatting Objects Processor (FOP) from Apache (`http://xml.apache.org/fop/`). FOP generates PDFs page by page, so it does basic page optimization and supports PDF version 1.3 (Acrobat 4). Another open source tool in Java is iText (`http://www.lowagie.com/iText/`); this tool converts XML directly into PDF documents and compresses for size but does not linearize.

Many commercial products including PDFLib (`www.pdflib.com`) enable you to create PDF documents on many platforms, including Windows with ASP and ASP.NET.

Saving PDFs

In Acrobat (the full version) or Distiller, you can reduce the resolution of bitmapped images to a fixed value and use JPEG or ZIP compression. Set the resolution to "screen" (72 dpi) to create the smallest files or "eBook" (150 to 300 dpi) for laptops and mobile devices (see Figure 13.10).

Figure 13.10
Distiller downsamples images to 150 and 300 dpi in eBook mode.

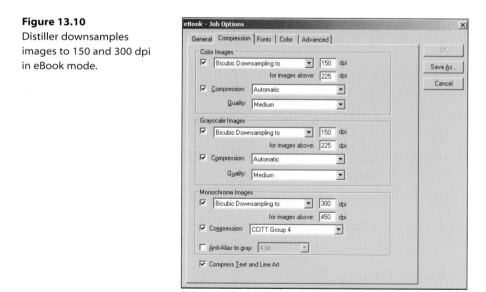

Adobe recommends using the default of eBook over the screen option, although eBook files are larger. Double-check your images for legibility after using the screen setting because they can become blurry. Table 13.2 compares various Distiller settings on a sample file with a number of images:

Table 13.2   Acrobat Distiller Output Setting versus File Size

	PostScript	Screen	eBook	Print	Press
File size	12.3MB	397KB	1.6MB	3.0MB	3.4MB
Image resolution	N/A	72 dpi	150 to 300 dpi	300 to 1200 dpi	2400 dpi

The text itself also can be compressed using ZIP compression in Distiller. Always subset your embedded fonts for the web. Font subsets contain only the glyph descriptions that are actually used in your document. If you don't subset your fonts, the entire font will be included in the PDF document, which can easily add 40KB per font to the file.

To minimize file size, turn off thumbnails when saving PDFs for the web.

For PDF files, the higher the version the smaller the file. Adobe has made Acrobat more efficient with each revision. Of course, using the latest PDF version will create compact files but require that your users have the latest plug-in.

Avoiding Fat Forms

In Acrobat 4, forms can become very large. Acrobat 5 forms are much smaller. For minimum size in Acrobat 5, you can use JavaScript to place the objects in the page. To use this feature, select Document > Set Page Action and select JavaScript from the Action types, and then press the Edit button and enter the JavaScript. See the JavaScript documentation in the Help menu for more details. The disadvantage of this form creation method is that the output is compatible only with Acrobat 5.

Optimizing PDF Files

Even after you've created your PDF, you must optimize the file for the web. Optimizing PDF documents does the following:

- Removes duplicate objects
- Removes old and unneeded versions of objects
- Linearizes the output per page

The result is a compact, linearized PDF that displays the first page (or an arbitrary page) quickly, while the rest of the file downloads. Although linearized PDFs are slightly larger, they also increase perceived speed.

One easy way to trim your PDF file is to Save As to a new file in Acrobat. This removes unnecessary objects automatically. Finally, use the Acrobat's PDF Consultant (select Tools > PDF Consultant) to analyze and remove elements, and select "Optimize Space" (select Tools > PDF Consultant > Optimize Space) to minimize file size.

Further Reading

For more information about PDF optimization, see these resources:

- *Adobe Acrobat 5 Master Class* (Adobe Press, 2002)—The best book on advanced Acrobat. Also includes a "Managing File Size" section on optimizing the size of PDF files.
- PDFzone (http://www.pdfzone.com/)—Devoted exclusively to PDFs and professionals.
- Planet PDF (http://www.planetpdf.com/)—All PDFs, all the time.
- For PDF optimization products, see this book's companion web site (http://www.WebSiteOptimization.com).

Summary

Here's a quick recap of what you have learned in this chapter. You learned about the multiple audio data types out there and found out why MPEG-4 is the new audio format to watch.

You then read about the many different video data types such as QuickTime, WMP, and Real, and learned about the strengths and weaknesses of each. Additionally, you learned about the different methods of delivering your audio or video through streaming, progressive downloading, or straight downloading, and discovered how to compress or encode your files for specific needs.

You covered all aspects of video—from discussions about which hardware to get, how to plan capturing video for use on the Internet, which players are better or worse, and how to optimize your video—and got suggestions for delivering it.

Here is a list of highlights from the chapter:

- QuickTime, RealMedia, and Windows Media Player are the leading video formats.
- Flash, Shockwave, Shockwave 3D, and Cult3D are the leaders in web animation.
- The limitations to multimedia are CPU speed and your customer's bandwidth.
- Remember to keep in mind your goals, your target audience, any limiting factors, and any potential copyright issues.
- When shooting video for the Internet, reduce outside and background noise and use professional equipment, a tripod or stabilizer, and a lot of light.
- When optimizing video, crop the edges, reduce the noise, adjust the gamma, and deinterlace.
- When compressing video, remember that the higher the data rate, the better the quality, but the bigger the file. Use the data-rate formula (W*H*FPS/35000) as a starting point, and always use 2-pass VBR and a multiple of 10 times your FPS for your keyframes.
- When optimizing Flash content, remember these variables: audio, bit rates, reuse symbols, keep animation to a minimum, and generate a file-size report to test.
- When optimizing Flash code, remember to code in Flash 4 whenever possible (version 4's coding style is faster), keep your scripts less than 64K, and use local variables.
- When optimizing Shockwave, remember that the majority of the file-size savings is in the bitmapped graphics and any imported audio.

- When creating PDFs, minimize the number of bitmapped images, objects, and fonts. Use default fonts where possible. Substitute vector images wherever you can.

- To optimize PDFs, eliminate unnecessary objects, subset your fonts, minimize bit depth, use 72 dpi for bitmapped images, and use compression where possible. Use the latest PDF version that most users have, and use Distiller or an optimization tool for minimum file size.

Online Resources

Here's a list of recommended online resources:

- `http://www.apple.com`—Apple Computer, makers of QuickTime.
- `http://www.electricimage.com`—Electric Image Universe.
- `http://www.discreet.com`—Discreet's Cleaner, the premiere streaming media optimization tool.
- `http://www.dvgarage.com`—dvGarage, 3D toolkits and resources.
- `http://www.sorenson.com`—The premiere video codec. Also offers Sorenson Squeeze for Flash MX and QuickTime.
- `http://www.cgchannel.com/`—CG Channel, an online magazine for computer graphic artists and professionals.
- `http://www.mkaku.org/`—Adventures in science.
- `http://www.ninjai.com`—Ninjai: The Little Ninja.
- `http://www.shift.jp.org/`—Shift Japan, an e-zine.
- `http://flasm.sourceforge.net/`—Flasm, Flash ActionScript bytecode assembler/disassembler.
- `http://hotwired.lycos.com/webmonkey/`—WebMonkey.com, Flash, and other developer-related tutorials.

14

Case Study: Apple.com

by Jason Wolf

In this case study, I'll put the techniques you learned in Chapter 13, "Minimizing Multimedia," to work optimizing a video that was done for Apple Computer.

First take a look at Figure 14.1. This is the movie that needs to be compressed. The raw video footage is about a minute long and over 500 megabytes in size. Realistically, this file needs to be under 20 megabytes to play well from a CD and even smaller to play off the Internet.

Figure 14.1
The raw, uncompressed video is over 500 megabytes in size.

This example uses Cleaner (http://www.discreet.com) for the compression because it is the best video encoder and allows one video to be compressed in many different formats.

Within Cleaner, there are tabs that categorize the functions you can perform on your movie. Each category holds a group of functions such as Audio or Encode that allow you to control that specific aspect of your compression.

Output

For this movie, the following settings are activated for the first category, Output:

- **File Suffix (.mov)**—This adds the .mov extension to all your files. This is necessary if your movies are going to be played on a PC.

- **Flatten, Cross-platform, Fast start**—Flatten removes the Macintosh resource fork from your file so that the file can play on a PC, and Fast start enables the playback calculations so that your movie will start playing as soon as enough content has arrived at the player.

- **Compress Movie Header**—This function compresses a portion of the movie that the player can automatically decode. I recommend using this for Internet-based movies, but not for CD-ROM or movies stored on hard drives.

Tracks

The next category is Tracks. Here are the settings that are used:

- **Video settings**—Process. This tells Cleaner that you want to compress the video track. Turning this on activates the Encode tab.

- **Audio settings**—Process. This is the same as the video track, except that it controls audio settings. Turning this on activates the Audio tab.

Image

The next tab category is Image. For the sample clip, the following settings are used:

- **Crop**—Cropping allows you to adjust the video manually to remove any fuzzy edges around the video.
- **Image size**—The size used for this clip is 600×380, to accommodate the UI in which the clip will be displayed.
- **Deinterlace**—Because this clip was shot with a video camera that thinks the video is going on TV, the interlaced frames are adaptively blended together using the "auto" function.
- **Adaptive Noise Reduction**—This is used to remove blockiness by blurring some pixels.

Adjust

In the Adjust tab, the following checkboxes are activated:

- **Gamma**—A gamma setting of 25 is used to help brighten the image on PCs.
- **Brightness**—The brightness is boosted to 10 to help compensate for the darkening effect that compression adds.
- **Contrast**—The contrast is boosted to 5 to help the brightness adjustment look correct.
- **Saturation**—The saturation is boosted just slightly to 2 to add more color overall.

Encode

In the Encode tab, the following settings are used to make the video look as good as possible:

- **Codec**—Sorenson Video 3 Pro is used.
- **Frame Rate**—30 FPS (frames per second).

- **Keyframes**—"every" 90 is used.
- **Video Data Rate**—2-pass VBR is used with a setting of 200Kbps. This is derived by multiplying the width and height by frames per second and then dividing by 35,000. This results in 195.4, which is then rounded up.

Audio

The final tab used is the Audio tab. Here are the settings:

- **Codec**—QDesign Music Pro 2. Each audio codec excels in different areas, and QDesign is great for audio delivery.
- **Sample Rate**—44.100Khz. 44.100 is the same sample rate that CD-ROMs use. The quality is high and the audio should sound good.
- **Depth**—16-bit. QDesign works only in 16-bit.
- **Channels**—Mono. If the file is a bit smaller than expected, you can make the channels stereo.
- **Speed**—The speed is 4Kbps.
- **Volume**—Normalize is selected and set to 95. This attempts to make the audio as loud as possible without distorting the sound.

Final Results

That's all there is to it. These settings produce a 15MB file that looks and sounds perfect. Granted, the size was too big for the web, but quick adjustments to the Size and Data Rate setting made the movie 4MB. To do this, scale the movie to 320×240, lower the frame rate to 15, and lower the data rate to 33Kbps.

V

Search Engine Optimization

15

Keyword Optimization

Search engine optimization (SEO) is about adding finely tuned keywords and phrases to your pages so that you can bring as many relevant visitors to your site as possible. Web site optimization (WSO) is the process of optimizing web sites for maximum speed, which ideally includes SEO as part of the optimization process. WSO and SEO are often used interchangeably, but they are different. WSO is an umbrella term that can optionally incorporate SEO, while SEO is devoted solely to raising search engine relevance to acquire relevant visitors. Now that we've got that straightened out, let's look at what we'll cover in this chapter.

To fully optimize a web site, you need to optimize its keywords. Although the focus of this book is on speed optimization, it's important that you optimize your keywords so that your audience can find your site. A lightning-fast web site won't succeed if no one can find it. This chapter summarizes keyword selection and placement techniques that you can use to maximize the search engine positioning of your site.

The Big Picture

The idea is to place keywords strategically within your pages that match both the gestalt of your site and the terms users actually enter when searching for content like yours. The strategy is to choose keywords that best match the overall theme of your site, but yield few enough appropriate search results that you can achieve competitive rankings. These are your optimum keywords.

WordTracker's Secret Weapon

WordTracker's Keyword Effectiveness Index (KEI) can help you identify the keyword phrases that are most likely to succeed (www.WordTracker.com). The KEI is the ratio of the number of times a term appears in the WordTracker database (its popularity) versus the number of pages that target that phrase (the competition). A keyword phrase with a KEI of 100 is "good," while a KEI of 400 is "excellent" and more likely to be successfully targeted.

Although many developers perform SEO after they've created a site, the best approach is to research keywords and keyphrases beforehand, and build your site around them. The best time to employ optimized keywords is when you are choosing a domain name and organizing your site. If possible, enhance your keyword relevance by using a domain name that contains your top keyphrases. Pay special attention to top-level directories and files because search engines give these higher relevance.

Target Multi-Word Phrases

Unless they are unique, targeting individual keywords is a losing proposition. The competition is intense, and single keywords can sometimes be misleading. Users know that they'll get better search results with multi-word phrases than with individual words (like "cruises in Caribbean" versus "cruises"). Unless you can effectively target unique words like "UNISYS," "JavaScript," or "your ACRONYM or product name here," stick with multi-word phrases for the best results.

NOTE

An NPD Group study of May 9, 2000 found that multiple keyword searching has become more popular than single keyword queries (`http://www.npd.com`).

How Search Engines Rank Sites

Fredrick Marckini, founder of iProspect.com, says that most search engines rank the relevance of your site by using the following keyword factors:[1]

- **Prominence**—How high in your HTML and DOM hierarchy your top keywords appear (`title`, `h1`, etc.).

- **Frequency**—How often your keywords appear.

- **Weight or density**—The ratio of keywords to the total number words within a web page, or a section of a web page (that is, `title` tag density). Used to detect "stuffing" of keywords by search engines.

- **Proximity**—How close keywords are to each other.

- **Placement**—Where you put your keywords within your HTML shows their relative importance and can indicate what your page is about. Search engines favor the following areas for keyword placement:

  - The `title` tag

  - Heading tags (`h1`, `h2`, and so on)

  - The keyword `meta` tag

  - The first 25 visible words

  - Hyperlinked text, URLs, and titles

  - `alt` attributes

- **Off-the-Page Criteria**—In some search engines, the way external sites refer to your page can be more important than what's inside your page:

---

1. Fredrick Marckini, *Search Engine Positioning* (Plano, TX: Wordware Publishing, 2001). The definitive guide for SEO professionals.

- *Inbound Links*—Google, Teoma, and other search engines rank relevance in part based on the number and popularity of inbound links to your page. These "virtual votes" by other webmasters are a good way to improve relevancy.

- *Term Vectors*—A data-mining technique that converts inbound and outbound link characteristics and page terms into numbers representing points in space (vectors) and compares these numbers against an existing database of term vectors to classify pages according to subject and "theme." Focusing your page content on two or three keyword phrases can better define your theme, and thus raise your relevance.

Inbound Link Popularity

Here are two tips for building inbound links to your site:

- Find sites similar to yours that rank highly on Google and other search engines, and ask for a link or an exchange of links.

- Outbound links can also help raise your relevance, so be generous with links to sites you recommend.

Keyword Optimization Guidelines

The following guidelines will help you optimize all of these factors, except inbound links. Maximizing the effects of this factor requires a lot of hard work and time spent gathering external links to your site. Here's a summary of the search engine optimization process, which I expand on in the sections that follow:

1. Determine your keyword phrases.
2. Sort by popularity.
3. Refine and combine keyword phrases.
4. Sort by popularity again (repeat steps 2 and 3 as needed).
5. Write a `title` using your top two to three phrases.

6. Write a `description meta` tag.

7. Write a `keywords meta` tag.

8. Add keywords into key tags and attributes, and mix well.

9. Submit to search engines.

10. Watch the hits roll in.

Step 1: Determine Your Keyword Phrases

The first and most important step is to determine your most important keywords. Ask yourself which keyphrases you want folks to use when finding your site. Include terms that people not familiar with your products and services will use. If you don't know what an *emulsion* is, you'll never look for it. Use *film* or *pictures* instead. Be careful to avoid general terms like *car* or *travel* because they are overused on the Internet. Instead, use more specific keyword phrases that closely match your offerings. Then determine whether people actually use these terms when looking for your site.

Brainstorm Keyphrases

Brainstorm a list of the top 10 terms that describe your site. Find similar terms with `www.Thesaurus.com` and `www.WordTracker.com`. List these terms by their relative importance. Using two or more words as a keyword phrase is best. Single keywords are much more common and are harder to target effectively than multi-word phrases, unless they are unique, such as *DARPA* or *DHTML*.

Use WordTracker's KEI to find the terms most likely to be targeted successfully. Choose terms with higher KEI values. These are popular phrases with fewer competing sites. To illustrate the process, I'll show you how I optimized the keywords for the companion web site for this book, `www.WebSiteOptimization.com`. Keyphrase List 15.1 is my initial stab at our top 10 keyphrases.

Keyphrase List 15.1   Initial Top 10 Terms for WebSiteOptimization.com

web site optimization

web page optimization

html optimization

continues

Keyphrase List 15.1   Initial Top 10 Terms for WebSiteOptimization.com   *continued*

graphics optimization

web speed

performance tuning

java script optimization*

fast web sites

download time

improved usability

*Note that I split the term *JavaScript* into two words after discovering the phrase *java script* is more popular. Note also that I'm using all lowercase phrases. This fits the habits of most users who usually don't capitalize words when search-ing. Most search engines are pretty insensitive when it comes to capitalization.

Step 2: Sort by Popularity

Next, use a search voyeur service like Overture.com's Search Term Suggestion Tool (formerly Goto.com) or WordTracker to find which of these terms are the most popular and most likely to succeed (`http://inventory.overture.com/d/searchinventory/suggestion/`). Figure 15.1 shows an example.

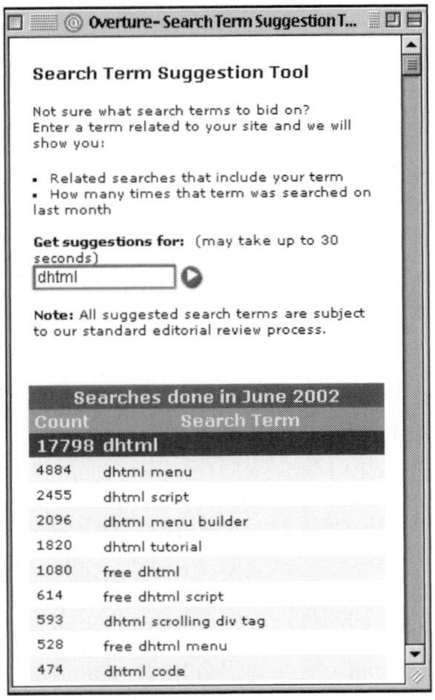

Figure 15.1
Overture.com's search term suggestion tool.

Here's our list of potential keyword phrases, sorted by popularity:

Keyphrase List 15.2   Sorted by Popularity

Number of Hits	Keyphrase
8,995	web site optimization
574	web page optimization
431	fast web site(s)
391	performance tuning
348	web speed
126	graphic(s) optimization
198	download time
39	html optimization
0	improved usability
0	java script optimization

NOTE

Commercial services like WordTracker (`http://www.WordTracker.com`) can help you brainstorm and refine keyphrases and sort by popularity and KEI. For more search voyeur services, see the list at Search Engine Watch (`http://www.searchenginewatch.com/facts/searches.html`).

This list tells you how often people searched for each term at Overture.com in the last month. As you can see, we have some work to do. A couple of the terms had no hits in the past month, and some terms are relatively popular. There is indeed a difference between the keywords we *think* people will use, and those they *actually* use. Let's brainstorm keyphrases again and see if we can improve our results:

Keyphrase List 15.3   Improved by Popularity

Number of Hits	Keyphrase
11,208	internet speed
8,995	web site optimization
1,714	fast internet

continues

Keyphrase List 15.3   Improved by Popularity   *continued*

Number of Hits	Keyphrase
574	web page optimization
431	fast(er) web site(s)
414	quick web page
391	performance tuning
348	web speed
126	graphic(s) optimization
68	java script performance
39	html optimization

This is much better, though some terms are still not as specific as they should be. There also are some near duplicates that we can discard. That's where techniques like *word stemming* and *proximity grouping* come in.

Word Stemming

Most search engines parse words for their roots, removing all prefixes and suffixes. By using longer words and plurals, you'll get more matches with fewer keywords. For example, use "*graphics* optimization," not "*graphic* optimization." Users searching on the word *graphic* will still get a hit if you use the plural, *graphics*.

Eliminate near duplicates and include or extend keywords to replace them. Don't use "stop words" like *a, and, it, of, that, the,* and *too* because they are filtered out by the search engines anyway. Also avoid "filter" words like *web* that are so popular they are routinely eliminated from non-quoted queries.

Proximity Grouping

Search engines rank web page relevance in part by keyword proximity; that is, by how close terms are to each other. You can use this creatively by combining similar terms into one longer phrase. If you tack keywords onto either end of popular phrases, you can combine multiple phrases into one. For example:

    11,208—internet speed

    2,720—faster internet

    1,002—speed boost

These can all be combined into:

14930†—(faster) internet speed (boost)
† means the total phrase value. Parentheses denote phrase combinations.

By using proximity grouping, you can get more phrase matches with fewer words.

Step 3: Refine Keyword Phrases

Now brainstorm on other relevant phrases for your site. Don't hold back.

Write down every keyword you can think of that could be used in searching for your site. Look at the `meta` tags of your competitors to see which terms they are using. Cross check your search logs to see what your users are actually searching for. Analyze your referrer logs to see which search phrases are bringing in search engine traffic. Break out that thesaurus (or use `www.Thesaurus.com`) to find similar words. Reuse online brainstorming services like WordTracker.com to refine keyword phrases. Then refine your list of terms with those on other search engines that display related searches, like AltaVista and HotBot, and cross check for related terms at Yahoo!.

Don't worry if your list gets too long. The popularity filter will bubble the better terms to the top. Go through your list again, and remove any terms that don't apply to your site or that you feel won't fare well with existing sites. Here's my updated list:

Keyphrase List 15.4   Brainstorming Other Possible Keywords

(optimizing) animated gif(s)

web page design

crazy fast web sites

advanced html

hyperspeed web pages

hyperspeed hypertext

(fast) internet speed

warp speed connections

web site ranking

fast web site

continues

Keyphrase List 15.4   Brainstorming Other Possible Keywords *continued*

fast flow state

web site search engine optimization

speed boost

optimized keywords

web page optimization

html compression

bandwidth

increased usability

accelerate the web

faster downloads

meta tag optimization

html optimization

jpeg compression

java obfuscation and optimization

javascript obfuscation and optimization

java script archive

web site performance

server performance tuning

Step 4: Sort by Popularity Again

As you can see, this is an iterative process. You'll find that certain terms will appear wildly popular for searches; for example, *computer, software, free,* and *web design.* Avoid the temptation to use those phrases. Use only the terms that accurately describe your site and are popular, but not too popular. Any terms with ratings over 100,000 hits are probably too popular and not worth pursuing. Also, reuse WordTracker's KEI to find terms most likely to be targeted effectively. The higher KEI, the better (over 400 is "excellent"). For each keyphrase, WordTracker will let you know potential referral traffic and the number of competing web pages for each search engine. You may go through the sort and refine steps 2 and 3 a few times until you are happy with your list.

Here's my refined list of keyphrases, sorted by popularity:

Keyphrase List 15.5 Refined Master List Sorted by Popularity

Number of Hits	Keyphrase
92,663	web site design
84,390†	(optimizing) animated gif(s)
39,303	web page design
34,438	bandwidth
14,415	web site development
11,208	internet speed
9,990	web site ranking
9,198	web site search engine optimization
8,995	web site optimization
8,253	bandwidth speed test
7,739	performance appraisal
7,351	web accelerator
3,946	faster downloads
2,926	improve search engine ranking
2,720	faster internet
1,725	speed up internet
1,714	fast internet
1,346	fast web
1,192	fast download
1,002	speed boost
980	advanced html
904	web usability
873	fast browser
858	web site load testing
776	compression software
711	image compression
706	increase web site ranking
638	optimization services

continues

Keyphrase List 15.5   Refined Master List Sorted by Popularity   *continued*

Number of Hits	Keyphrase
583	increase internet speed
574	web page optimization
564	optimize keyword
505	meta tag optimization
488	web optimization
483	keyword optimization
479	java script archive
466	jpeg compression
441	jpeg optimizer
431	fast web site
414	quick web page
401	web site optimization services
391	performance tuning
357	web site performance
348	web speed
337	file size
320	java script validation
319	internet optimization
268	maximum performance
263	optimized meta tag
254	web site usability
745	lzw compression algorithm
277	gif optimizer
242	url optimization
214	slow response
210	jpeg compressor
200	zip compression
196	optimize web site
187	jpeg compression
179	performance optimization
164	web server performance

Number of Hits	Keyphrase
160	lossless compression
145	lossy compression
127	gif compression
126	graphic(s) optimization
106	professional web page optimization
99	web site optimization consultant
92	high speed web site
77	html compression
62	html compress
52	optimized web site design
43	compress html
39	html optimization
28	shrink web page size

† denotes terms and scores that were combined.

Now you have your master list. Let's combine and refine these terms strategically, using the proximity technique you learned earlier and weed out the terms that don't apply to your site. The crossed-out terms in Keyphrase List 15.6 have been discarded for more popular and relevant terms.

Keyphrase List 15.6   Combine and Refine

Number of Hits	Keyphrase
84,390†	(optimizing) animated gif(s)
42,691†	bandwidth (speed test)
14,930†	(faster) internet speed (boost)
10,034†	web site optimization (services)
9,990	web site ranking
9,198	web site search engine optimization
~~8,253~~	~~bandwidth speed test~~
~~7,739~~	~~performance appraisal~~

continues

Keyphrase List 15.6   Combine and Refine   *continued*

Number of Hits	Keyphrase
7,351	web accelerator
1,777†	fast web site(s)
~~1,714~~	~~fast internet~~
~~1,002~~	~~speed boost~~
980	advanced html
904†	(improved) web usability
853†	(html) compression software
748†	web site performance (tuning)
745	lzw compression algorithm
711†	(jpeg gif lzw) image compression
~~638~~	~~optimization services~~
574	web page optimization
564	optimize keyword(s)
~~505~~	~~meta tag optimization~~
~~488~~	~~web optimization~~
~~483~~	~~keyword optimization~~
~~479~~	~~java script archive~~
~~466~~	~~jpeg compression~~
~~441~~	~~jpeg optimizer~~
414	quick web page
~~401~~	~~web site optimization services~~
~~391~~	~~performance tuning~~
~~383‡~~	~~(page) file size~~
348	web speed
~~319~~	~~internet optimization~~
~~277~~	~~gif optimizer~~
254	web site usability
~~242~~	~~url optimization~~
~~210~~	~~jpeg compressor~~
~~196~~	~~optimize(d) web site~~
~~187~~	~~jpeg compression~~

Number of Hits	Keyphrase
~~179~~	~~performance optimization~~
~~164~~	~~web server performance~~
~~160~~	~~lossless compression~~
~~145~~	~~lossy compression~~
139†	html compress(ion)
~~127~~	~~gif compression~~
126	graphic(s) optimization
~~106~~	~~professional web page optimization~~
~~99~~	~~web site optimization consultant~~
92	high speed web site
~~62~~	~~html compress~~
68	java script performance
~~52~~	~~optimized web site design~~
~~43~~	~~compress html~~
39	html optimization
~~28~~	~~shrink web page size~~

† denotes terms and scores that were combined.

You should now have a list of approximately 20 to 50 prime keyword phrases that describe your site, sorted by popularity. You'll use these keywords to craft your key HTML tags. If you've really planned ahead, you can use them to choose your domain name and URLs, because search engines place a high value on keywords in these locations.

Start with Your Home Page

The home page of your site is the most important page search engines index. You need to ensure that your home page has a keyword-rich URL (if possible), `title` tag, `meta` tags, headers, `img` tag `alt` attributes, filenames, links and link text, and other information that makes effective use of your key terms.

Step 5: Write a *title* Using the Top Two to Three Phrases

Other than your domain name, the `title` tag is the most important item that search engines index. Title tags should use your top two or three terms and total between 7 to 15 words, ideally 10 words or less. Search engines and directories generally index the entire title but display only 55 to 90 characters of your title, with most averaging 70 to 80 characters in length. Put your top keyphrases first. Don't use "Home Page" or "Welcome to our Company.com." For example:

```
<title>WebSiteOptimization.com · speed up your site with web site optimization and
optimized html</title>
```

Note that our top term is also our domain name. This optimum placement of keywords is not by coincidence. Using your top term as part of your domain name is the best way to ensure that you'll be found on the Internet. I also repeat my top term later on, and include the book title.

Due to the overuse of the `keywords meta` tag, most search engines place lower importance on its contents. Therefore, it's important to spend time crafting a good `title` tag that concisely conveys the message of your site and top keyword phrases. And, if that's not enough, you also need to make your site sound irresistible. Search engines use the `title` tag to create a link to your site in their results list, so you need to make your title text appealing. Because your `title` tag carries a lot of weight, you need to spend some time on it to make it count. So instead of this meaningless `title`:

```
<title>Welcome to our company!</title>
```

Do this:

```
<title>Sprockets, gears, and gizmos · Sprockets.com gets you in gear</title>
```

Step 6: Write a *description meta* Tag

Next, you need to craft a succinct description of your site, reiterating your most important keyword phrases. Don't just repeat your `title` tag, because search engines often use the `description` tag to annotate your link. The same title copy would yield the same sentence twice! The description should be no more than 25 words (search engine display limits range from 150 to 200 characters and index from 200 to 250 characters). Make this description an attractive summary of your content without marketing hype. Again, weave in the keyphrases by which you want to be known. For example:

```
<meta name = "description" content = "Web site optimization speeds up web page downloads
and increases website rankings. Optimizing web pages increases website speed and decreases
bailout rates, using advanced html, image, javascript and java optimization and
compression.">
```

This paragraph has 32 words, which is close enough to the 25-word limit. Descriptions typically are used by search engines on results pages and in some directory listings. Make sure that your most important descriptive text is in the first 25 words (or 150 to 200 characters) because some search engines may cut off your description at this point.

Step 7: Write a *keywords meta* Tag

The `keywords meta` tag contains keyword phrases that describe topics covered within the page. Make sure that you include the top terms by which you want your site to be found, plus any key terms already within your page. The `keywords meta` tag should be 200 characters or less. Here is an example:

```
<meta name = "keywords" content = "web site optimization services faster internet speed
boost bandwidth speed fast web site search engine optimization web page optimization
ranking advanced html compression http web site usability image compression quick web page
performance tuning">
```

Commas can be used to delineate phrases, and you can omit spaces after commas to save space. I prefer not to use commas and to carefully place important phrases next to each other for more proximity hits from search engine algorithms. Be careful, however, because omitting commas can yield new combinations with unexpected meanings. You can add commas as needed to clear up any ambiguities.

Note also that we include terms here from our home page, which we analyzed using a word frequency summarization tool in our favorite text editor. If you include terms that appear within your page, you can raise your relevancy in search engines by "magnifying" these terms. Do not repeat the same term more than three times.

Search engines now emphasize `title` tags over the `keywords meta` tag, so you can save some bytes by shortening the `keywords` tag. For household names like Yahoo! or AOL, you can even omit these `meta` tags altogether or use conditional `meta` tags, which are discussed in Chapter 17, "Server-Side Techniques."

Step 8: Add Keywords into Key Tags and Attributes, and Mix Well

Make sure that your top keyphrases are well represented throughout your page. Liberally, but not too liberally, add your top phrases within your `body` text, especially in `h1`s, the first 25 words, link text, URLs, and `alt` attributes. This should occur naturally in relevant pages. Search engines generally know every trick in the book and can penalize or banish sites for keyword "spamming" techniques (or "spamdexing"). Avoid using artificial techniques like double `title` tags, keyword-rich comments, and `alt` attributes stuffed with keywords.

Keyword Density

Shorter pages generally rank higher than longer pages because with fewer total words per page, the percentage of relevant keywords increases. However, search engines may flag extremely short pages because they look for realistic pages based on average page lengths. Optimal page length varies from around 400 to 700 words, according to WebPosition Gold's reporter. So don't stuff in too many keywords, or search engines may flag your page. Depending on which search engine you target, the *keyword density* (keywords/ visible word ratio) should be lower than 3 to 10 percent or you'll risk banishment. Search engine designers favor naturally occurring patterns in web pages rather than artificial ones.

Keyword Placement Priority

Search engines vary in the way they calculate relevance, but they all place more importance on the following factors:

- **Domain**—Keywords in domain
- `title`—Keywords in title
- `h1 to h6`—Keywords in headline elements
- **HTML**—Keywords in the first 2KB to 3KB of your page
- `meta` **tags**—Keywords in `description` and `keywords` meta tags

- **Links**—Keywords in anchor URLs, text, and `title` attribute
- **`alt` attribute values**

Some of the newer search engines like Google.com and Teoma.com also take external and internal links into account. Google's PageRank algorithm is seemingly immune to influence and "keyword spam." Instead, it relies in part on the inbound links to your site.

But all links are not created equal. Links are relevant only if the theme of the linking site matches yours. A link from an off-topic site carries little weight compared to a link from a similar site. Strive to get targeted links from sites like yours.

In my experience, there is no substitute for longevity on the web. The older your site, the more external links you'll generally have (assuming that you have some up-to-date content worth linking to). It's important to get your site out there and publicized as soon as it's ready.

Step 9: Submit to Search Engines

Once you're happy with your new and improved keywords and have placed them strategically throughout your pages, it's time to submit. The best way to submit your pages to search engines and directories is to do it by hand. Automated services can help, but would you trust your listing in AltaVista or Yahoo! to some automated spider?

Make sure that you check out the search engine's help pages first, *before* you submit. Each has different rules and guidelines with which your site must comply. Some search engines require only that you submit your top-level URL, while others require more information.

Don't over submit! If a page is already listed, don't submit it again. Check whether the page has been indexed using the `link:` or `url:` syntax (see the search engine's help page for specifics).

For details on which sites to submit to and other search engine topics, I recommend Danny Sullivan's SearchEngineWatch.com (`http://www.searchenginewatch.com`) and Fredrick Marckini's iProspect.com (`http://www.iProspect.com`).

Step 10: Watch the Hits Roll In

Anywhere from a few minutes to weeks later, you'll start to see referral traffic from the search engines that have added your site to their databases. By the time you read this, Google will probably have overtaken Yahoo! for search referral traffic. However, getting a high listing in Google doesn't happen overnight. Google's PageRank algorithm weighs external links from popular sites heavily when ranking web site relevance. So before you submit to Google, be sure you first have some links to your site—the more the better. I have found that there is no substitute for one-to-one networking and time.

SEO should be followed up every month. Check your server logs to see what people and spiders are doing on your site. Adjust the site accordingly. Perhaps introduce extra keywords, or expand popular topic areas, or create new content in topics users are searching for. Check the positioning of your pages in all major search engines and any specialized directories and search engines in your topic area. Webposition Gold (www.WebPosition.com) is a valuable tool for monitoring your progress.

Spider-Friendly Design Tips

Most search engine spiders don't index everything you embed in a web page. Flash, Java, Shockwave, graphics, and frames are a few of the roadblocks automated spiders run up against when parsing pages. Spiders don't read graphics or many embedded objects, but text is easily digested. Text is the universal language of spiders. Here are a few spider-friendly design tips to keep in mind:

- **Dynamic content**—Avoid the question mark (?) for dynamically generated content, as most search engines don't follow these links. CMS tools like Vignette Story Server (http://www.vignette.com) can generate pages without the query command.

- **Flash**—Flash content is not indexed; instead, only the alternate content or HTML page is indexed. Make sure that you provide alternatives. Flash MX addresses these accessibility issues to some degree.

- **Frames**—Some spiders don't support frames. Avoid frames, especially on home pages. They can degrade usability and slow page display.

- **Images**—Provide text alternatives for all functional images. Substitute styled text for graphic text where possible.

- **Links**—Always use an anchor tag to link pages (such as `<a href="...">`), not a `javascript:` link. Most spiders don't follow `javascript:` or Flash links; they understand only HTML.

- **JavaScript and CSS**—Use external JavaScript and CSS files to maximize relevance. External JavaScript and CSS files are search engine friendly and move your content higher up in your code. You also can use keywords in `class` and `id` names.

- **Structure**—Favor breadth over depth for site hierarchy. Spiders don't crawl more than two or three links deep, which means that sites with deep site hierarchies may not be fully indexed. Avoid splash screens because they add another level.

- **Hidden text**—Avoid using text that is the same color as the background. Search engines flag this common keyword "stuffing" technique.

Page Characteristics of High-Ranking Results

Axandra (`http://www.axandra.com/`), a German company, has studied which factors affect high rankings in popular search engines, including Google, AllTheWeb, iWon/Inktomi, Wisenut, Teoma, and AltaVista. Their April 2002 "Google Ranking Study"[2] looked at the characteristics of pages that ranked in the top 10 for 1,721 popular keyphrases.

Johannes Selbach, cofounder of Voget Selbach Enterprises GmbH, says about the study: "We want to give our readers accurate data on what kind of web pages Google (and other search engines) currently rank in the top 10 so that they can make their own conclusions."[3]

---

2. André Voget and Johannes Selbach, "Google Ranking Study, Q2/2002," [online], (2002), available from the Internet at `http://www.axandra.com/search-engine-studies/`. An empirical analysis of top 10 results on Google.com.
3. Johannes Selbach, email to author. 22 August 2002.

They analyzed more than 100,000 web pages for various measurable characteristics such as matching keyphrases, placement, frequency, and more. Some of their findings may surprise you. Figure 15.2 shows you what their JavaScript Usage section looks like.

Figure 15.2
Axandra.com Google ranking study—JavaScript usage.

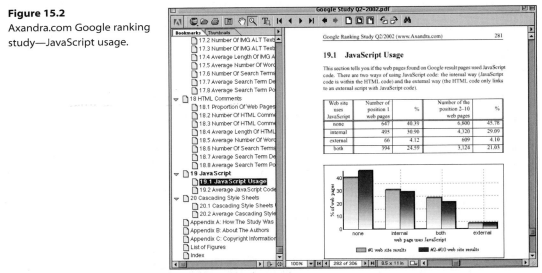

http://www.axandra.com/

For example, most results pages on Google ranking in the top 10 have these characteristics:

- Have zero or one matching keyphrase in the `title` or `h1` tags.
- Have `head` sizes from 50 to 700 bytes.
- Are older than three or four years.
- Use two or three `meta` tags.
- Average 20.4KB per page.

In addition, the following is true of the top 10 results:

- Nearly 85 percent have search term densities of around 0 percent.
- 94 percent have search term densities of less than 5 percent.
- 4.3 percent use Flash or Shockwave.
- Less than 3 percent use Java.
- Over 81 percent don't have search terms in hyperlink URLs.

So the typical high-ranked page on Google is over three to four years old (this provides external links to your site), and low-tech (few use Flash or Java). It uses two or three `meta` tags in a trim `head` from 50 to 700 bytes in size, averages around 20KB, and uses keywords sparingly. Fat keyword-filled pages clearly don't rank well on search engines like Google.

There's an entire industry of firms that are built around attaining high search engine rankings. Some of these firms are bogus, while others are legitimate. Choose wisely, because the reputation of your site may hang in the balance. By applying what you've learned in this chapter, you'll have a solid keyword foundation that will attract qualified customers interested in buying your products instead of undifferentiated traffic.

Summary

The purpose of search engine optimization is to make finding your site easy for users who are interested in your topic areas. By tagging your pages with the phrases that best match the overall theme of your site, you can ensure that users will find your site when searching for content like yours. Choose popular—but not too popular—phrases that best describe your site, and use them strategically within your pages. Studies have shown that a restrained approach works best with popular search engines like Google.

Here is a list of this chapter's highlights:

- Target multi-word phrases unless your keywords are unique.
- Gather external links on high-ranking sites like yours through tireless PR and compelling up-to-date content.
- Use word stemming and proximity grouping to maximize hits and minimize words.
- Find your optimum keywords through iteration, popularity, and WordTracker's KEI.
- Write a keyword-rich `title` tag. Put the top keyphrase up front.
- Use your optimum phrases in your `title`, `h1` through `h6`, `meta description`, `meta keywords`, and `body` text, and link URLs, text, and `title` attributes.

- Include your top keyphrase(s) in your domain name—ideally, your optimum keyphrases would determine your domain name choice and top-level directory and filenames.
- Minimize the `head` section for maximum relevance.
- Use external JavaScript and CSS files to raise relevance.
- Use meaningful `alt` attribute values (`alt="company.com"`, not `alt="logo image"`).
- Don't overdo it. Target one or two keyphrases that describe your site.
- Practice spider-friendly design—Avoid spider-stopping technology like ? and JavaScript in links, frames, and Flash.
- Watch your keyword density or risk banishment.

Online Resources

Try these sites for more information:

- `www.iProspect.com`—Search engine positioning firm.
- `www.Pandia.com`—An SEO portal with many useful resources.
- `www.PositionPro.com`—Web-based submission service.
- `www.se-optimizer.com`—The Search Engine Optimizer program checks web pages for optimum relevancy.
- `www.SearchEngineWatch.com`—Danny Sullivan's search engine information portal.
- `www.SearchEngineWorkshops.com`—SEO workshops and information from John Alexander and Robin Nobles.
- `www.Thesaurus.com`—Helps find similar words.
- `www.WebPosition.com`—WebPosition Gold Software is the gold standard for SEP. It includes a suite of integrated modules designed to raise relevance, including page generation and critique, and submission.
- `www.WordTracker.com`—Brainstorm keywords with this subscription-based service. Choose phrases with a high KEI (Keyword Effectiveness Index).

16

Case Studies: PopularMechanics.com and iProspect.com

In this chapter, you apply the techniques you learned in Chapter 15, "Keyword Optimization," to two web sites. The first site, PopularMechanics.com, shows what *not* to do when optimizing your site for maximum relevance. The second, iProspect.com, demonstrates the right way to select and place keywords within your pages.

PopularMechanics.com

First let's look at what not to do. For that, we turn to the PopularMechanics.com home page (see Figure 16.1).

Here's the (first) head section of the PopularMechanics.com home page:

```
<html>
<head>
<title>Popular Mechanics</title>
<meta http-equiv="Content-Type" content="text/html; charset=iso-8859-1">
<meta name="site" content="PM_Zone">
<meta name="Description" content="">
<meta name="Keywords" content="">
<meta name="department" content="">
<meta name="date" content="">
<meta name="display" content="">
```

```
<SCRIPT LANGUAGE="JavaScript">
function formHandler(form){
var URL = document.form.site.options[document.form.site.selectedIndex].value;
window.location.href = URL;
}
</SCRIPT>
</HEAD>
```

Figure 16.1
PopularMechanics.com
(May 7, 2002).

http://www.popularmechanics.com/

Popular Mechanics is a magazine devoted to do-it-yourselfers and handymen and women, with automotive, science and technology, home improvement, and the outdoors listed as some of their main topic areas. Unfortunately, their online companion site, PopularMechanics.com, takes little advantage of this rich set of keywords within their pages. Keyword-free title tags, blank `meta` tags and `alt` attributes, an oversized `head` section, commented code, and syntax errors highlight this poster child for web site optimization. Let's start at the top and work our way down.

Term-Limited *title*

`<title>Popular Mechanics</title>`

This is a good start, but Hearst Communications is wasting a perfectly good `title` tag by omitting their prime search terms. Let's take them at their word and use their main topic headings:

```
<title>Popular Mechanics - automotive, science and technology, home improvement news
outdoors</title>
```

This is much better. Another improvement would be to put their top keywords up front, before their name. Remember from our Keyword Optimization Guidelines to write a `title` using your top two to three phrases. It goes downhill from there, however.

Empty *meta* Tags

PopularMechanics.com includes many `meta` tags, but most of them are blank. All but the `description` and `keywords` tags can be deleted. So instead of this:

```
<meta http-equiv="Content-Type" content="text/html; charset=iso-8859-1">
<meta name="site" content="PM_Zone">
<meta name="Description" content="">
<meta name="Keywords" content="">
<meta name="department" content="">
<meta name="date" content="">
<meta name="display" content="">
<SCRIPT LANGUAGE="JavaScript">
function formHandler(form){
var URL = document.form.site.options[document.form.site.selectedIndex].value;
window.location.href = URL;
}
</SCRIPT>
</HEAD>
```

They should do this:

```
<meta name="description" content="Popular Mechanics is a magazine devoted to ...">
<meta name="keywords" content="automotive do-it-yourself science technology outdoors
handyman house repair ...">
```

Be sure to include your top keyword phrases in the `description` and `keywords` `meta` tags. All the other `meta` tags are superfluous or can be accomplished more efficiently with server settings.

Big *head*

Search engines generally give higher relevance to pages that get to the point within the first 2KB to 3KB of code. The `head` section of a web page should be minimized both to decrease load time and to increase relevance.

PopularMechanics.com uses 1,783 lines of CSS and JavaScript before you get to the body tag. This 60KB+ block of code must be loaded before any content can be displayed and before visible text can be indexed. Their head section alone is twice as large as many home pages. Highlights include internal overspecified CSS, iSyndicated content place-holders and instructions, profuse comments, and JavaScript galore (some of which is not used).

So instead of this (imagine a long jumble of JavaScript, CSS, and comments):

```
<!-- first head section here - ABK -->
</SCRIPT>
</HEAD>
<!-- second head section starts here - ABK -->

<style type="text/css">
<!-- lots of CSS and JavaScript here - ABK -->


...
</script>
<!--  End rollovers (yellow_navigational_buttons)   -->
<!-- PowerAd -->
<!-- PowerAd -->
</head>
<!-- feed name ="Top New" -->
<!-- article -->

<BODY OnUnLoad="checkCount()"  leftmargin="0" topmargin="0" marginwidth="0"
marginheight="0"
onLoad="MM_preloadImages('/images/b_auton.gif','/images/b_himpon.gif','/images/b_scion.gif'
,'/images/b_outon.gif','/images/b_techon.gif','/images/b_srcon.gif','/b_whton.gif','/images
/b_shpon.gif','/images/b_crron.gif','/images/b_emlon.gif','/images/b_advon.gif','/images/b_
msgon.gif')">
```

They should do this:

```
<html><head><title>Popular Mechanics - automotive, science and technology, home
improvement news</title>
<meta name="description" content="Popular Mechanics is a magazine devoted to ...">
<meta name="keywords" content="outdoors automotive do-it-yourself science technology do it
yourself handyman house repair ...">
<link rel="stylesheet" type="text/css" href="/css/global.css">
<script src="/js/global.js" type="text/javascript"></script>
</head>
<body>
```

This simplified `head` section saves PopularMechanics.com nearly 60KB of code, from 61,569 characters down to less than 500 characters. Most of the JavaScript can be eliminated, optimized, moved to external scripts, or shunted into server-based scripts. The overspecified CSS can be simplified, optimized, and moved to an external style sheet.

Search engines will now get to the visible text much earlier in the page, and users won't resort to home-improvement projects while waiting for the page to display. The lesson? Remember to minimize your `head` section.

Sharp-eyed readers will notice that PopularMechanics.com has two closing `</head>` tags, which means that not all their CSS is HTML 4 compliant. They also specify their `body` styles twice, with a huge `body` tag that appears to be generated by Dreamweaver. I'd eliminate the rollovers entirely, or use a more efficient alternative, such as one from Doc JavaScript (`http://www.docjs.com`), `www.DHTML.com`, or `xml.apache.org`—or even better, use CSS rollovers (see Chapter 8, "Advanced CSS Optimization," for more information).

Missing *alt* Attributes

PopularMechanics.com uses graphic text for their primary navigation, but they do not provide text alternatives for the visually challenged or for folks with images turned off (which is likely if they return a second time). Alternative descriptions (`alt` attributes) are a required attribute of image elements in HTML 4.x and XHTML.

Here PopularMechanics.com misses on two counts:

- Search engines rank link text and URLs higher than regular text.
- Search engines also look inside `alt` attributes for keywords.

Search engines can't read a graphic "automotive" or "technology" button, so they will not see these keywords. Vision-impaired users need descriptive `alt` attributes to help navigate a site.

So instead of this automotive menu item:

```
<tr>
            <td width="1" height="17" align="left" valign="top"></td>
            <td width="123" height="17" align="left" valign="top"><a
href="/automotive/index.phtml" onMouseOver="HISpopUp('HISelMenu2',event);
img_act('red_automotive')" onMouseOut="HISpopDown('HISelMenu2');
img_inact('red_automotive')" style="color:fefefe"><img name=red_automotive
src="/images/b_autoff.gif" width=119 height=17 alt="" border=0></a></td>
        </tr>
```

They should do this:

```
<tr>
<td width="1"><img src="/t.gif" width="1" height="17" alt=""></td>
<td width="123"><a href="/automotive/" onMouseOver="HISpopUp('HISelMenu2',event);
img_act('automotive')" onMouseOut="HISpopDown('HISelMenu2'); img_inact('automotive')"
style="color:#fefefe"><img name="automotive" src="/images/b_autoff.gif" width="119"
height="17" alt="automotive" border="0"></a></td>
</tr>
```

Notice that I've used defaults (`align="left"`) and simplified the image names to use the `'automotive'` keyword. I also simplified the unnecessary 1-pixel spacer cell. To prepare PopularMechanics.com for XHTML, I've added quotes on all the attributes.

Most importantly, I added a meaningful `alt` attribute value of `"automotive"`.

Even better, remove the DHTML menus entirely and use style sheets:

```
<tr>
<td width="123"><a href="/automotive/" class="r">Automotive</a></td>
</tr>
```

This HTML could be optimized further, but this should give you an idea of the savings you can achieve. These improvements would dramatically improve the search engine rankings of PopularMechanics.com.

iProspect.com

The home page of a professional search engine optimization firm is a good place to learn positioning techniques. One of the better ones is iProspect.com (see Figure 16.2).

Founded by Fred Marckini, author of *Search Engine Positioning* (Wordware Publishing, 2001), iProspect.com offers search engine optimization services to high-profile clients.

Figure 16.2
The iProspect.com
home page.

http://www.iprospect.com/

Let's take a look at the `head` section:

```
<html>
<head>
<TITLE>iProspect: Search Engine Optimization and Search Engine Positioning Professional
Services</TITLE>
<META NAME="description" CONTENT="iProspect's search engine optimization strategies
increase Web traffic and market reach. iProspect offers comprehensive search engine
optimization services to drive qualified visitors.">
<META NAME="keywords" CONTENT="search engine optimization, search engine positioning,
search engine positioning firm, search engine optimization, iprospect, search engine
optimization, search engine positioning, iprospect.com">

        <script language="JavaScript" src="http://www.iprospect.com/ref.js"></script>
        <link rel="stylesheet" type="text/css" href="includes/iprospect.css">
<script language="JavaScript" src="http://www.iprospect.com/oc.js"></script>
</HEAD>
```

This is much better than the PopularMechanics.com `head` section. The `title` tag highlights their prime keyword phrase. The `description` and `keywords` `meta` tags are carefully
crafted and use external JavaScripts and style sheets to help minimize the `head` size for
maximum relevance.

Title with Keywords

People generally search for topics and services rather than particular company names. iProspect.com designers naturally chose to highlight the term "search engine optimization" in their `title` and throughout their home page. They chose to place their company name first, followed by their most important phrase:

```
<TITLE>iProspect: Search Engine Optimization and Search Engine Positioning Professional
Services</TITLE>
```

Putting their company name first emphasizes their brand, although putting their top term first would emphasize their top keyword phrase more. For example:

```
<title>Search Engine Optimization from iProspect - professional search engine positioning
services</title>
```

The exception is when your company name contains a keyword phrase that you want to target. Ideally your domain name should also contain the keyword phrase that you want to target.

Keyword-Rich *meta* Tags

iProspect.com shows the right way to use `meta` tags. They only include the `description` and `keywords` meta tags, and they are well-crafted, as you would expect:

```
<META NAME="description" CONTENT="iProspect's search engine optimization strategies
increase Web traffic and market reach. iProspect offers comprehensive search engine
optimization services to drive qualified visitors.">
```

```
<META NAME="keywords" CONTENT="search engine optimization, search engine positioning,
search engine positioning firm, search engine optimization, iprospect, search engine
optimization, search engine positioning, iprospect.com">
```

The 220-character `description` tag highlights their key phrase "search engine optimization" early on in the description, and again a second time. They emphasize the benefit of increased traffic and include their company name. The 227-character `keywords` tag highlights the two main phrases they are targeting; that is "search engine optimization" and "search engine positioning." They use commas to separate phrases and they also include their company name and URL. There's no question what this firm is about.

Minimal *head*

The `head` section is 792 characters. This is nearly two orders of magnitude smaller than the `head` section of PopularMechanics.com, but it could be reduced further. The JavaScript files could be combined into one, and the URLs could be shortened, but these are minor quibbles. iProspect.com uses absolute URLs, no doubt to increase the relevance of their company name.

So this:

```
<script language="JavaScript" src="http://www.iprospect.com/ref.js"></script>
<link rel="stylesheet" type="text/css" href="includes/iprospect.css">
<script language="JavaScript" src="http://www.iprospect.com/oc.js"></script>
</HEAD>
```

Could become this:

```
<script type="text/javascript" src="/refoc.js"></script>
<link rel="stylesheet" type="text/css" href="/i.css">
</head>
```

As you can see, there's a tradeoff between maximum search engine optimization and maximum speed. You can make your pages fast, but then they'll likely be less relevant. Or you can make your pages more relevant as iProspect.com has naturally chosen to do, and they'll be slower. What you choose within this range is up to you, but most webmasters do not have to go as far as iProspect.com has gone.

Meaningful *alt* Attributes

Here is one area where iProspect.com could use some improvement: They have no `alt` attributes in their `img` tags. The logo and home buttons have no `alt` attributes. The spacer GIFs need blank `alt` attribute values, and their URLs could use some shortening.

So instead of this:

```
<img src="images/logo_iprospect.gif" width="253" height="62">
```

They should do this:

```
<img src="images/logo_iprospect.gif" width="253" height="62" alt="iprospect.com">
```

Add Keywords into Key Tags and Attributes, and Mix Well

Remember Step #8 of the Keyword Optimization Guidelines: Add your keywords into `key` tags and attributes, and mix well. Here iProspect.com does an admirable job of adding keyword phrases within URLs, link text, and top-level headers. Here are some examples:

```
<td><a href="search_engine_placement/seo_industry.htm">the industry</a></td>
...
<td><a href="search_engine_ranking/research.htm">research</a></td>
```

Notice that they use keyword-rich URLs throughout the page, varying the names of the file and directory to maximize relevance. This is admittedly an extreme example, as the organizational structure is sacrificed for relevance. Let's take a look at their first main heading:

```
<p><b>The Original™ Search Engine Positioning Firm</b>
```

This heading has their tag line and one of their top keyphrases, which is good. But it isn't a heading at all. They miss an important opportunity here by not using a styled `h1` element that could achieve the same effect, and give higher relevance. Their previous home page used a styled `h1` with a link to their most important phrase. Perhaps they are trying to confuse their competitors here. Let's look at their first main link (they have a row of toolbar links up at the top, with strategically named directories and filenames):

```
<a href="search_engine_positioning/search_placement_clients.htm"><span class="blue-text">blue-chip client list</span></a>
```

Their first link includes two terms in the URL, and subsequent links include key terms in the text, giving them a double dollop of relevance. Link text generally ranks higher than regular text.

Keywords in *body* Text

The designers have liberally added their top keyphrases throughout the body text. Overall, iProspect.com has done a good job of weaving the theme of their site through-out their home page. They use text for text menus, and with the exception of the home button and the logo, they use graphics mainly for items that cannot be represented as text. My recommendation would be to add meaningful `alt` attribute values, substitute styled heading elements instead of styled body text, and optimize the page for speed. Nevertheless, their 24,469-byte home page is a huge improvement over PopularMechanics.com's 136KB behemoth.

VI

Advanced Optimization Techniques

17

Server-Side Techniques

Client-side optimization techniques can only take you so far. You can squeeze only so many bytes out of that GIF, JavaScript, or XHTML page. But as you'll discover, with server-side techniques, you can squeeze even more speed and HTTP requests out of popular pages. The idea is to shunt code from the client to the server, and let the server do more of the work. This chapter covers the following topics: conditional includes, browser sniffing, automatic URL abbreviation, form and CGI optimization, and faster Perl scripts with mod_perl.

These server-side techniques can save you and your users both time and space. They increase speed by reducing HTTP requests and shaving 20 to 30 percent off file sizes. They save maintenance costs by including site-wide code snippets. Best of all, these tools can help spice up your site with dynamic or randomized content.

As the name implies, server-side techniques require different levels of server access. Some technologies, such as XSSI, are probably already installed on your server, while others (mod_rewrite, configuration files) may require initial installation by your system administrator. But don't worry; you'll find instructions and sample configuration settings in this chapter. Note that this chapter shows how to configure the Apache server; Microsoft's IIS server can also perform SSI and URL rewrites with ISAPI filters.

Like most things in web design, each of these techniques involves tradeoffs. Each time you shunt more code (long URIs, CGI defaults) and work ([X]SSI) to the server, you make it work a little harder. For high-traffic pages like home pages, the tradeoff favors smaller page size and fewer HTTP requests over any server speed considerations.

Server-Side Includes

Server-side includes (SSI) are a wonderful device for saving time and space in web page design.[1] SSI are placeholders that dynamically include data within your page as the server parses the file. Here's the syntax of an SSI command:

```
<!--#element attribute="value" -->
```

The `element` is a predefined SSI function, like `echo`, `exec`, or `include`, that uses the attribute and value parameters. You can include and change snippets of HTML site-wide with one SSI in each page. You also can add optimized dynamic content with SSI based on time or browser characteristics. That's where XSSI comes in.

Conditional SSI

With eXtended Server-Side Includes (XSSI), available in Apache 1.2 and above, Apache added the ability to include conditional logic within your pages, based on environment variables set by the server or within the HTML page itself. Conditional if/else logic adds "flow control" to your pages, allowing you to jazz up your site—with browser-dependent content, randomized links or messages, and timestamps in various formats—and ultimately create modularized pages.[2]

---

1. Apache Software Foundation, "Apache Tutorial: Introduction to Server-Side Includes" [online], (Forest Hill, MD: Apache Software Foundation, 2002 [cited 13 November 2002]), available from the Internet at `http://httpd.apache.org/docs-2.0/howto/ssi.html`.

2. Webmonkey, "HotWired's XSSI Extensions" [online], (Waltham, MA: Terra Lycos, 1999), available from the Internet at `http://hotwired.lycos.com/webmonkey/99/10/index0a.html`.

Here is a simple example:

```
<!--#if expr="${HTTP_USER_AGENT}= /Mac/" -->
    Mac code goes here
<!--#else -->
    Non-Mac code goes here
<!--#endif -->
```

Setting and Testing Environment Variables

The CGI specification introduced the notion of a standard set of environment variables that are used to communicate between servers and CGI scripts.[3] Environment variables include SERVER_NAME, QUERY_STRING, and CONTENT_LENGTH. In addition, the server sets environment variables based on the headers received from the client, prefixed with the string HTTP_.[4] The HTTP_USER_AGENT string holds information about the client requesting the resource from the server (browser, version, and platform). For example, for Internet Explorer 5.0 on my Macintosh PowerBook, the HTTP_USER_AGENT string looks like this:

```
Mozilla/4.0 (compatible; MSIE 5.0; Mac_PowerPC)
```

You can parse this user agent string to extract information about the client requesting a particular page. Apache extends the standard set of environment variables with their own named variables and gives you the ability to set your own with the set directive.[5]

```
<!--#set var="isDOM" value="true" -->
```

You can use these variables within the same HTML file or automatically pass them to included HTML files to create nested includes. Here is an example:

```
<!--#if expr="${HTTP_USER_AGENT} = /Gecko/" -->
    <!--#set var="isDOM" value="true" -->
<!--#endif -->
```

3. NCSA, "The CGI Specification" [online], (Champaign, IL: NCSA, 1995), available from the Internet at http://hoohoo.ncsa.uiuc.edu/cgi/interface.html.

4. Roy T. Fielding et al., "Hypertext Transfer Protocol—HTTP/1.1," RFC 2616 [online], (Reston, VA: The Internet Society, 1999), available from the Internet at http://www.ietf.org/rfc/rfc2616.txt. Defines the HTTP 1.1 protocol for "stateless" web server software. Also specifies what header information is sent from the client to the server.

5. Apache Software Foundation, "Environment Variables in Apache" [online], (Forest Hill, MD: Apache Software Foundation, 2002 [cited 13 November 2002]), available from the Internet at http://httpd.apache.org/docs-2.0/env.html.

To reference variables, you use the dollar sign ($). To use this new `isDOM` variable, you would write:

```
<!--#if expr="${isDOM}" -->
    DOM code goes here
<!--#else -->
    non-DOM code goes here
<!--#endif -->
```

Once you've got your variables set up, you can perform comparison operations, like AND (&&) and OR (||). Here is an example:

```
<!--#if expr="(${isIE5} && ${isMAC})" -->
```

You can see where this is going: server-side browser sniffing.

Advantages of SSI: Speed and Broad Compatibility

The advantages of using SSI over externally loaded files (like HTML, CSS, or JavaScript files) are speed (fewer HTTP requests), broad compatibility, and reduced maintenance costs. Here's an example from WebReference.com:

```
<script language="JavaScript1.2" type="text/javascript">
<!--#include virtual="newsflipper.js" -->
</script>
</body>
```

This SSI embeds our DHTML newsflipper just before the end of our front page. This avoids an extra HTTP request and lets the content load first.

We use SSI throughout WebReference.com for things like navigation bars, dynamic footers, copyrights, and news tickers. WebReference.com's home page is pre-assembled from numerous includes created by `cron` jobs. This keeps the front page content fresh and delivers it fast (kind of like Domino's, but we don't take 30 minutes to load). Interior pages include dynamically generated headers and footers. Even with 10 million impressions per month, we have received no complaints about page display speed.

Disadvantages of SSI

The downsides to SSI are increased overhead, security issues, limited environment variables, and limited programmability. Parsing files and inserting content does put a load on the server, although only heavily loaded sites will experience any noticeable slowdown. Enabling the exec option can pose a security risk. SSI can interfere with the caching of your documents. For browser sniffing, only the HTTP_USER_AGENT environment variable is set by default. However, there are ways to work around these limitations.

Tuning mod_include

SSI commands are handled by the mod_include module, which comes with the standard Apache distribution.[6] The mod_include filter is controlled by special SGML directives that allow conditional includes of files or programs. You can set, check, and print environment variables to sniff browsers or perform time-based tasks. (You can skip the next section if you don't have access to Apache configuration files.)

Here are some ways you can speed up mod_include:

- Consider XBitHack or .shtml.
- Run mod_include per virtual server.
- Use AllowOverride None to avoid .htaccess queries.
- Enable caching with XBitHack Full or mod_expires.

Consider *XBitHack* or *.shtml*

To tell Apache which files to parse for SSI commands, you can use .shtml and .html suffixes:

```
# To use server-parsed HTML files
AddType text/html .html
```

---

6. Apache Software Foundation, "Apache Module mod_include" [online], (Forest Hill, MD: Apache Software Foundation, 2002 [cited 13 November 2002]), available from the Internet at http://httpd.apache.org/docs-2.0/mod/mod_include.html.

```
AddType text/html .shtml
AddHandler server-parsed shtml
AddHandler server-parsed html
```

However, telling Apache to parse all `.html` files for SSI is inefficient. Using `.shtml` or `XBitHack` to parse only files with the execute bit set to `On` is more efficient, as you see here:

```
<VirtualHost          xxx.xx.xx.xx>
    DocumentRoot      /www/webref/webref
    ServerName        www.webreference.com
    ErrorDocument     404 /_404.html
    DirectoryIndex    index.html index.shtml index.wml
    XBitHack On
</VirtualHost>
```

Run mod_include per Virtual Server

To enable includes, you use the `Options Includes` directive. You can either place this directive in the root directory section, which enables includes for the entire server, or you can place it within a `Virtual Host` section with a `Directory` entry for speed:

```
<Directory /www/webref/webref>
    Options FollowSymlinks Includes
    Options IncludesNOEXEC
    order deny,allow
    deny from all
</Directory>
```

Note that we use the `IncludesNOEXEC` version, which closes a possible security hole.

Use AllowOverride None

The `AllowOverride` directive controls how the `.htaccess` files work, one per directory. By using the `httpd.conf` file, we can ignore `.htaccess` files and speed up the server. Without this directive, Apache traverses the directory tree above the requested resource, looking for `.htaccess` directives that apply, slowing down each request:

```
<Directory />
    AllowOverride None
    Options FollowSymLinks
```

```
    order deny,allow
    deny from all
</Directory>
```

Enable Caching with *XBitHack Full* or mod_expires

By default, Apache does not send the last modified date for SSI pages, which can prevent your pages from being cached. There are two solutions, XBitHack Full, and mod_expires. XBitHack Full sends the last modified date of the original file, ignoring any included files. mod_expires allows you to set expiration times for your files, allowing them to be cached. For more details, see the Apache documentation.[7]

Now that you've got your server tuned to run SSI, let's look at some more advanced ways to use SSI. Besides creating SSI templates and nested includes, you can perform browser sniffing with SSI to include conditional code.

Server-Side Browser Sniffing

You can use flow control to test for different browsers and display conditional code. This is especially useful for external JavaScript files that are optimized for various platforms. Using conditional SSI and the set command, you can create environment variables that closely mirror common client-side JavaScript sniffing techniques. Let's take a real-world example, using our own DHTML hierarchical menus (see Figure 17.1).

For his hierarchical menus, Peter Belesis uses an external JavaScript "loader" file to conditionally load two other JavaScript files, for a total of three HTTP requests. This ingenious method avoids some compatibility problems Belesis found with older browsers. Here is the JavaScript code that filters out browsers that support the level of DHTML he needs for his menus (available at http://www.webreference.com/dhtml/hiermenus/latest/loader.html):

```
HM_DOM   = (document.getElementById) ? true : false; // includes Opera
HM_NS4   = (document.layers) ? true : false;
HM_IE    = (document.all) ? true : false;
```

---

7. Apache Software Foundation, "Introduction to Server-Side Includes" [online].

```
  HM_IE4    = HM_IE && !HM_DOM;
  HM_Mac    = (navigator.appVersion.indexOf("Mac") != -1);
 HM_IE4M    = HM_IE4 && HM_Mac;

 HM_Opera    = (navigator.userAgent.indexOf("Opera")!=-1);
 HM_Konqueror = (navigator.userAgent.indexOf("Konqueror")!=-1);

HM_IsMenu    = ((HM_DOM || HM_NS4 || (HM_IE4 && !HM_IE4M)) && !HM_OPERA);
```

Figure 17.1
Peter Belesis' DHTML
hierarchical menus.

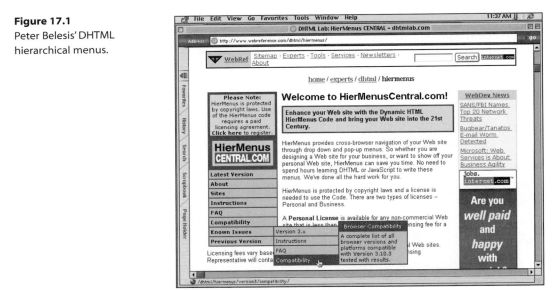

http://www.webreference.com/dhtml/hiermenus/

Let's try and replicate that logic with conditional SSI (see Listing 17.1).

Listing 17.1   XSSI Browser Sniffing

```
<!--#if expr="${HTTP_USER_AGENT} = /Mac/" -->
    <!--#set var="isMAC" value="true" -->
<!--#endif -->

<!--#if expr="${HTTP_USER_AGENT} = /Opera/" -->
    <!--#set var="isOPERA" value="true" -->
<!--#endif -->

<!--#if expr="${HTTP_USER_AGENT} = /Konquerer/" -->
    <!--#set var="isKONQUERER" value="true" -->
<!--#endif -->
```

```
<!--#if expr="${HTTP_USER_AGENT} = /MSIE [4-9]/" -->
    <!--#set var="isIE" value="true" -->
    <!--#if expr="${HTTP_USER_AGENT} = /MSIE [5-9]/" -->
        <!--#set var="isIE5" value="true" -->
        <!--#if expr="(${isIE5} && ${isMAC})" -->
            <!--#set var="isDOM" value="true" -->
        <!--#elif expr="${HTTP_USER_AGENT} = /MSIE.5\.[5-9]/" -->
            <!--#set var="isDOM" value="true" -->
        <!--#elif expr="${HTTP_USER_AGENT} = /MSIE [6-9])/" -->
            <!--#set var="isDOM" value="true" -->
        <!--#endif -->
    <!--#endif -->
<!--#elif expr="${HTTP_USER_AGENT} = /Mozilla\/[4-9]/" -->
    <!--#set var="isNS" value="true" -->
    <!--#if expr="${HTTP_USER_AGENT} = /Gecko/" -->
        <!--#set var="isDOM" value="true" -->
    <!--#endif -->
<!--#endif -->

<!--#if expr="(${isNS} && !${isDOM})" -->
    <!--#set var="isNS4" value="true" -->
<!--#endif -->

<!--#if expr="(${isIE} && !${isDOM})" -->
    <!--#set var="isIE4" value="true" -->
<!--#endif -->

<!--#if expr="(${isIE4} && {isMAC})" -->
    <!--#set var="isIE4M" value="true" -->
<!--#endif -->

<!--#if expr="(${isDOM} ¦¦ ${isNS4} ¦¦ (${isIE4} && !${isIE4M}))" -->
    <!--#set var="isMENU" value="true" -->
<!--#endif -->
```

Whew! That's a fair amount of code, but it closely approximates the client-side JavaScript. We know that MSIE 5.0 (Mac) and MSIE 5.5 and above support the W3C DOM (at least enough for Peter's menus), and that anything using the Gecko engine by AOL/Netscape supports the DOM. By first checking for MSIE4+ and then Mozilla4+, we filter out older browsers that don't support DHTML and group non-MSIE browsers into the isNS camp. Then we use some AND NOT operators to assign all non-DOM Netscape, Explorer, and Mac Explorer browsers to isNS4, isIE4, and isIE4M variables, respectively. Note that IE 4 to 5.4 is grouped in IE4, because W3C DOM support begins with IE5.5.

Opera can use a slash or a space before the version number, depending on whether it is spoofing:

```
Opera/6.0 (Windows NT 4.0; U) [en] - as Opera
Mozilla/5.0 (Windows NT 4.0; U) Opera 6.0 [en] - as Mozilla 5
```

To add Opera, you could use the following logic:

```
<!--#if expr="${HTTP_USER_AGENT} = /Opera *\/* *[5-9]/" -->
    <!--#set var="isDOM" value="true" -->
<!--#endif -->
```

Next, you would use these new environment variables to conditionally include external JavaScript files, like this:

```
<!--#if expr="${isMENU}" -->
    <!--#include virtual="/scripts/ARRAYS.js" -->
    <!--#if expr="${isDOM}" -->
        <!--#include virtual="/scripts/DOM.js" -->
    <!--#elif expr="${isIE4}" -->
        <!--#include virtual="/scripts/IE4.js" -->
    <!--#elif expr="${isNS4}" -->
        <!--#include virtual="/scripts/NS4.js" -->
    <!--#endif -->
<!--#endif -->
```

However, in this case, we found that Opera 5 and 6 do not support all the features we need for the menus. The code is simplified somewhat for illustrative purposes, because we'd normally filter out Opera 0-6 here. Because Opera can disguise itself as MSIE or Mozilla, your first test should be for Opera, and then check for MSIE/Mozilla *and not* Opera, like this:

```
<!--#if expr="${HTTP_USER_AGENT} = /Opera/" -->
    <!--#set var="isOPERA" value="true" -->
<!--#endif -->

<!--#if expr="${HTTP_USER_AGENT} = /MSIE [4-9]/" -->
<!--#if expr="!${isOPERA} -->
    <!--#set var="isIE" value="true" -->
...
```

One improvement would be to merge the arrays file with each of the API files to reduce the number of includes from two to one. You learned about shrinking JavaScript in Chapter 9, "Optimizing JavaScript for Download Speed."

Faster Browser Sniffing with *BrowserMatch*

A better way to assign custom environment variables is to embed the regular expressions in the httpd.conf file for speed. Apache can assign environment variables with the BrowserMatchNoCase or BrowserMatch directives, which apply a regular expression check to the environment variable HTTP_USER_AGENT. As with the XBitHack and Options directives, you can add this code to the general section or virtual host section of your httpd.conf file. Listing 17.2 shows the same sniffing logic using BrowserMatchNoCase.

Listing 17.2   Setting Environment Variables with BrowserMatchNoCase for Speed

```
BrowserMatchNoCase Mac isMAC
BrowserMatchNoCase Opera isOPERA
BrowserMatchNoCase Konquerer isKONQUERER

BrowserMatchNoCase "MSIE [4-9]" isIE
BrowserMatchNoCase "MSIE [5-9]" isIE5

BrowserMatchNoCase "MSIE.5\.[5-9]" isDOM
BrowserMatchNoCase "MSIE [6-9]" isDOM
BrowserMatchNoCase "Mozilla\/[4-9]" isNS
BrowserMatchNoCase Gecko isDOM
```

> **NOTE**
>
> These directives are the same as setting isXXX=1 or 0 or true or false.

With these new environment variables embedded in your server, you can then use in your HTML files an abbreviated version of the code used earlier (see Listing 17.3):

Listing 17.3   Improved SSI Browser Sniffing

```
<!--#if expr="(${isNS} && !${isDOM})" -->
    <!--#set var="isNS4" value="true" -->
<!--#endif -->

<!--#if expr="(${isIE} && !${isDOM})" -->
    <!--#set var="isIE4" value="true" -->
<!--#endif -->
```

continues

Listing 17.3   Improved SSI Browser Sniffing   *continued*

```
<!--#if expr="(${isIE4} && {isMAC})" -->
    <!--#set var="isIE4M" value="true" -->
<!--#endif -->

<!--#if expr="(${isDOM} || ${isNS4} || (${isIE4} && !${isIE4M}))" -->
    <!--#set var="isMENU" value="true" -->
<!--#endif -->
```

You then can conditionally include external JavaScript files like this (see Listing 17.4):

Listing 17.4   Conditionally Including JavaScript Files

```
<!--#if expr="${isMENU}" -->
    <!--#include virtual="/scripts/ARRAYS.js" -->
    <!--#if expr="${isDOM}" -->
        <!--#include virtual="/scripts/DOM.js" -->
    <!--#elif expr="${isIE4}" -->
        <!--#include virtual="/scripts/IE4.js" -->
    <!--#elif expr="${isNS4}" -->
        <!--#include virtual="/scripts/NS4.js" -->
    <!--#endif -->
<!--#endif -->
```

By embedding the HTTP_USER_AGENT string comparisons within the server configuration file, you shrink and speed up your SSI code. Of course, once Microsoft or AOL revs their browsers above 9, you'll need to tweak the regular expressions to handle versions 10–99, but that won't happen for a while.

PHP Browser Sniffing

Embedded server-side scripting languages like PHP and JSP also can be used to sniff browser environment variables and capabilities. PHP has been called "SSI on steroids," because it allows you to use a real programming language within your pages.

To do simple sniffing for conditional CSS in PHP, you'd do something like this (see Listing 17.5).

Listing 17.5   Conditional CSS in PHP

```php
<?php

if (preg_match("/Opera (\d)/i",$HTTP_USER_AGENT,$v)) {
    if (($version=$v[1])>4) $type=1;
    else $type=2;
}
elseif (preg_match("/MSIE (\d)/i",$HTTP_USER_AGENT,$v)) {
    if (($version=$v[1])>4) $type=1;
    else $type=2;
}
elseif (preg_match("/Mozilla(?:\/|\s)(\d)/i",$HTTP_USER_AGENT,$v)) {
    if (($version=$v[1])>4) $type=1;
    else $type=2;
}
else {
    $version="unknown";
    $type=2;
}

switch ($type) {
    case 1: $StyleSheet=compliant.css; break;
    case 2: $StyleSheet=older.css; break;
    default: StyleSheet=older.css; break;
}
?>
```

A number of pre-written PHP browser sniffers are available:

- The Horde Project: http://cvs.horde.org/co.php/horde/lib/Browser.php

- phpSniff: http://phpsniff.sourceforge.net/

- SniffBrowser: http://www-student.eit.ihk.dk/instruct/php-sniffer.php

The open source Horde Project provides a browser sniffer as part of their application framework in PHP. Their browser class provides capability information for the current browser using the HTTP_USER_AGENT string.

Let's try and duplicate our JavaScript code with Horde's PHP browser class (see Listing 17.6).

Listing 17.6   Sniffing with the Horde Project's PHP Browser Class

```php
<?php

require_once 'Browser.php';
$browser = new Browser();

$isOPERA     = $browser->isBrowser('opera');
$isKONQUERER = $browser->isBrowser('konqueror');

$isDOM  = $browser->hasFeature('dom');
$isNS4  = $browser->isBrowser('mozilla') && $browser->getMajor() == 4;
$isIE   = $browser->isBrowser('msie') && !$isOPERA;
$isIE4  = $isIE && !$isDOM;
$isMAC  = stristr($HTTP_SERVER_VARS['HTTP_USER_AGENT'], "Mac");
$isIE4M = $isIE4 && isMAC;

$isMENU = ($isDOM || $isNS4 || ($isIE4 && !isIE4M));

if ($isMENU) {

include($DOCUMENT_ROOT . "/scripts/ARRAYS.js ");
if ($isDOM) {
    include($DOCUMENT_ROOT . "/scripts/DOM.js");
    } elseif ($isIE4) {
        include($DOCUMENT_ROOT . "/scripts/IE4.js");
    } elseif ($isNS4) {
        include($DOCUMENT_ROOT . "/scripts/NS4.js");
    }
}

?>
```

Of course, we'd have to make sure that the browser class matched our definition of DOM support. (They say it mirrors the document.getElementById test.) Note that we've added in an Opera exclusion test for MSIE here for safety (even though the Horde sniffer doesn't identify Opera as being DOM compliant). Once Opera provides sufficient DOM support for our menus, we could add it back to the isMENU test.

PHP also provides a built-in function called get-browser.php. This function matches the HTTP_USER_AGENT string to the browser's capabilities using the browscap.ini file, which we'll discuss next. The function returns an object, which contains various data elements representing browser capabilities. Unfortunately, you've got to be sure you keep your `browscap.ini` file up to date. For more information on PHP's get-browser function, see `http://www.php.net/manual/en/function.get-browser.php`.

Faster PHP Scripts

Zend Technologies offers software tools to optimize your PHP code at `http://www.zend.com`.

Advantages and Disadvantages to Server-Side Browser Sniffing

The main advantage to server-side browser sniffing is that both these techniques save three HTTP requests over the client-side technique of loading external JavaScript files. For high-traffic pages, this can make a big difference in response rate.

Unlike external files, conditionally included scripts and CSS are not cached for subsequent pages. Some webmasters use a hybrid approach, using SSI on their home page and external files for the rest of the site.

Unlike JavaScript browser sniffing, this technique is limited by the information the browser sends to the server; in this case, the `HTTP_USER_AGENT` string. The problem with this approach is that the DOM category is under-represented. The DOM test is not as elegantly inclusive as the JavaScript DOM test (`isDOM = (document.getElementById) ? true : false;`), which catches all browsers that support this technique of element referencing. This test is often used as a surrogate for DOM support. It is close enough for our purposes. I've approximated this by testing explicitly for MSIE 5/5.5+ and Gecko browsers that we know support the DOM. MSIE, Mozilla, and Gecko variants account for nearly 90 percent of the users who are browsing WebReference.com.[8] The other 10 percent are Lynx, robots, iCab, and the like.

There are two ways to include any DOM-compliant agents in this group: through brute force and by sending JavaScript tests from the server.

---

8. WebReference.com, "WebReference.com Statistics" [online], (Darien, CT: Jupitermedia Corporation, 2002 [cited 13 November 2002]), available from the Internet at `http://webreference.com/stats/`.

browscap: The Browser Capabilities File

The good folks at cyScape, Inc. created a browser capabilities file (browscap.ini) that recognizes many of the browsers in use today by way of HTTP_USER_AGENT strings (http://www.cyscape.com/browscap/).

The file maps these strings to various browser capabilities. Be sure to get the latest version, because the file isn't updated very often. Juan Llibre keeps his version of browscap pretty up to date. You can check out that version at http://asp.net.do/browscap.zip.

By correlating these strings with the browsers that support the DOM, you could in theory make a brute-force XSSI DOM test that exactly matched the JavaScript equivalent. You could create a list of browser id strings based on the HTTP_USER_AGENT environment variable and embed them in your httpd.conf or php.ini file.

When new browsers enter the arena, however, you've got a problem. You would have to update your browscap.ini file and your regular expressions.

A better brute-force approach would be to flag all the browsers that *don't* support the DOM and negate them to find those who do. This would be a matter of finding all non-MSIE/Mozilla/Gecko browsers that support the DOM, finding the version number where they started, and listing these browsers just below that version, along with those browsers (Lynx, for example) that don't support the DOM.

Let's take a generic example. Suppose that you have a new DOM-compliant Mozilla competitor called Mothra. At version 7, Mothra starts to support the DOM, so you would do something like this:

```
<!--#if expr="${HTTP_USER_AGENT} = /Mothra [0-6]/" -->
    <!--#set var="notDOM" value="true" -->
<!--#endif -->

... other non-DOM-compliant browsers here ...

<!--#if expr="(!${notDOM} && !${isIE4} && !${isNS4})" -->
    <!--#set var="isDOM" value="true" -->
<!--#endif -->
```

For either brute-force technique, especially the first, you'd throw in a safety check for DOM support in the JavaScript file, like this:

```
isDOM = (document.getElementById) ? true : false;
if isDOM {
    //DOM code goes here
}
```

This would filter out any browsers that weren't listed in the database but nevertheless squeaked through and didn't support the DOM. The !notDOM approach would require fewer updates of the browscap.ini file. This approach would match the JavaScript DOM sniffing technique, even after a new DOM-compliant browser came out. The disadvantage to this technique is the need to update the browscap.ini file as new browsers appear (although less often than the previous approach). Wouldn't it be nice if there were a way to do this automatically? That's where products like BrowserHawk come in.

BrowserHawk: Advanced Server-Side Sniffing

BrowserHawk from cyScape, Inc. is the next step up in server-side browser sniffing. The brainchild of Richard Litofsky, BrowserHawk can detect almost everything about your browser on the server, including JavaScript capabilities.

BrowserHawk is available for Active Server Pages (ASP), Coldfusion (CF), and Java Server Pages (JSP) and servlets (as a Java Bean), and it can be used on any web server that supports Active Server Pages, JavaServer Pages, or servlets such as Microsoft IIS and Apache. BrowserHawk uses an object-based binary file for its browser database. This provides faster browser detection than browscap.ini.

The database includes over 120 properties, compared to 15 or so in browscap. It can be updated automatically with the Professional and Enterprise Editions (see Figure 17.2).

With BrowserHawk, you can use Java Server Pages (JSP) to do sophisticated browser sniffing on the fly. For our browser-sniffing example, the BrowserHawk database has all the browser details it needs. Listing 17.7 shows the example browser sniffing code in JSP.

Figure 17.2
BrowserHawk detecting
environment variables.

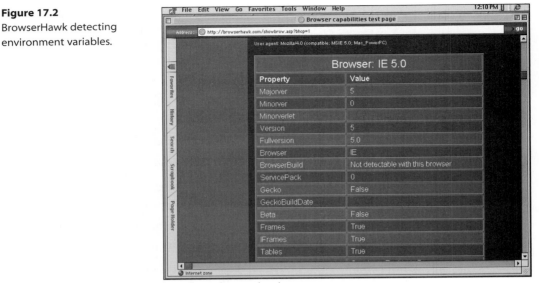

http://www.browserhawk.com

Listing 17.7   Sniffing with JSP and BrowserHawk

```
<%@ page import = "com.cyscape.browserhawk.*" %>
<%
  BrowserInfo b = BrowserHawk.getBrowserInfo(request);

  // This code sets some basic browser properties
  boolean isMac = b.getPlatform().startsWith("Mac");
  boolean isIE  = b.getBrowser().equals("IE");
  boolean isNS  = b.getBrowser().equals("Netscape");
  boolean isOpera = b.getBrowser().equals("Opera");
  boolean isKonqueror = b.getBrowser().equals("Konqueror");

  // This code sets the isDOM and isMenu vars
  boolean isIE4Plus = isIE && b.getMajorver() >= 4 && b.getVersion < 5.5;
  boolean isIE5Plus = isIE && b.getMajorver() >= 5;
  boolean isIE55Plus = isIE && b.getVersion() >= 5.5;
  boolean isIE5Mac = isIE5Plus && isMac;
  boolean isIE55NoMac = isIE55Plus && !isMac;

  boolean isNS4Plus = isNS && b.getMajorver() >= 4 && b.getMajorver() < 5;
  boolean isNS6Plus = isNS && b.getMajorver() >=6;
  boolean isMozilla = b.getBrowser().equals("Mozilla");
  boolean isGecko   = b.getGecko();

  boolean isDOM = isIE55NoMac || isNS5Plus || isIE5Mac || isMozilla;
```

```
    boolean isMenu = isDOM || isNS4Plus || (isIE4Plus && !isMac);
%>

<% if (isMenu) { %>
<%@ include file="/scripts/ARRAYS.js" %>
<% } %>

<% } if (isDOM) { %>
<%@ include file="/scripts/DOM.js" %>
<% } else if (isIE4Plus && !isMac) { %>
<%@ include file="/scripts/IE4.js" %>
<% } else if (isNS4Plus) { %>
<%@ include file="/scripts/NS4.js" %>
<% } %>
```

This JSP code performs the same function as the PHP and XSSI examples—only faster. Using JSP with BrowserHawk gives better performance than JavaScript includes and conditional SSI, assuming that you don't mind the additional overhead of running JSP or ASP.

What About Standards?

Of course, if we all wrote for the W3C's DOM, we wouldn't need this elaborate browser detection. This is true for (X)HTML and CSS in large part, but JavaScript is a special case. Accommodating older browsers and the DOM can be done in one file or separate files. DHTML developers typically either separate their code into three parts (IE4, NS4, and DOM), use an API that abstracts these differences, or ignore older browsers altogether.

The problem with the multi-file approach is that you've got at least two external files to load (data arrays and the browser APIs, for example) adding two HTTP requests to every page. By using server-side sniffing and conditional includes, you can eliminate extra HTTP requests and dramatically speed up high-traffic pages.

For More Information

For more information on the topic of client-side versus server-side browser sniffing, visit http://cyscape.com/developer/workshop/article/bh_vs_js.asp.

Conditional *meta* Tags

For maximum speed, you can optionally omit meta tags from your high-traffic pages. Here is an example from WebReference.com's home page:

```
<!DOCTYPE HTML PUBLIC "-//W3C//DTD HTML 4.01 Transitional//EN">
<html>
<head>
<title>WebReference.com - The Webmaster's Reference Library - Web Authoring Tips &
Tutorials for Developers</title>
<!--#if expr="$HTTP_USER_AGENT = /^Mozilla/" --><!--#else -->
<meta name="keywords" content="authoring web development web
design java script graphic design html tutorials javascript dynamic html tutorial
authoring tools ...">
<meta name="description" content="The definitive guide to web
development with tutorials on all aspects of web design ...">
<!--#endif -->
...
</head>
```

If the server detects a Mozilla-based browser it sends no meta tags; otherwise, it does send them (presumably to a spider). You learned how to optimize meta tags for search engine relevance in Chapter 15, "Keyword Optimization."

URL Abbreviation with mod_rewrite

URL abbreviation is one of the most effective techniques you can use to optimize your HTML. First seen on Yahoo!'s home page, URL abbreviation substitutes short redirect URLs (like r/ci) for longer ones (like Computers_and_Internet/) to save space. The Apache and IIS web servers, and Manila (http://www.userland.com) and Zope (http://www.zope.org) all support this technique. In Apache, the mod_rewrite module transparently handles URL expansion. For IIS, ISAPI filters handle URL rewrites. Here are some IIS rewriting filters:

- ISAPI_Rewrite (`http://www.isapirewrite.com/`)
- OpCode's OpURL (`http://www.opcode.co.uk/components/rewrite.asp`)
- Qwerksoft's IISRewrite based on mod_rewrite (`http://www.qwerksoft.com/products/iisrewrite/`)

Cocoon

Many of these fancy browser detection and performance techniques can be handled elegantly with Cocoon. Cocoon is an open source web-application platform based on XML and XSLT. Actually a big Java servlet, Cocoon runs on most servlet engines. Cocoon can automatically transform XML into (X)HTML and other formats using XSLT. You can set up a style sheet and an output format for certain types of browsers (WAP, DOM, etc.), and Cocoon does the rest. It makes the difficult task of separating content, layout, and logic trivial. Cocoon can handle the following:

- Server-side programming
- URL rewriting
- Browser detection
- PDF, legacy file formats, and image generation
- Server-side compression

You can read more about Cocoon at `http://xml.apache.org/cocoon/`.

URL abbreviation is especially effective for home or index pages, which typically have a lot of links. As you will discover in Chapter 19, "Case Studies: Yahoo.com and WebReference.com," URL abbreviation can save anywhere from 20 to 30 percent off of your HTML file size. The more links you have, the more you'll save.

> **NOTE**
>
> As with most of these techniques, there's always a tradeoff. Using abbreviated URLs can lower search engine relevance, although you can alleviate this somewhat with clever expansions with mod_rewrite.

The popular Apache web server[9] has an optional module, mod_rewrite, that enables your server to automatically rewrite URLs.[10] Created by Ralf Engelschall, this versatile module has been called the "Swiss Army knife of URL manipulation."[11] mod_rewrite can handle everything from URL layout, load balancing, to access restriction. We'll be using only a small portion of this module's power by substituting expanded URLs with regular expressions.

The module first examines each requested URL. If it matches one of the patterns you specify, the URL is rewritten according to the rule conditions you set. Essentially, mod_rewrite replaces one URL with another, allowing abbreviations and redirects.

This URL rewriting machine manipulates URLs based on various tests including environment variables, time stamps, and even database lookups. You can have up to 50 global rewrite rules without any discernible effect on server performance.[12] Abbreviated URI expansion requires only one.

9.   Netcraft, Ltd, "Netcraft Web Server Survey" [online], (Bath, UK: Netcraft, Ltd., October 2002 [cited 13 November 2002]), available from the Internet at `http://www.netcraft.com/survey/`. For active sites, over 65 percent use Apache.

10. Ralf S. Engelschall, "Apache 1.3 URL Rewriting Guide" [online], (Forest Hill, MD: Apache Software Foundation, 1997 [cited 13 November 2002]), available from the Internet at `http://httpd.apache.org/docs/misc/rewriteguide.html`. Ralf Engelschall is the author of mod_rewrite, the module used for URL rewriting. See also `http://www.engelschall.com/pw/apache/rewriteguide/`.

11. Apache Software Foundation, "Apache Module mod_rewrite" [online], (Forest Hill, MD: Apache Software Foundation, 2001 [cited 13 November 2002]), available from the Internet at `http://httpd.apache.org/docs-2.0/mod/mod_rewrite.html`. An URL rewriting engine.

12. Ralf S. Engelschall and Christian Reiber, "URL Manipulation with Apache" Heise Online [online], (Hanover, Germany: Heise Zeitschriften Verlag GmbH, 2001), available from the Internet at `http://www.heise.de/ix/artikel/E/1996/12/149/`. English translation.

Tuning mod_rewrite

To install mod_rewrite on your Apache Web server, you or your IT department needs to edit one of your server configuration files. The best way to run mod_rewrite is through the `httpd.conf` file, as this is accessed once per server restart. Without configuration file access, you'll have to use `.htaccess` for each directory. Keep in mind that the same mod_include performance caveats apply; `.htaccess` files are slower as each directory must be traversed to read each `.htaccess` file for each requested URL.

The Abbreviation Challenge

The strategy is to abbreviate the longest, most frequently accessed URLs with the shortest abbreviations. Most webmasters choose one, two, or three-letter abbreviations for directories. On WebReference.com, the goal was to create a mod_rewrite rule that would expand URLs like this:

`r/d`

Into this:

`dhtml/`

Like Yahoo!, `r` is the flag we've chosen for redirects. But why stop there? We can extend this concept into more directories. So turn this:

`r/dc`

Into this:

`dhtml/column`

and so on. Note that the lack of a trailing forward slash in this second example allows us to intelligently append column numbers.

With the right `RewriteRule`, the abbreviation of `/r/c/66` expands into the string `/dhtml/column66/`.

The *RewriteRule* Solution

To accomplish this expansion, you need to write a RewriteRule regular expression. First, you need to find the URI pattern /r/d, and then extract /d and turn it into /dhtml. Next, append a trailing slash.

Apache requires two directives to turn on and configure the mod_rewrite module: the RewriteEngine Boolean and the RewriteRule directive. The RewriteRule is a regular expression that transforms one URI into another. The syntax is shown here:

```
RewriteRule <pattern> <rewrite as>
```

So to create a RewriteRule to solve this problem, you need to add the following two mod_rewrite directives to your server configuration file (httpd.conf or .htaccess):

```
RewriteEngine    On
RewriteRule      ^/r/d(.*)    /dhtml$1
```

This regular expression matches a URL that begins with /r/ (the ^ character at the beginning means to match from the beginning of the string). Following that pattern is d(.*), which matches one or more characters after the d. Note that using /r/dodo would expand to /dhtmlodo, so you'll have to make sure anything after r/d always includes a /.

So when a request comes in for the URI <a href="/r/d/diner/">DHTML Diner</a>, this rule expands this abbreviated URI into <a href="/dhtml/diner/">DHTML Diner</a>.

The *RewriteMap* Solution for Multiple Abbreviations

The RewriteRule solution would work well for a few abbreviations, but what if you want to abbreviate a large number of links? That's where the RewriteMap directive comes in. This feature allows you to group multiple lookup *keys* (abbreviations) and their corresponding expanded *values* into one tab-delimited file. Here's an example map file at (/www/misc/redir/abbr_webref.txt):

```
d     dhtml/
dc    dhtml/column
pg    programming/
h     html/
ht    html/tools/
```

The MapName specifies a mapping function between keys and values for a rewriting rule using the following syntax:

```
${ MapName : LookupKey ¦ DefaultValue }
```

When you are using a mapping construct, you generalize the RewriteRule regular expression. Instead of a hard-coded value, the MapName is consulted, and the LookupKey accessed. If there is a key match, the mapping function substitutes the expanded value into the regular expression. If there is no match, the rule substitutes the default value or a blank string.

To use this external map file, we'll add the RewriteMap directive and tweak the regular expression correspondingly. The following httpd.conf commands turn rewriting on, show where to look for your rewrite map, and show the definition of the RewriteRule:

```
RewriteEngine    On
RewriteMap       abbr    txt:/www/misc/redir/abbr_webref.txt
RewriteRule ^/r/([^/]*)/?(.*)    ${abbr:$1}$2    [redirect=permanent,last]
```

The first directive turns on rewrites as before. The second points the rewrite module to the text version of our map file. The third tells the processor to look up the value of the matching expression in the map file. Note that the RewriteRule has a permanent redirect (301 instead of 302) and last flags appended to it. Once an abbreviation is found for this URL, no further rewrite rules are processed for it, which speeds up lookups.

Here we've set the rewrite MapName to abbr and the map file location (text format) to the following:

```
/www/misc/redir/abbr_webref.txt
```

The RewriteRule processes requested URLs using the regular expression:

```
^/r/([^/]*)/?(.*)        ${abbr:$1}$2
```

This regular expression matches an URL that begins with /r/. (The ^ character at the beginning means to match from the beginning of the string.) Then the regular expression ([^/]*) matches as many non-slash characters it can to the end of the string. This effectively pulls out the first string between two slashes following the /r. For example, in the URL /r/pg/javascript/, this portion of the regular expression matches pg. It also will match ht in /r/ht. (Because there are no slashes following, it just continues until it reaches the end of the URL.)

The rest of the pattern /?(.*) matches 0 or 1 forward slashes / with any characters that follow. These two parenthesized expressions will be used in the replacement pattern.

The Replacement Pattern

The substitution (${abbr:$1}$2) is the replacement pattern that will be used in the building of the new URL. The $1 and $2 variables refer back (backreferences) to the first and second patterns found in the supplied URL. They represent the first set of parentheses and the second set of parentheses in the regular expression, respectively. Thus for /r/pg/javascript/, $1 = "pg" and $2 = "javascript/". Replacing these in the example produces the following:

```
${abbr:pg}javascript/
```

The ${abbr:pg} is a mapping directive that says, "Refer to the map abbr (recall our map command, RewriteMap abbr txt:/www/misc/redir/abbr_webref.txt), look up the key pg, and return the corresponding data value for that key." In this case, that value is programming/. Thus the abbreviated URL, /r/pg/javascript, is replaced by the following:

```
/programming/javascript/
```

Voila! So you've effectively created an abbreviation expander using a regular expression and a mapping file. Using the preceding rewrite map file, the following URL expansions would occur:

```
"r/dc" becomes "dhtml/column"
"r/pg" becomes "programming/"
```

The server, upon seeing a matching abbreviation in the map file, will automatically rewrite the URL to the longer value.

But what happens if you have many keys in your RewriteMap file? Scanning a long text file every time a user clicks a link can slow down lookups. That's where binary hash files come in handy.

Binary Hash *RewriteMap*

For maximum speed, convert your text `RewriteMap` file into a binary *DBM hash file. This binary hash version of your key and value pairs is optimized for maximum lookup speed. Convert your text file with a DBM tool or the txt2dbm Perl script provided at `http://httpd.apache.org/docs-2.0/mod/mod_rewrite.html`.

> **NOTE**
>
> Note that this example is specific to Apache on Unix. Your platform may vary.

Next, change the `RewriteMap` directive to point to your optimized DBM hash file:

```
RewriteMap    abbr    dbm:/www/misc/redir/abbr_webref
```

That's the abbreviated version of how you set up link abbreviation on an Apache server. It is a bit of work, but once you've got your site hierarchy fixed, you can do this once and forget it. This technique saves space by allowing abbreviated URLs on the client side and shunting the longer actual URLs to the server. The delay using this technique is hardly noticeable. (If Yahoo! can do it, anyone can.) Done correctly, the rewriting can be transparent to the client. The abbreviated URL is requested, the server expands it, and serves back the content at the expanded location without telling the browser what it has done. You also can use the /r/ flag or the `RewriteLog` directive to track click-throughs in your server logs.

This technique works well for sites that don't change very often: You would manually abbreviate your URIs to match your `RewriteMap` abbreviations stored on your server. But what about sites that are updated every day, or every hour, or every minute? Wouldn't it be nice if you could make the entire abbreviation process automatic? That's where the magic of Perl and cron jobs (or the Schedule Tasks GUI in Windows) comes in.

Automatic URL Abbreviation

You can create a Perl or shell script (insert your favorite CGI scripting language here) to look for URLs that match the lookup keys in your map file and automatically abbreviate your URLs. We use this technique on WebReference.com's home page. To make it easy for other developers to auto-abbreviate their URLs, we've created an open source script called shorturls.pl. It is available at `http://www.webreference.com/scripts/`.

> **NOTE**
>
> XSLT gives you another way to abbreviate URLs automatically. Just create the correct templates to abbreviate all the local links in your files.

The shorturls.pl script allows you to abbreviate URLs automatically and exclude portions of your HTML code from optimization with simple XML tags (`<NOABBREV>` `...</NOABBREV>`).

Using this URL abbreviation technique, we saved over 20 percent (5KB) off our 24KB hand-optimized front page. We could have saved even more space, but for various reasons, we excluded some URLs from abbreviation.

This gives you an idea of the link abbreviation process, but what about all the other areas of WebReference? Here is a truncated version of our abbreviation file to give you an idea of what it looks like (the full version is available at `http://www.webreference.com/scripts/`):

```
b     dlab/
d     dhtml/
g     graphics/
h     html/
p     perl/
x     xml/

3c    3d/lesson
dd    dhtml/dynomat/
ddd   dhtml/dynomat/dialogs/
dc    dhtml/column
...
i     http://www.internet.com/
ic    http://www.internet.com/corporate/
...
jsc   http://www.javascript.com/
jss   http://www.javascriptsource.com/
jsm   http://www.justsmil.com/
...
```

Note that we use two and three-letter abbreviations to represent longer URLs on WebReference.com. Yahoo! uses two-letter abbreviations throughout their home page. How brief you make your abbreviations depends on how many links you need to abbreviate, and how descriptive you want the URLs to be.

The URL Abbreviation/Expansion Process: Step by Step

In order to enable automatic link abbreviation (with shorturls.pl) and expansion (with mod_rewrite), do the following:

1. Create an abbreviation map file (RewriteMap) with short abbreviations that correspond to frequently used and longer directories separated by tabs. For example:

```
d     dhtml/
g     graphics/
dc    dhtml/column
gc    graphics/column
...
```

2. Add the following lines to your httpd.conf file to enable the mod_rewrite engine:

```
RewriteEngine    On
RewriteMap       abbr    txt:/www/misc/redir/abbr_yrdomain.txt
RewriteRule^/r/([^/]*)/?(.*)        ${abbr:$1}$2    [redirect=permanent,last]
```

3. Try some abbreviated URLs (type in /r/d, etc.). If they work, move on to step 4; otherwise, check your map and your rewrite directives. If all else fails, contact your system administrator.

4. Convert your RewriteMap text file to a binary hash file. See http://httpd.apache.org/docs-2.0/mod/mod_rewrite.html for the txt2dbm Perl script.

5. Change the preceding RewriteMap directive to point to this optimized *DBM hash file:

```
RewriteMap       abbr    dbm:/www/misc/redir/abbr_yrdomain
```

6. Now your rewrite engine is set up. To automate URL abbreviation, point shorturls.pl to the text version of your RewriteMap file, input your home page template and output your home page, and schedule the job with cron on UNIX/Linux, or the Schedule Tasks GUI in Windows:

```
echo "\nBuilding $YRPAGE from $YRTEMPLATE\n"
/www/yrdomain/cgi-bin/shorturls.pl $YRTEMPLATE $YRPAGE
```

That's it. Now any new content that appears on your home page will be automatically abbreviated according to the `RewriteMap` file that you created, listing the abbreviations you want.

Use Short URLs

You could name your directories using these short, cryptic abbreviations. Using descriptive names for directories and file names has advantages, however, in usability and search engine positioning. Using URL abbreviation, you can have the best of both worlds for high-traffic pages like home pages.

For front page or frequently referenced objects like single-pixel GIFs, logos, navigation bars, and site-wide rollovers, however, you can use short URLs by placing them high in your site's file structure, and using short filenames. For example:

```
/i.gif (internet.com logo)
/t.gif (transparent single pixel gif)
```

I've seen some folks carry the descriptive-names-at-all-cost idea to extremes. Here's a surreal-world example:

```
transparent-single-pixel-gif1x1.gif (actual file name)
```

Some search engine positioning firms sprinkle keywords wherever they are legal—and in some places where they're not. Again, it's a tradeoff. Bulking up your pages with keyword-filled `alt` values and object names may increase your rankings, but with the advent of backlink-based search engines like Google and Teoma, these practices are fading in effectiveness.

You could even use content negotiation or your `srm.conf` file to abbreviate file type suffixes. This technique is pretty extreme, seldom used, but perfectly valid. Here's an example:

```
i.g (.g = .gif, srm.conf directive of AddType  image/gif     g)
i (content negotiation resolves to i.gif, could later use i.png)
```

Form and CGI Optimization

Forms can be used for anything from feedback and e-commerce applications to web-based services. However, they are seldom optimized for speed.

There is one required attribute to the form element: action. The action attribute specifies the URI of the application that will receive and process the form's data.

```
<form action="/cgi-bin/search.cgi">...</form>
```

The method attribute sets the HTTP method the browser uses to send the form's data to the server. There are two methods of sending data: POST or GET. With the POST method, the browser sends the data in two steps—first it contacts the server's action script; then it sends the data to the server in a separate transmission. The data is hidden from the user using this method.

In the GET method (the default) the browser contacts the server's action script and appends the data onto the URL, all in one transmission. GETs are more efficient than POSTs, but less secure because the data appears and can be modified in the browser's address field.

Hidden controls often are used to pass default values to the server's CGI script using either method. However, these can quickly add up. Here's an example:

```
<form method=get action="/cgi-bin/search.cgi">
<td align="right">
<span class="c"><a href="/cgi-bin/search.cgi">Search &gt;</a></span> 
</td>
<td align="right" width="5%">
      <input type="hidden" name="what" value="local">
      <input type="hidden" name="engine" value="au">
<input type="hidden" name="summary" value="1">
<input type="hidden" name="startnumber" value="0">
<input type="hidden" name="batchsize" value="25">
<input type="hidden" name="relevancethreshold" value="50">
<input type="text"  name="query" size="12">
</td>
<td align="right" width="1%">
<input type="hidden" name="Submit" value="Search"> <!-- for returns -->
<input type="submit" name="Submit" value="Search">
</td>
</form>
```

A better way to set defaults is to shunt them to your CGI script. Here's an example based on WebReference.com's `search.cgi` Perl script (`http://www.webreference.com/scripts/`):

```
# search.cgi - default entries for parameters

my $What_DEF         = 'local'; # search where?, locally, usenet, the web?
my $Engine_DEF       = 'au';    # which search engine to use
my $QuerySummary_DEF = '1';     # display summaries? 1=yes 0=no
my $Startnumber_DEF  = '0';     # where to start output
my $Batchsize_DEF    = 25;      # number of results to return
my $Relevancethreshold= 50;     # relevance threshold, 0-100
my $Sort_DEF         = '';      # type of autonomy sort
#                                   empty means Relevance, Date


# form variables - from CGI
my $webinfo      = new CGI;
    $webinfo->autoEscape(undef);     # turn off automatic escaping of values
my $What         = $webinfo->param('what');     # search Usenet, web, locally?
my $Engine       = $webinfo->param('engine');   # which search engine to use
my $Query_clean  = $webinfo->param('query');    # the query w/o special chars
my $Query        = uri_escape($Query_clean,"^A-Za-z"); # the query with special chars
my $QuerySummary = $webinfo->param('querysummary');    # display summaries?
my $Startnumber  = $webinfo->param('startnumber');     # where to start output
my $Batchsize    = $webinfo->param('batchsize'); # number of results to return
my $Relevancethreshold=$webinfo->param('relevancethreshold'); # rel thrshld0-100
my $Sort         = $webinfo->param('sort');       # type of autonomy srch 2 perf


# replace with defaults any unsupplied params
$What           = $What_DEF          unless ($What);
$Engine         = $Engine_DEF        unless ($Engine);
$QuerySummary   = $QuerySummary_DEF  unless ($QuerySummary eq "0");
$Startnumber    = $Startnumber_DEF   unless ($Startnumber);
$Batchsize      = $Batchsize_DEF     unless ($Batchsize);
$Relevancethreshold=$Relevancethreshold_DEF unless ($Relevancethreshold);
$Sort           = $Sort_DEF          unless ($Sort);
```

Note you can still specify the `hidden` defaults in your forms, but this code allows you to omit the defaults. Now you can remove the hidden fields and shrink the form dramatically:

```
<form method="get" action="/cgi-bin/search.cgi">
<td align="right">
<span class="c"><a href="/cgi-bin/search.cgi">Search &gt;</a></span> 
</td>
```

```
<td align="right" width="5%">
<input type="text" name="query" size="12">
</td>
<td align="right" width="1%">
<input type="hidden" name="Submit" value="Search"> <!-- for returns -->
<input type="submit" name="Submit" value="Search">
</td>
</form>
```

But don't stop there. By abbreviating the `action` URI and simplifying your layout, you can shrink it even more:

```
<form class="tb" method="get" action="/r/cs">
<table border="0" cellspacing="0" cellpadding="0">
<tr><td><input type="text" name="query" size="20"></td><td width="1%" align="right"><input
type="submit" value="search"></td>
</tr></table></form>
```

Note that we've expanded the search field from 12 to 20 characters for better usability here. You could go even further, because `get` is the default `method`, `text` is the default `input` type, and `submit` is the default value for `submit`-type inputs:

```
<form class="tb" action="/r/cs">
<table border="0" cellspacing="0" cellpadding="0">
<tr><td><input name="query" size="20"></td><td width="1%" align="right"><input
type="submit"></td>
</tr></table></form>
```

This method saves 485 bytes or 70 percent from the original (685 to 200 bytes). The form will say "Submit" instead of "Search" now of course, which isn't too specific. But for some forms, this would be appropriate. Strip out the presentation, and the original 18-line form fits into one line:

```
<form action="/r/cs"><input name="q" size="20"><input type="submit" value="search"></form>
```

Parameter-free forms like this one save space and are required by some third-party web services, like Apple's Sherlock search service for the Macintosh OS.

Use mod_perl to Speed Up Perl Scripts

Another useful module for speeding up Apache-based sites is mod_perl. The mod_perl module embeds a Perl interpreter within your web server, avoiding the overhead of starting the Perl interpreter for each CGI request. Popular sites like Slashdot.org, Wired.com, and IMDB.com use mod_perl to speed their content delivery by orders of magnitude. mod_perl avoids the need to fork a new process for each script request, which can overload your server's RAM and process limits.

Existing scripts can be used with the Apache::PerlRun module and with a little tweaking moved to Apache::Registry for better performance. mod_perl is second only to PHP for module popularity, with over 36 percent share, according to SecuritySpace.com. For more information, see `http://perl.apache.org/`.

No More *www*

You can shave a few bytes off your URLs and make them friendlier by not requiring the www. at the beginning of your domain name. Have your system administrator set your DNS server to resolve yourdomain.com and www.yourdomain.com, like this:

```
ServerName www.yourdomain.com
ServerAlias yourdomain.com
```

This allows users to type in yourdomain.com to get to www.yourdomain.com. If you are on a server with named-based virtual hosting, you also need to add a ServerAlias directive inside the appropriate VirtualHost, like this:

```
NameVirtualHost ip.of.yourdomain.com:80
<VirtualHost ip.of.yourdomain.com:80>
    ServerName www.yourdomain.com
    ServerAlias yourdomain.com
    [...]
</VirtualHost>
```

The ServerAlias directive in Apache specifies alternate names for a host. Some system administrators also provide misspellings and other alternate domains, like this:

```
ServerAlias foo.com foo.net ww.foo.com wwww.foo.com
```

You also can use a wildcard to match anything before the dot like this:

```
ServerAlias foo.com *.foo.com
```

It is important to provide an IP address for your domain; otherwise, Apache will be forced to perform a reverse DNS lookup.

You always need the DNS configuration; otherwise, the client won't find the server. The web configuration is needed only if you use name-based virtual hosting on the IP. Some high-profile sites still require the www. to access their sites. Three examples at press time are gannett.com, morningstar.com, and wendys.com. Requiring users to type in the www. to get to your site is like throwing traffic away.

Summary

Client-side web site optimization can take you only so far. To fully optimize high-traffic pages, you've got to turn to the server-side. By configuring your server to accommodate conditional SSI and browser sniffing, abbreviated URLs, and shunting defaults to the server, you can dramatically speed up your pages. Here is a list of key points in this chapter:

- Use SSI to minimize HTTP requests on high-traffic pages.
- Where possible, pre-merge dynamic content without SSI for maximum speed.
- Use server-side browser sniffing to minimize HTTP requests, especially for JavaScript files. Use the fastest technology available (JSP > PHP > XSSI).
- Conditionally include meta tags.
- Abbreviate your links, manually or automatically, with mod_rewrite and shorturls.pl (20 to 28 percent savings).
- Optimize your forms and CGI scripts to shunt defaults to the server.
- Use mod_perl to speed up Perl scripts.
- Don't require www. for your domains.

Further Reading

For more information on the Apache server, modules, URL rewrites, and other server-side tuning topics, see the following:

- Apache.org—The Apache server home page. The place for the most up-to-date information and documentation at `http://www.apache.org`.

- "Apache Performance Notes" by Dean Gaudet on tuning the Apache server for speed (applies more to version 1.3) at `http://httpd.apache.org/docs-2.0/misc/perf-tuning.html`.

- *Apache Server 2.0: The Complete Reference* by Ryan Bloom (Osborne McGraw-Hill, 2002)—The first book on Apache 2.0 by one of the developers.

- "Extreme HTML Optimization" by Andy King (2000)—Radical reductions with no-holds-barred techniques, including URL rewriting, at `http://www.webreference.com/authoring/languages/html/optimize/`.

- "URLS! URLS! URLS!" by Bill Humphries (2000)—An article on URL rewriting at `http://www.alistapart.com/stories/urls/`.

- *Web Performance Tuning, 2nd ed.* by Patrick Killelea (O'Reilly, 2002)—Has numerous server-side tuning tips. More at `http://www.patrick.net/`.

18

Compressing the Web

by Konstantin Balashov

Compression is one of those technologies where it seems like you get something for nothing. Compression saves bandwidth and speeds up web sites by removing redundancy to reduce the amount of data sent. Although the cost of compression is certainly not zero, over networked environments like the Internet, transmission time is usually the limiting factor. This chapter will show you how to compress the text in your content to minimize bandwidth costs and maximize speed. See Chapter 12, "Optimizing Web Graphics," and Chapter 13, "Minimizing Multimedia," for graphics and multimedia compression information.

Compression algorithms trade time for space by pre-processing files to create smaller versions of themselves. This compressed file is then decompressed to reconstruct the original, or an approximation thereof. The compression process naturally includes two components: encoding, and decoding. Encoding compresses the data, while decoding decompresses the data, usually at a faster rate. With Moore's Law leading Metcalf's, bandwidth concerns usually trump any CPU speed considerations.

Covert Compression

Compression works behind the scenes to make many of the products we use more efficient and even feasible. The images and multimedia that make the web so compelling use compression for fast delivery. MP3 players deliver compressed audio for music on the go. Modems use compression to speed transmission. Digital cameras use JPEG compression. Set-top boxes, HDTV, and DVD players use MPEG video compression. Operating systems use compression to save space. Even spies use compression and encryption to send short "spurts" to the homeland. But some forms of compression, mainly text, are underutilized yet quite effective on the web.

Text Compression Algorithms

There are three major approaches to text compression:

- Dictionary-based (LZ stands for *Lempel* and *Ziv*)
- Block sorting-based (BWT, or Burrows-Wheeler Transform)
- Symbol probability prediction-based (PPM, or Prediction by Partial Matching)

Most file-compression formats like arj, zip, gz, lzh, and rar (including GIF and PNG) are based on dictionary algorithms of previously occurring phrases. By substituting the distance to the last occurrence and the length of the phrase, they save space. The LZW (Lempel, Ziv, and Welch) algorithm used in the GIF format is different—it substitutes a dictionary index for the phrase. LZ-based algorithms are very fast, with moderate compression ratios and modest memory requirements (< 100KB).

BWT algorithms make a block-sorting transform over the text. The result of the transform is text of the same size, but letters are magically grouped. It can then be efficiently compressed with a very fast and simple coding technique. Block-sorting transforms make sense when they are applied to a big data block. BWT algorithms are fast, with high compression ratios and moderate memory requirements (1MB+).

PPM algorithms calculate the probability distribution for every symbol and then optimally encode it. Most PPM implementations are slow, sophisticated, and memory intensive (8MB+).

The efficiency of these lossless algorithms is measured in bits per character (bpc), or the number of bits needed to encode each character. The English language has an effective bits/char of 1.3,[1] so theoretically if a compression algorithm "knew" all the idioms and structure of this language, it could approach this figure. To give you an idea of how effective the current web compression algorithms are, here is a table of lossless compression algorithms and their efficiencies (see Table 18.1).

Table 18.1   Lossless Compression Ratios for Text Compression on the Calgary Corpus[1,2]

Date	Implementation	Algorithm	Author	Ratio, bpc
1977	LZ77	LZ	Ziv, Lempel	3.94
1984	LZW (GIF, V42/44b)	LZ	Welch	3.27
1987	Deflate (PNG, gzip)	LZ	Katz	2.63
1997	BOA	PPM	Sutton	1.99
2000	RK	PPM	Taylor	1.82
2002	SBC	BWT	Taylor	1.88

bits per character (bpc)

Other than multimedia- or plug-in–based formats, the compression algorithms currently used on the Internet are pretty old and far from state-of-the-art. Will they be replaced with newer and better ones? Not likely anytime soon. Even if somebody came up with the world's-best compression algorithm and the algorithm was patent-free, it will be hard to convince the major browser developers to add this algorithm to their browser code. But even if they do, it will be hard to convince webmasters to use compression that is not supported by older browsers.

1. Guy E. Blelloch, "Introduction to Data Compression" [online], (2001 [cited 12 November 2002]), available from the Internet at http://www-2.cs.cmu.edu/afs/cs.cmu.edu/project/pscico-guyb/realworld/www/compression.pdf. A draft of a chapter on data compression.

2. Timothy Bell, Ian H. Witten, and John W. Cleary, "Modeling for Text Compression," *ACM Computing Surveys* 21, no. 4 (1989): 557–591.

So we've got to work with what we have. Let's see how we can squeeze the maximum advantage out of these algorithms.

Content Compression

Most browsers released since 1998–1999 support the HTTP 1.1 standard known as IETF "content-encoding" (although content encoding was included in the HTTP 1.0 specification: RFC 1945.[3]) Content encoding (also known as *HTTP compression*) is a publicly defined way to compress (that is, deflate) HTTP content transferred from web servers to browsers using public domain compression algorithms, like gzip.

Here's how it works…

Browsers tell servers they would prefer to receive encoded content with a message in the HTTP header, like this:

```
Accept-Encoding: gzip
```

The server should then deliver the content of the requested document using an encoding accepted by this client. If the client isn't lying (like early versions of Netscape 4.x can), the compressed data is decompressed by the browser. Modern browsers that support HTTP 1.1 content-encoding support ZLIB inflation of deflated documents and benefit from HTTP compression. Older browsers that don't send the Accept-Encoding header automatically receive the uncompressed version of your files.

You can create gzipped versions of your files beforehand and let server add-ons like mod_gzip or mod_deflate do the negotiation for you (that is, .html.gz or .html, and .js.gz or .js), or let software like mod_gzip compress your data on the fly (letting Apache do the negotiation alone is possible but problematic).

---

3. Tim Berners-Lee, Roy T. Fielding, and Henrik F. Nielsen, "Hypertext Transfer Protocol—HTTP/1.0," RFC 1945 [online], (1996), available from the Internet at http://www.ietf.org/rfc/rfc1945.txt. This RFC includes a content encoding section.

The net effect is dramatically smaller files, faster page response, and lower bandwidth bills. In fact, webmasters who have employed content encoding on their servers have realized bandwidth savings of 30 to 50 percent. The compression ratio depends on the degree of redundancy in your site's content, and the ratio of text to multimedia. Most importantly, compressed pages display much faster as the browser downloads less data. As browsers decompress compressed content with ZLIB, a dictionary-based algorithm, decompression speed is very fast.

GZIP Compression

The easiest way to employ content encoding on your server is to use software specifically designed for this purpose. Mod_gzip, mod_hs, and mod_deflate-ru are software modules that automate the entire process for Apache, as does PipeBoost and Hyperspace i for Microsoft's IIS server. These server add-ons can work with static or dynamic content, and the predefined installation files take care of most common server and browser configurations. Later in this chapter, we'll compare the strengths and weaknesses of these and other compression modules and filters available for the Apache and IIS servers.

How good is gzip compression? Some say that the improvement can be up to 90 percent; others are happy with 25 percent. They just measure it in a different way. HTML files are typically compressed by 80 percent (5:1 ratio), while JavaScript and CSS files average 70 and 80 percent compression, respectively.

A typical HTML page consists of an HTML file, several image files, sometimes a CSS file, and a couple of JavaScript files. Images are already compressed, so it doesn't make sense to apply content compression to them. Because images and multimedia objects take more than half of total web page size,[4] even if you compress the HTML file by 90 percent, the total compression ratio will be less than 50 percent.

---

4. Eric Siegel of Keynote Systems, email to author, 25 September 2002. The median KB40 site has over 50 percent graphics, and without JavaScript, over 60 percent. See also a previous study at http://www.keynote.com/ solutions/assets/applets/Performance_Analysis_of_40_e-Business_Web_Sites.pdf.

To give you an idea of how effective compression can be, take a look a Table 18.2. This table shows the potential compression ratios for five of the most popular high-tech companies, five online newspapers, five web directories, and five sports resources.

Table 18.2   Content Encoding: Average Compression Ratios for Different Web Site Categories

Web Site Type (Average for 5 Web Sites)	Number of Files	HTML, CSS, and JS Files Only			All Files Including Graphics		
		Original Size	Compressed Size	Savings	Original Size	Compressed Size	Savings
High-Tech Company	14	26,531	5,092	79%	60,650	39,211	35%
Newspaper	37	74,688	16,218	79%	15,0220	91,749	40%
Web Directory	11	36,096	13,296	69%	50,168	27,368	46%
Sports	24	41,011	10,167	74%	11,0530	79,686	27%
Average	22	44,582	11,193	75%	92,892	59,504	37%

High-tech: www.cisco.com, www.hp.com, www.ibm.com, www.microsoft.com, www.oracle.com
Newspapers: www.latimes.com, www.nytimes.com, www.usatoday.com, www.washingtonpost.com, www.wsj.com
Web directories: www.altavista.com, www.looksmart.com, www.lycos.com, www.netscape.com, www.yahoo.com
Sports: www.espn.com, sports.yahoo.com, sportsillustrated.cnn.com, www.sportsnetwork.com, www.usatoday.com/sports/front.htm

On average, the text portion of these sites was compressed by 75 percent. Overall, compression would save 37 percent in total file size.

Modem Compression Is Not Enough

Most dial-up modems use V42bis or V44bis compression based on the LZW algorithm. If modems already compress data, you might ask, why do we need any additional compression? First, because of the speed and limited memory of modems, modem compression has relatively low compression ratios. In my experience, V42b provides a compression ratio of about 2:1 on most text files. As you learned earlier, gzip compression gives much higher compression ratios of 3:1 or higher. Second, modems do not compress SSL-encrypted files. Most importantly, dial-up connections are only one way to connect to the Internet. DSL, cable, and T1 modems as well as network cards do not have compression onboard. That is why HTTP content compression is so important.

Content Compression: Client Side

As you learned in the "Content Compression" section, browsers and servers have brief conversations about what kind of content they would prefer to accept and deliver. The browser tells the server that it can accept content encoding, and if the server is capable, it will then compress the data and transmit it. The browser decompresses the data and then renders the page. Clients that don't understand compressed content don't request encoded files and, thus, receive files uncompressed (assuming that the content is offered conditionally). By definition, HTTP 1.1-compliant browsers support gzip compression. Most modern browsers support gzip content encoding (see Table 18.3).

Table 18.3   Browser Content Encoding Support

Browser	Encoding Support
Microsoft Internet Explorer	4.x+ gzip, deflate. Macintosh versions do not understand coding by the methods gzip and deflate. They do not transfer the "Accept-Encoding" header.
	There is a caching issue with compressed content in Internet Explorer. Fortunately, all the content compression software vendors are aware of this and know how to work around it. The only software that works incorrectly with MSIE is Microsoft Internet Information Server.
Netscape 4.06+	Supports HTTP/1.0, but Netscape 4.06 and later versions send "Accept-Encoding: gzip" in the header. There are some limitations, however. It works consistently only for content type "text/html" or "text/plain." JavaScript and CSS files ("application/x-javascript" and "text/css") will not be decompressed properly.
Mozilla m14-m18, 0.6-0.9.3, Netscape 6.0-6.1, Galeon, and SkipStone	Error in implementation.
Mozilla 0.9.4+, Netscape 6.2+	Good
Opera 5.12+	Good
Lynx 2.6+	Good
Konqueror	gzip only

What is the difference between gzip and deflate? Both are based on the same compression algorithm, deflate,[5] implemented in the compression library zlib.[6] Deflate encoding assumes that you are sending only the compressed data. gzip[7] adds a 10-byte header to the compressed data. It also adds a CRC32 checksum and the length of the compressed data (4+4=8 bytes) to the end of compressed file. The image of transferred data is a valid .gz file.

There is one more content-encoding compression algorithm: compress, which utilizes a compression algorithm implemented in the UNIX compress utility. This algorithm is supported only by Lynx, Netscape, and Mozilla.

Because some versions of Konqueror have an error in deflate decoding and gzip is widely supported, most compression solutions use gzip content encoding.

HTML and Compression

HTML and other text files can be compressed on the server and automatically decompressed with HTTP 1.1-compliant browsers. Because HTML files must be downloaded before your content appears, fast delivery of this page framework is critical to user satisfaction.

Because HTML text files can be highly redundant (especially tables), compression rates for HTML files can be dramatic, with savings up to 90 percent. Most modern browsers support decompression of HTML files compressed with gzip.

5. L. Peter Deutsch, "DEFLATE Compressed Data Format Specification Version 1.3," RFC 1951 [online], (Alladin Enterprises, 1996), available from the Internet at http://www.ietf.org/rfc/rfc1951.txt.

6. L. Peter Deutsch and Jean-Loup Gailly, "ZLIB Compressed Data Format Specification version 3.3," RFC 1950 [online], (Alladin Enterprises, 1996), available from the Internet at http://www.ietf.org/rfc/rfc1950.txt.

7. L. Peter Deutsch, "GZIP File Format Specification version 4.3," RFC 1952 [online], (Alladin Enterprises, 1996), available from the Internet at http://www.ietf.org/rfc/rfc1952.txt.

The ZLIB Saga

After CompuServe and Unisys rattled their GIF copyright sabers in late 1995, browser manufacturers rushed to add PNG support to their browsers.[8] Luckily, the PNG format uses public domain GZIP/ZLIB[6] compression algorithms (deflate and inflate), which are based on the older, non-proprietary Lempel-Ziv algorithm (LZ77).[9] GIFs use the less efficient Lempel-Ziv-Welch algorithm (LZW),[10] which is based on LZ78.[11] So in order to receive and display PNG files, the browser manufacturers had to add ZLIB inflation to their browsers. CompuServe subsequently backed down, but the deed was done. Now browsers had ZLIB support.

Developers at Microsoft and Netscape realized that they already had ZLIB on board to handle inflating PNG files. Why not implement IETF content encoding? Why not indeed.

Their first attempts went badly (browsers would report "Accept-Encoding" but then botch things when the compressed data arrived), but after a few more browser releases, they both got it right. The outcome is that any browser that can display PNG files can usually decompress anything sent with IETF content encoding: gzip.

---

8. Michael C. Battilana, "The GIF Controversy: A Software Developer's Perspective" [online], (Las Vegas: Cloanto Italia, 1995 [cited 12 November 2002]), available from the Internet at http://www.lzw.info.

9. Jacob Ziv and Abraham Lempel, "A Universal Algorithm for Sequential Data Compression," *IEEE Transactions on Information Theory* 23, no. 3 (1977): 337–343. LZ77 described.

10. Terry A. Welch, "A Technique for High-Performance Data Compression," *IEEE Computer* 17, no. 6 (1984): 8–19. The LZW algorithm described.

11. Jacob Ziv and Abraham Lempel, "Compression of Individual Sequences via Variable Rate Coding," *IEEE Transactions on Information Theory* 24, no. 5 (1978): 530–536. LZ78 described.

CSS Compression

In theory, you can also compress external style sheets using content encoding. In practice, webmasters have found that browsers inconsistently decompress .css files. Apparently, style sheets were hacked into some browsers in a non-HTTP-compliant way. So when these browsers receive a 'Content-Encoding: gzip' header in the response for a .css file, they don't realize that they are supposed to decompress it first.

This is not always the case, however, and no one to my knowledge has been able to nail down which browsers can actually handle the decompression of style sheets and under what circumstances. The problem seems to involve a mixture of variables. Therefore, I recommend that you exclude compression of .css files in any configuration files for programs such as mod_gzip:

```
mod_gzip_item_exclude           file         \.css$
```

Most .css files are smaller than .js files anyway, so the need for compression is usually greater for .js files. In fact, CSS files are usually so small that the two HTTP headers needed to request and respond can add up to a significant portion of the total traffic (up to 750–1,000 bytes). So for smaller CSS files on high-traffic pages, it may be more efficient to embed them directly into your (X)HTML files or use SSI, where they can *then* be compressed.

JavaScript Compression

Like HTML files, external JavaScript files can be compressed with IETF content encoding. Unlike external .css files, support for decompressing compressed JavaScript files is good in modern HTTP 1.1-compliant browsers, as long as they are placed within the head of your HTML documents. Although it is possible, I don't recommend using proprietary compression methods to deliver external JavaScript files (.jar, CHM/ITS, etc.). The standards-based method described in this chapter requires at most only one additional file—not four—to maintain.

JavaScript Compression Gotcha: Use Your *head*

External scripts must be referenced in the head element of (X)HTML documents to be reliably decompressed by modern browsers. The story goes like this. Netscape's original specification for JavaScript 1.1 implied that the inclusion of JavaScript source files should take place in the `head` section, because that is the only place where they are pre-loaded and pre-processed.[12] For some reason, browser manufacturers stopped decompressing any compressed files after leaving the `head`.

As scripts grew larger, developers started moving `script` elements down into the `body` to satisfy impatient users. In HTML, the "head-only" rule was then relaxed to allow `script` elements within the `body`, but the die was cast. Developers subsequently discovered that certain JavaScript inclusion operations must be in the `head` section or problems can occur.

Browsers continue to decompress scripts only when they are located within the `head` element. Some companies get around this limitation by adding "_h" to the names of JavaScript include files in the `head` section of HTML documents. Using this technique, a script author can use server-side filtering logic to find whether a request for a certain JavaScript file is coming from the `head` section of a HTML document (where it is OK to send it compressed) versus somewhere in the `body` (where it is not OK to send the script compressed). You can optionally use the `defer` attribute to compensate for this requirement.

JavaScript Compression Gotcha: Premature *onload* Events

Internet Explorer 5 has a known bug when loading compressed JavaScripts.[13] IE mistakenly triggers the `onload` event after it downloads the compressed file, but *before* it is decompressed. This can lead to unexpected behavior. The way around this bug is to include another variable at the end of your external file and poll for its presence in the `onload` event handler.

13. Kevin Kiley and Andrew Jarman, "Compressing .js files, from a lurkers point of view" [online], (Mod_gzip mailing list, 17 March 2001), available from the Internet at `http://lists.over.net/pipermail/mod_gzip/2001-March/001708.html`.

12. Netscape Communications, "JavaScript Guide for JavaScript 1.1" [online], (Mountain View, CA: Netscape Communications, 1996), available from the Internet at `http://wp.netscape.com/eng/mozilla/3.0/handbook/javascript/`. Implied in the section "Specifying a File of JavaScript Code" that external files should be in the `head` section.

Content Compression: Server Side

So it sounds like all you need to do is compress your content on the server and deliver it, right? Unfortunately, it is not that simple. You have three options for choosing the type of compression you want to use:

- Static pre-compressed content
- Dynamic real-time server-side compression
- Proxy-based compression

Static pre-compressed content makes sense for heavily loaded web sites with more or less static content. Some news web sites keep all their news in a database and convert it to static HTML files once every several minutes. These sites send responses faster than sites with ASP, JSP, or PHP pages. The best thing to do here is to keep a compressed copy of the pages ready to send. If an HTTP request contains the Accept-Encoding line, send a compressed file; otherwise, send an HTML file.

Dynamic real-time server-side compression compresses files before sending them to the client. It can be implemented as a plug-in to a web server or as a part of standalone proxy server.

Proxy-based compression compresses files between the server and the client, alleviating the need to compress files on the server. This reduces server load and gives ISPs and enterprise operations more power and flexibility.

Content Compression in Apache

In Apache, you can pre-compress content or install a module to compress content on the fly.

There is a special administration tool written in Perl to pre-compress content on your Apache web site and properly set up the .htaccess file. It is available at http://www.chatologica.com/site/eWSA.htm.

You can pre-compress content manually as well. The process is pretty straightforward:

1. gzip your .htm files to .htmz.

2. Add to httpd.conf following line:

   ```
   AddEncoding gzip htmz
   ```

3. Add index.htmz as a default directory index:

   ```
   DirectoryIndex index.htmz index.htm index.html index.html.var
   ```

4. In the mime.types file, add **htmz** to the text/html line:

   ```
   text/html               html htm htmz
   ```

But how do you address links? Links in the .htmz files point to .htm; so the index file will be compressed, and the other files will not. You can copy the web site, change links to .htmz, and then compress. This will work, but it is a lot of work. There is a better way that is based on Apache content negotiation and the Multiviews feature.

Since version 1.2, the Apache web server has supported content negotiation as defined in the HTTP 1.1 specification. Apache 1.2 supports server-driven content negotiation, while Apache 1.3.4 supports transparent content negotiation. In order to negotiate a resource, the server needs to know about the *variants* of each resource.

Multiviews implicitly maps variants based on filename extensions, like .gz. Multiviews is a per-directory option that can be set within .htaccess files or within the httpd.conf file for one or more directories. Setting the Multiviews option within the .conf file is more efficient because the server doesn't have to access an .htaccess file every time it accesses a directory. Here's how you turn on Multiviews in the httpd.conf file:

```
Options    Multiviews
```

In a real configuration file, it will look like this:

```
<Directory />
    Options FollowSymLinks Multiviews
    AllowOverride None
</Directory>
```

Apache recognizes only encodings that are defined by an `AddEncoding` directive. So to let Apache know about gzip encoded files, you'd add the following directive:

```
AddEncoding gzip .gz
```

With `Multiviews` set, authors need only create filename variants of resources, and Apache does the rest. So to create gzipped compressed versions of your `.html` or `.js` files, you zip them up like this:

```
gzip -9 index.html
gzip -9 script.js
```

Then you link to the uncompressed `.html` or `.js` files, and Apache would negotiate to the `.gz` variant for capable browsers.

Some Browsers Lie

Apache (through 2.0x) checks to see whether browsers have sent the `Accept-Encoding:` header and assumes that any pre-compressed files are OK to send. This isn't always the case, however, because some browsers lie. Netscape 4.x sends the following message, yet it is incapable of receiving compressed data for some file types:

```
Accept-Encoding: deflate, gzip
```

For More Information

To learn more about content negotiation and how to combine content encoding with other features like content language, see this document: `http://httpd.apache.org/docs-2.0/content-negotiation.html`.

Content negotiation produces significant overhead, slowing server response by as much as 25 percent. But as long as the Apache reply time is just several milliseconds, there is no way your users will notice the response time when requesting pages with their browsers.

Apache and Microsoft's IIS server can perform content negotiation, but to avoid any headaches due to misleading browsers, it is best to use a tool designed specifically for the job, like mod_gunzip or mod_gzip.

Serving Static Pre-Compressed Files with mod_gunzip

As long as only a tiny percent of requests come from older browsers, it may make sense to save only compressed versions of your content. If an old browser requests a page, your server can decompress it in real time before sending.

For More Information

A mod_gunzip module is available for the Apache web server. It is available at `http://www.oldach.net/`. You can find configuration information for mod_gunzip at `http://www.innerjoin.org/apache-compression/howto.html`.

To use mod_gunzip, create a second gzipped version of your HTML or JavaScript (`.html.gz` or `.js.gz`) file, like this:

```
gzip -9 index.html
gzip -9 script.js
```

Then link to the uncompressed file as normal, using the `href` or `src` attribute:

```
<a href="/index.html">Home</a>
<script src="/script.js" type="text/javascript"></script>
```

Now when a browser reports that it can understand IETF content encoding, the server can deliver the compressed version of your text file.

Serving Static Pre-Compressed Files with mod_gzip

Mod_gzip also can be used to deliver pre-compressed files to appropriate browsers. By turning on the `mod_gzip_can_negotiate` switch, you can deliver compressed files to the right browsers. You can run mod_gzip in "negotiation-only" mode by also omitting any include rules. These rules tell mod_gzip which files to compress dynamically. Here's a snippet from mod_gzip's Apache 1.3x configuration file:

```
# use mod_gzip at all?
    mod_gzip_on                   Yes
# ..................................................................
# let mod_gzip perform 'partial content negotiation'?
    mod_gzip_can_negotiate        Yes
```

Netscape 4.x in particular has spotty support for compressed JavaScript. You can use two general approaches to deal with Netscape 4:

- Include HTTP 1.0 browsers (like Netscape 4.x) that support content encoding and exclude .js files (and optionally SSI .js files so they'll be compressed with the HTML), or

- Require HTTP 1.1-compliant browsers to exclude Netscape 4.x and deliver compressed .html and .js files.

You can specify these two scenarios easily in the filters section of the mod_gzip configuration file. Here's how you'd set mod_gzip for the first scenario:

```
##############
### filters ###
##############
# ..................................................................
# Required HTTP version of the client
# Possible values: 1000 = HTTP/1.0  1001 = HTTP/1.1, ...
# This directive uses the same numeric protocol values as Apache internally
    mod_gzip_min_http            1000
# ..................................................................
# which files are to be compressed?
#
# phase 1: (reqheader, uri, file, handler)
# =====================================
# NO:   include files / JavaScript & CSS (due to Netscape4 bugs)
    mod_gzip_item_exclude        file      \.js$
    mod_gzip_item_exclude        file      \.css$
#
# phase 2: (mime, respheader)
# ==========================
# YES:  normal HTML files, normal text files, Apache directory listings
    mod_gzip_item_include        file      \.html$
    mod_gzip_item_include        mime      ^text/html$
```

```
      mod_gzip_item_include          mime        ^text/plain$
      mod_gzip_item_include          mime        ^httpd/unix-directory$
...
```

To exclude Netscape 4.x and include .js files for compression for the second scenario, bump up the minimum HTTP level and include .js files, like this:

```
      mod_gzip_min_http              1001
      mod_gzip_item_include          file        \.js$
      mod_gzip_item_exclude          file        \.css$
```

For More Information

For more details on configuring mod_gzip, consult the documentation available at the following sites:

- http://www.ehyperspace.com/
- http://sourceforge.net/projects/mod-gzip/

You also can find more details at the following sites:

- Mod_gzip mailing list: http://lists.over.net/mailman/listinfo/mod_gzip/
- Michael Schröpl's mod_gzip site:
  http://www.schroepl.net/projekte/mod_gzip/

Pre-compressed content has some advantages. By pre-compressing your files, you can save CPU resources on your server. Dynamic compression of data requires some CPU horsepower. For higher loads on slower servers, dynamic compression can be too CPU intensive, so pre-compression makes more sense. On faster servers with dynamic content, however, dynamic compression is a better choice.

Pre-compressed content also has some disadvantages: It requires more maintenance and cannot deliver dynamic content.

How to Compile and Install an Apache Module

Most of the custom Apache modules including mod_gunzip are provided in source code form. If you want to get the maximum performance from your Apache server, be prepared to compile them. However, to save time I recommend that you download a precompiled module instead of source code when one is available.

You can attach a module to Apache in two ways: by static or dynamic linking. Statically linking to a module means that every time you want to add, remove, or update the module, you have to rebuild Apache. Dynamic linking, although it is about five percent slower, does not require recompiling. You can easily update or unplug dynamically linked modules, although you must recompile Apache to unplug static modules. Static linking is better for security reasons because it is much harder to replace part of the code, which is important for commerce sites (SSL). For flexibility, consider dynamic linking. For maximum performance and security, consider static linking.

Here are the steps for static linking:

1. Add the following line near the bottom of the src/Configuration file:
   ```
   AddModule modules/mod_gunzip/mod_gunzip.c
   ```

2. Put the module source code here:
   ```
   modules/mod_gunzip/mod_gunzip.c
   ```

3. Rebuild the Apache server.

For a dynamic link, you only need to build the module. Here are the steps:

1. Decompress the source with `tar` if it is compressed:
   ```
   tar -zxvf mod_gunzip.tar.gz
   ```

2. Compile the module:
   ```
   /usr/local/apache/bin/apxs -i -a -c -lz mod_gunzip.c
   ```

   Option `-c` compiles, `-i` installs, and `-a` activates. Activating means adding the proper lines to the Apache config file and restarting.

   The apxs tool is described here:
   ```
   http://httpd.apache.org/docs/programs/apxs.html.
   ```

3. Place the resulting file `mod_gunzip` in the `/usr/httpd/modules` directory (or the `/usr/lib/apache/` directory, depending on your version or distribution). For Windows, it will be something like this:

   `C:\Program Files\Apache Group\Apache2\modules\.`

4. Add the following line into the `httpd.conf` file:

   `LoadModule gunzip_module /usr/httpd/modules/mod_gunzip.so`

For More Information

More information about compiling Apache modules can be found at `http://httpd.apache.org/docs-2.0/dso.html`.

Dynamic Compression

If you need to generate every page on the fly, there is no way you can statically pre-compress it. Pre-compressed content wouldn't work well for a site like Google, for example.

Fortunately there are a number of real-time Apache compression modules. Notice, however, that none are perfect (see Table 18.4).

Table 18.4   Apache Modules for Dynamic Content Compression

Module	Advantages	Disadvantages
Mod_gzip from RemoteCommunications, Inc. (now an open source SourceForge project)	Lots of documentation. Lots of parameters for fine-tuning. Free.	Save compressed content to temporary file—works slower than other modules.
Mod_gzip from VIGOS AG	The first product on the market, includes whitespace removal, improved gzip algorithm (30 percent faster than RCI's mod_gzip), only in-memory compression, and browser auto-detection.	Only available for Apache 1.3. A commercial product. Same name as SourceForge mod_gzip. VIGOS encourages using their reverse proxy Website Accelerator instead.

continues

Table 18.4   Apache Modules for Dynamic Content Compression   *continued*

Module	Advantages	Disadvantages
Mod_deflate ru by Khrustalev and Sysoev	Lots of parameters for fine-tuning. Fast and efficient.	Documentation is poorly translated to English. Name violation with Apache mod_deflate. Distributed in source only. No Windows version available. Incompatible with Apache 2.
Mod_deflate from the Apache Software Foundation	Included in Apache 2.0. No compilation required.	Not flexible.
Mod_hs from HyperSpace Communications, Inc.	Improved commercial version of mod_gzip. Fast and efficient.	Incompatible with Apache 2.
Gzip_cnc by Michael Schröpl	Can be installed on a shared hosting with restricted access to Apache settings.	Written in Perl; does not handle dynamic content.

There are two different mod_deflate modules. Which module is the real one? Igor Sysoev claims he created his module in April 2001, while Apache created its module in August 2001. In any event, make sure that you use the right documentation for the appropriate module.

These modules all use essentially the same gzip algorithm, so the compression ratio is the same. I recommend that you use the maximum compression level of 9 instead of the default of 6 when possible. It may save you 100 bytes on a 100KB HTML file. The modules vary in how fast they compress and deliver content, and how specifically you can target browsers and file types.

What is the speed difference for compressed versus uncompressed content? It is hard to believe, but Apache responds with the compression module only about two times slower than Apache configured to send pre-compressed content.

Dynamic compression of content does have some advantages. In full content negotiation mode, mod_gzip and similar modules handle everything: They negotiate the compression of content on the fly and then deliver the data. Maintenance costs are reduced because separate compressed files are not necessary. More importantly, you can deliver compressed dynamic content, which is not possible with pre-compression.

Dynamic compression also has some disadvantages. It requires some CPU power to compress files on the fly. However, mod_gzip and others deflate very efficiently with their compiled C code. CPU concerns are a factor only on slower servers.

Mod_deflate, Apache Version

Mod_deflate from Apache is the easiest solution for dynamic content compression because you don't need to find or compile it—it's already there in Apache 2.0. Just add the following lines to `httpd.conf`:

```
LoadModule deflate_module modules/mod_deflate.so
SetEnv gzip-only-text/html 1
SetOutputFilter DEFLATE
```

And enjoy the compression!

All the HTML files requested with appropriate Accept-Encoding headers will be compressed from now on.

Unfortunately, there is no way you can fine-tune the Apache mod_deflate module to configure which file types are compressed and which browsers are targeted.

mod_deflate is included in the Apache 2.0 distribution at
`http://httpd.apache.org/docs-2.0/mod/mod_deflate.html`.

Mod_gzip—Configurable Compression

If you really need fine-tuning and advanced statistics, use mod_gzip instead. Mod_gzip is currently an open source SourceForge project at
`http://sourceforge.net/projects/mod-gzip/`.

Mod_gzip has one minor disadvantage: It temporarily saves the compressed versions of files to disk before serving them, which can slow the response by up to 30 percent. On the other hand, it is the most extensively tested module with proven reliability.

To install mod_gzip, see the section, "How to Compile and Install an Apache Module," and substitute mod_gzip filenames for mod_gunzip. Note that recent versions of mod_gzip at SourceForge are no longer in a single-file distribution.

You can make the entire compression process transparent by letting mod_gzip do the compression on the fly. Without pre-compressed variants, you can turn off negotiation to save one file access for each request, as shown here:

```
# let mod_gzip perform 'partial content negotiation'?
    mod_gzip_can_negotiate          No
```

Next, set mod_gzip's include rules to specify which types of files to compress:

```
mod_gzip_item_include       file        \.js$
mod_gzip_item_exclude       file        \.css$
mod_gzip_item_include       file        \.html$
...
```

Once installed, mod_gzip will compress the data that you specify automatically. Browsers that can handle compressed data will receive it, and browsers that don't, won't.

Although static files can be compressed with gzip's maximum setting of 9, mod_gzip actually uses the more moderate compression setting of 6, which gives a good compromise between file size and decompression speed.

Mod_hs—The Commercial Version of mod_gzip

mod_hs is a commercial product based on mod_gzip that was created by HyperSpace, Communications, Inc. HyperSpace claims a 30 percent performance increase achieved by in-memory compression and elimination of disk I/O operations. For more information, see http://www.ehyperspace.com.

Mod_deflate ru

If you need fine-tuning and the best possible performance, try mod_deflate from sysoev.ru. It is more flexible than mod_gzip and allows you to add the compression method (deflate or gzip), uncompressed file size, compressed file size, and compression ratio to the Apache log file.

According to the authors, the module's installation fixes some bugs in the Apache source code, so you'll need to re-build Apache after you configure the module.

To install mod_deflate:

1. Unpack it with `tar` and run the configuration script:

```
tar zxf mode_deflate-mod_deflate-1.0.12.tar.gz
cd mod_deflate-mod_deflate-1.0.12
./configure --with-apache=<apache_dir>   -- with-zlib=<zlib_dir>
make
```

ZLIB is available for free download here: `http://www.gzip.org/zlib/`.

2. Rebuild Apache and activate the module:

```
cd <apache_dir>
./configure
    ...
    --activate-module=src/modules/extra/mod_deflate.o
    ...
```

3. The default configuration works great, but I recommend that you change the compression ratio from 1 to 9 or at least 6 for higher compression:

```
DeflateCompLevel 9
```

Mod_deflate ru from Khrustalev and Sysoev is available at the following sites:

- `http://sysoev.ru/mod_deflate/mod_deflate-1.0.15.tar.gz`

- `http://pflanze.mine.nu/~chris/mod_deflate/`
  `mod_deflate_readme_EN.html` (documentation)

- `http://sysoev.ru/mod_deflate/` (in Russian)

Gzip_cnc—For Those Without Apache System Access

Most web sites are hosted on shared servers. In this case, you cannot access the `httpd.conf` and "modules" folder, so there is no way to install an Apache module. Web hosting companies usually refuse to install additional components, especially third-party products. I understand them; they care about the 99.9 percent uptime they promised.

There is still a way to compress content if you can edit your `.htaccess` files. Gzip_cnc is not an Apache module, but rather a content handler written in Perl. This program requires that gzip be on your server in a place where you can access it.

To install Gzip_cnc, follow these steps:

1. Copy the source code from
   `http://www.schroepl.net/projekte/gzip_cnc/program.htm`.

2. Create a new file `gzip_cnc.pl` in your cgi-bin folder and paste the source code there.

3. Add the following lines into the `.htaccess` file and test it:
   ```
   <Files ~ \.html?$>
     Action text/html /cgi-bin/gzip_cnc.pl
   </Files>
   ```

   If it does not work, verify the path to gzip in the source code.
   ```
   my $gzip_path              = '/usr/bin/gzip';
   ```

You can specify parameters for the Gzip_cnc two ways. The first way is by modifying the code—all the settings are in the very top of the program. The alternative way is to set up environment variables.

For More Information

To learn more about gzip_cnc, see Michael Schröpl's site at `http://www.schroepl.net/projekte/gzip_cnc/`.

Choosing a Compression Module

How do you choose the appropriate compression module for your Apache server? It's easy for Apache 2; mod_deflate is the only current option. For Apache 1.3, if you are looking for a commercial product, try mod_hs or mod_gzip from VIGOS; otherwise, try mod_gzip (RCI) or mod_deflate ru for maximum speed. On a shared server, try gzip_cnc.

There are some other ways to compress the output in the Apache server:

- For PHP version 4.0.4+, add the line:
  ```
  output_handler = ob_gzhandler ;
  ```

  in `php.ini` to turn on content compression (but only for PHP files, of course).

- To turn on compression only for particular files, add the following statement:
```
ob_start("ob_gzhandler");
```

- If you use an older version of PHP, you will have to implement a gzip handler by yourself. It's easy:
```
function gzip_output($output) {
    return gzencode($output);
}
// if browser supports compression
if (strstr($HTTP_SERVER_VARS['HTTP_ACCEPT_ENCODING'], 'gzip')) {
    ob_start("gzip_output"); // set handler
    header("Content-Encoding: gzip");  // tell browser
}
```

For More Information

More information about PHP compression is available at `http://zend.com/zend/art/buffering.php`.

Here are some tools to compress Perl output for Apache:

- Apache::Dynagzip—`http://search.cpan.org/author/SLAVA/Apache-Dynagzip-0.06/Dynagzip.pm`

- Apache::GzipChain—`http://search.cpan.org/author/ANDK/Apache-GzipChain-0.06/GzipChain.pm`

I recommend that you to use an Apache compression module or a reverse proxy instead because they offer more complete solutions for compressing all your content.

Content Compression in Microsoft's IIS Server

With some help, Microsoft's IIS server can deliver compressed content to HTTP 1.1-compliant browsers. The best way to enable content encoding on IIS is to use an ISAPI filter specifically designed for this purpose. For pre-compressed content, IIS doesn't have any built-in mechanism like Apache's `Multiviews`.

Dynamic Content Compression for the IIS Server

Microsoft's IIS server has content compression onboard. To turn it on, follow these steps:

1. Open the Computer Management window.

2. Select Internet Information Services.

3. Right-click and select Properties (see Figure 18.1).

Figure 18.1
Setting up compression for IIS.

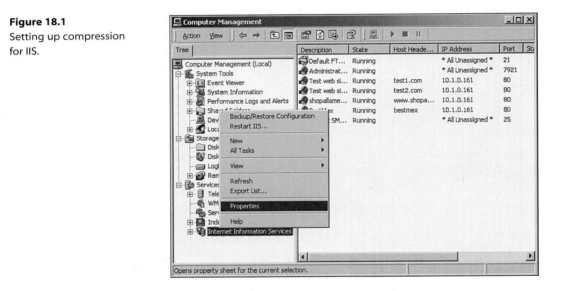

4. In Internet Information Services Properties, click Edit in the Master Properties section.

5. In WWW Service Master Properties, check the Compress application files option and click OK (see Figure 18.2)

6. Restart the IIS server.

Ironically, this works with all browsers except Microsoft Internet Explorer. It is a caching problem. Internet Explorer displays the compressed file properly for the first time, but the refresh button ruins it. The file is there, and you can save it to disk, but you cannot properly see it.

Figure 18.2
Setting up compression for
IIS—final step.

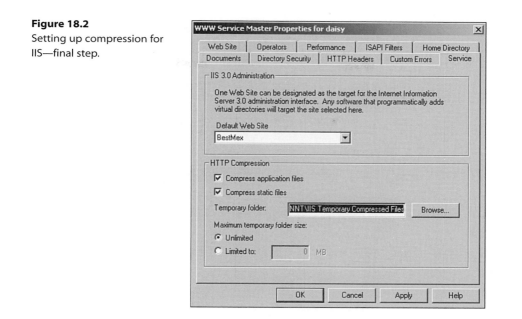

A number of dynamic content compression solutions allow you to work around this limitation. All these tools are implemented as an ISAPI filter. The difference is flexibility.

PipeBoost

PipeBoost is a powerful, flexible, and easy-to-use commercial content compression solution for Microsoft IIS.

In PipeBoost, you can configure literally everything. You can set individual configurations for every web site and every folder. You can assign individual content type handling rules for each browser (see Figure 18.3).

You can even set custom compression levels for each file type (see Figure 18.4).

The other good thing about PipeBoost is that it includes a powerful analyzing and monitoring system (see Figure 18.5), a cache performance analyzer, and some other useful tools.

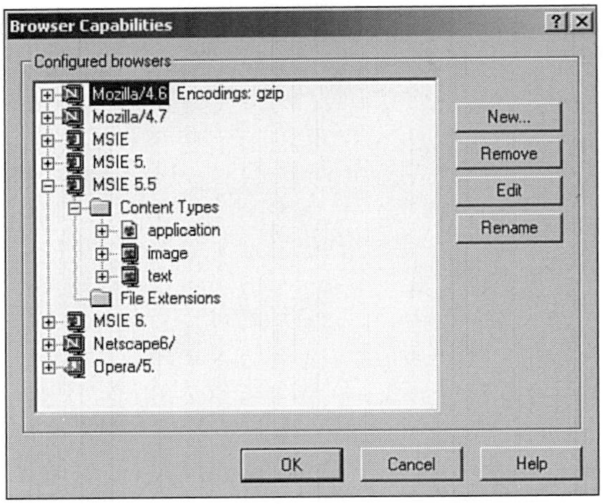

Figure 18.3
PipeBoost—setting up
browsers.

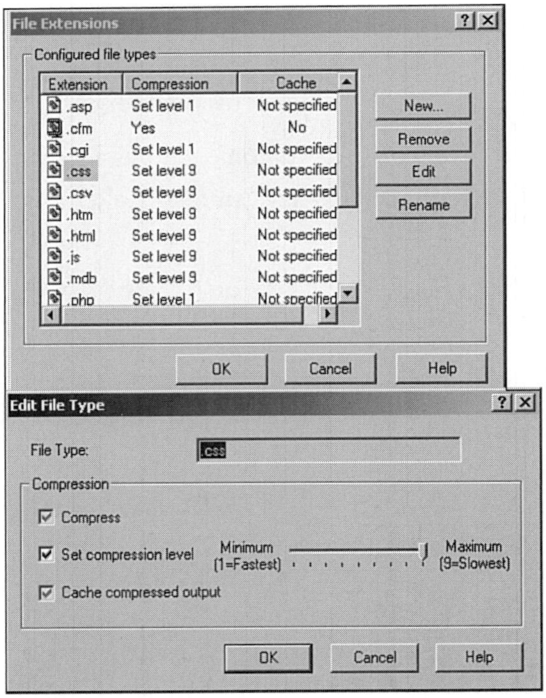

Figure 18.4
PipeBoost—setting up
MIME types.

Figure 18.5
PipeBoost performance
monitor.

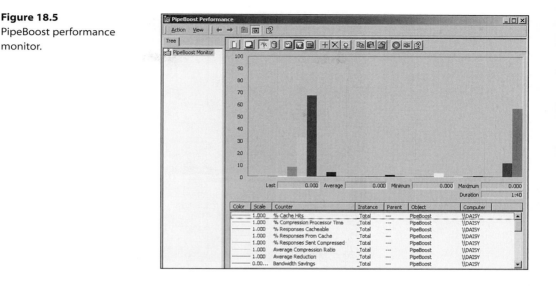

For More Information

To find out more about PipeBoost, see http://www.pipeboost.com/.

Inner Media SqueezePlay

SqueezePlay from Inner Media, Inc. is another commercial content compression solution for Microsoft IIS. It consists of Configurator and Accelerometer.

Configurator is a GUI tool with a lot of dialogs and settings. You can configure browser types and content types (see Figure 18.6).

The Accelerometer is a graphics analysis tool with column diagrams. It shows sent data size and savings.

In addition to the HTTP content compression, SqueezePlay provides image optimization. An LZW license to optimize GIF files is not included; you have to buy it separately.

Figure 18.6
SqueezePlay Configurator.

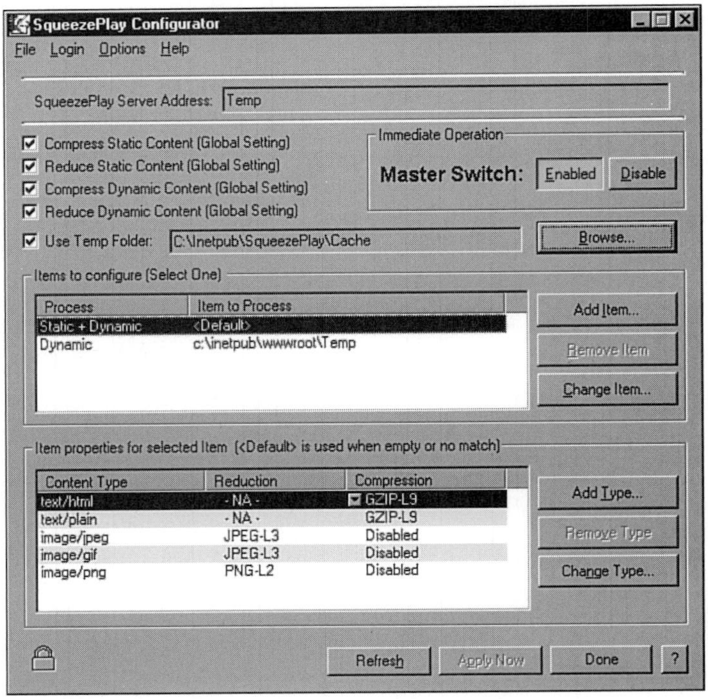

For More Information

To find out more about SqueezePlay, see http://www.innermedia.com/.

HyperSpace i

If you don't mind editing text configuration files, try HyperSpace i from eHyperSpace (http://ehyperspace.com/solutions/hyperspacei.html).

This tool is pretty flexible. You can set up browser types and versions, MIME types, minimum file size to be compressed, and so on. You also can add information like compressed file size and compression ratio to your log file.

This tool is not for everybody, however. There is no GUI, which means that configuring the configuration files is similar to editing Apache's httpd.conf for mod_gzip.

VIGOS IIS Accelerator

This ISAPI filter has all the configuration options from the VIGOS Website Accelerator, excluding the proxy specific ones. The filter can remove whitespace before compression, auto-detects browsers and MIME-types to avoid incompatibilities, and includes graphics optimization. It is configured with a text file, but comes with a handy configuration tool for editing this file.

HTTP Burst

There is one more tool in the market. HTTP Burst is free and looks pretty powerful and flexible. It is not easy to use, however; the authors suggest configuring it with `regedit.exe`.

The other problem—there is no English documentation. You can find more information at the following sites:

- `http://www.timax.net.ua/~httpburst/download.htm`
- `http://www.timax.net.ua/~httpburst/opisanie.htm`

Summary: IIS ISAPI Compression Filters

As long as all this software uses the same compression algorithm and the same ISAPI technology, you'll find no relevant difference in performance or compression ratio. Just keep in mind that the tools will slow down server response about 1.5 times (for example, 1.5 versus 1-second latency). On the majority of web sites, however, this added overhead is more than made up with the time saved sending compressed content. Therefore, I recommend that you make a decision based on the functionality you need, the added maintenance you are ready to take on, and the price you are willing pay.

Proxy Server-Based Content Compression

Compression does not necessarily need to be done by the web server. It can be implemented as a proxy server installed on the same or on a standalone server. Such a server can work with any web server. It can run on a different platform under a different operating system.

If you can install a compression server on the server side and decompression on the client side, you can use better compression algorithms. Proxy-based solutions give you real power, but they usually are more sophisticated. I recommend that you use them only in the following cases:

- To move compression to separate servers to reduce web server CPU load.

- To compress an Internet line with traffic when web servers are not available for administration.

- To use with a web server that does not support content compression.

There are several proxy-based solutions. Most of these companies have solutions for ISPs and enterprise-size networks:

- Fourelle provides several compression solutions, including server- and client-side proxy: `http://www.fourelle.com/`

- HyperSpace has a compression proxy server: `http://www.ehyperspace.com/`

- Packeteer has AppCelera a "compression, conversion, and caching" proxy: `http://www.packeteer.com/`

- VIGOS has the Website Accelerator, reverse-proxy software that compresses and optimizes content: `http://www.vigos.com/`

For maximum compatibility, consider one of these proxy solutions. They avoid problems with SSL and dynamic content. VIGOS Website Accelerator is a reverse-proxy software solution that automatically removes whitespace, optimizes graphics, compresses content, and includes their SmartShrink database, which they say eliminates HTTP compression compatibility problems.

For maximum speed, consider a hardware compression proxy. Packeteer's AppCelera ICX is a hardware/software appliance that automatically adjusts the optimization level based on the user's browser type and connection speed. It uses compression, image optimization, and conversion from GIFs to PNGs or JPEGs, caching, and SSL processing to minimize page size. AppCelera reports on user and server response times, load, and connection profiles. Packeteer also incorporates delta encoding in their latest products.

Benchmarking Tools

Benchmarking tools can show you how content encoding can benefit your web site. These tools quickly show how much you will save by adding compression to your web server.

PipeBoost Analyzer

PipeBoost Analyzer is the most convenient and easy-to-use content compression benchmarking tool (see Figure 18.7). It adds a toolbar to Internet Explorer and displays complete compression statistics. Unlike other tools, it takes into account not only HTML files, but also all the images that appear on the page. Table 18.2 was prepared with this tool.

Figure 18.7
PipeBoost Analyzer— compression benchmarking tool.

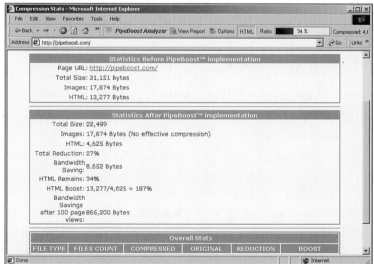

ApacheBench

ApacheBench, enhanced by Remote Communications, Inc. is a good tool for Unix and Windows, available at `http://www.remotecommunications.com/apache/ab/`.

This tool provides information about request and response, a hexadecimal image of the response, compression rate, transfer rate, performance increase, and connection time.

VIGOS Website Analyzer

VIGOS offers a free compression benchmarking tool for Windows. It can spider your entire site and estimate the total potential speed improvement. All objects like images, HTML, and Flash files are analyzed. The Analyzer includes a ROI calculator and a load-time monitor. This tool is available at `http://www.vigos.com`.

Web-Based Benchmarking Tools

Some web-based compression benchmarking tools are also available:

- HyperSpace Communications' connection speed test: `http://ehyperspace.com/solutions/performance.html#` (Tests your browser for content compression capabilities.)
- XCompress online analyzer: `http://www.xcache.com/home/default.asp`

On the Horizon

As you've seen, the ability to compress both static and dynamic content by more than 80 percent can be incorporated into all major web servers. Users are already seeing significant improvement in download speeds. Nowhere is this more evident than when searching the web. Those of us who use Google can see the accelerated response times.

Even though compression offers significant improvements, there is still much work to be done in the area of content acceleration. Delta encoding is a proposed extension to the HTTP 1.1 protocol (RFC 3229)[14] that will allow browsers to receive only content that has changed relative to other content on the page. Although companies are starting to embrace this technology, it has several limitations when delivering dynamic content, which by its very nature generates entirely new pages rather than smaller sections.

Of more interest is the ability to reduce the latency effect incurred while requesting web pages. Latency (the amount of time taken for the response to reach the web server and

14. Jeffrey C. Mogul et al., "Delta Encoding in HTTP," RFC 3229 [online], (Reston, VA: The Internet Society, 2002), available from the Internet at `http://www.ietf.org/rfc/rfc3229.txt`.

for the web server to reply) is significant in wireless infrastructures (narrowband). Often referred to as *pipelining*, this new feature is available in some browsers, but the majority of web servers (nearly the entire installed base) does not know how to process this request.

A more innovative approach would be the use of a special thin client that communicates directly with a modified server, allowing not only the numerous GET requests to be joined into a single request but also provide the ability to offer bi-directional optimization of other protocols from within the client. For example, the ability to send HTML email already pre-compressed from your client device over a narrowband connection would be of tremendous benefit to the wireless community. Once at the server, it can be decompressed and forwarded to a regular SMTP server.

Summary

Here's what to keep in mind when you are designing your system. If your system is not expected to be heavily loaded, use simple solutions and default settings to save time. Enabling content compression can save you 30 to 50 percent off bandwidth costs; further fine-tuning may save another 1 percent. And it is a very time-consuming black art.

Remember that gunzip works much faster than gzip, so it is better to keep content compressed and decompress it on demand than compress it on the fly. Use server-side caching for compressed files where possible.

HTML and JavaScript file decompression is well supported by mainstream browsers, although decompressing external CSS files is not. Make sure that you link to any compressed JavaScript files in the head of your documents for reliable decompression.

Here's a summary of web compression tips discussed in this chapter:

- For lighter loads, use simple solutions and default settings.
- Pre-compress content for maximum speed.
- For dynamic content, use a module or ISAPI filter specifically designed for this, like mod_gzip, mod_deflate-ru, or mod_hs for Apache and PipeBoost, VIGOS, or Hyperspace i for IIS.

- For Apache 2.0x, there's only one choice: mod_deflate.

- In a shared hosting situation, try gzip_cnc.

- Compress HTML files and external JavaScript files referenced in the head. Avoid CSS compression.

- For maximum speed or for other servers like Sun or iPlanet, consider a reverse proxy compression solution like AppCelera or VIGOS Website Accelerator.

Further Reading

- ACT compression test—http://compression.ca/

- Data compression resources—http://datacompression.info/

- Dr. Dobb's Journal Data Compression Resources—http://www.ddj.com/topics/compression/

- "HTTP Compression Speeds the Web" by Peter Cranstone—http://www.webreference.com/internet/software/servers/http/compression/

- "Introduction to Data Compression" by Guy Blelloch—http://www-2.cs.cmu.edu/afs/cs.cmu.edu/project/pscico-guyb/realworld/www/compression.pdf

- Official comp.compression FAQ—http://www.faqs.org/faqs/compression-faq/

19

Case Studies: Yahoo.com and WebReference.com

Now let's take the URL abbreviation technique you learned in Chapter 17, "Server-Side Techniques," and put it to work. As you recall, you can use the mod_rewrite module to automatically expand abbreviated URLs to save space. For pages with lots of links, this can make a big difference in file size. Because your home page is usually the busiest page on your site, it is especially important to ensure that it displays quickly.

Let's look at some real-world examples of sites before and after link abbreviation. For these case studies, we turn to Yahoo.com and WebReference.com.

Abbreviating Yahoo.com

Yahoo! was one of the first sites on the web to employ URL abbreviation. As one of the most popular pages on the web, Yahoo! does everything possible to save bandwidth and maximize speed. Yahoo! uses unquoted abbreviated URLs to squeeze their home page down to the bare minimum, which violates (X)HTML but still works (see Figure 19.1).

Figure 19.1
Yahoo.com—abbreviation central.

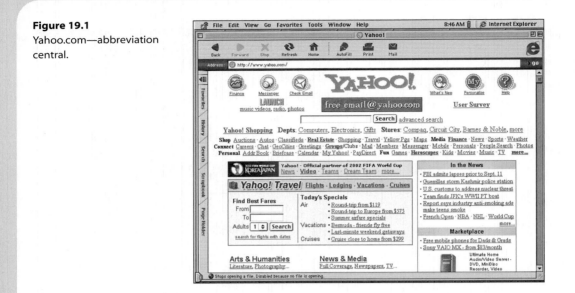

Yahoo! created mod_rewrite rulesets that allow URLs like this:

```
Computers_and_Internet/
```

To be abbreviated into this:

```
r/ci
```

But why stop there? You also can represent multiple directories with short abbreviations. So instead of this:

```
Computers_and_Internet/Internet/World_Wide_Web/
```

They do this:

```
r/ww
```

Behind the scenes, Yahoo!'s webmaster created a mapping file or `RewriteMap` that looks something like this:

```
r/bs  http://dir.yahoo.com/Business_and_Economy/Shopping_and_Services/
r/jo  http://dir.yahoo.com/Business_and_Economy/Employment_and_Work/
r/ci  http://dir.yahoo.com/Computers_and_Internet/
r/ww  http://dir.yahoo.com/Computers_and_Internet/Internet/World_Wide_Web/
...
```

Using mod_rewrite, a binary hash version of this RewriteMap, and a RewriteRule similar to the one discussed in Chapter 17, Yahoo! can serve up abbreviated links that automatically expand on request.

Here's a truncated version of Yahoo.com's home page before abbreviation. So instead of this:

```
<a href=http://dir.yahoo.com/Business_and_Economy/Shopping_and_Services/>Shopping</a>,
<a href=http://dir.yahoo.com/Business_and_Economy/Employment_and_Work/>Jobs</a>
...<br><br><font size=3 face=arial><a href=r/ci><b>Computers & Internet</b></a></font><br>
<a href=http://dir.yahoo.com/Computers_and_Internet/Internet/>Internet</a>,
<a href=http://dir.yahoo.com/Computers_and_Internet/Internet/World_Wide_Web/>WWW</a>,
<a href=http://dir.yahoo.com/Computers_and_Internet/Software/>Software</a>,
<a href=http://dir.yahoo.com/Recreation/Games/Computer_Games/>Games</a>...<br><br><font
size=3 face=arial><a href=http://dir.yahoo.com/Education/><b>Education</b></a></font><br>
<a href=http://dir.yahoo.com/Education/Higher_Education/>College and University</a>,
```

They do this:

```
<a href=r/bs>Shopping</a>,
<a href=r/jo>Jobs</a>...<br><br><font size=3 face=arial><a href=r/ci><b>Computers &
Internet</b></a></font><br><a href=r/in>Internet</a>,
<a href=r/ww>WWW</a>,
<a href=r/sf>Software</a>,
<a href=r/ga>Games</a>...<br><br><font size=3 face=arial><a
href=r/ed><b>Education</b></a></font><br><a href=r/un>College and University</a>,
```

Yahoo! saves over 8.3KB (over 28 percent) by abbreviating the 273 links on their home page.[1] Note that Yahoo! uses subdomains for nearly all their links, making redirects all the more effective. Redirects save space, and help distribute the load.

Abbreviating WebReference.com

WebReference.com uses automatic link abbreviation on their home page to maximize display speed. Like Yahoo!, WebReference.com uses mod_rewrite to create auto-expanding URLs.

---

1. Andrew King, author calculation of abbreviated Yahoo.com home page size (30 May 2002).
   30,177 bytes–21,639 bytes=8,538 bytes=28.3 percent smaller.

Here is a `RewriteMap` snippet:

```
b       dlab/
d       dhtml/
g       graphics/
h       html/
p       perl/
x       xml/
```

Unlike Yahoo!, WebReference uses a `RewriteRule` that allows intelligent expansion of URLs. By ending popular directory values without slashes, and crafting the right regular expression, this `RewriteMap` entry:

```
dc      dhtml/column
```

allows URLs like this:

```
/r/dc/66
```

to expand into this:

```
/dhtml/column66/
```

Here is a truncated version of WebReference.com's home page before abbreviation. So instead of this:

```
... top navigation bar snippet ...

<tr><td class=y align=center><a
href="/services/reference/"><b>Reference</b></a></td></tr><tr><td><a
href="/html/reference/color/">Color Codes</a><br><a href="/html/reference/character/">HTML
Characters</a><br><a href="/xml/reference/">XML</a></td></tr>
<tr><td class=y align=center><a href="/services/"><b>Services</b></a></td></tr><tr><td><a
href="http://refer-it.com/main.cfm">Affiliates</a><br><a href="/tools/browser/">Browser
Sniffers</a><br>
<a href="/services/dns/">Domains</a><br><a
href="http://forums.internet.com/">Forums</a><br><a
href="/services/graphics/">Graphics</a><br>
<a href="http://jobs.webdeveloper.com/">Jobs</a><br><a href="/services/news/">RSS
News</a><br><a href="/scripts/">Scripts</a><br><a href="/cgi-
bin/search.cgi">Search</a><br><a href="/services/validation/">Validation</a><br><a

... main body content snippet ...
```

```
<dt><a href="/js/column110/">JScript .NET, Part IV: Inheritance</a></dt><dd>Contrary to
Mom&#39;s instructions,...
<dt><a href="/programming/java/webservices/">Book Excerpt: Professional Java Web
Services</a></dt><dd>Move over Microsoft...
<dt><a href="/xml/column56/">Google SVG Search, Part II</a></dt><dd>Another module,
another dozen lines,

... nav bar snippet (Web Dev Sites)...

<a href="http://www.flashkit.com">FlashKit</a><br>
<a href="http://www.gif.com">GIF.com</a><br>
<a href="http://javaboutique.internet.com">Java Boutique</a><br>
<a href="http://www.javascript.com">JavaScript.com</a><br>
<a href="http://www.javascriptsource.com">JavaScript Source</a><br>
<a href="http://jobs.webdeveloper.com">Jobs</a><br>
<a href="http://www.justsmil.com">JustSMIL</a><br>
...
```

Do this:

```
<tr><td class=y align=center><a href="/r/sr"><b>Reference</b></a></td></tr><tr><td><a
href="/r/hrc">Color Codes</a><br><a href="/r/hrh">HTML Characters</a><br><a
href="/r/x/reference/">XML</a></td></tr>
<tr><td class=y align=center><a href="/r/s"><b>Services</b></a></td></tr><tr><td><a
href="r/rfi/main.cfm">Affiliates</a><br><a href="/r/tb">Browser Sniffers</a><br>
<a href="/r/sd">Domains</a><br><a href="r/sf">Forums</a><br><a
href="/r/sg">Graphics</a><br>
<a href="r/jwd">Jobs</a><br><a href="/r/sn">RSS News</a><br><a
href="/r/ss">Scripts</a><br><a href="/r/cs">Search</a><br><a href="/r/sv">Validation</a>
...
<dt><a href="/r/jc/110/">JScript .NET, Part IV: Inheritance</a></dt><dd>Contrary to
Mom&#39;s instructions,...
<dt><a href="/r/pg/java/webservices/">Book Excerpt: Professional Java Web
Services</a></dt><dd>Move over Microsoft...
<dt><a href="/r/xc/56/">Google SVG Search, Part II</a></dt><dd>Another module, another
dozen lines,
...
<a href="r/fkt">FlashKit</a><br>
<a href="r/gif">GIF.com</a><br>
<a href="r/jbt">Java Boutique</a><br>
<a href="r/jsc">JavaScript.com</a><br>
<a href="r/jss">JavaScript Source</a><br>
<a href="r/jwd">Jobs</a><br>
<a href="r/jsm">JustSMIL</a><br>
...
```

In my quest for speed, I saved 5KB (over 20 percent) off WebReference.com's front page using abbreviated URLs. (We don't have quite as many links as Yahoo!.)

Overall, this auto-abbreviation technique saves from 20 to 28 percent off the HTML of these home pages. This savings makes URL abbreviation one of the most effective HTML optimization techniques available (other than converting to CSS and cutting out unnecessary fluff). The more links you have, the greater the savings.

Chapter 1, excerpted from

Search Engine Visibility

Shari Thurow

0-7357-1256-5

Search Engine Visibility is about designing, writing, and creating a web site primarily for your site's visitors, and helping them find what they are searching for via the major search engines, directories, and industry-related sites. This book teaches developers, designers, programmers, and online marketers what pitfalls to avoid from the beginning so they can provide their clients with more effective site designs.

part 1

Before You Build

Introduction

Search engine optimization (SEO) is a powerful online marketing strategy. When done correctly, millions of online searchers can find your site among millions of top search results.

Many web site owners consider SEO as an afterthought—after a site has already been built. If you are about to create a new site or redesign an existing one, understanding how the search engines work, how your target audience searches, and how best to design your site from the onset can save your company thousands of dollars in time and expenses.

Why Search Engine Visibility Is Important

Search engines and directories are the main way Internet users discover web sites. Various resources confirm this statement, and the percentages generally range from 42 percent of Internet users to 86 percent.

A January 2001 study conducted by NPD Group, a research organization specializing in consumer purchasing and behavior, tested the impact of search engine listings and banner advertisements across a variety of web sites to determine which marketing medium was more effective. In each situation, search engine listings came out on top. They found consumers are five times more likely to purchase your products or services after finding a web site through a search engine rather than through a banner advertisement.

Jupiter Media Metrix, another Internet research firm, determined that 28 percent of consumers go to a search engine and type the product name as a search query when they are looking for a product to purchase online.

Search engines and directories average over 300 million searches per day. Therefore, regardless of whether the percentage value is as low as 28 percent or as high as 86 percent, millions of searches are performed every day. Properly preparing your web site for search engine visibility increases the probability that web searchers will visit your site.

Additionally, think about your own personal experience. Where do you go to search for information about a company or a product on the web? Where do you go to find a site whose web address you do not know or cannot remember? In these cases, you probably use a search engine or directory to find the information.

Web searchers are not random visitors. When searchers enter a series of words into a search engine query, they are actively searching out a specific product or service. Thus, the traffic your site receives from the search engines is already targeted. In other words, web searchers are self-qualified prospects for your business.

Of course, search engines are not the only way in which people discover web sites. People may find a web address in offline sources such as print, television, or radio. They might click a link to a web site in an email document or a banner advertisement. Word of mouth (referral marketing) also is a popular method of bringing visitors to sites. In addition, people locate sites by clicking links from one site to another, commonly known as surfing the web.

Because millions of people use the search engines and directories to discover web sites, maximizing your site's search engine visibility can be a powerful and cost-effective part of an online marketing plan. A properly performed search engine marketing campaign can provide a tremendous, long-term return on investment (ROI).

Understanding the Search Services

Search services can generally be categorized into two types of sources: directories and search engines. Many people confuse the two terms, often referring to Yahoo! as a search engine. (Yahoo! is a directory.)

The reason for the confusion is understandable. People see a Search button on a web site and assume that when they click the button, they are using a search engine. Both Yahoo! and Google have search boxes, as shown in Figure 1.1.

The search services use two main sources to obtain their listings. The first type of search service is called a directory, and a directory uses human editors to manually place web sites or web pages into specific categories. A directory is commonly called a "human-based" search engine.

The other type of search service is called a search engine, and a search engine uses special software robots, called *spiders* or *crawlers*, to retrieve information from web pages. This type of search service is called a "spider-based" or "crawler-based" search engine.

Figure 1.1

Although both Yahoo! and Google enable people to search, the information they provide in their search results is different.

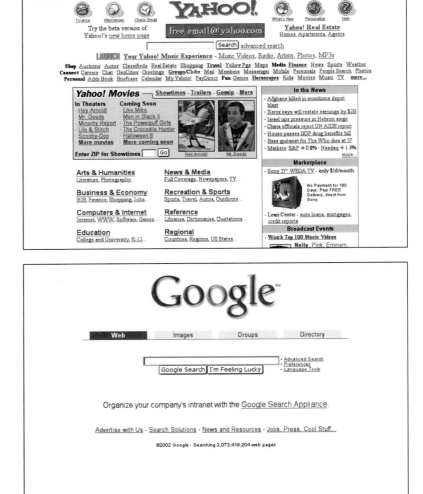

Many search services are a hybrid of a search engine and a directory. A hybrid search service usually gets most of its listings from one source; thus, hybrid search services are classified according to the main source used. If a hybrid search service gets its primary results from a directory and its secondary results from a search engine, the search service is generally classified as a directory.

MSN Search is classified as a directory. Its primary results come from the LookSmart database, and its secondary (fall-through) results currently come from Inktomi, a search engine.

Most search engine marketers label both search engines and directories as "search engines," even though search engines and directories have unique characteristics. Web site owners need to understand the differences between the two terms because the strategies for getting listed well in search engines are quite different from the strategies for getting listed well in directories.

Search Engines

What differentiates a search engine from a directory is that the directory databases consist of sites that have been added by human editors. Search engine databases are compiled through the use of special software robots, called spiders, to retrieve information from web pages.

Search engines perform three basic tasks:

- Search engine *spiders* find and fetch web pages, a process called crawling or spidering, and build lists of words and phrases found on each web page.

- Search engines keep an index (or database) of the words and phrases they find on each web page they are able to crawl. The part of the search engine that places the web pages into the database is called an *indexer*.

- Search engines then enable end users to search for keywords and keyword phrases found in their indices. Search engines try to match the words typed in a search query with the web page that is most likely to have the information for which end users are searching. This part of the search engine is called the *query processor*.

How do search engines begin finding web pages? The usual starting points are lists of heavily used servers from major Internet service providers (ISPs), such as America Online, and the most frequently visited web sites, such as Yahoo!, the Open Directory, LookSmart, and other major directories. Search engine spiders will begin crawling these popular sites, indexing the words on every single page of a site and following every link found within a site. This is one of the major reasons it is important for a web site to be listed in the major directories.

What Is a URL?

A uniform resource locator (URL) is an address referring to the location of a file on the Internet. In terms of search engine marketing, it is the address of an individual web page element or web document on the Internet.

Many people believe a URL is the same as a domain name or home page, but this is not so. Every web document and web graphic image on a web site has a URL. The syntax of a URL consists of three elements:

- The protocol, or the communication language, that the URL uses.
- The domain name, or the exclusive name, that identifies a web site.
- The pathname of the file to be retrieved, usually related to the pathname of a file on the server. The file can contain any type of data, but only certain files, usually an HTML document or a graphic image, are interpreted directly by most browsers.

For example, the URL for a home page is commonly written as follows: http://www.companyname.com/index.html.

- The http:// is the protocol (Hypertext Transfer Protocol).
- The www.companyname.com is the domain name.
- The index.html is the pathname. In this example, it is a Hypertext Markup Language (HTML) document named index.

The URL for an About Us page for a company called TranquiliTeas is commonly written as this: http://www.tranquiliteasorganic.com/about.html.

- The http:// is the protocol.
- The www.tranquiliteasorganic.com is the domain name.
- The about.html is the path name.

As a general rule of thumb, whenever you see Add URL or Submit URL to the search engines, remember that every web page has a unique URL.

Figure 1.2 outlines the search engine crawling process for a single web page.

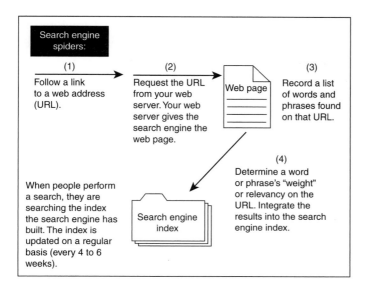

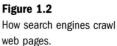
Figure 1.2
How search engines crawl web pages.

Because search engine spiders are continuously crawling the web, their indices are constantly receiving new and updated data. Search engines regularly update their indices about every four to six weeks.

The search engine index contains full-text indices of web pages. Thus, when you perform a search query on a search engine, you are actually searching this full-text index of retrieved web pages, not the web itself.

To determine the most relevant URL for a search query, most search engines take the text information on a web page and assign a "weight" to the individual words and phrases on that page. An engine might give more "weight" to the number of times that a word appears on a page. An engine might assign more "weight" to words that appear in the title tags, meta tags, and subheadings. An engine might assign more "weight" to words that appear at the top of a document. This assigning of "weight" to a set of words on a web page is part of a search engine's algorithm, which is a mathematical formula that determines how web pages are ranked. Every search engine has a different formula for assigning "weight" to the words and phrases in its index.

Search engine algorithms are kept highly confidential and change almost every day. Thus, no search engine optimization expert can ever claim to know an exact search engine algorithm at a specified point in time.

Submission Forms Versus Natural Spidering

Search engines also add web pages through submission forms, generally labeled as Add URL or Submit URL. The Submit URL form enables web site owners to notify the search engines of a web page's existence and its URL.

Unfortunately, unethical search engine marketers (called spammers) created automated submission tools that bombard submission forms with thousands of URLs. These URLs point to poorly written and constructed web pages that are of no use to a web site owner's target audience.

Most of the major search engines state that 95 percent of submissions made through the Add URL form are considered spam.

Because of the overwhelming spam problems, submitting a web page through an Add URL form does not guarantee that the search engines will accept your web page. Therefore, it is generally more beneficial for web pages to be discovered by a search engine spider during its normal crawling process.

However, a search engine optimization expert can do the following:

- Ensure that targeted words and phrases are placed in a strategic manner on the web pages, no matter what the current algorithms are.

- Ensure that spiders are able to access the web pages.

The key to understanding search engine optimization is comprehending Figure 1.2. Why? Because search engine spiders are always going to index text on web pages, and they are always going to find web pages by crawling links from web page to web page, from web site to web site. *Anything that interferes with the process outlined in Figure 1.2 will negatively impact a site's search engine positions.* If a search engine spider is not able to access your web pages, those pages will not rank well. If a search engine can access your web pages but cannot find your targeted keyword phrases on those web pages, those pages also will not rank well.

Pay-for-Inclusion Models

With a pay-for-inclusion model, a search engine includes pages from a web site in its index in exchange for payment. The pay-for-inclusion model is beneficial to search engine marketers and web site owners because (a) they know their web pages will not be dropped from a search engine index, and (b) any new information added to their web pages will be reflected in the search engines very quickly.

This type of program guarantees that your submitted web pages will not be dropped from the search engine index for a specified period of time, generally six months or a year. To keep your guaranteed inclusion in the search engine's index, you must renew your payment.

Submitting web pages in a pay-for-inclusion program does *not* guarantee that the pages will appear in top positions. Thus, it is best that pages submitted through pay-for-inclusion programs be optimized.

Search engine marketers find pay-for-inclusion programs save them considerable time and expense because a web page cannot rank if it is not included in the search engine index. Furthermore, pay-for-inclusion programs enable dynamic web pages to be included in the search engine index without marketers having to implement costly workarounds.

Pay-for-Placement Models

In contrast to pay-for-inclusion models, a pay-for-placement search engine guarantees top positions in exchange for payment. With pay-for-placement search engines, participants bid against each other to obtain top positions for specified keywords or keyword phrases. Typically, the higher the bid, the higher the web page ranks.

Participants are charged every time a person clicks through from the search results to their web sites. This is why pay-for-placement search engines are also referred to as "pay-per-click" search engines. Participants pay each time a person clicks a link to their web site from that search engine.

Many pay-for-placement search engines have excellent distribution networks, and the top two or three positions are often displayed in other search engines and directories. Paid placement advertisements are generally marked on partnered sites as "Featured Listings," "Sponsored Links," and so on.

If no one bids on a particular search term, the free, fall-through results are generally displayed from a search engine partner. For example, currently, the fall-through results for Overture.com come from Inktomi.

Participating in pay-for-placement programs can get expensive. Part 3, "Page Design Workarounds," discusses how to best utilize this type of service.

Search Engine Optimization Strategies

Search engine optimization is the process of designing, writing, coding (in HTML), programming, and scripting your entire web site so that there is a good chance that your web pages will appear at the top of search engine queries for your selected keywords. Optimization is a means of helping your potential customers find your web site.

To get the best overall, long-term search engine visibility, the following components must be present on a web page:

- Text component
- Link component
- Popularity component

All the major search engines (Google, FAST Search, MSN Search, and other Inktomi-based engines) use these components as part of their search engine algorithm. Figure 1.3 illustrates the "ideal" web page that is designed and written for the search engines.

Very few web pages can attain the "ideal" match for all search engine algorithms. In reality, most web pages have different combinations of these components, as illustrated in Figure 1.4.

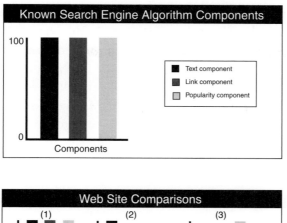

Figure 1.3
Known search engine
algorithm components:
text, link, and popularity.

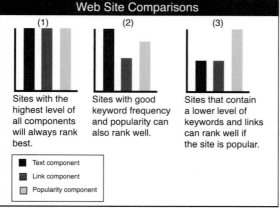

Figure 1.4
Web site comparisons.

Sites perform well in the search engines overall when they have (a) all the components on their web pages and (b) optimal levels of all the components.

Text Component—An Overview

Because the search engines build lists of words and phrases on URLs, it naturally follows that to do well on the search engines, you must place these words on your web pages in the strategic HTML tags.

The most important part of the text component of a search engine algorithm is keyword selection. For your target audience to find your site on the search engines, your pages must contain keyword phrases that match the phrases your target audience is typing into search queries.

After you have determined the best keyword phrases to use on your web pages, you will need to place them within your HTML tags. Different search engines do not place emphasis on the same HTML tags. For example, Inktomi places some emphasis on meta tags; Google ignores meta tags. Thus, to do well on all the search engines, it is best to place keywords in all the HTML tags possible, without keyword stuffing. Then, no matter what the search engine algorithm is, you know that your keywords are optimally placed.

Keywords need to be placed in the following places:

- Title tags

- Visible body text

- Meta tags

- Graphic images (the alternative text)

The title tag and the visible body text are the two most important places to insert keywords because all the search engines index and place significant "weight" on this text.

Keywords in Your Domain Name

Many search engine marketers believe that placing keywords in your domain name and your filenames affects search engine positioning. Some search engine marketers believe that this strategy gives a significant boost whereas others believe that the boost is miniscule.

One reason people believe the position boost is significant is that the words or phrases matching the words you typed in a query are highlighted when you view the search results. This occurrence is called *search-term highlighting* or *term highlighting*.

Search engines and directories might use term highlighting for usability purposes. The process is done dynamically using a highlighting application. This application simply takes your query words and highlights them in the search results for quick reference. Term highlighting merely indicates that query terms were passed through the application. In other words, in search results, just because a word is highlighted in your domain name does not necessarily mean that the domain name received a significant boost in search results.

Many other factors determine whether a site will rank, and the three components (text, link, and popularity) have more impact on search engine visibility than using a keyword in a domain name.

Link Component—An Overview

The strategy of placing keyword-rich text in your web pages is useless if the search engine spiders have no way of finding that text. Therefore, the way your pages are linked to each other, and the way your web site is linked to other web sites, does impact your search engine visibility.

Even though search engine spiders are powerful data-gathering programs, HTML coding or scripting can prevent a spider from crawling your pages. Examples of site navigation schemes that can be problematic include the following:

- **Poor HTML coding on all navigation schemes:** Browsers (Netscape and Explorer) can display web pages with sloppy HTML coding; search engine spiders are not as forgiving as browsers.

- **Image maps:** Many search engines do not follow the links inside image maps.

- **Frames:** Google, Inktomi, and Lycos follow links on a framed site, but the manner in which pages display in search results is not ideal.

- **JavaScript:** The major search engines do not follow many of the links, including mouseovers/rollovers, arrays, and navigation menus, embedded inside JavaScript.

- **Dynamic or database-driven web pages:** Pages that are generated through scripts or databases, or that have a ?, &, $, =, +, or % in the URL, pose problems for search engine spiders. URLs with CGI-BIN in them can also be problematic.

- **Flash:** Currently, only Google and FAST Search can follow the links embedded in Flash documents. The others cannot.

Therefore, when designing web pages, be sure to include a navigation scheme so that the spiders have the means to record the words on your web pages. Usually that means having two forms of navigation on a web site: one that pleases your target audience visually and one that the search engines spiders can follow.

For example, let's say that a web site's main navigation scheme is a series of drop-down menus coded with JavaScript. Figure 1.5 illustrates why sites without JavaScript in the navigation scheme consistently rank higher than sites with JavaScript in the navigation scheme.

In Figure 1.5, note that both the text and the popularity component levels are equal in all three graphs. A web page that uses JavaScript in its navigation can rank well in the search engines as long as a spider-friendly navigation scheme (text links, for example) is also present on the web page. However, because some scripts can "trap" a spider (prevent it from indexing the text on a web page), the link component level is lower than a site that does not use JavaScript in its navigation.

Figure 1.5

How a site with JavaScript and a site without JavaScript might rank in the search engines.

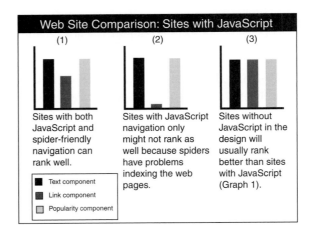

Popularity Component—An Overview

The popularity component of a search engine algorithm consists of two subcomponents:

- Link popularity
- Click-through or click popularity

Attaining an optimal popularity component is not as simple as obtaining as many links as possible to a web site. The quality of the sites linking to your site holds more weight than the quantity of sites linking to your site. Because Yahoo! is one of the most frequently visited sites on the web, a link from Yahoo! to your web site carries far more weight than a link from a smaller, less visited site.

To develop effective link popularity to a site, the site should be listed in the most frequently visited directories. Yahoo!, LookSmart, and the Open Directory are examples of the most frequently visited directories.

More importantly, it can boost your search engine position if a directory that is associated with a search engine lists your site. For example, a site that is listed in LookSmart can be given higher visibility in an MSN Search.

Obtaining links from other sites is not enough to maintain optimal popularity. The major search engines and directories are measuring how often end users are clicking the links to your site and how long they are staying on your site and reading your web pages. They are also measuring how often end users return to your site. All these measurements constitute a site's click-through popularity.

The search engines and directories measure both link popularity (quality and quantity of links) and click-through popularity to determine the overall popularity component of a web site.

If a single page (web page 1) ranks well in the search engines and end users click the links to that web page and browse your site, web page 1's popularity level increases. If a different web page (web page 2) ranks well in the search engines for a different keyword phrase, web page 2's popularity level increases. The total page popularity of your site will increase your overall site's online visibility.

One of the reasons that a site's home page is more important than any other web page is that search engines assign a higher "weight" to it. In all likelihood, the home page is going to be the URL listed in the major directories, and the home page has more links to it from within the web site.

Figure 1.6 illustrates the popularity within a web site. Pages with more links pointing to them have a higher page popularity "weight."

Figure 1.7 illustrates the popularity of a web site, which search engines do not always measure. Search engines measure a web page's popularity; a web site owner also will measure a web site's popularity. Sites with more links pointing to them have a higher site popularity "weight."

Figure 1.6

How search engines measure web page popularity.

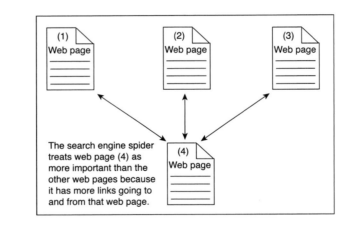

Figure 1.7

How web site owners measure web site popularity.

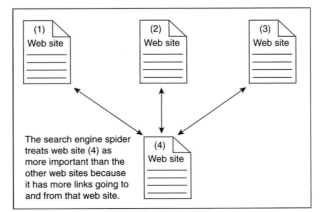

Because popularity consists of multiple subcomponents and these subcomponents are always fluctuating, the popularity measurement is dynamic and cumulative.

All search engine marketing campaigns should begin with the popularity component because all the major search engines measure popularity as a part of their search engine algorithms. The quickest way to achieve an initial, effective popularity component is to have your site listed in what search engines consider reliable sources: the major directories.

Web Directories

Web directories use human editors to create their listings. When you submit a site to be included in a directory, a human editor reviews your site and determines whether to include your site in the directory. Human editors also discover sites on their own through searching or browsing the web.

Every web page (or site) listed in a directory is categorized in some way. The categories are typically hierarchical in nature, branching off into different subcategories. Web searchers can find sites in directories by browsing categories, or they can perform a keyword search for information.

For example, a company that sells "organic teas" might be listed in this Yahoo! category: Business and Economy > Shopping and Services > Food and Drinks > Drinks > Tea > Organic. If we place the categories in a vertical hierarchy, it will look like this:

Business and Economy

    Shopping and Services

        Food and Drinks

           Drinks

                Tea

                    Organic

In this example, the top-level category is called "Business and Economy." A subcategory of "Business and Economy" is "Shopping and Services." A subcategory of "Shopping and Services" is "Food and Drinks," and so on. As we move down (drill down) the category structure, notice that the categories get more and more specific.

A company that sells "herbal teas" might be listed in a different Yahoo! category: Business and Economy > Shopping and Services > Food and Drinks > Drinks > Tea > Herbal. Let's place this categorization into a vertical hierarchy:

Business and Economy

    Shopping and Services

        Food and Drinks

            Drinks

                Tea

                    Herbal

A company that sells a variety of teas might be listed in a less specific Yahoo! category:

Business and Economy

    Shopping and Services

        Food and Drinks

            Drinks

                Tea

Directories are structured in this manner to make it easier for their end users to find sites.

Web pages are generally displayed in directories with a Title and a Description. The Title and Description originate either from the directory editors themselves (upon reviewing a site) or are adapted from site owner submissions. It is important to remember that directories do *not* necessarily use the HTML <title> tag or the description contained in your site's meta tags.

Because most web directories tend to be small, directory results are often supplemented with additional results from a search engine partner. These supplemental results are commonly referred to as *fall-through* results. In fact, many people mistakenly believe that their sites are listed in a directory when they are actually appearing in the fall-through results from a search engine.

Directories usually differentiate their directory listings and their fall-through listings. If you perform a keyword search on a directory, the directory results might appear under a heading titled "Web Site Matches" or "Reviewed Web Sites." Sites that are listed in directories generally have a category displayed with them.

When a web directory fails to return any results, fall-through results from a search engine partner are usually presented as the primary results. Fall-through results are typically labeled "Web Page Matches" or something similar.

One way you can tell if your site is listed in a directory is to perform a keyword search on your company name or URL. If you see a "Powered by Google" or "Powered by Inktomi" near your web site listing, then in all likelihood, your site is listed in the search engine fall-through results but not in the directory (see Figure 1.8).

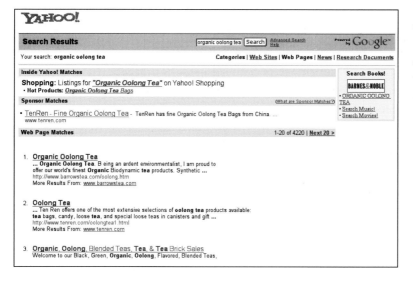

Figure 1.8

The "Powered by Google" image indicates that the search results came from the search engine (Google), not the directory (Yahoo!).

Finally, directories tend to list web sites, not individual web pages. A web site is a collection of web pages that generally focuses on a specific topic. In other words, a web page is part of a web site. A directory is most likely to list only your domain name (www.companyname.com), not individual web pages. In contrast, search engines can list all individual web pages from an entire web site, not just a single home page.

If a particular web page (or set of pages) within a site contains unique, valuable information about a particular topic, that page can be listed in a different directory category. Glossaries and how-to tips are examples of content-rich sections of web sites that can receive additional directory listings.

Paid Submission Programs

A search engine or directory that uses a paid submission program charges a submission fee to process a request to be included in its index. Payment of the submission fee guarantees that your site will be reviewed within a specified period of time (generally 48 hours to 1 week).

If you want to have individual, content-rich web pages included in separate categories, in most cases, you must pay an additional submission fee for another review. Some directories accept content-rich pages without payment, but directory editors generally do not review these pages as quickly as the paid submissions.

The main advantage of paid submission is speed. You know your web site is being reviewed quickly, and, if the editors find your site acceptable, your site is added to the directory database quickly. Furthermore, after your site is added to the directory, the listing gives your site a significant popularity boost in the search engines. Yahoo! is an example of a directory that has a paid submission program.

How Directories Rank Web Sites

When you perform a keyword search in a directory, the search results are displayed in order of importance. Top directory listings are based on the following criteria:

- The directory category

- The web site's title

- The web site's description

If the words you searched for appear in a category name, the category name appears at the top of a directory's search results. For example, if we searched for "organic teas" on Yahoo!, the category that has both the word "organic" and the word "tea" appears at the top of the search results, as shown in Figure 1.9.

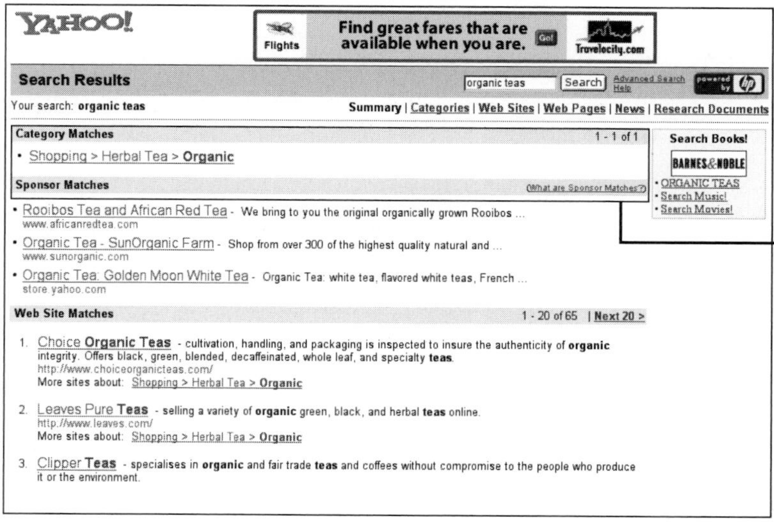

Figure 1.9

Matching category results for the phrase "organic teas" in Yahoo!.

Immediately following the category listings are Sponsor Matches, which are pay-for-placement advertisements (see Figure 1.10).

If the words in a search query do not appear in a directory category, the search results display sites that use these words in their titles and descriptions. Figure 1.11 shows the results of scrolling down the Yahoo! search results page.

Sites that have keywords in the category name, title (company name), and description are displayed at the top of the page. Figure 1.11 shows how Yahoo! provides access to some web sites that it feels are directly relevant to the search.

Sites that have keywords in their company name and description appear next, and sites that have only keywords in the description appear after that.

Figure 1.10

Paid advertisements appearing in Yahoo! search results.

Sponsor matches for "organic teas"

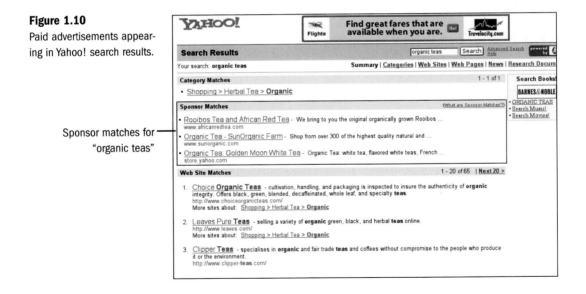

Web Site Matches   1 - 20 of 65 | **Next 20 >**

1. Choice **Organic Teas** - cultivation, handling, and packaging is inspected to insure the authenticity of **organic** integrity. Offers black, green, blended, decaffeinated, whole leaf, and specialty **teas**.
   http://www.choiceorganicteas.com/
   More sites about: Shopping > Herbal Tea > **Organic**

2. Leaves Pure **Teas** - selling a variety of **organic** green, black, and herbal **teas** online.
   http://www.leaves.com/
   More sites about: Shopping > Herbal Tea > **Organic**

3. Clipper **Teas** - specialises in **organic** and fair trade **teas** and coffees without compromise to the people who produce it or the environment.
   http://www.clipper-**teas**.com/
   More sites about: United Kingdom > Shopping > Tea

4. Nub Circus Chai Tea Company - **organic teas**, potent herbs, and other feats of synergistic fancy!
   http://www.nub.com
   More sites about: Shopping > Chai > Brand Names

5. Tea Herb Farm - seeds, **organic** produce, and herbs.
   http://www.serve.com/teaherbfarm/
   More sites about: Missouri > Tea > B2B > Nurseries

6. Star of Roses **Organic** Farm - **organic**ally grown herbs used for processing tinctures, healing balms, infused oils, skin care products, and herbal **teas** using principles of aromatherapy and therapeutic herbalism.
   http://www.starofroses.com/
   More sites about: Hawaii > Ahualoa > B2B > Nurseries

7. Virtuous **Teas** - offers a selection of loose oolong, green, black, **organic**, and herbal **teas**. Also carries tea accessories and a variety of teapots.
   http://www.virtuousteas.com/
   More sites about: Massachusetts > Newtonville > Shopping > Coffee and Tea

8. Republic of Tea - offers full-leaf, **organic**, green, oolong, and other types of **teas**.
   http://www.republicoftea.com

Figure 1.11
Web site matches in Yahoo! for the phrase "organic teas."

How Directory Editors Evaluate Web Sites

Directory editors look at a submitted web site to determine (a) whether unique, quality content is present on the web site, and (b) how this content is presented. Great content is the most important element of any web site, and that content needs to be delivered to your target audience in the most effective way possible. Figure 1.12 illustrates the directory submission process.

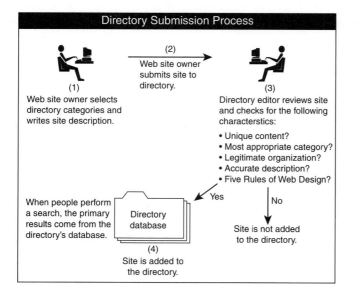

Figure 1.12
How directory editors evaluate a web site.

Directory editors are looking for particular characteristics before including a site in the directory. We discuss those characteristics next.

Unique Content

Directory editors do not want to place sites with identical information in the same category. Thus, before you submit your site to a directory, check out the other sites in your targeted category. Make sure your site contains unique information so that it will add value to that directory category.

You can point out any unique content to the directory editor using your description or the extra comments field in the submission form.

Most Appropriate Category

To select the most appropriate category (or categories) for your web site, type your selected keywords in the directory search box and study the results. If multiple categories appear, view many of the web sites listed under each category. Your site's actual content must accurately reflect the category or categories you wish to be listed under and be similar to the other sites listed in those categories.

You will probably be listed under the same categories your competitors are listed under, though it is important to understand that from directory editors' perspectives, your site belongs in a category that they deem appropriate, not necessarily in a category in which you believe your target audience is searching.

Legitimate Organization/Company

Editors want legitimate organizations and companies listed in their commercial categories. They do not want a small start-up company that will not be around next year. This would result in a dead link to a URL in the directory.

Having a virtual domain (www.companyname.com) is an indication that you are a legitimate organization or business. Having all your contact information (address, telephone number, fax number, and email address) readily available on your site is also an indication that you have a legitimate business. Directory editors will perform a WHOIS lookup (www.netsol.com/cgi-bin/whois/whois) to see if the information there matches the information you gave in your submission form.

If you have an e-commerce site, directory editors are looking for such items as secure credit card processing (for sites that accept credit cards), a return policy or a money-back guarantee (for sites that sell products), and a physical address, not a post office box.

Accurate Description

The description you submit to directory editors should accurately reflect the content of your web site. Directory editors should be able to determine that the description is accurate just by viewing your home page.

For example, if you sell organic tea on your web site and you specialize in three types of tea (oolong, black, and green teas), those three specialties should be obvious to an editor just by his viewing your home page. Furthermore, if directory editors navigate your site or perform a search on a site search engine, they should easily be able to find the pages that show the items used in your description.

Part 2 of this book, "How to Build Better Web Pages," details how to write effective directory descriptions.

Index

www.informit.com

YOUR GUIDE TO IT REFERENCE

New Riders has partnered with **InformIT.com** to bring technical information to your desktop. Drawing from New Riders authors and reviewers to provide additional information on topics of interest to you, **InformIT.com** provides free, in-depth information you won't find anywhere else.

Articles

Keep your edge with thousands of free articles, in-depth features, interviews, and IT reference recommendations— all written by experts you know and trust.

Online Books

Answers in an instant from **InformIT Online Books'** 600+ fully searchable online books.

POWERED BY

Catalog

Review online sample chapters, author biographies, and customer rankings and choose exactly the right book from a selection of over 5,000 titles.

www.newriders.com

VIEW CART search ▶

▶ Registration already a member? Log in. ▶ Book Registration

OUR AUTHORS

PRESS ROOM

web development	design	photoshop	new media	3-D	server technologies

EDUCATORS

ABOUT US

CONTACT US

You already know that New Riders brings you the **Voices that Matter**.

But what does that mean? It means that New Riders brings you the

Voices that challenge your assumptions, take your talents to the next

level, or simply help you better understand the complex technical world

we're all navigating.

Visit **www.newriders.com** to find:

▶ 10% discount and free shipping on all purchases

▶ Never-before-published chapters

▶ Sample chapters and excerpts

▶ Author bios and interviews

▶ Contests and enter-to-wins

▶ Up-to-date industry event information

▶ Book reviews

▶ Special offers from our friends and partners

▶ Info on how to join our User Group program

▶ Ways to have your Voice heard

WWW.NEWRIDERS.COM

VISIT OUR WEB SITE

W W W . N E W R I D E R S . C O M

On our Web site you'll find information about our other books, authors, tables of contents, indexes, and book errata. You will also find information about book registration and how to purchase our books.

EMAIL US

Contact us at this address: **nrfeedback@newriders.com**

- If you have comments or questions about this book
- To report errors that you have found in this book
- If you have a book proposal to submit or are interested in writing for New Riders
- If you would like to have an author kit sent to you
- If you are an expert in a computer topic or technology and are interested in being a technical editor who reviews manuscripts for technical accuracy
- To find a distributor in your area, please contact our international department at this address. **nrmedia@newriders.com**

- For instructors from educational institutions who want to preview New Riders books for classroom use. Email should include your name, title, school, department, address, phone number, office days/hours, text in use, and enrollment, along with your request for desk/examination copies and/or additional information.
- For members of the media who are interested in reviewing copies of New Riders books. Send your name, mailing address, and email address, along with the name of the publication or Web site you work for.

BULK PURCHASES/CORPORATE SALES

The publisher offers discounts on this book when ordered in quantity for bulk purchases and special sales. For sales within the U.S., please contact: Corporate and Government Sales (800) 382-3419 or **corpsales@pearsontechgroup.com**. Outside of the U.S., please contact: International Sales (317) 581-3793 or **international@pearsontechgroup.com**.

WRITE TO US

New Riders Publishing
201 W. 103rd St.
Indianapolis, IN 46290-1097

CALL US

Toll-free (800) 571-5840 + 9 + 7477
If outside U.S. (317) 581-3500. Ask for New Riders.

FAX US

(317) 581-4663